French-Canadian Nationalism

An Anthology

French-Canadian Nationalism

An Anthology

Edited by
RAMSAY COOK

Macmillan of Canada / Toronto / 1969

The publisher gratefully acknowledges the contribution by the Canada Council toward the cost of publishing this book.

Printed in England by
Hazell Watson & Viney Ltd
for The Macmillan Company of Canada Limited
70 Bond Street, Toronto

To the memory of
André Laurendeau
(1912-1968)

Contents

Acknowledgments

Grateful acknowledgment is made to the following individuals and publishers for permission to reproduce in English material contained in this book:

The editor, Canadian Historical Association *Report*, for 'Cultural and Political Implications of French-Canadian Nationalism' by J.-C. Bonenfant and J.-C. Falardeau; the Right Honourable Pierre Elliott Trudeau for 'La Province de Québec au moment de la grève'; Fernand Ouellet for 'Les Fondements historiques de l'option séparatiste dans le Québec'.

Mme Anne Bourassa for 'Le Patriotisme canadien-français, ce qu'il est, ce qu'il doit être' and 'La Langue française et l'avenir de notre race' by Henri Bourassa; les Editions Bellarmin for 'L'Industrie dans l'économie du Canada français' by Olivar Asselin.

M. François-Albert Angers, Directeur, La Ligue d'Action Nationale for 'Si Dollard Revenait . . .' and 'Why We Are Divided' by Canon Lionel Groulx, 'Et nos frères de la dispersion' by J.-M.-R. Villeneuve, 'Enquête sur le nationalisme' by Antonio Perrault, 'Le Corporatisme et le national' by Esdras Minville, 'Pourquoi nous n'accepterons *jamais* la conscription pour service outre-mer' by François-Albert Angers, and 'Y a-t-il une crise du nationalisme?' by André Laurendeau.

Mme Paul-Emile Borduas for 'Refus Global' by Paul-Emile Borduas; Editions Fides for 'Canadians et Canadiens' by Michel Brunet; Léon Dion for 'Le Nationalisme Pessimiste: Sa source, sa signification, sa validité'; les Presses de l'Université Laval for 'Le Néo-nationalisme, où conduit-il?' by Jean-Marc Léger; and L'Association Générale des Etudiants de l'Université de Montréal for 'De l'humiliation à la révolution' by Jean-Marc Piotte.

Every reasonable care has been taken to trace ownership of copyrighted material used in this book. The editor and publisher will welcome information that will enable them to rectify any errors or omissions.

Finally, I wish particularly to thank my wife, Eleanor, who helped me in numerous ways, but especially by assuming the tedious task of preparing the index.

Introduction

This is a book in which French Canadians, past and present, speak for themselves – in translation. What they are talking about – analysing or advocating – is French-Canadian nationalism. The first section contains a series of essays that attempt, from a variety of viewpoints, to interpret and define the French Canadians' collective sense of identity. The second section brings together statements by individuals actively involved in the struggle for French-Canadian survival.

The distinction between the two sections is not an entirely satisfactory one as every reader will quickly perceive. The authors of the articles in the first section are by no means coldly detached scientists dissecting the ideology of their community. Since each writer is a member of that community, he is to a greater or less degree involved in the very evolution he describes. But in each of the essays in the opening section the emphasis is on analysis. Each of the contributors in the second section offers some analysis, but the emphasis here is on advocacy. In short, the essays in the second half of the anthology represent attempts to formulate an ideology of survival for French-Canadian society.

The principles of selection, in bringing these essays together, have been threefold, although one of the principles has not been adhered to with total consistency. Since the collection is intended to illustrate the intellectual history of French-Canadian nationalism, I have attempted to exclude writers who were primarily concerned with defending a political party or program. This has meant that certain prominent French Canadians are not represented – Louis-Joseph Papineau, Honoré Mercier, Sir Wilfrid Laurier, and Maurice Duplessis, to take the most obvious examples. But one major exception to this rule was obviously necessary: Henri Bourassa. The fact is, of course, that Bourassa is such a major figure in the intellectual history of French Canada that a collection of this kind that excluded him would read like *Hamlet* without the Prince of Denmark. Moreover, Bourassa was primarily a journalist and an educator, not a politician. For these reasons, then, Henri Bourassa is well represented in this anthology despite his direct involvement in politics at several important stages in his career. It is also true that another French-Canadian politician is represented here: Pierre Elliott Trudeau. But he was not engaged in active politics when his article was first published, and therefore represents no serious exception to this editorial principle.

My second concern in selecting these essays has been to illustrate the historical development of the idea of nationalism in French Canada. My intention, then, has been to show how French-Canadian intellectuals have been preoccupied with the survival of their community for more than a century. Indeed nearly every other intellectual pursuit – philosophical, religious, literary, historical, social, economic, and political – has been subordinated to, or at least interwoven with, the national question. Like nationalist ideologues everywhere, French Canadians have been concerned, at least since the publication of Garneau's *Histoire du Canada*, to delineate at once the uniqueness of their society and its relationship to the universality of mankind.

Finally, and most important, I wanted to demonstrate through the selection of essays in both sections of this book the varieties of French-Canadian nationalism. The point here is to suggest that French-Canadian nationalism has not been monolithic. There has never been full agreement about the character of French Canada's uniqueness and therefore there has been disagreement about its mission. Instead controversy over the meaning of the French-Canadian past has been continual. And out of this controversy has grown, at every stage of French Canada's development, equally vigorous disputes about how best to deal with present problems in order to ensure French Canada's future. Thus French-Canadian nationalism can best be seen as an attempt, repeated in every generation, to bring past, present, and future into harmony.

Naturally, the limits of space have necessitated the exclusion of some essays that might well have deserved a place in this anthology. And a greater number of individual contributors might have been included had the editor's scissors been applied more vigorously. I decided, however, that in the main the integrity of the author's thought demanded that the whole selection be reprinted. Both historical development and ideological variety are fully represented here, though a few minor tendencies had to be ignored. It seemed better to reprint, in nearly every case, the complete argument presented by an author, and limit the number of contributions, than to present a greater number of edited selections which would, of necessity, have destroyed the full development of the argument.

There is no need to extend this introduction by offering a lengthy exposition of the meaning of French-Canadian nationalism. This has been done by others, and by myself, elsewhere. The purpose of the anthology is to allow French Canadians to speak for themselves. I only hope that the collection gathered together here will provide readers with a new opportunity to understand the complex minds and emotions of French Canadians as they debate the question that has been central to their entire history – *la survivance*.

Ramsay Cook

French-Canadian Nationalism

An Anthology

Part One
Interpretations

I Jean-C. Bonenfant and Jean-C. Falardeau
Cultural and Political Implications of French-Canadian Nationalism

This paper attempts to single out some basic points of reference for a sociological analysis of French-Canadian nationalism.[1] Our specific purpose is to consider this development from its origins, in terms of its successive symbols, leaders, trends, and expressions; to analyse the psychological, social, and political factors which made it possible at different periods, as well as the institutional or associational devices which canalized it. Particular reference is made to the various segments of the local society which it actually touched. The attempt is broad and perhaps too ambitious. This essay can hardly be more than a sketchy survey and it may very well frustrate both the historians and the sociologists. It can, though, at least raise questions if it does not bring coherent answers. This in itself, we assume, may be worth while, particularly so if the historians' and the sociologists' interest is stimulated toward further investigation of this complex aspect of French-Canadian history.

For the sake of clarity, an important distinction must first be made between nationalism, as such, and patriotism. Basically, patriotism means devotion to one's country. It is a sentiment of loyalty by virtue of which one feels identified with the political community.[2] It implies a spontaneous reference to the sharing of a common soil, language, culture, history, folkways, customs, and values, all of which result in a sense of pride as well as a sense of duty to the group. Sociologically, it means the satisfaction of belonging, on the national level, to a 'we-group' and to live with the 'insiders', as Sumner puts it, 'in a relation of peace, order, law, government and industry to each other'.[3]

On the other hand, neither the word nor the fact of nationalism are simple things. Historically, the word was born in most languages around the turn of the nineteenth century to give expression to an individual or collective

Reprinted from the Canadian Historical Association *Report, 1946*, pp. 56–71.

phenomenon which had oftentimes existed long before. Its meanings have nowadays in many countries become subtly varied and are apt to create great confusion. This has happened in Canada and especially in French Canada. Thus, very often, nationalism may refer only to an acute sense of group-consciousness developed among a people and it can hardly be differentiated from plain patriotism. It implies 'the tendency to place a particularly excessive, exaggerated, and exclusive emphasis on the value of the nation at the expense of other values, which leads to a vain and unfortunate overestimation of one's nation and thus to a detraction of others'.[4] Nationalism in this sense generally also implies a closer drawing together within a group, most frequently within the framework of a political structure, with its leaders, its symbols, and its historical myths. It can be defensive, militant, offensive, or bitterly aggressive. It is connected more closely with the notion of 'race' and, to that extent, springs from or leads to ethnocentricism and chauvinisms of all sorts. It is also very often related to the idea of a 'national mission', supposedly vested by God in the group conceived as the object of divine election and the true bearer of a millennial responsibility of some sort. The people comes to consider itself, to use Dostoievski's word, a 'God-bearing' people.

Such may be the political or sociological components of nationalism. We have to see to what extent French-Canadian nationalism historically has combined these elements in a more or less continuous pattern in the course of its successive phases. These dialectical phases fall, in our opinion, under three characteristic headings: (1) the preliminary growing of defensive nationalism with Papineau, followed by the crystallization of constitutional nationalism under the Union regime; (2) the rebound of nationalism on the racial level during the Mercier episode, around 1885; (3) finally, the 'Canadian', anti-imperialist nationalism of Bourassa, at the beginning of this century till the end of the First World War.

1: The Development of Constitutional Nationalism

1. The Growing of Defensive Nationalism

It is true that the complicated canvas of history often makes it hard to single out the threads of patriotism from those of nationalism. They intertwine and may be reciprocal functions of each other. Their difference may not amount to much more than that between shades along the spectrum. Even so, one could hardly say that nationalism existed in French Canada before the moment of the British conquest. Patriotism itself, during the French regime, was more latent than explicit. The soil-tilling habitants, the adventurers, the soldiers, the bureaucratic seigneurs as well as the clergy, busy as they were at their respective parts in the defence and the shaping of a growing society, nevertheless developed, during this century and a half, collective traits which made the French of Canada different from those of France. Montcalm in his diary notices many biases and resentments of the 'Canadians' against the French.

Group-consciousness and patriotic feeling really developed only after the

British conquest, as a result of isolation, contrast, and struggle with the
culturally-alien conquering group. The history of the French-Canadian society
during the first thirty or forty years of English domination is one of great
internal diversity and gradual shifting of attitudes. The incoming English-
speaking group was, on the whole, of two sorts. There were, first, the politically
liberal-minded British military officers and functionaries sent to Canada in the
last period of George II who tried, often with partial success, to gain the
sympathy of the local population. There were, on the other hand, the merchants,
and the adventurers, mostly from New England, who descended on the new
British colony and showed openly hostile ambitions and attitudes toward both
the local population and even the British administrators. French-Canadian
attitudes toward the 'English' developed variously among the segments of an
emerging new French-Canadian society. The clergy, still imbued with the
absolutist tradition of the French monarchy, ideologically linked with Rome
and always respectful of the established authority, accepted the British government of the country with moderation, strength, and tact and did more than
any other group to rally the rural mass to the conqueror and have them accept
the new regime. The local nobility, professionally a functionary caste which, it
is now acknowledged, remained in much greater numbers than had been
formerly assumed, found great affinities with the English aristocracy of
functionaries and professional soldiers. There were gradually English-French
intermarriages. There were also some between English and the two other
important French-Canadian upper social classes, the wealthy merchants and
the professional group. These people were almost all on the side of the British
governors and administrators, and against the Anglo-American party. They
remained, however, critical of the new regime as well as of its functionaries
whenever they felt these were wrong. The significant fact is that this process
of gradual identification of the well-to-do French Canadians with the British
ruling group also meant an ever-widening gap between the French-Canadian
rural and city masses and their intellectual or commercial leaders – a gap which
became even greater than the one which had existed during the French
regime.[5]

During the last part of the eighteenth and the first part of the nineteenth
centuries, especially around the time of the Quebec Act of 1774 and the
Constitution of 1791, national solidarity grew into an acute form of political
consciousness. French Canadians sensitively felt their minority political status
while, at the same time, they remained quite naturally aware of being what
Everett C. Hughes describes as 'the charter members' of the country.[6] This
was a period of strife against the ruling power, stimulated by the struggle for
the recognition of civil and constitutional rights.[7] This culminated in the
events of 1837-8 and the name of Papineau dominates this period. Papineau
later became a violent symbol of nationalism and it is generally assumed that
he was himself a nationalist, that French-Canadian nationalism actually
originated from him. Filteau in his *Histoire des Patriotes* overly stresses this
idea.[8] Papineau was actually a nationalist, but we may question whether, in the
first part of his life, that is, the active part which he lived here before his stay

in Paris and which is really important in our history, he was profoundly under the influence of contemporary European trends of thought regarding the principle of nationality.[9] He was, rather, a great parliamentary liberal, a great patriot forced by the circumstances to be a nationalist.

During the elections of 1827, the former Canadian party became officially known, under the lead of Papineau, as the Patriots' party, being, as they said, 'the friends of the king, of the constitution and of the country'.[10] A few years later the party adopted a rallying flag which consisted of three horizontal stripes bearing the colours of green, white, and red, not dissimilar to the French revolutionary tricolour. The party was reshaped and systematically organized for national political action in 1834 at the moment of the '92 Resolutions'. It then included a most impressive array of political leaders and orators: Lafontaine, Viger, Morin, Nelson, Duvernay, Parent, and, above all, Papineau. Its philosophy was largely derived from the prevalent continental catchwords of social progress, democracy, reform, and liberty. It was liberal with a view to integrating the Canadian tradition into a fully worked out framework of British parliamentary institutions. Some newspapers shared its cause and diffused its ideas among the population: in Montreal, the *Vindicator*, *La Minerve* published by Duvernay and having as its regular collaborators most of the leaders of the Patriots' party; in Quebec the *Liberal*, *Le Canadien*, published by the firmly reasonable Etienne Parent who had coined as his motto the patriotic slogan: 'Nos institutions, notre langue et nos droits'; the *Echo du Pays*, the *Township Reformer*, *Le Fantasque*, etc. Besides, the party included as its central feature the over-all body of the Comité Central et Permanent, which centralized information and propaganda and which, through the channels of a hierarchical structure of local sub-committees, had the duty of organizing meetings, providing speakers and literature, and otherwise uniting and stimulating the 'popular forces'.

The so-called nationalism of Papineau and of his followers expressed itself on the political and economic levels. Economically, the Patriots' attitude took the form of boycotting British products. But, on the whole, in our opinion, the events of 1837–8 were of too local a character, and too hopeless to be described as a large-scale nationalist movement. The aggressive and intensive patriotism of Papineau and of his followers represents, more truly, an extreme form of the reaction of a minority group deprived of their rights and struggling for recognition.

Another movement, grown out of the events of 1837–8, deserves special mention. It is the Saint-Jean-Baptiste Society, which originated in Montreal in 1834 owing to the initiative of Duvernay and Jacques Viger and first took the form of banquets gathered to 'unite the French Canadians and give them a rallying cry'.[11] The meetings were stopped during the dark days of '37–8', then resumed in Quebec in 1842, and finally again in Montreal. The Saint-Jean-Baptiste Society was hoped, in the minds of its founders, to be the first great associational device binding strongly together the masses and the élite among French Canadians who had gradually drifted more and more apart. It was rationalized as the sanction of a 'sacred alliance' between these two groups and was even, afterwards, compared to the Magna Carta, which had sanctioned the alliance between the Norman Barons and the Britons.[12] The Saint-Jean-Baptiste Society had a motto, a flag, an emblem, and a definite patriotic purpose. The motto was that of 'Nos institutions, notre langue et nos droits', which Duvernay borrowed from Etienne Parent. The flag had the same green, white, and red colours as the Patriots' flag. The emblem was the maple leaf, conceived as 'the symbol of the destiny of the French-Canadian people'. As Viger had said at the first national banquet in Montreal (later to be quoted by numberless speakers again and again): 'This tree – the maple – which grows in our valleys . . . at first young and beaten by the storm, pines away, painfully feeding itself from the earth, but it soon springs up, tall and strong, and faces the tempest and triumphs over the wind which cannot shake it any more. The maple is the king of our forest; it is the symbol of the Canadian people.'[13] It is mostly from the ranks of the Saint-Jean-Baptiste Society that the leaders of the Patriots' party's Permanent Committee came and, to that extent, the Saint-Jean-Baptiste Society originally had for a while a semi-political character. This Society also did much, from the very beginning, to make explicit and to over-emphasize the unconscious relationship which always exists between national feeling and religion. Simultaneously, through its annual lyrical speeches and demonstrations, it glorified and popularized, along with a true reverence for tradition and the institutions of the past, an emotional and myth-like interpretation of the historical development of the French Canadians, which later developed into the recurrent theme of a 'national mission' of the people.

These features of early official French-Canadian patriotism are symptomatic of one basic stratum of collective feeling on which, under the stimulus of politically defined situations of 'national emergency', nationalist leaders were later able to capitalize and to which they could give stereotyped, exuberant forms.

2. Constitutional Nationalism under the Union Regime

It appears that Quebec nationalism as a political expression of the French Canadians on the Canadian scene actually came to life against the assimilation attempt of the Union Act. The Durham Report and the Union Act had left the French Canadians in a state of great pessimism, which cannot be described more dramatically than by Etienne Parent's article in *Le Canadien* of October 1839. After having recalled that French Canadians had faith in the establishment, in Lower Canada, of an independent nation different from those of the surrounding states, Parent goes on, in an unexpectedly pessimistic mood, to say that French Canadians, in their own interest as well as that of their children, have nothing more to do than 'work as hard as they can to bring forth an assimilation which will crush the barrier separating them from the population pressing upon them from every side'.[14]

French-Canadian nationalism then took a strong political orientation within the context of British parliamentary institutions. This marks a turning-point in the history of group relations in Canada. Lafontaine was responsible for it.

He and many other contemporary French-Canadian political leaders were, above all, clever jurists and they enjoyed, along with their patriotic feelings, playing the game of British political institutions. It was felt necessary in the British world, about this time, to sanction the principle of ministerial responsibility, that is, of the control of the executive by the people's representatives. The Durham Report acknowledged the necessity of applying this principle in the colonies as it had been in the metropolis a few years earlier. Lafontaine understood that ministerial responsibility would mean partial control of the executive by the French-Canadian representatives and, to attain his aim, he had the extraordinary opportunity of being able to become allied with the Reformers of Upper Canada. Once the political victory was obtained, it had important consequences on every level of the public administration. French Canadians experienced a considerable development under the Union regime. It seems as though the nationalism of former years had, during that period, become less aggressive, less vocal, and more oriented toward practical developments in the educational, municipal, and agricultural fields. The ethnic groups in Canada then seem to have come to a sort of equilibrium which made possible the bargaining which preceded Confederation.

Without going too far beyond the scope of this study, we must briefly mention here certain features of contemporary French-Canadian life which may help us grasp in truer perspective the series of political events we have to investigate. The population of the whole of Canada, according to the 1861 census, was 2,507,657, of whom 883,568 were French-speaking. Lower Canada alone had a population of 1,100,000, of which seventy-five per cent, viz. 847,000, were French. The province was almost exclusively rural, despite the constant flow of emigration toward, first, the United States, then, in a scattered fashion, toward the new West. There were only three or four communities deserving the name of cities: Montreal, with a population of 90,333; Quebec, with 58,319, Three Rivers, and Sorel. Numerous classical colleges had been founded in the province, either by the local secular clergy or by teaching orders from Europe: Nicolet in 1804, Saint-Hyacinthe in 1811, Saint-Thérèse and Chambly in 1824, Joliette in 1846, Sainte-Marie in Montreal in 1850. The Ecole Littéraire of Quebec had been fostering an ardent group of writers, poets, historians, and novelists, like Garneau, Gérin-Lajoie, LaRue, Crémazie, and others,[15] who exalted the ideals, the symbols, and the values of the French Canadians: the history of the race, the Mother Country, the Roman Catholic Church, the language and the folklore, the cult of the soil. The voluminous writings of Garneau and Ferland aroused interest around 1860 in the reading and the teaching of Canadian history. Textbooks for college students were published which consisted mostly, at first, of chronological tables, deliberately underlining the ecclesiastical and religious landmarks of the history of the French in Canada.[16]

Less refreshing than these blossoming literary achievements were the ideological cleavages which had been, for some time, splitting, in harsh controversies, notable portions of the French-Canadian élite of journalists, political writers, and politicians. Let us evoke only the clash between the two schools of thought, the ultramontanes and the liberals, which were very influential in conditioning the emergence of the two main political parties of the Conservatives and the Liberals. Mgr Bourget, the authoritarian Bishop of Montreal, none the less a pro-Patriot, had been the leader of the local Catholic reaction to the French Revolutions of 1830 and 1848, and he did much to infuse such views in the Quebec mentality by his importation of teaching orders: Jesuits, Christian Brothers, etc., all of whom were imbued with the idea that the new democracy was incompatible with Catholicism. When Papineau indoctrinated the 'rouges' with the new democratic ideas after his return from Paris, the long struggle began between the ultramontanes and the liberals. The latter were thought of as too radical, too democratically-minded, too free-thinking and anticlerical.[17] The historical fights between their extreme wing, the Institut Canadien, and Mgr Bourget are well known. Out of their milder wing came men like Laurier. But, curiously enough, as Mason Wade points out, ultramontanism, which was anti-nationalist in Europe, became highly nationalist in Canada, while the liberal, Gallican-minded group were internationalist.[18] The fusion of political ideas with religious ones, with Catholicism yielding to nationalistic symbols in case of conflict, is evident in Mgr Laflèche, Mgr Bourget's right-hand man, who was inspired by the ideas of Rohrbacher, an apologist for the Catholic reaction to the events of 1830 and 1848.[19] Mgr Laflèche is among the earliest, if not the first, to over-emphasize the idea that the French Canadians constitute a Catholic nation, that they have a providential mission, and that as such it is their duty to remain defensively self-centred under the leadership of their bishops, who as leaders of the sacred society stand above the political leaders in temporal affairs. It is amid these controversies that political conservatism grew up, whose politicians, during so many years, fought fights which Mercier was later to describe as 'fratricides'.

11: The Rebound of Political Nationalism on the Racial Level During the Mercier Episode, 1885

The equilibrium already mentioned between English and French lasted for a few years in Canada after Confederation. French Canadians seemed politically happy to grow within their new provincial institutions, and in Ottawa they played an important role within the powerful Conservative party. This equilibrium was broken by events happening not inside, but outside, Quebec, viz., by facts inherent in the spreading and growth of the French-speaking population in the rest of Canada. The Quebec reaction to these events crystallized around Mercier.

Honoré Mercier already had strong nationalist tendencies. He was, as early as 1871, one of the original members of the first political group to be officially known as the 'national' movement. The latter was composed of young liberals and eager conservatives who were all ardent patriots. Its inception was due to the partial dissatisfaction with federal economic policies, particularly to resentment against the recent inclusion, under the name of Manitoba, of the former

Northwest Territories into Confederation. This event had a bad press in Quebec owing to the fear of spoliation of the rights of the French-Canadian minority in this area. The aim of the rising national movement was to create a 'united French-Canadian front erasing the former party lines, for the defense of French-Canadian rights'. The original platform of the party emphasized, along with an elaborate program of electoral reform and administrative readjustments, the ideas of provincial autonomy, decentralization, tariff protection, and opposition to the Canadian Pacific project.

It was actually the outcome of the Riel affair, in 1885, which stimulated Mercier's nationalist movement. The execution of Riel in November 1885 created great irritation among the Quebec population against the federal Conservative Cabinet of Sir John A. Macdonald and especially against its French-Canadian ministers, Langevin, Caron, and Chapleau. Riel, although a semi-neurotic and megalomaniac character with whom the French-Canadian Bishop of Saint-Boniface, Mgr Taché, had had trouble, was built up by the press and the politicians into a 'racial' symbol. Being, as he was, the chief of the French half-breeds of the West, he stood as a 'French' martyr, a 'brother' (– 'Louis Riel, mon frère' – Mercier would repeatedly proclaim –)[20] who had, in the hands of fanatic Orangists, been the victim of an unjust trial and condemned to unjust death. Popular meetings were held in a great many communities and villages.[21] There was an uproar throughout the province. It was at the first of these meetings, in Montreal, that Mercier announced the formation of a new great national party which would gather in all those who resented the Riel 'outrage'. The first objective would be to overthrow, by all constitutional means possible, the Macdonald government. The national movement thus reinforced and capitalized on the dramatic rebirth of the French-Canadian feeling of solidarity created by the 'affair'. The political offensive, led by Mercier, included all the Liberals, the Nationalist Conservatives detached from their party by the Riel affair, and the Ultramontanes of Quebec and Montreal, against the die-hard Conservatives, the Ultramontanes of Three Rivers, and the English-speaking Quebec minority. Mercier, in 1886, as leader of the national party, won the election which was to make him for five years a leader and active symbol of French-Canadian political unity.

Mercier's nationalist movement was rhetorical and political. It was opposed to the Ottawa Conservatives. It also materialized in positive action. With the help of Sir Oliver Mowat, Premier of Ontario, in whom he found an ally against Sir John A. Macdonald, Mercier took pleasure in reaffirming the rights of the provinces. He also, interestingly enough, foreshadowed the future political theories of Bourassa on two main points: (1) the interest in French Canadians in Canada outside Quebec; (2) the opposition to British imperialism of a new brand then being put forward by Joseph Chamberlain. Speeches made by Mercier on many occasions unmistakably illustrate the extent to which the last forms of his own nationalism connect up with Bourassa's nationalism to come.[22] Mercier's nationalism, spectacular and political as it was, aroused a certain amount of popular fervour but did not reach down to a very large portion of the population. It was Mercier as a man who was popular – to the point of becoming legendary even during his lifetime – rather than his nationalism. The tempo and intensity of communication with the country were not what they are today. Moreover, the main political issue which the always influential clergy had been stressing to the rural and even the urban population for years was anti-liberalism. It was mostly among college and university students that the rationale of nationalism could gain adherents. Mercier's slogans and catchwords were spread by the press, especially by the two exclusively 'national' newspapers, *La Vérité* in Quebec and *L'Etendard* in Montreal. Both stood for 'national' causes like provincial autonomy, the development of agriculture, the protection of French minorities outside Quebec, the official recognition of the French language, etc.

Other factors also did much to popularize the word 'national' with a French-Canadian connotation. Again, the Saint-Jean-Baptiste Society, for one, with its festive annual meetings officially gathering representatives from all the significant walks of French-Canadian life – clergy, politicians of all colours, journalists, writers, professionals, merchants, and students – was potent in developing an impressive nationalist symbolism for mass consumption. It has already been suggested that the slightly nationalist view of French-Canadian history originally implied the notion of a special divine mission granted to the French Canadians in North America. Such a view is a natural outcome of the theological-mindedness of the French-Canadian clerical leaders, particularly of those who shared the conception of history of Bossuet and De Maistre, according to whom Providence intervenes directly in human affairs, or, as Alfred de Vigny pleasantly remarked, 'plays checkers with kings and people'. The idea of a French-Canadian providential mission was recurrent in the writings of such men as Fréchette and the Abbé Casgrain who wrote that the French Canadians would 'lead back under the aegis of Catholicism the errant peoples of the New-World'. This idea had by this time become an oratorical commonplace. In 1879, Mgr Laflèche, in a letter to the President of the Saint-Jean-Baptiste Society of Quebec, was saying: 'I am of those who firmly believe that nations have a providential mission and that nothing can stop in their march those which tend constantly, without deviating to right or to left, toward the end which has been prescribed for them, no more than anything can save those which have prevaricated and finally left the paths which the Providence has traced for them. The teaching of the Church is, on this point, in harmony with that of history.'[23] This *leit-motiv* is amplified in such famous speeches as that of Justice A. B. Routhier at the national convention of the Saint-Jean-Baptiste Society in Quebec in 1880;[24] and in sermons preached on Saint-Jean-Baptiste days in Montreal, Quebec, and elsewhere, even outside the province, by lyrical guest orators.[25] A frequent implication of these religious deliveries is that an additional evidence of the French Canadians' inescapable divine mission lies in the fact that France has abdicated, in modern times, by becoming secular and atheistic, her former God-given mission on earth. They held that it is now up to French Canada to take on where old France has left off. An outstanding figure among the religious orators was Mgr L.-A. Pâquet, who was to become French Canada's foremost theologian and whose sermons on Saint-Jean-Baptiste days in 1887[26] and especially in 1902 remain the classics of patriotic literature and messianic nationalism. On the last occasion of the celebration of the Quebec Saint-Jean-Baptiste Society's diamond jubilee, Mgr Pâquet held that not only does each nation have its providential mission but that some of them have the honour of being called to a sort of priesthood among the others. They have a divine 'vocation' and such is the case of the French-Canadian people.[27]

Thus there evolved a French-Canadian body of national thought closely integrating the sacred with the secular. This philosophy, officially voiced by the clerical leaders, was implicitly or explicitly taken up and played upon with symphonic variations by the political leaders whose desire to utilize the national feeling made them sensitive to the people's accepted definition of national life. This trend of thought is sociologically significant because it helps us understand how the kind of halo which magnified Bourassa into a mystic figure could ever be possible.

iii: The Canadian, Anti-Imperialist Nationalism: Bourassa

Whenever Quebec nationalism is referred to, it is chiefly in connection with the Bourassa-worshipping movement which was born around the turn of the century and was to disappear or substantially transform itself at the end of the First World War. This period offers us the paradox of a man, Bourassa, who on the one hand came closest to being the French-Canadian equivalent of a charismatic leader, and whose nationalism on the other hand had officially little more than a broad Canadian connotation. Nationalism in this tumultuous phase took the form of a revival, gathering a wide range of supporters and followers, ideological, mystical, and political. It is a phase of, first, militant and aggressive, then opportunistic, nationalism.

Recent events in Canadian life had once more intensified the French-Canadian sense of solidarity. The way in which the Manitoba school question had been unsettled since 1890, and was finally decided in a way unfavourable to the French-speaking minority, became a matter of national discussion. The Canadian 'racial' conflict sprang to a new height. The Quebec French Canadians, on the whole, took sides with their ostracized compatriots, while on the other side an extremist English-speaking group outside Quebec entrenched itself behind an anti-French attitude not unrelated, as has been pointed out by many students of Canadian affairs, to the anti-Catholic dissatisfaction aroused among many Anglo-Protestant groups by Mercier's indemnity to the Jesuits in 1888. It was in large part around the Manitoba school question that Laurier had become prime minister in 1896. Later, in 1899, the Canadian official decision to participate in the South African war caused the recrudescence of a strong anti-imperialistic wave. Bourassa immediately resigned his seat in protest.

The Ligue Nationaliste (Nationalist League) grew up in Montreal around 1900 out of meetings organized by a group of combative patriots dissatisfied with the national attitude of the two great parties.[28] Bourassa was their idol.

The League was officially founded at a great mass meeting in Montreal in 1903, and in 1904 Asselin started publishing its official newspaper, *Le Nationaliste*. This nationalist revival was consciously strongly linked with the past.[29] Bourassa did not forget that he was Papineau's grandson, and his lieutenants never missed a chance of recalling it. The political program of the movement centred around the basic themes of integral bilingualism, anti-imperialism, the autonomy of Canada within the Empire and the autonomy of the province within Canada, opposition to mass European immigration, and the settlement of the minority school problems. The League also campaigned for the reorientation along nationalist lines of French-Canadian economic life. It was supported, on many issues, by a great number of the Quebec newspapers, among which were *L'Evénement* in Quebec, *L'Action Sociale* founded in 1908, *La Vérité* edited by Omer Héroux, and *La Libre Parole*.

In 1904 there was also founded in Montreal, under the auspices of the Jesuits, the A.C.J.C. (Catholic Association of Canadian Youth), which was a non-political association but which soon gave strong ideological support and dynamic following to the nationalist movement. It aimed at including all the male youth of the province, but at the beginning and for a long time afterwards consisted only of college study groups. Their official purpose, under the motto of 'Piety, Study, Action', was the study of national problems, but they soon began echoing the political campaigns of Bourassa and participating in organized, large-scale nationalist action and public demonstrations of their own. They organized campaigns for the recognition of bilingualism. They popularized the hero-worshipping of myth-transformed historical characters like Dollard, and of 'national' defenders or 'martyrs' like Papineau, Riel, etc. They generally appealed to public opinion for defensive action against all enemies of the French Canadians.

There existed then in Quebec, for the first time, a rather strongly organized body of nationalist political action which was active in federal, provincial, and even municipal elections. As suggested, it was still more a movement than a party in the true meaning of the word. Bourassa, for one, always protested that he had never wanted to create a real party, but it remains a fact that the movement of his followers played an important role between the Conservative and the Liberal parties. It was as a political group that nationalism drew to itself many political opportunists who saw in it the only means of fighting against Laurier, who had become the idol of the whole province, while the Conservatives alone could hardly do anything about it. On the other hand, the Liberal party was experiencing the handicap of all strong parties that remain long in power. The young Liberals were getting more independent and themselves felt, although to a lesser extent than the Conservatives, the appeal of Bourassa's nationalism. Many provincial political leaders sided in with the nationalists. One remembers the historical political campaigns of 1910–11 against Laurier's navy program and participation in imperial wars. The atmosphere was fierce and mystical. Lavergne, one of the champions of the movement, refers to himself and Bourassa as the then 'bishops' of nationalism.[30] This climax culminated in the defeat of Laurier in 1911. Soon after, when in power, many of the former nationalist, 'raisin-blue' Conservatives forgot their recent golden alliance with the nationalist movement.

French-Canadian nationalism during this whole period was given a manifold content by the various groups who directly or indirectly felt bound to it. Bourassa's followers on various levels interpreted his postulates according to their own respective perspectives, from mild anti-British feeling to ultra-nationalism. He was the prophet whose teachings are faithfully distorted by his proselytic disciples.

Formally, Bourassa's personal interpretation of nationalism forms a well-integrated ideology in which the French-Canadian approach as such is only secondary, the main emphasis being made on a broad Canadianism. First of all, Bourassa was never a separatist himself. Separatism at that time was represented by a lone wolf whom Bourassa occasionally attacked, J.-P. Tardivel, editor of the newspaper *La Vérité*.[31] Bourassa was, above all, historically always a fierce 'Canada-firster', in a constitutional and emotional way. His statements on this can be found anywhere in his innumerable writings and particularly in his articles in *Le Devoir*, the daily newspaper he founded in 1910. In a pamphlet on the 1911 tariff agreement between Canada and the United States Bourassa wrote that 'The general and superior interests of Canada must have priority over the more particular class or provincial interests; they must not be left under the predominance of American industry and transport; they must not be subordinated to a false imperial idea either. Now or never is the time to say: Canada to the Canadians and, in so saying, to yield neither to the Americans nor to the other parts of the Empire. Such is the true nationalist doctrine. It is as such that we have suggested its adoption long before the founding of *Le Devoir*.'[32] His concept of Canadian citizenship and Canadian patriotism is similarly well known. 'We do not have the right,' he says in a speech in Montreal in 1915, 'to make Canada an exclusively French country more than the Anglo-Canadians have the right to make it an English country....'[33] And again in his pamphlets entitled *Independence or Imperial Partnership?*:

> ... the preservation and simultaneous growth of two national languages and two different types of mental culture, far from being an *obstacle* to the progress of Canada, *constitute its most powerful factor and our greatest national asset*. The moment the English-speaking majority have found that much, they will make this other discovery: that the French Canadians are much more *Canadien* than *French*, and therefore, once left alone in the development of their *ethnical* propensities, always prepared to cooperate with the English majority, provided the latter prove also that they are more *Canadian* than *English* or *Imperial*. Then, the racial quarrel will be at an end or very near it. *So long as the majority of Canadians have two countries, one here and one in Europe, national unity will remain a myth and a constant source of internecine quarrels.*[34]

Bourassa's doctrinal nationalism awakened in Quebec diverse echoes which are still hard to appraise justly. The most crucial social class to consider in this connection is the clergy. From the very beginning of the nationalist movement, at the time of the South African war, diverse attitudes are noticeable among the clergy; one would almost say between the higher and the lower clergy. The clergy in general shared the feelings of the people who were anti-imperialist and sympathetic to the Boers, while the bishops and the Church official spokesmen expressed loyalty to the British Crown.[35] It is indubitable that the rural and the urban as well as the teaching clergy in the colleges were later gradually moved by Bourassa when he crusaded for the western schools, for the rights of the French language, and for a provincial policy of a wider and more technical colonization, and also when he showed a personal attitude of submissiveness to the Church.[36] His famous speech at the Montreal Eucharistic Congress in 1910, which identified the Catholic faith of the French Canadians with the French language and, later, the intellectual charm of *Le Devoir*, were influential in seducing the clergy. They, in their turn, were influential in galvanizing their flock or their students with messianic symbols. There was also, in 1910 in Quebec, the much-publicized first Congress of the French Language in America (Congrès de la Langue française en Amérique), which gathered, in a fascinating context, delegates from all the French-speaking groups in North America and helped sublimate official clerical inhibitions. When the 1914 war broke out and when passions became aroused it was discovered that a great part of the clergy was nationalist.[37] The Church hierarchy, however, as soon as the end of September 1914, published a joint pastoral letter stressing the fact that Canada's destiny was linked with that of England.[38] Typical divergent attitudes of the lower clergy are revealed in the polemics between two anonymous priests, one of them attacking Bourassa and nationalism, the other vigorously defending the 'true French-Canadian patriotism'.[39]

Given the direct influence of the clergy over the rural population and the appeal of the nationalist political campaigns, the country became, more than ever, consciously exalted by ambivalent patriotic symbols.[40] The permeation of nationalism into the cities is harder to appreciate. There, more than in the country, the political campaigns left their imprint. Young intellectuals were, on the whole, vibrating in unison with Bourassa's ideas. In the last years of the nationalist sawdust trail it was the 'school question', still more than the imperialist problem, which made of Bourassa a sort of champion of French Canadians. It was the Ontario school problem, the Regulation XVII, which, more than the war itself, did bring about the 'clash' between the two Canadian 'races'. To this vicarious struggle the French Canadians gave various meanings according to the stereotypes of their respective milieus. Hugh MacLennan's Marius Tallard is symptomatic of one, but only one, of them.

To sum up, one might say that Bourassa was the catalytic spirit who precipitated sour patriotism into a rationalized objective. French-Canadian collective thought could not, after this period, be the same. One of the very last official expressions of this phase was the motion presented by J. N. Francoeur, member for Lotbinière, in the Quebec legislature in January 1918.[41] This was the anti-climactic episode of a period of dynamism and frustration.

Already, another type of exclusively French-Canadian-centred nationalist movement was expressing itself. The Abbé Groulx had started his lectures and public speeches. The *Action française* began to be published in 1917. A considerable nationalist and parochial literature began to appear – Groulx's books, Brother Marie-Victorin's short stories, etc.; another phase was emerging which is too close to be considered objectively. It constitutes a landmark at which we must stop.

The history of French-Canadian nationalism, which still has to be written, appears to us, like the social history of any minority group, as a combative, stubbornly composed, unfinished symphony. It offers a wide field of investigation to historians, to political scientists, to sociologists, to economists, and to social psychologists. We notice that its growth has not been in a rectilinear, regularly widening pattern. It has been sporadic. A relevant way to approach it, in our opinion, is to see it as an acute political form of the French Canadians' interpretation of their minority status in a painfully growing country. It has emerged under the stimulus of events outside Quebec, which were interpreted either as threats to or as breaches of promise of the covenant assumed to sanction the recognition of the French Canadians as equal partners in the life of the nation. It has also emerged as a by-product of the self-centredness of the French-Canadian group, ideologically and culturally guided by a segregating clergy. It has been historically a paramount factor in the social outlook of Quebec. Like any social problem, it must be considered through neither an apologetic nor an antipathetic looking-glass.

2 Pierre Elliott Trudeau
Quebec on the Eve of the Asbestos Strike

The Ideas

It may seem a little arbitrary to try to analyse separately, at this point, the social thinking of French Canadians, and, farther on, the public institutions that our people evolved. Normally, a society's dominant ideas tend to become embodied in, and identified with, its institutions; so that an account of the leaders' ideas would, in effect, also indicate the nature of the institutions, which provide a framework for the leaders' actions.

In Quebec, however, during the first half of the twentieth century, our social thinking was so idealistic, so *a priori*, so far removed from reality – and, to be blunt, so ineffectual – that it practically never became a real part of the community's living and evolving institutions. To point out some of the underlying components of this thought may therefore help the reader to see how inadequately people were prepared – on the eve of the Asbestos strike – to face up to and to influence the true state of affairs in this highly industrialized province as described in a foregoing section.

I shall make little reference to the few sources of free and realistic thought that did exist on the fringes of what I shall call our monolithic ideology. This is not because I deny their existence. On the contrary, the far-reaching echoes of the Asbestos strike in many different circles show retroactively the farsightedness and the courage of those who had refused to accept our official philosophy as the embodiment of eternal wisdom. But, after all, I am attempting here not so much to draw up an honours list as to describe a society at a turning-point. And, to my mind, the scope and meaning of the upheaval . . . are linked less to the fact that a very few enlightened minds managed to understand and to sway developments than to the fact that a whole people were, by the force of events, propelled into a new way of life quite against the mainstream of their intellectual and moral outlook, which was leading them in a totally different direction. For this I shall now produce the evidence.

Translated from 'La Province de Québec au moment de la grève', in P. E. Trudeau (ed.), *La Grève de l'amiante*, Editions Cité Libre, Montreal, 1956, pp. 10–37.

1. The Main Pivot

Right up to the end of the period studied in this book, nationalism provided the pivot around which nearly all the contemporary social thinking of French Canadians revolved. This undisputed fact needs no elaborate explanation here. A people vanquished, occupied, leaderless, kept aside from business life and away from the cities, gradually reduced to a minority role and deprived of influence in a country which, after all, it had discovered, explored, and settled, could have but a limited choice of attitudes that might help it to preserve its own identity. A system of self-defence[1] was thus developed; but, as it grew out of bounds, it invested French Canadians' every distinguishing characteristic with inordinate value and made them hostile to all ideas for change, or even for possible improvement, that came from the outside.

That is why, pitted against an English, Protestant, democratic, materialistic, business-minded, and later industrial environment, our nationalism's system of self-preservation glorified every contrary tendency; and made a cult of the French language, Catholicism, authoritarianism, idealism, the rural way of life, including later, the myth of a 'return to the land'.

Out of these values, gravitating around the nationalist pivot, our social thinkers created an astrology designed to order the destinies of French Canada with the precision expected of a celestial system. Thus would our God-given mission be accomplished.

But while our theorists were, in the twentieth century, busy erecting a superstructure that would clearly and uniformly weld together all the social ideas that had served the French-Canadian group over a past period of its history, the people were, on their side, busy meeting the challenge of everyday life. A man's first compulsion is to stay alive and to provide a livelihood for his family, whatever the risk of upsetting current ideological niceties. In practice, therefore, the tenets of nationalism were applied so selectively that it survived as best it could. In the last century, for instance, a pretty pastoral dream cherished by the professional nationalists was tragically shattered by the exodus to the industrial centres of the United States. And authoritarianism lost much of its weight after Laurier was brought to power by a people to whom Mgr Laflèche had preached, during the 1896 electoral campaign, that 'a Catholic may not, under pain of grievous sin, vote for a party leader'[2] of Laurier's ilk.

I must therefore point out that I shall not go into what is sometimes (incorrectly) called 'our practical, down-to-earth nationalism' (which is nothing else than the exercise for better or for worse of everyday common-sense patriotism by an ethnic group, though political figures occasionally, *in retrospect*, claim to have been guided by it). What I *shall* be dealing with is our 'theoretical nationalism' – the one elaborated and applied by those who, in our group, took on the task of writing and teaching, and who were generally recognized as our mentors and leaders.

In the present context I can only refer to a few of these men, generally recognized as typical; and I cannot of course do full justice to the whole of their thinking. Perhaps I should therefore make it clear that, almost without exception, I believe them to merit respect. They lacked neither honesty of intent, nor courage in action, nor firmness of purpose; nor was their approach altogether lacking in originality. Surrounded by a materialistic civilization, and up against frequently callous politicians, the nationalist school was practically alone in elaborating a *system of thought*. Since I shall concentrate mainly on its economic and social aspects, I shall have little occasion to point out the worthwhile sides of this conceptual approach. But it would be quite wrong to assume that I am underrating its useful role. Perhaps it was first necessary to 'sauver la race' – save our people – as a preliminary step to later finding out what was worth 'saving' in the human race as a whole. And – since the growth of a culture spans several generations – might not today's generation have adopted yesterday's attitudes had it been born twenty years ago? Perhaps . . . However, since I intend to pass judgment on no one, I shall not let myself wander off into historical might-have-beens. That is also why I shall not quibble at singling out from nationalist thinking those elements which, today, burden the present and jeopardize free and straightforward action. In all fairness, however, I cannot start to criticize the nationalist school of thought without paying a tribute to its partisans; there have been many kinds of 'nationalists', but most of them were blessed with a sense of loyalty, a faith in the minds of men (if not invariably in men themselves!), and a certain respect for culture. Had such men taken no interest in public life, our people would less often have had the benefit of disinterested leadership.

It was, alas, the very idealism of the nationalists that most hurt them. They 'loved not wisely but too well'; and in their anxiety to obtain nothing but the best for French Canadians, they developed a social outlook impossible to put into practice, and which, to all intents and purposes, left the people without effective intellectual guidance. This is what I shall now analyse.

2. Nationalism as an Intellectual Discipline

In a 1902 sermon, which became 'the French Canadian's daily prayer-book', Mgr Paquet stated: 'We have the privilege to be entrusted with this social priesthood, granted but to select peoples . . . Our mission is less to handle capital than stimulate ideas; less to light the furnaces of factories than to maintain and spread far and wide, the glowing fires of religion and thought. . . . While our rivals are struggling for . . . the power that stems from industry and finance, our aspirations shall above all aim to uphold the honour of the doctrine and to gain the palms of apostleship.'

It is impossible to define in fewer words and more forcefully the curriculum of the school of idealism to which our intellectuals had to subscribe. All of them, one after another, strove 'to uphold the honour of the doctrine' – which, in the end, came to sterilize their minds. For the only 'truths' that might be expounded had to proceed from the most unproductive traditionalism.

Within a century of each other, two of the foremost teachers of 'the doctrine' established a rigid framework for all research. In the conclusion to his *History of Canada*, F.-X. Garneau wrote: 'Let Canadians be true to themselves; let them be wise and persevering, and let them not be seduced by the gleaming novelties of social and political life! They are not strong enough to make their fortunes thus. It is to larger nations that must fall the testing of new theories.' In 1945 the preaching of such excessive caution had become, in the hands of Esdras Minville, an imperative *Gleischaltung*:[3] 'It is not enough for all to will the good of the nation; it is important to seek *unanimously* the methods needed to achieve it . . .'[4] As we shall see, *unanimous* thinking, as envisaged by our nationalists, could only consist of timorous and reactionary thinking.

If anyone, therefore, ventured to think beyond the bounds of official nationalism, or even to restate it with a change in any of its basic tenets, he would automatically become suspect; he would be cornered and his ideas would undergo far-reaching search and scrutiny. Were he to renounce nationalism, he would find himself discredited and without an audience; were he to profess his faith in it, he would see his ideas emasculated and swallowed up in the mainstream.

This is what happened to Edouard Montpetit and to several other young professors on their return from Europe, before the First World War, bringing with them the then novel belief that our people should turn toward industry and finance. In this, they were only repeating an idea put forward a century earlier by Etienne Parent, Edmond de Nevers, and Errol Bouchette. But the idea was still unsanctioned, even though the lack of industry was causing an annual exodus of twenty thousand people to the United States. The young professors therefore came across only hostility and distrust; they were accused of atheism for the unanswerable reason that they were pronouncing the economic theories of liberalism.

But their stand was gradually worn down; they eventually came round to seeing their subject in 'nationalistic' and stationary terms – 'to think nationally' – [5] so that the official outlook on social matters got the chance to catch up with their thinking and to swallow it up. A few decades later they could thus imperturbably dispense outdated subject matter in our schools; all the more so as a growing number of our thinkers had already begun to take an interest in economic problems, quite obviously along nationalistic lines.

In 1921 Joseph Versailles, a Montreal financier, addressed a convention of the Catholic Association of Canadian Youth, saying: 'Let us stop serving our enemies. Material power must support moral strength, so that our people may stand up proudly and honourably . . . To succeed, we must do our utmost to launch our brightest young people in economic and financial careers.' That same year Action Française, then under the leadership of Abbé Groulx, undertook a protracted study of the economic question. Olivar Asselin in 1927 returned to the subject of the economic position of French Canadians, and concluded that, while they represented two-sevenths of the Canadian population, they owned only one-seventh of the national wealth. 'Our economic wealth,' he wrote, 'barely corresponds to half our numerical size.'[6]

During the depression years, economic nationalism was a lively subject of discussion. Thus, in 1934, according to *Le Devoir* of October 30, Abbé Groulx asked: 'Is there any inherent or unavoidable reason why, with 2,500,000 French

Canadians in Quebec, all big business, all high finance, all the public utilities, all our water rights, forests and mines, should belong to a minority of 300,000?' (This, of course, referred to an *ethnic* minority; no support must be read into it for the theory that property is theft.) That same year Athanase David, Provincial Secretary of Quebec, in his book *En Marge de la politique*,[7] dared to state: 'Isn't it about time for the graduates of our classical colleges to stop seeing, in business, industry and finance, occupations unworthy of their culture and training? I am convinced of the need for money, because it will allow us to fulfil the great tasks which our destiny requires of us on this continent.' In 1936 Victor Barbeau sized us up in his *Mesure de notre taille*, and argued (p. 24) that 'besides the land, the abandoned, the unhappy land, besides the few little islands we hold on to through force of inertia, we have nothing, we are left with nothing at all. We cannot even enjoy the yields of the boundless resources that God placed within our reach.'

So, in a province where sixty-three per cent of the population lived in the cities, in a fairly industrialized society, in a city which in 1933 had an unemployment rate of thirty per cent and had 280,000 persons receiving direct assistance, the inadequacy of pinning hopes upon 'the honour of the doctrine and the palms of apostleship' at the expense of the industrial phenomenon was gradually becoming apparent. People were beginning to see that the engineer, the tradesman, and the businessman played as important a social role as the priest, the doctor, and the lawyer. But, since these truths were looked at solely from within the nationalist context, infinite care was taken to adopt no solution that might upset any of the traditional assumptions.

As an example, let us look at the views concerning agriculture. After having suggested settling our economic problems through 'Buy French Canadian', Edouard Montpetit stated: 'This will do for secondary industry, since it is largely supplied by agriculture which will remain the basic industry, the provider of raw materials.'[8] Two months later, Olivar Asselin wrote a moving appeal against selling out our natural resources and against the population exodus to the United States, but came to this strange conclusion: 'To keep the natural increase of our population in this country, we will not need new industries, provided we find a means of attaching the sons of farmers to the land.' He advocated new settlements in the Abitibi area, and felt that the involvement of our people in major industry could be postponed until some later date.[9] Then, in 1928, presenting the conclusions of his 1927 study (mentioned above) in *Action française*, Asselin dwelt mainly on rural questions; while he did, in fact, favour a revolutionary policy of the eventual return to the state of the natural resources exploited by private enterprise, his main emphasis was nevertheless on agricultural reforms and improvements, on rural labourers and rural schools, as well as on fisheries. Victor Barbeau[10] proclaimed that agriculture would have spared us the humiliations of economic depression, and actually *criticized* us for having 'rushed towards the fires that industry was kindling throughout our hills and vales'. Athanase David[11] was careful not to forget that 'Quebec is farmland above all else; it is and will remain an agricultural province.' Henri Laureys, in spite of being principal of the Ecole des Hautes Etudes Commerciales, went scarcely any farther: 'To develop and reach its full potential, Quebec agriculture must seek through a certain extension of industry the expansion that its geographical situation does not permit.'[12] And in 1945, Father Arès, S.J., dealing with 'our national question' in a book by that title,[13] wrote that the industrial revolution 'could only have a disastrous effect on our people ... [because] we have neither the capital, nor the industrial and business traditions, nor the great technical schools; and, above all, we have no clearly defined social and national doctrine.' To fill the gap, this nationalist thinker put forward a social doctrine of his own, based on the following principles: 'The countryside's lessening role is a great misfortune, because of the primary importance of rural areas in the life of nations in general, and of our nation in particular. Indeed, as Minville writes, "the countryside has always provided, and particularly in our restless and disoriented age still provides, a reservoir of physical and moral strength upon which a nation can draw. . . ." From the social and ethical point of view [Father Arès continued], large cities, particularly in times of unemployment, wear down men's bodies and souls, disrupt families, breed quarrels and hatreds, foment revolutionary ideas and social unrest.'[14]

After having thus impressed city workers with their innate inferiority, and having declared that a province, barely five per cent of whose land could qualify as arable,[15] should pursue an agricultural destiny, the theorists nevertheless had to come to the point of suggesting some cures for the 'evils' of industrialization.

Unfortunately, practically no one was equipped for this task. Clergymen, journalists, lawyers, and accountants all tried their hand at sociology and economics; but they were unable to free themselves from a heritage that was traditionalist, anti-modern, and imbued with authoritarianism and haphazard methods.

And so, when they had energetically diagnosed our intellectual poverty as well as our social and economic inadequacies; when they had castigated the inertia of our people and exhorted them to initiative and perseverance; when they had done with preaching family, rural, and national virtues; when they had talked sufficiently about educational reforms and assiduously covered every inch of familiar ground – their social thinking came to an abrupt end. It fell singularly short of saying anything about our adjustment to the realities of the industrial revolution.

Their obsession with caution and self-preservation, which had inhibited their search for original solutions to the problems of changing times, also prevented them from studying the solutions worked out in other countries.

There is in fact something astounding about the persistence with which our official thinkers shied away from all contemporary thought in the social sciences. To judge by their writings, it is no exaggeration to say that, until very recently, they were innocent of any acquaintance with the newer world-wide trends in legal theory from Dubuit to Pound; in sociology from Durkheim to Gurvitch; in economics from Wallas to Keynes; in political theory from Bosanquet to Laski; in psychology from Freud to Piaget; in educational theory from Dewey to Ferrière.

With what, then, did they fill in the gaps in their social thinking? With a collection of ideas that they called the social doctrine of the Church.

3. 'Our' Catholic Social Doctrine

We must here distinguish clearly between the social ethics of Catholicism, as expounded by some of the popes who devoted special study to the profound changes occurring in contemporary society, and the social doctrine of the Church as conceived of and applied in French Canada.

The former lies outside my present scope; but the latter is precisely what I shall be dealing with. In effect it amounts to an extension of our traditionalist assumptions, adorned by the cloak of papal authority. Indeed, with their lack of readiness to acknowledge, and in no way prepared to understand, the new phenomena of industrialization and proletarianization, our official thinkers could not easily grasp the far-reaching scope of the social encyclicals promulgated to abolish what Pius XI had called the scandal of the Church. Our theoreticians therefore simply singled out, in the social teaching of the popes, those formulas which might confer a semblance of prestige on our own group prejudices.

This spurious use of papal authority to support nationalism was abetted by a misunderstanding of the popes' pronouncements against the abuses of capitalism. The popes censured the capitalist system for keeping part of the proletariat in a state of abject poverty and for preventing the development among a great many people of truly human values; whereas our clerical-nationalist doctrine seemed mainly to hold it against the system that it kept French Canadians in a state of economic subjection, and prevented the development among them of predominantly nationalist values. Abbé Groulx was quoted approvingly by Father Arès[16] as saying: 'It is not only certain classes that are being subjected to oppression, it is a whole nation'; and yet Abbé Groulx took a more realistic stand than many others, for he also said: 'I am not claiming, mind you, that had the captains of industry and finance come from our own people, we would have been better off socially . . . but social ills would have remained social ills; the emotional element that dangerously exacerbates them would have been absent.'[17]

The inference is that a native capitalism would have spared us all the misfortunes that may be compounded by an 'emotional element'! Our captains of industry would have protected us from world-wide economic depression; but had they failed to do so, the unemployed would have eschewed any grudges against bosses of their own blood! Thus, for our social thinkers, industrialization had produced no serious problem not already known at the time of *Maria Chapdelaine* – which they were all fond of quoting; their lament remained unchanged : 'Around us strangers have come, whom we are wont to call the barbarians; they have taken hold of nearly all the power; they have taken over nearly all the money . . .' As a result, it was beyond their understanding that, to fit into a world changed by the industrial revolution, they would need to change some of their traditional concepts and methods of action. 'That is why we must stay in the Province where our fathers stayed, and live as they lived . . . Nothing must change . . .'[18]

In this way the social doctrine of the Church – which, in other countries, had openly welcomed popular democracy, the emancipation of workers, and social progress – in French Canada was called upon to support authoritarianism and xenophobia. And, worse still, our 'doctrine' helped make it impossible for us to solve our problems. For, on the negative side, it rejected all solutions that could be successful against our 'enemies': the English, the Protestants, the materialists, etc. And, on the positive side, it remained content with elaborating theoretical systems, devoid of any objective link with reality and often totally inapplicable in practice.

4. Negative Effects of the Doctrine

In the economic field we rejected the correctives to capitalism thought out by the liberal economists of Sweden and England and suggested to us by federal civil servants in Ottawa. Thus our own dismayed helplessness toward the problem of unemployment, together with our adamant opposition to any constitutional amendment that might allow Ottawa to cope with the problem, represents one of the most tragic episodes of the thirties. Our economists even saw to it that Quebec's unemployed got less help than the jobless in other provinces: as Esdras Minville notes, Quebec 'received less because it asked for less . . . In some way it instinctively feared excessive demands in return . . . The other provinces, who have a *traditionally different attitude toward expenditures*, seemed on the contrary, to have wanted to take the greatest possible advantage of federal disbursements, such as public works, etc.'[19]

In the social sector, too, our inconsistency was great. For instance, in line with papal doctrine we had long been in favour of a 'just family wage'. But our very feeble influence over the capitalist world on the one hand, and on the other our unremitting view of the State as an ogre eager to devour families, stood in the way of this reform; so we failed to introduce it either through pressure on private enterprise or through appropriate social legislation. As a result, family allowances – favoured by the Church, and fully with the province's constitutional rights – finally came to French-Canadian families by grace of the federal and 'Protestant' State. It is an interesting sidelight that François-Albert Angers, the most impressive economist in our nationalist group, decided, in support of the claim that family allowances are an infringement upon paternal authority, to set the example of personally refusing them.

The case of old-age pensions is also worth quoting: federal legislation in the matter goes back to 1927, and the provinces one by one decided to make the plan available to their older citizens. The last province to act was Quebec, which waited until 1936. It will not be surprising to remember that up to 1939 the best-known sociologist in French Canada preached the traditional doctrine in these terms: 'The organization of *social welfare services* in the Province of Quebec rests upon private initiative. And it is the consensus among Catholics that this should continue to be so. The State must only supplement, fill the gaps, and not displace or dominate . . . The urgency or the need for various social measures varies from people to people and from era to era.'[20]

Finally, in the political field, we similarly condemned ourselves to a no less appalling paralysis. Our political ideas were shot through with authoritarianism, and we persistently envisaged the State as an entity independent of its citizens. This congenital belief that even the provincial government (notwithstanding its dependence on the electoral will of a French-Canadian majority) could neither serve our interests nor be brought under our control may even be seen in a social thinker who did, however, patiently try to rehabilitate democracy in the eyes of a public that placed scant faith in it. Maximilien Caron analysed the greatness and the subservience of the State in these terms: '. . . *The masses* can thus snatch [from political parties] a series of concessions, which may finally *exasperate the authorities*, seriously jeopardize the finances of *the State*, and bring about the ruin of the system . . . The State, while a witness to such fratricidal struggles [between rich and poor], is *nearly always a helpless* bystander.'[21] Discussing corporatism, the same author refers to the legislative function of the State: 'Corporative arrangements are a thousand times preferable to cartels or to direct State control over the economy. Corporative rules are adopted openly, with the consent of a majority of the interested parties, under the supervision of both public authorities and of groups responsible for protecting the consumers.'[22] But how else, then, did this lawyer envisage the legislative process in a democratic State?

This state of mind, together with the papal condemnation of atheistic socialism, served us as a pretext for rejecting a new Canadian social democratic party, the Co-operative Commonwealth Federation (C.C.F.) – little as it dabbled in either atheism or philosophy, and much as it put forward quite specific political remedies designed to end the very economic colonialism that our nationalism found so offensive.

Altogether, our political thinking was pretty fairly summed up in a lecture by Cardinal Villeneuve on the social doctrine of the Church, where we find the following conclusions: 'The C.C.F. doctrine has been condemned in a pastoral letter by Monsignor Gauthier, Archbishop of Montreal. The C.C.F. differs from communism mainly in that it does not seek to achieve its ends by violent means . . . [As to Social Credit], the Church is neither for nor against the Social Credit Party . . . With respect to fascism, [Mussolini] greatly contributed to saving the peace of Europe through his presence at Munich. The Italian system of government presents certain dangers, it is true, but we must not forget that democratic government also has its dangerous aspects.'[23]

It will be clear that this kind of pronouncement – in a climate where a bishop's 'may' was as good as his 'shall' – did not tend to encourage people in the objective search for facts, or in the exercise of that free judgment which must underlie the practice of democracy. Basically, in fact, our thinkers seemed to harbour a far-reaching distrust of the people, who – by abandoning the land where starvation lay in wait – had in some way betrayed their God-given mission and were courting disaster by looking for jobs in the cities. At bottom, no doubt, the social doctrine of the Church in Quebec envisaged political society in terms of élites and leaders, rather than in terms of the political education of the masses.

This was, indeed, a time when Les Editions de l'A.C.J.C. (Catholic Association of French-Canadian Youth) published a book entitled *On demande les chefs.*

Elsewhere Abbé Groulx, dealing with 'language and survival', wrote: 'And yet we have a splendid army of teachers ready to serve us. All they need is a doctrine, a method, a stimulus. Who will supply the impulse, the energy and inspiration, the will? Who will be the national leader? Who will prove to be a de Valera, a Mussolini, whose policies may be disputed – but who, over a ten-year span, psychologically made a new Ireland and a new Italy, just as Dollfuss and Salazar are building a new Austria and a new Portugal? It is, alas, necessary to recognize that no such national leader is in sight. Will we ever have one? . . . Let us, with humble hearts, ask Providence for this leader without whom no people can forge their destiny; and, meantime . . .', etc.[24]

The editors of *L'Action nationale* also stated: 'French Canada needs a leader . . . a leader, a true leader, imbued with our traditions, strong in our faith, clearminded, strong-willed, warm-hearted; that is what our survival imperiously calls for. May Providence bring him forth.'[25]

Albert Lévesque, a publisher of nationalist literature, wrote in the same vein: 'For a number of years in fact, young people have clamoured for leaders; indeed, they feel they have been bereft of proper guidance; and they look for it among their elders.'[26] And Esdras Minville, who in 1945 wrote two volumes entitled *Le Citoyen canadien-français*, in which he called on the élite to play its full part, had already mentioned, as one of the 'special characteristics' of our popular attitudes, 'a practically spontaneous acceptance of authority and hierarchy in the family, in society, and in the State. *French Canadians like to be ruled . . .*'[27]

A final characteristic of our social doctrine, which must be mentioned before analysing its positive content, is an idealism bordering on the schizophrenic. Climbing upward was admittedly perhaps the only way out of the blind alley in which our thinking had trapped itself.[28] On the one hand, in fact, our ethnic group had no influence whatever on the private sector of the economy: we could always seek consolation in the 'palms of apostleship', but they were of little help in correcting a situation in which we were limited to a subservient role. And, on the other hand – on top of our deep-seated horror of anything that smelled of State intervention – we shunned any political action liable to produce economic reforms, for the irrefutable reason that the reforms favoured by liberal economists were advocated by 'Anglo-Saxons', whereas socialist reforms were the brain-children of 'materialists'. Indeed, the insolvency of our social sciences hardly discouraged us from our ambitious search for the ideal solutions: 'A Catholic is too rich to go borrowing ideas from socialists or communists.' We had scant success in the field of social policies; yet we must 'keep [political power] in our hands, entirely in our hands. We must win it back from the grasp of financiers and free it from Ottawa's tentacles.' We had produced little but company-dominated unions, but 'let us not abandon our workers to foreign organizers'.[29]

Esdras Minville, answering a questionnaire on '25 years of national life',[30] summed up our economic position thus: 'the obvious inability of the capitalist system to solve the painful problems to which it itself gives rise, on the one hand; on the other, the inhuman character of the so-called reforms advocated by the supporters of communism and totalitarianism of every hue, have convinced [French Canadians] of a basic truth, namely that they can expect no one but themselves to come forward with a solution to their problems. Consequently, for some years now, instead of turning abroad for guidance, for a line of thought or a doctrine, they have started searching for these within, in their own social philosophy and in a study of their actual situation.'

As for national pride, the young did not lag far behind their elders. André Laurendeau, tolling 'an alarm for French Canadians',[31] criticized Mr. Godbout for having accepted an amendment to the Constitution that would allow the federal government to deal (at last) with the problem of unemployment; and he explained why Ottawa had to be kept out of the field of social legislation: '[Ottawa's interference] would mean that reforms undertaken or needed to bring social life into closer conformity with Catholic ethics would come under the scrutiny of a Protestant majority. This would mean the end of all hope of corporatism, and for a long time set aside all hope of adjusting social legislation to family needs (the Anglo-Saxon outlook being geared more to the interests of the individual than to those of the family) as well as of meeting the need of a particular group and area (since Ottawa legislates for the country as a whole rather than for its individual parts) . . . We cannot, therefore, under any pretext whatsoever, bargain away any of our social legislation; *we need it all.*' (Mr. Laurendeau's italics and parentheses.)

This is a rather startling attitude in view of the long-standing backwardness of Quebec's social policies. Self-government is an admirable aim, of course – provided a people really intend to govern themselves. Now, let us look at the positive home-grown measures considered to offer an alternative to the array of perilous reforms suggested to us from the outside.

5. The Positive Message

Obviously no exhaustive list can be drawn up of every panacea put forward by French Canada's thinkers over the last half-century. Some of these, like the revival of handicrafts, were too clearly insignificant to merit much attention. Others, like our views on immigration, in effect amounted to a rejection which may be listed among the negative products of our doctrine. Others still, like some of the statements about State control and nationalization, were too sporadic, too timid, and above all too inconsistent to amount to a truly 'positive' message. It may therefore be said in short that our nationalist 'Catholic' social doctrine proposed renewing our economic and social structures in five ways – by promoting: a return to the land, small businesses, co-operatives, Catholic trade-unionism, and corporatism.

A return to the land

'Colonization' – the settling of new land – and campaigns to encourage a 'return to the land' almost invariably received prominent billing whenever we re-opened the search for remedies to the ills of industrialization. I have already shown above that agriculturalism[32] was part and parcel of our nationalism; and I have also shown that whoever wanted to discuss our economic problems had first to offer up sacrifices to the rural deities, so I shall merely add a few typical examples at this point.

In a series of articles on the economic crisis, written in September 1931, Henri Bourassa advocated the prime remedy of a 'return to the land'.[33] And in May 1933 *L'Action nationale* informed us that the Ecole Sociale Populaire had elaborated a program of social rehabilitation, which inspired Father Alexandre Dugrès, S.J., to say: 'We must toil or die, sow or go jobless . . . Our race will be agricultural, or it will cease to grow, it will perish.'

Finally, in 1938, in the previously mentioned study on 'Labour Legislation and the Social System in the Province of Quebec', Esdras Minville – who had the clear-sightedness to be fairly early aware of Quebec's industrial vocation – nevertheless speaks of reforms as follows: 'From the sociological point of view, unemployment insurance, as well as a certain number of other legislative social measures, appear to be *more or less called for* in the Province of Quebec. In an appendix to our brief on the trade-union movement, we dwelt at some length on the seriousness of Quebec's *rural problem*. We consider, and we know that most economists and sociologists who have studied the situation share this view, that the desertion of our farms and the extreme congestion in our cities, particularly Montreal, lie at the root of our present economic instability. Any measure that might tend towards *further improving the life of the industrial workers*, or at any rate that might foster the illusion that the urban workers' existence is becoming easier and more secure, would almost inevitably accelerate the *tendency to abandon the farms*, unless the rural population were given equivalent advantages . . .'[34]

Small business

Edouard Montpetit stated: 'In the field of production, a study of our needs has long convinced me that, for the time being, we should *concentrate upon medium and small industry*.'[35] Maximilien Caron covered practically all our reforms in one paragraph when he wrote: 'Let us develop small and medium industry; and in order to succeed, let us apply the principles of co-operatism. We will then manage to create in our fellow citizens this deep belief that a healthy prosperity must be based upon principles of healthy corporatism.'[36] An American sociologist thus relates the sermon of a small-town parish priest delivered on Saint-Jean-Baptiste Day: 'The true French Canadian [must] practice thrift and become the owner of a small property. Anglo-Saxon methods are not for us. It was small savings and small business that made the French powerful. Beware of applying alien business methods here.'[37] And Henri Laureys, concluding the address quoted from previously, hoped that 'French Canadians would resolutely participate in small and medium enterprise'.

Mr. Minville also reports that many people stressed 'Let us get control of small business'; but he quite correctly demolishes this aspect of our doctrinal myth when he adds: 'besides the fact that economists have never provided a satisfactory definition of small business, the question arises how small business might withstand the competition of big business, and particularly how can a community ever, through the control of small business alone, gain adequate independence in an economic system designed and oriented in terms of big business and dominated by it.'[38] Needless to say, this crucial question was never answered. But the strangest thing is that it even seems to have been forgotten by its author. In 1945 he suggested reforming the economy's industrial structure by incorporating part-time industrial workshops within the rural set-up: agriculture, forestry, and fisheries . . .[39]

The co-operative movement

Credit must certainly be given to our theorists for having understood that co-operatives could have become – had we gone about it otherwise – a tool for the emancipation of a people who were short of capital but long on numbers. Alphonse Desjardins and his disciples were admirable pioneers in this respect.

But while co-operative ideas met with a certain success in rural areas and among fishermen, they failed sadly in urban centres, and small wonder that they did. Co-operatives presuppose a respect for democratic responsibilities and for collective ownership, two concepts which the fear of socialism, particularly lively in the cities, led us to reject lock, stock, and barrel. Moreover, promotion of the co-operative idea seems to have been undertaken in the worst of all possible ways. Some of the apostles of the movement appeared to address their special appeals to the Saint-Jean-Baptiste Societies and to other groups of small owners and tradesmen who were particularly unlikely to commit economic suicide for the sake of a dubious nationalism. Others, it is true, sought to convert the workers, but they appeared at too late a stage in our economic development; the co-operative movement could no longer by itself (i.e. without active political support) fend for itself in an economy already wholly dominated by capitalistic institutions. And, to make matters worse, the Society of Jesus led a vigorous campaign to institutionalize the religious character of co-operatives – which in no way promoted their acceptance in urban communities whose people were of various faiths and languages. As the then-Provincial of the Dominicans wrote in defence of Father Lévesque, who had been attacked by the Jesuits for having favoured the non-confessional character of the co-operatives: 'Without going as far as to assert it positively, I have reason to fear that in certain circles the religious character of secular institutions is being used as a cover up for narrow nationalism.'[40]

Catholic trade-unionism

The role of Catholic and French-Canadian trade-unionism in creating workers' self-awareness in Quebec should not be underrated; it is mainly due to this movement that the Quebec worker came to formulate, in his own language and in terms of his own ideas, the problems and solutions applicable to his particular industrial world. But this result, one might almost be tempted to say, was achieved by chance rather than by design.

In fact, Catholic trade-unionism did not stem primarily from a generous urge to find some solution to the real hardships of our Catholic proletariat in Quebec. Like much of the rest of our social doctrine, our trade-union ideas were born of a nationalist reaction against outside reforms, after their timely application had been unconscionably delayed by our own neglect. The birth of our denominational trade-unionism, a product of artificial insemination, is hardly a page to be proud of in Labour's history. To perceive the movement's xenophobic, authoritarian, and unrealistic roots, we need only listen to the indefatigable promoter of the Ecole Sociale Populaire, attempting to justify our long-standing blindness: 'The need [to stand united after the Conquest] made French Canadians into one great family without caste distinction or class rivalries. Gradually, with the growth of our population, social differences did arise; but they were barely perceptible, and lacked the glaring inequalities that elsewhere divide the rich from the wage-earners, and that create such bitter animosities. These are the circumstances that here delayed the Church's participation in the setting up of trade unions. When . . . under the impulse of new economic conditions, such as the growing cost of living and the development of industries based on anonymous foreign capital, the Church *thought the time had come* for workers' associations – nearly all the difficulties it came up against originated [*sic*] with the American organization. The employers, who had already suffered from the activities of the Workers' International, and whose sense of social responsibility was, indeed, minimal, generally proved hostile to the movement. On their side, a good number of workers who belonged to their own unions, or who, without actually being members, were nevertheless influenced by the concept of neutrality which the unions were propagating among the masses, proved unresponsive to the Church's initiative . . . The hardest times, however, were over. Thanks to the clear instructions of the Episcopate, based upon the teachings of Rome, thanks to the energy of chaplains and to the faith of several employers and of a *sizeable number of workers*, Catholic workers' organizations are now developing satisfactorily.' And the good Father concludes that 'the élite influences the masses' and that – in order to serve 'our people and the Church' – the doctrine needs to be preached in all circles, in churches, Parliament, the press, financial and industrial circles, and *even* (!) 'in the factories where an all-too-often bitter and threatening proletariat is rife'.[41]

During the same Semaine Sociale, Mgr Lapointe, one of the founders of our Catholic trade-unionism, stated, without turning a hair: 'The clergy, at the right moment, as soon as it proved feasible, did for the workers what it had done for all other classes of citizens . . . It once again acted here, I am sure everyone will recognize, as a far-sighted and well-inspired initiator.'[42]

One may well wonder what inspired Cardinal Taschereau to condemn the Knights of Labour, a gesture which Alfred Charpentier (before his 'conversion' and appointment as first president of the Catholic trade unions) described as the result of 'thoughtlessness, hastiness and a lack of competent familiarity with the subject'.[43] And we may wonder at the 'farsightedness' which – for instance in Chicoutimi and Jonquière in 1913 – had led 'the Catholic authorities' to launch 'an all-out appeal' against the international unions, calling upon 'the workers to unite and chase them out, as a pre-requisite to preserve their Catholic faith'.[44]

With the years the aggressive tone became somewhat subdued, but the attitude remained the same. Thus, in 1937, during a strike in the garment industry in Montreal, the religious authorities firmly supported the Catholic unions against the I.L.G.W.U., the Catholic unions having accepted a collective agreement that violated the minimum-wage legislation.[45]

Again in 1938, Father Arès wrote in the *Petit Catéchisme d'éducation syndicale*: 'In the Province of Quebec, may a Catholic worker decide to belong to a neutral union rather than to a Catholic union? No; unless he should suffer serious injury were he to leave the neutral union in order to join the Catholic one, e.g. if he thereby ran the risk of losing *the only job open to him*' (p. 28, italics added). And the following year, Mr. Minville, referring to the international (American) labour movement, wrote: 'The a-religious character of the unions almost inevitably confronts their members with a choice between two loyalties: to their religion, or to their labour association.' And, a little further on: 'The international labour movement, in view of its doctrinal sources, no more guarantees order than does the revolutionary individualism from which it flows; no more, indeed, than does communism, towards which this movement's ideas lead by a natural, so to speak, progression'. To which Mr. Minville candidly added the comment that his line of argument 'in effect amounted to a summary of the vast campaign in favour of Catholic and national trade unionism carried out in November [1937] by the French and Catholic press and by the radio'. Finally, moving into the realm of fact, the same sociologist admitted that the 'trade unionism' he so nonchalantly slandered 'certainly went neither as far nor as fast as its principles would have allowed it to do. All the same, its inclination is to the left. Its tendencies are shown clearly enough by the trend of its claims: before 1872, it fought for the 9-hour work day . . . [and today] it favours the 6-hour work day and the 30-hour week.' No doubt about it: a clear portent of progression towards undisguised bolshevism! The argument closes with a plea in favour of 'the employer who has as much right to a decent life as the worker'.[46]

What better indictment against this phalanx of social thinkers than the words of a 'neutral' trade-unionist quoted by Mgr Lapointe? 'We have, Father . . . for many years suffered, laboured, worked for starvation wages. When we protested our misery and were met with gun-fire like rebels and revolutionaries, where were you? You exhorted us to patience, talking about salvation, and delivered fine sermons about respect for the social order. Well, Father, you failed to show us any solution. Then, organized labour stretched out its hand to us from the United States; we were glad to grasp it. Today, you tell us this is no good. Why couldn't you have said so sooner?'[47]

The truth is that the hardship of our workers only became apparent to our sociologists when their nationalism led them to denounce the international unions. Then, with a clerical and employer-oriented paternalism, they preached denominational trade-unionism, because 'without this method, *no authority will be able to impose* Christian principles upon these associations, where men of all opinions mix.'[48] And, forgetful of the deep scars they had left upon the labour movement, and the profound dismay they had created in Christian consciences, our social thinkers once again found refuge in the comfortable myth of our God-sent mission. Bourassa concluded a series of articles on trade-unionism with an appeal to workers' nationalism, isolationism, and social conservatism.[49]

It is not surprising that the following year he again denounced 'the gaping wound of industrialization, and its inevitable consequence, the abandonment of the farms'.[50] And Alfred Charpentier, after having addressed to *Le Devoir* a public profession of faith in the 'workers' nationalism', later wrote: 'It would indeed seem that God has allowed our people to grow in this corner of the country, despite past persecutions, so that it might become the purifying element of the whole Canadian nation . . . Our Catholic workers are also called upon by Providence to do their share in the task of protecting the working classes of the country against the dangers that lie in wait.'[51]

Corporatism

Corporatism is, without doubt, the most important of the reforms envisaged by our social thinkers. The single-mindedness, constancy, enthusiasm, and futility with which different men, in the most varied circumstances, with the most divergent aims, preached the corporatist gospel provides the most crushing evidence of our monolithic ideology.

Year after year, in and out of context, the lecturers at the Semaines Sociales grasped every opportunity to eulogize corporatism: starting with Mgr Paquet and the future Mgr Desranleau in 1921, through Jean Bruchési (1936), up to Maximilien Caron (three times from 1938 to 1942). Mr. Caron relied upon authorities as disparate as Cardinal Villeneuve ('Corporatism to the full!') and the premier of the province ('Whatever leads us towards corporatism represents progress'). In 1942 Gérard Picard still referred to trade-unionism as a method of furthering the corporative organization of society.

The contributors to *L'Action nationale* also went through a period of ardent corporatism. In November 1937 Roger Duhamel envisaged the victory of nationalism through national and Catholic trade-unionism, which would reach its pinnacle in corporatism. The following year a long study of corporatism was undertaken, in which the most diverse authorities reached agreement: Abbé J. B. Desrosiers (who, during a Semaine Sociale at the Collège Jean-de-Brébeuf in November 1937, had also advocated instituting the just family wage through corporatism), François Hertel (later a supporter of corporatist personalism, which he would continue to advocate as late as 1945 in his *Nous ferons l'avenir* (We Shall Mould the Future)), F.-A. Angers (the trade unions must move towards corporatism); other adepts who participated in this study were Messrs. Hermas Bastien, Gérard Filion, Esdras Minville. Father G.-H. Lévesque was also of their number: he advocated close ties between the co-operative and the corporatist movements.

Father Arès drew up the corporatist catechism. Indeed, in his trade-union catechism, he had not omitted to point out (Question 45) that trade-unionism represents a first step toward corporatism. Victor Barbeau concluded his outstanding study of Quebec's economic misery by a plea in favour of economic and political corporatism.[52] That same year Dostaler O'Leary published a book entitled *Séparatisme* (in the Jeunesses Patriotes collection) and asked for 'the establishment of a corporative system in the free French State' (p. 125). The Bloc Universitaire, at its Duchesnay meeting in 1939, advanced the hope that each of our Social Science Schools would try to awaken every student's interest in, specifically, corporatism.

The list of references might be extended indefinitely. But isn't the picture of our philosophical idealism already sufficiently clear? Several decades of social thought can practically be summed up in a single word: corporatism. It was enough that the expression should have been used by a pope, and that the English should never have sung its praises, for us to seize upon it as a universal panacea. So everyone happily recommended this miraculous cure-all, whose advocacy had the added advantage of not requiring any deep personal thought. Everyone felt relieved of the obligation to search for social solutions appropriate to the trend of the times, since it was enough to invoke the currently favoured prejudice to win recognition as a Catholic and a national sociologist.

Whether or not the corporatist doctrine has anything to contribute to a political theory based on progress is a matter I need not discuss here. But there is no doubt whatever that objective economics and sociology have as yet failed to show how a legal superstructure, which introduces no basic changes into capitalist institutions, might reconcile the opposite interests of capital and labour, except in specific and limited instances. But then the inevitable rise of social and economic cartels, inherent in the corporative system, might well create conflicts of interests (e.g. cartel versus cartel, or cartel versus consumers) which only oligarchic arrangements or even a dictatorship might prove capable of settling or checking. That is why it would surely be extremely dangerous to experiment with the system anywhere but among a people with the most deeply ingrained democratic reflexes, so that there would be unfailing subordination of individual interests (lying within the purview of the corporations) to the common interest (which is the responsibility of the State).

Now, on the contrary, most of our thinkers saw in corporatism a way of taming the 'democratic strength of trade unionism'; and they only accepted trade-unionism because they envisaged it as a stepping-stone to corporatism. In fact, our corporatism was conceived of in terms of an élite, which might use it to discipline popular forces and to preserve its authority over the organized masses. The people, however, were not taken in. When, finally, an objective study was carried out of the results of almost half a century of theoretical corporatism, it was realized that its failure had been complete: 'There is practically no organization in existence whose administrative structure comes at all close to the model described by the theorists.'[53]

It is still in Ecclesiastes where perhaps the best comment can be found on our over-all social ideas during the half-century that preceded the Asbestos strike: '*mataiotès mataiotètôn, ta panta mataiotès*'

3 Fernand Ouellet
The Historical Background of Separatism in Quebec

For the past few years our nationalism has been going through another of these periods of crisis in which separatism is, once again, given a free rein. But isn't this a usual development in times of economic recession or of serious military tension? And may we not therefore assume that, after our present economic difficulties have been ironed out, nationalism will once again resume its traditional course? This is probably what André Laurendeau had in mind when he asked readers of *Le Magazine Maclean*: 'Will nationalism take root more successfully now than in 1936?' Of course it is no easy task to recognize, among the multitude of basic options open to French Canada today, precisely those that spring irrepressibly from the pattern of tradition. Upon analysis, however, it is not impossible to distinguish basically vital aspirations (those with lasting intrinsic value) from those fitful bouts of fever that are simply the signs of temporary uneasiness, divorced from any permanent cause. In the present circumstances, might not the current wave of separatism be merely a secondary symptom of our feverish revision of traditional values? Even if nationalism is still French Canada's leading ideology, it is no longer our only answer to the challenging problems of a modern world. Moreover, this nationalism is so heavily saturated with tradition that it may well lack the necessary buoyancy to catch up with our fresh outlook on world horizons and everyday realities. This may be all the truer of separatism, whose historical roots are far less securely anchored.

How far back does French-Canadian nationalism date? The question may seem superfluous to those who refuse to treat nationalism as a very recent phenomenon in the evolution of mankind. After centuries of rallying round the uniting ideal of 'Christianity', the Western world later took to clustering about an 'obedience-to-the-king' concept. The monarchist ideal then gained the upper hand until the beginning of the nineteenth century, when men were proffered a new set of standards. Those wishing to rebuild the world on a different basis

Translated from 'Les Fondements historiques de l'option séparatiste dans le Québec', first published in *Liberté*, IV, No. 21, March 1962, 90–112, and reprinted in the *Canadian Historical Review*, XLIII, No. 3, September 1962, 185–203.

now found a source of inspiration in the 'principle of nationalities', giving peoples the right to self-determination, as also in the new 'ideas of freedom'.

Canada, in the early nineteenth century, did not escape this wind of change. From 1802 to 1830, the terms 'nation', 'nationality', 'liberalism', and 'French Canadian' were commonly applied to the French-Canadian community. As for the word 'nationalism', it only came into common usage during the next two decades. To date our nationalism back to the French regime, or even to the latter half of the eighteenth century, would be to ascribe to the men of that period a scale of values of which they were not yet aware. The use of terms such as *Canadiens*, meaning French Canadians, and 'old' or 'new' subjects – frequently applied after 1760 – does not imply adherence to nationalism. It just reflects, at best, a consciousness of obvious differences.

Besides, there were very few elements in that second half of the eighteenth century that could be used to further an active nationalism.[1] Apart from the substitution of Englishmen for Frenchmen at certain government levels, the Conquest did not bring about any significant disturbance in the colony's economic and social structures. They were to remain the same for another forty years or so. The fur trade, at one time threatened by the Royal Proclamation of 1763, kept its predominant status. The trade was not just one form of economic activity among many others; it also provided a source of social integration for individuals. Though outwardly simple, it was actually a highly diversified field for the handling of valuable goods. Whether they were traders, boatmen, or backwoodsmen, the people engaged in the fur trade shared common interests, common tastes, and also common enemies. As in the French era, the enemy remained the New England trader and the Hudson's Bay Company. By settling on the banks of the St. Lawrence, British traders were embracing the same way of life as Canadians of French origin. Such a community of interests, and the coexistence of French Canadians and Britishers in the St. Lawrence Valley, made cultural differences readily acceptable. The fur-trading world suffered no racial prejudice; if anything, it encouraged racial co-operation.

A similar situation prevailed in the agricultural sector, which encompassed a major part of the population. After 1763, as before, many peasants continued to combine cultivation of the soil with fur-trading. Not only was the seigniorial system maintained but, thanks to a gradual expansion of foreign trade, agriculture climbed, from decade to decade, to an ever-increasing degree of prosperity. Population was certainly expanding fast, but it was fairly easy to clear new land reclaimed from acres of available territory. All in all, except when the harvest was poor or in periods of military crisis, the peasants had no cause to complain about the new regime – fortunately so, in view of their inborn xenophobia. On the contrary, there developed a growing tendency to attribute their prosperity to the arrival of the English. This even reached the point of Anglomania. Mgr Hubert and Mgr Plessis praised the new regime unreservedly. What is more they went so far as to consider the Conquest a godsend. Of course they mostly had in mind the fact that repercussions of the French Revolution were being countered by England; but few would have dared to contradict them. It was not until the nineteenth century that such praise began to seem immoderate.

These economic factors gave the political picture quite a curious aspect, considering its colonial context. After a few years, however, the objectives put forward by the Royal Proclamation of 1763 were abandoned. English merchants, too few in numbers, could not gain acceptance for their personal idea of the colony's future. On the contrary, the slow rate of economic development during the regime's first twenty-five years, coupled with the absence of mass immigration, compounded by the American revolutionary movement and the governors' own sympathetic attitude, focused policies on meeting the requirements of the French sector. And this is where the 'persecution myth' loses ground. First in practice, then officially through the Quebec Act, French Canadians were granted full religious freedom. They acquired it at least sixty years before England, and long before they themselves had learned the rudiments of religious tolerance. The only concessions of any significance that were made to the English trading minority were the application of English criminal law and unlimited testamentary rights. Such a policy was true to the tradition of British realism, with its propensity to pragmatism, at least as regards Canada. The only organized demonstrations of discontent came from the English merchants and, to a lesser extent, from a few French-Canadian businessmen, rising against a government that set such small store by commercial interests.

The English rulers' views on Canada's future affected their social attitude, too. Not content with seeking the support of the Church, whose influence was not underestimated, the State was interested in winning over to its side genuine members of the aristocracy – the sole lay élite in a predominantly French society. This explains why the governors went to such pains to restore the waning prestige of the seigneurs and the old nobility. In the existing monarchist context, these basic preoccupations prevailed until the early nineteenth century.

Despite certain inherent inequalities in the colonial system, whose worth, however, no one would have dreamed of questioning, English policies thus turned out to favour the French segment of the community. Bilingualism mainly affected the Anglo-Saxon minority. In actual fact, annexation to the British Empire had hardly interfered with the established political institutions. With the exception of a few changes in points of detail, they were maintained as of old. French Canadians objected to the parliamentary system; England refrained from introducing it until forced by the Loyalist influx to take into account the aspirations of a now sizeable English minority, and until such time as, thanks to an active group of merchants, colonial life became sufficiently imbued with capitalism. But there again, the decisions made in 1791 were stamped with the greatest caution, and were aimed solely at giving recognition to a dynamic middle class who needed a parliamentary system to make its influence felt. Yet the introduction of such a system in an illiterate population gave rise, in the long run, to tremendous problems. England's mistake in 1791 was to allow too large a proportion of the population voting rights which, by suddenly opening up a free field for extremist views, prevented the French Canadians' gradual adjustment to the new system.

The friendly relationship existing between the two races when the parliamentary system was established had given grounds to suppose that it would work without too much trouble. But economic and social changes at the very end of the eighteenth century considerably altered the climate in the colony. Since 1784 the French Canadians' economic position had weakened markedly. French-Canadian traders had been unable to adapt to new conditions in the fur trade. In a situation requiring a pooling of effort and capital, they had remained staunchly individualistic. Their conservative, unenterprising attitude prevented them from making investments in new sectors of the economy. So much so that, by the turn of the century, French Canadians had no high-calibre businessmen capable of defining their common objectives to meet new rather than past conditions. The period was a critical one indeed, with the mainstays of the economy and of society swinging in different directions. And this within a span of but a few years, when all that French Canadians were left with to guide their destinies was a lower middle class made up of notaries, lawyers, physicians, landsurveyors, and small businessmen in the towns and countryside who were hardly even conscious of the new requirements, let alone ready to lead their countrymen toward meeting them.

This rising middle class was doubtless our most striking social phenomenon at the end of the eighteenth century. Mostly of peasant extraction, our *petite bourgeoisie* had neither the breadth of view nor the necessary education to master the meaning of Canada's general needs, lost as they were in a maze of complications beyond their understanding. While the fur trade had started to decline, the lumber trade was picking up by leaps and bounds. Whereas cereal production was constantly favoured by foreign and domestic markets, agriculture in Lower Canada dropped off sharply from year to year, to the point where it became dependent on Upper Canada. If we add to this the considerable population growth and the accelerating Anglo-Saxon immigration at a time when seigniorial lands were becoming scarcer, then we have the perfect backdrop for our original nationalism's first scene of action. Yet, any perceptive French Canadian might have recognized these new developments as being full of concrete challenges. Renovating agricultural techniques, abolishing the seigniorial system, reforming the civil law, generalizing primary education, training skilled workers, forming a managerial class, changing the concept of the role of the State – such were the most pressing tasks involved in a clear-sighted adjustment to circumstances. What is more, for these basic reforms to materialize fairly quickly an efficient parliamentary system required the rapid emergence of a political élite who, with the help of English merchants, would be in a position to promote this complete remodelling of traditional institutions. Despite the efforts of certain French Canadians to adapt to the parliamentary process, over-all progress was far too slow. Our first parliamentarians sorely lacked not so much talent for abstract reasoning as ability to grasp the concrete basis for parliamentary action. Several members knew their Blackstone, of course, and their Montesquieu, their Rousseau, and their Locke. But was that likely to give them enough insight into the practical purpose of a Canadian Parliament?

In such straits, relations between the two ethnic groups began to deteriorate. Middle-class French Canadians were no better prepared than the peasantry to welcome in their society the radical changes dictated by the encroachment of capitalism. Did they see any real need for it? As a people ever dependent on the static values they had been raised on and to which they were still clinging, were they psychologically ready for it? It seems not.

The fact remains that our nationalism struck root in a ground highly conducive to national self-awareness and to the defensive isolation of the middle class against collective danger. From now on, the enemy became the English merchant, who through his control over the country's economy had an impact on politics. He was even passed off as a persecutor. The English merchant was seen not only as a political rival and a social competitor, but also as the propagator of standards potentially harmful to French-Canadian culture. The lower middle class started shaping a vocation of their own, wherein were consecrated both their role as a lay élite and their right to act as spokesmen for an agricultural, feudal society. The future of Canada, they argued, lies in agriculture, and we mustn't delude ourselves into looking for it in trade or industry. Since neither the clergy nor the legitimate aristocracy seemed to be aware of the perils threatening the French-Canadian community, the middle class would take it upon themselves to head the opposition to the English. As seen from this new angle, Parliament no longer served as anything but a convenient device for keeping national institutions alive, whatever their worth, and for protecting class interests. It is to this lapse in parliamentary action, far more than to any original flaw in the system adopted in 1791, that we owe the political chaos we are in the habit of pompously referring to as 'our parliamentary struggles'. Growing racial conflicts gradually bared the deep-seated roots of the agricultural crisis, and fostered a climate in which constitutional principles became but a barn where each faction in turn gathered grist for the mill of its own goals.

Fortunately our first wave of nationalism was not exclusively absorbed in the rejection of progress and the pursuit of immediate or selfish interests. By teaming up with liberal ideas, it gained a much more positive attitude. Probably with a view to emphasizing this trend, the *parti canadien* also took the title of the Reform Party. In this new capacity it gave rise to a movement of political and social reform which clearly revealed the middle class's firm determination to set itself up as the lay élite in French-Canadian society. Had it not been for an unholy fear of the English, these efforts, given time, would have proved rewarding. The same also applied at a strictly political level, where the bourgeoisie advocated structural improvements which, in the long run, would have redressed certain all-too-obvious abuses. But racial prejudice on both sides raised insuperable barriers to the settlement of problems which, in normal circumstances, would have been solved with greater dispatch.

Our first nationalism was not, as we might tend to believe, an enemy of colonialism. Quite the contrary, the French-Canadian middle class generally, along with the clergy and the seigneurs, shared a sincere admiration for England. England had not as yet projected her 'wicked stepmother' image, evoked at a later stage by a certain politician of ours. Their mistrust of revolutionary

France and American democracy led them to value British liberty. In their view, however, this liberty, striking the balance between monarchic principles and democratic freedom, could only find fulfilment through the establishment of a fully representative parliamentary system in England's colonies. This meant going as far as claiming a right to ministerial responsibility, while at the same time subjecting English merchants to French-Canadian representation. It also meant, at a juncture where Canada depended on the mother country's help for her progress, demanding a revision of the colonial system which, in the final analysis, could only turn out to be detrimental to the Canadian economy. Keeping faithfully to her role as arbiter between opposing factions, England chose to make only minor concessions. Her reaction was exactly the same when, in 1822, English merchants were to advocate a union of the Canadas. The mother country only conceded certain strictly necessary reforms. Her extreme caution in handling the solutions to serious problems was only provisionally successful in placating restless minds.

From 1826 onward, French-Canadian nationalism steadily shifted toward more extreme positions. This may have been due to certain failings in the colonial system, as well as a more aggressive attitude on the part of a good many of the British. But these could not have been the only reasons. One should not underestimate, of course, the decisive influence of the leaders' increasingly ruthless behaviour; but neither should one forget that nationalism, at that point, was no longer limited to the middle class. It had gradually seeped through to the peasantry, whom the agricultural crisis had, by then, made more receptive to the nationalist message. For there does seem to be close correlation between the spread of nationalistic ideas among the masses and the sorry state of agriculture in Lower Canada, whose dire effects were felt equally by the professional and the trading classes. How is an impoverished farmer to pay his bills at the general store, or his notary's, lawyer's, and doctor's fees? When a people as a whole start realizing that their traditional structures are crumbling, it is not surprising that they should look for someone to blame, rightly or wrongly, for their predicament. And they immediately became extremely sensitive to anything likely to intensify, in any way, their instability. In such cases, alternating periods of political and social tension tend to coincide roughly with the shifting balance of deficits or surpluses in agricultural production. Now, between 1826 and 1837, agriculture in Lower Canada produced a surplus only in two years. If we add to this the land shortage and the massive immigration from the British Isles, we have an explanation for the people's mounting anxiety right up to the 1837 rebellion. Had it not been for the counterbalancing effects of the lumber and shipbuilding trades, there is no doubt that a much more serious economic depression would have been experienced. One might almost say that it was due to these two fields of economic activity, built up by the bourgeoisie with the aid of preferential tariffs, that the British regime was able to survive the onslaught of our first great separatist wave.

Against such a discouraging background, national grievances rapidly acquired a bitter turn that they had seldom exhibited on previous occasions, whereupon relations between the two ethnic groups seriously deteriorated. The fact that the

Patriots' party was founded during this transition period was a clear indication of the dogged determination to protect the traditional heritage at all cost. Whatever its actual importance, any incident involving cultural differences or conflicting interests was immediately exaggerated out of all proportion. Even outside events, such as the Paris revolution of 1830, sparked the most explosive reactions. Liberalism, true enough, had made enormous strides in the middle class; but the pursuit of strictly liberal goals was hanging more than ever on the outcome of the hostile attitude toward the English. Certain institutions – a readjustment of whose aims might otherwise have been contemplated for the sake of liberty – were now being revered as sacrosanct. This hostility monopolized all energies, including those of the laity. A few men did manage, in the thick of the turmoil, to continue their cry for compromise if not for final agreement, but they were voices in the wilderness. Others, on the contrary, turned coat and by the same token earned the derisive title of *chouaguen*. Any ideological deviation, however slight, was considered a heinous crime.

Not that this national feeling, vented through violence, was devoid of all ferment for more constructive self-expression. Members of the Patriots' party were constantly voicing their desire to remodel their society entirely. They talked of the physical and moral rehabilitation of a French-Canadian nation crippled, they claimed, under the weight of persecution, compounded by all kinds of privileges granted to the British and by a crushing colonialism. Very soon Patriots began to pledge their allegiance to democracy. In their opinion the future of the nation could only be secured through democratic freedom. Not content with calling democratic institutions to its aid, the nationalist program started clamouring for either a very generous measure of autonomy within the empire, or complete independence.

Patriotic leaders, or at least most of them, were still far from becoming confirmed revolutionaries. At first they felt convinced they could achieve their goals without having to resort to arms, hence their cherishing the hope that political obstruction and verbal agitation would win them all the freedom needed to start rebuilding their society from scratch. But was England likely to accept the establishment of a French-Canadian republic on the banks of the St. Lawrence? Not only would such a decision have placed the colonial system in serious jeopardy, but the fate of Upper Canada and that of the Lower Canadian British minority would also have been at stake.

Little by little, some of the leaders of the Patriots began to perceive the need for revolutionary action. As for the others, they maintained their original positions. Then came the day when England decided to settle the issue once and for all. Following Lord Russell's resolutions in the spring of 1837, the Patriots were suddenly faced with the following choice: either to back up their claims by a resort to arms, or to give up their contentions. In the autumn of 1837 rebellion broke out in Lower Canada.

How should we interpret the revolutionary events of 1837 and 1838? These insurrections, producing many more victims than heroes, ended in rather pathetic failure. We might seek the reasons for this failure in the faulty organization of the rebellion itself, in the rivalries that divided its leaders both before and after the uprising, in certain individual acts of cowardice, or in the fact that the movement was only localized. We could also put forward the clergy's decisive influence. Yet, notwithstanding the capital importance of such factors, they cannot be considered as the true key to the problem.

In actual fact, the 1837 outburst was not an expression of the intense vitality of French-Canadian society. It was too narrowly based upon a passing phase of discontent, and on gaining certain immediate advantages, to be capable of achieving lasting goals. The revolutionary option – or the choice for independence to which it can be equated – had been fostered by a long series of economic difficulties which only a complete reshaping of French-Canadian society could sweep aside. None of the major reforms that the situation called for would, in practice, have required either separation from the British Empire or even a high degree of autonomy. On the contrary, most of these innovations merely needed a strong indigenous desire for constructive change which, to succeed, had to find a basis in certain existing structures of the Empire. Thus, for instance, the revolutionizing of agricultural techniques was in no way hampered by the colonial framework; without this framework, in fact, there would probably never have been any incentive for improvement. The same applies to the over-all picture of French-Canadian economic inferiority, which really acquired its full significance during that period. It had its roots in the society's educational structures and in the mentality of individuals. Similarly, the people's adjustment to the parliamentary system and the development of effective politicians depended first and foremost on the French-Canadian community's own initiative. With a minimum of political education and a better-informed leadership, *Jean Baptiste* – the man in the street – would surely not have gone on voting so long against registry offices and the St. Lawrence canals.

Lastly, what would independence and democracy have meant, in 1837, to an illiterate population lacking in any managerial business class, corseted in feudal-type institutions, and, moreover, living off a crippled agriculture that limped on the crutches of antiquated techniques? Independence, and the ensuing abolition of the preferential tariff system, would inevitably have barred access to the English market. This, at a time when the American market offered very few opportunities, would have doomed French Canadians to a long period of under-development without any possible compensations, wherein any serious attempts to establish democratic institutions would necessarily have remained barren, thus creating a hotbed for the growth of a theocracy. It is obvious that the revolution would have served the immediate interests of the professional classes without solving their fundamental problems. It would have given birth to a new 'family compact' devoid of real administrative or middle-class traditions. The champions of independence in 1837 harboured too much faith in the abstract virtues of democracy, and not enough in the concrete values with which these are cemented. It would have been most interesting to see how responsible government would have worked under Pierre Bédard, and democracy under Papineau.

The rebellion's failure forced French-Canadian nationalism to relax its rigid position, and to settle for certain compromises it had previously refused to consider. Dread of a re-enactment of the revolution's ordeal, as well as the fact that political control came into more realistic hands, might explain this change of heart. The foremost political leaders recognized the need to accept certain major reforms, if the imbroglio caused by the separatist crisis was to be cleared up. These concessions to the spirit of capitalism – accepted more or less willingly by different groups – paved the way for a policy of mass investment in projects such as the St. Lawrence canals. After its bitter experience of 1837, it took United Canada less than ten years to complete the network of canals, thanks to which the country could later enjoy a long period of prosperity stretching from 1851 to 1873. Apart from re-establishing some degree of co-operation between the two ethnic groups, the spirit of compromise exemplified by Lafontaine also promoted the expansion of a Canadian economy fairly independent of the United States. This conciliatory attitude toward certain matters of broad Canadian interest (failing at times a more positive approach) became typical of French-Canadian nationalism throughout the latter half of the nineteenth century. Such an attitude may not have been shared by all concerned, yet it definitely reflected the general tendency, as was borne out by the Lafontaine–Baldwin, Macdonald–Cartier, Macdonald–Langevin–Chapleau coalitions. And these, in turn, were a proof of the gradual shaping up of a Canadian identity. Confederation in 1867 thus fitted into the general context of the times which doubtless called for an acceptance of diversity, but felt a far more urgent need for a strong central government.

But French-Canadian nationalism was not limited to a single course of action. It spread among the clergy during the decade prior to the rebellion, and thus gained access to a new source of inspiration drawn from the theocratic legacy of the past. Nationalist ideology, already deeply coloured by clerical tenets in spite of its liberal ties, acquired a strong propensity for social, political, and economic conservatism, as it came into contact with the ultramontane movement influencing both the clergy and the laity. Reinforcement of Church authority after 1840 – a direct consequence of an ineffectual middle class – played a decisive role in moulding nationalist philosophy. The ideology now stood ready to fend off any signs of liberalism or of campaigns for material gain; but it also had its more concrete pursuits. Clerical nationalism not only preached in the abstract. It borrowed from the former era's nationalism its compensating myth of an agricultural vocation for French Canadians, and sought to apply this doctrine to the practical solution of such concrete problems as the rural exodus and emigration to the United States. The only weak point in responding thus to the demographic peril was that the ideology was defined purely in terms of agriculture and colonization. While the rest of Canada considered railroad construction as an indispensable step towards future Canadian industrialization, the majority of French Canadians thought of the railways merely as an aid to settlers. Now, colonization was surely meant only as a temporary, albeit occasionally useful, solution. Yet the importance it was given tended to overshadow the possibility of more fruitful long-term solutions, such as a more realistic appraisal of the role of agriculture and a positive adaptation to Canada's commercial and industrial structures. Whatever the reasons, selfish or otherwise, that motivated the clerical-nationalist philosophy, it seemed firmly intent on cloistering up all the population in a static world where progress could only be exceedingly slow. Without attaching undue importance to the influence of these ideological pressures, it must nevertheless be noted that they seriously cut down the French-Canadian community's chances of adapting to and acting in Canadian society.

Strangely enough, this particular brand of nationalism, though highly conducive to cultural isolationism, did not show any leaning toward separatism. By this time the foe was hardly any longer symbolized by 'the English', but rather by 'the liberals', namely those bent on converting institutions and society to a broader view of world affairs. When the enemy happens to be in your own home, far less attention is paid to outside threats. This particular slant of nationalism toward unswerving conservatism finally tended to provide favourable ground for compromise, thanks to which coexistence between the two races was to become quite effective.

Does this imply that separatism had all this time been consigned to oblivion? True, the rebellion's failure had dealt a heavy blow to a nationalism strongly tinged with liberalism. Yet this did not stamp out the liberal spirit altogether and, though weakened, it survived the revolutionary movement. The ranks of its faithful followers had thinned almost to the point of depletion. But, under cover of the period of crisis during the commercial revolution of 1846–50, the liberal movement regained some of its old vitality. This recovery coincided with a revival of separatist fervour. The rapid abolition of preferential tariffs had given rise to grave concern among the capitalists, who blamed England's new trade policies for their current economic problems. Having lost all hope of being able to compete with the United States in the international market, a good many businessmen speculated that it would probably be best to link arms with the American economy, after all. On the horns of this dilemma, with the agricultural crisis still besetting Lower Canada, the 1849 annexation crisis broke out, rallying the support of the radical liberals, the extreme nationalists, and a part of the capitalistic managerial class. However, the financial struggles turned out to be nothing but growing-pains and, with a return to prosperity a few years later, businessmen recovered their faith in the country's future. By the same token, the annexation movement, though still popular with the professional classes, lost its most powerful protagonists.

On the other hand, liberal nationalists, now banded together in the Institut Canadien, continued to campaign for secularization of French-Canadian social structures and annexation to the United States. The nationalist left wing was not only opposed to Church control; it advocated a whole series of economic and social reforms aimed at democratizing French-Canadian institutions. As for the ideal of annexation to the United States, shared by the more doctrinaire elements only, it stemmed from a desire to anchor Canada's future more firmly in its North American traditions and destiny. These supporters of liberal nationalism eyed England as the enemy whose influence and intents were viewed with suspicion. The attitude of certain liberals both before and at the time of Confederation revealed a hatred of England that had become an obsession for many of them and continued to haunt the minds of countless twentieth-century nationalists.

Actually, liberal nationalism never gained the support of the masses. It grew to considerable proportions during periods of crisis, but never won over the majority. The party spirit contributed, indeed, to swelling liberalism into such an active power that the countering of its attacks required a full mobilization of all ecclesiastic forces. However, the party only succeeded in recruiting followers among young people and members of the professions. Youth, and poverty during their start in life, and lasting failure in certain cases: such were the trademarks of most of those who joined the liberal movement then. The latter therefore never gained enough power to tear down the traditional organization. Besides, progressive reinforcement of Church authority and growing Canadian national self-awareness prevented liberal nationalism from expressing anything but the feelings of an agitated minority. Since it was supposed to reflect the movement's objectives on a political level, the party needed to abandon a good many of its more doctrinaire policies if it was to gain popular support. This complete reshuffling of liberal plans fell into the realistic hands of Wilfrid Laurier. The party's long-term aims were first pruned of the policies of annexation to the United States and free trade. Secularization measures for the Province of Quebec were also discarded, since a nation-wide party could not very well justify keeping purely local reforms in its program. Laurier therefore left it strictly up to provincial Liberals to promote changes in Quebec's own institutions. In actual fact, the period since 1886 had witnessed a similar trend at the provincial level. Hence the dwindling hope that liberal nationalism might be likely to play an important political role. There were still a few ardent supporters of liberal doctrines, but they could no longer be considered as anything but free-lance elements. The same applied to the annexation ideal, which soon became a cause for individualists or for unstable business concerns.

Having maintained its conventional outlook over a fairly lengthy period of time, French-Canadian nationalism in the late 1800s was gradually forced to face new realities, notably the revival of imperialist tendencies, and in particular the gradual emergence of an industrial society. For the imperial concepts, springing around 1850 from the adoption of economic liberalism policies, had favourably strengthened the colonies' autonomy. For forty years or so the mother country had been receptive to Canada's plea for greater freedom of action. And yet, as early as 1890, it seems that rivalry between European imperialist powers was driving England into trying to burden its dependencies with a heavier share of the risks inherent in its international activities. About the same time Canada began to show a keener interest in international affairs. Now that its economy had become more sensitive to external factors, how could Canada continue to ignore what was going on in the outside world? Would its politicians have to confess their country's total indifference to problems involving the western world? The time had obviously come for carefully weighed, realistic decisions.

Not only was this shift in policy on the part of the mother country a source of legitimate French-Canadian concern. It also roused the old anti-English hatred which, since the ordeal of the 1837 revolution, had been lying dormant in French-Canadian hearts, while it had never ceased to find expression among liberal nationalists and their immediate or remote descendants. French-Canadian nationalism was now to embark upon another of its long, exalted crusades that lasted, in spite of frequent vagaries, right to the end of the Second World War. This intense nationalistic feeling, sensitive as it already was to economic difficulties, became even more suspicious of military measures and events. Over-demanding imperialism is bound to breed anti-imperialism as a natural reaction of self-defence. But such a reaction might well have been further provoked by frustrated internal pressures capable of exploding at the slightest outside provocation. Certain politicians doubtless tried to turn the situation to their own advantage, though they had certainly not themselves built it up from scratch. Yet it can be said that this pent-up French-Canadian fear of the imperialist peril and its violent release through ethnic prejudice produced practically total blindness to what the last two world conflicts really meant. Still, this tendency of French-Canadian nationalism did not influence all individuals alike. In spite of many a bitter argument and hostile reaction, a modicum of solidarity still filtered through to Canadians of all persuasions. And for a very long time this new brand of nationalism was not in the least prone to separatism. It was still linked to the broader movement that swept beyond cultural differences and called for 'national unity'.

The relentless campaign against British imperialism to some extent diverted French-Canadian attention from the vast problems arising in their society from the soaring growth of cities and of industrialization; though it can be argued conversely that anti-imperialism may have served as a convenient outlet for the feeling of helplessness produced by the onset of the industrial era. At any rate, throughout the long phase of prosperity that lasted without a break from 1896 to the end of the First World War, French Canada was only partly aware of the tremendous challenge of keeping up with the Canadian economy's quickening pace. Such projects as the construction of hydro-electric plants, mines, and pulp-and-paper mills, carried out at an opportune moment for the inflow of British and American capital, only revealed more than ever the economic weakness of the French sector. Despite its progress since 1840, the French-Canadian community had neither the required technical task-force nor the necessary teams of capitalists and scientists to enable it to play an active part in developing the province's natural resources. Lack of initiative, narrow individualism, a preference for strictly safe investments, an aversion to long-term planning, along with a love of routine and extravagant tastes, were the typical characteristics of most of our business executives. The happy exceptions (and there were some) were all too rare; and though much admired, they were little emulated. Moreoever, government did not assert its authority as actively as it should. The same goes for the élite, who were neither dynamic nor clear-sighted enough to correct the main shortcomings of the educational system, or to promote a reassessment of cultural values. In other words, ideology and outlook sorely lagged behind material progress. And so French-Canadian society, noted for its abundance of cheap labour and for its excellent supply of men in the liberal professions, became particularly vulnerable to adverse conditions between the two world wars.

The recession that began in 1920, despite a few years' improvement from 1926 to 1929, hit French Canadians particularly hard. But the hardship it caused was by no means limited to Quebec: the depression spread all over Canada; farmers in the West and in Ontario, and industrial workers generally, all suffered from its effects. The political unrest, sparked by the military crisis and kindled further by the economic crisis of 1920, re-awakened left-wing tendencies. Faced with a society shaped to the demands of liberal capitalism, farmers and workers made an attempt at collective action outside the framework of trade-unionism. The fact that the Progressive party was founded when the two main parties were in obvious need of redefining their objectives reflected a firm resolve to influence nation-wide economic and social decisions. Yet, despite their lightning ascent, Progressive forces never flourished in the Canadian political field. Economic recovery soon showed this political and social outburst to have been nothing but a short-lived flare-up. French-Canadian nationalism, on the other hand, was to experience quite a different fate.

In Quebec the trouble was more deep-seated. It revealed French Canada's maladjustment to the new capitalistic structures, as well as the French Canadians' current economic difficulties, prolonging the old tensions created by the military situation. We therefore witnessed, at the end of the war, an effort to revive the nationalist philosophy. Certain nationalist circles at this point proceeded to analyse the past development and future prospects of French Canada's national identity. Soon a realignment of national forces was seen to be necessary. People were still clinging to their anti-imperialist attitudes. But since such attitudes served merely as a tool for advocating national unity, it soon became apparent that anti-imperialism was too limited in scope. Besides, was imperialism really the root of the evil? The prime concern of our liveliest post-war wave of nationalism seems to have been with taking stock of the situation by re-appraising the past, preserving only the permanent trends in our history, and planning the future in terms of reassessed national values. But such an enterprise was not likely to stir and convert anyone to final adherence, unless it also promoted a surge of national pride. Abbé Groulx, the movement's most outstanding personality, was also its most heeded historian. No other nationalist wing has ever attached so much importance to history.

Was this attempt at rearrangement of nationalist goals and thought at all in line with the over-all pattern of Canadian development? Was it not too highly influenced, perhaps, by a past that preached self-denial in material matters and the submission of the laity to a pervasive Church control? Despite its generally invigorating effects, the movement, nourished on tradition, sought little support from its contemporary industrial setting. Not that it remained impervious to social questions; but the conservative nature of its basic aspirations made these difficult to adapt to new social requirements.

In the face of a trying economic situation, nationalism was to fall back once again on the option for independence and separation. As early as 1923, Father Ceslas Forest was explaining the common ideal to a whole gathering of intellectuals: 'We are at last beginning to realize the need to sever our destiny from that of our neighbours, in order to guide it freely along its own traditional path. Will this separation stretch as far as political independence? Our staunchest and best-informed leaders predict it, wish it, and even suggest that all efforts be devoted to this ideal.'[2] The ideal continued to wind its way among intellectuals and youth circles. It even resisted the brief economic revival between 1926 and 1929. But it was not till later, at the climax of the depression during the Taschereau regime's waning years, that the separatist movement entered a phase of exceptional vitality. The atmosphere created by the depression brought about a rude awakening to certain harsh realities about the French-Canadian community. First of all (as André Laurendeau wrote in the French-language edition of *Maclean's*[3]) French Canada's poor representation within federal institutions; then, the decisive factor of economic inferiority, followed, moreover, by the 'knowledge that such a dependence was a serious disease'. The Jeune Canada movement, recruiting its members from among youth groups and certain intellectuals, was not content with a mere diagnosis; it also wished to cure the nation's ills. Aside from independence, its favoured solutions were to 'nationalize trusts' and 'buy French-Canadian'. There was also the *La Nation* group headed by Paul Bouchard which, being Maurrasian in doctrine, was looking for solutions along right-wing national-socialist lines, and favoured a strengthening of the role of the State. The new separatist trend, bred by the straitened circumstances of the times and the French Canadians' newly gained awareness of their economic position, gradually lost its impetus with the growing improvement of the country's economy. In André Laurendeau's words: 'The period was not sufficiently single-minded in its purpose, and reactions seemed to vary a great deal according to men and circumstances.' This explanation, though incomplete, is none the less a part of the truth. There was, indeed, a later spurt of enthusiasm for independence from 1942 to 1945. But there again, the reaction was simply caused by the military situation and the burning question of conscription. The separatist ideal did not then, any more than in former days, really represent a basic trend in our historical evolution. It only rallied a minority, and did not reach those who might have been most affected by such a step. In fact, as had now been the case for some years, the time was ripe not for independence, but for autonomy.

Ever since 1920, federal-provincial relations had taken a different turn. Confederation had been achieved under the pressure of historical circumstances that called for a strong central government. And these same circumstances had continued to prevail until the end of the First World War. The St. Lawrence canals, the construction of a railroad network, along with the protectionist commercial policy, had all been intended as foundations for the nation's industrial development. These objectives were only achieved on the eve of 1914. Then the war itself strengthened the role of the central government. However, accelerated industrialization during the two previous decades had helped to set up regional economic structures adapted to local requirements. Post-war financial difficulties had failed to disrupt this process, and the period thus saw an intensification of provincial powers. Born out of this long-term trend, autonomist tendencies then started to spread throughout Canada. Though hardly pronounced at the outset, they gradually gained firmer ground with successive years. Consequently the spirit of autonomy was not a mere product of Hepburn's and Duplessis's invention, although these two capable and realistic men were the first to grasp its full significance.

Thus, by 1939, the autonomist position had already started to take over from the much more stringent and hazardous leaning toward separatism. In any case, the French-Canadian population was far from ready for a separatist venture. Then came war again, with its usual horde of hostile reactions, and with it, also, prosperity. Though defeated in 1939 when he tried to gain the support of all those opposing participation in the war, Duplessis was returned to power at the next election. He then embarked with his Union Nationale party, at a time when the majority feared an imminent return to crisis, on a sixteen-year term of domination over Quebec life. Under this profoundly conservative government and at the height of prosperity, nationalism became identified with provincial autonomy, just as it had formerly been identified with anti-imperialism.

But in the meantime the Province of Quebec had gradually come to realize its precarious position in the midst of industrialization. This newly gained awareness dictated a reappraisal of all the old traditional standards in the various political, social, religious, and educational fields. The survey was not limited to the past only; an inventory was also made of modern requirements. Nationalism was not, as previously, used as the sole yardstick for such a revision; a greater variety of solutions could be derived from other patterns. Originally banded together against the Union Nationale establishment, the opposition also began to point its guns at the ruling classes. Duplessis's disappearance made way for a series of reforms which the Liberal party's coming to power multiplied. Attention was focused on education, hospital insurance, political and administrative reform, and the like. But, even if it did command a large measure of general support, the reform movement did not proceed in an altogether peaceful atmosphere. The difficulties inherent in so ambitious an undertaking coincided with the new economic recession that began in 1957. A business slow-down and unemployment added their weight to the inevitable unrest felt at the modernizing of administrative methods. Even nationalism fell victim to such tensions. Once more it resorted to separatism. Once more the separatist movement rallied only a minority, and a very checkered one at that. Despite widespread propaganda it never gained a firm foothold among workers, farmers, and capitalists. Support for the movement came mostly from young people, with a few intellectuals thrown in. Haven't we often before witnessed this familiar phenomenon? With improved economic conditions, nationalism will almost certainly revert to supporting autonomy – a very promising tool indeed, though a dangerous one when used merely to satisfy short-term interests. Shouldn't Quebec itself pay the price of its own backwardness? There seems to be an overriding need for the majority to concentrate on introducing domestic reforms and on carrying them through. It seems essential that all available energy be mobilized. Will a dynamic, progressive society place Quebec on the same footing as the rest of Canada? Then, and only then, shall we find out whether Confederation was really a hoax.

Notes
Part One

Bonenfant and Falardeau
Cultural and Political Implications of French-Canadian Nationalism

[1] Cf. the Abbé Arthur Maheux, 'Le Nationalisme canadien-français à l'aurore du XXᵉ siècle', *Canadian Historical Association Report* (1945), pp. 58–74.

[2] Francis W. Coker, article on 'Patriotism', *Encyclopedia of the Social Sciences*, XI, 26.

[3] W. G. Sumner, *Folkways* (Boston, 1906), p. 12.

[4] Max Hildebert Boehm, article on 'Nationalism', *Encyclopedia of the Social Sciences*, XI, 231.

[5] Léon Gérin, 'L'Intérêt sociologique de notre histoire au lendemain de la conquête', *Revue Trimestrielle Canadienne*, I (May 1915), 3ff.

[6] Everett C. Hughes, *Rencontre de deux mondes* (Montreal, 1946), foreword.

[7] It has been suggested that the year 1806, in which the first issue of the newspaper *Le Canadien* was published, might be considered as the original date in the history of French-Canadian nationalism. The actual role of the press in French Canada's political life will be better appreciated when the complete history of French-Canadian newspapers will have been systematically studied as an integral part of our total social history. See Séraphin Marion, *Lettres canadiennes d'autrefois* (Ottawa, 1939).

[8] Gérard Filteau, *Histoire des Patriotes* (Montreal, 1939), especially Vol. I, Book II; Vol. III, Book VIII, ch. I, II.

[9] Papineau and his lieutenants were undoubtedly acquainted with the contemporary French political theories. Lamennais's *Les Paroles d'un croyant* was being circulated and read in Canada at that time. A copy of this book, published in 1834, now part of the Chauveau Collection at the Quebec Provincial Parliament Library, bears the following handwritten note by Chauveau: 'importé en grande quantité à cette époque (1835) par les chefs du mouvement et distribué dans toutes les campagnes du Canada. Ou plutôt imprimé à Montréal?'

The two names which occur most often in Papineau's letters of this period are those of Lamennais and, especially, Jefferson. The influence of the Jeffersonian ideology on the contemporary Canadian political leaders is of no small significance and should be studied more thoroughly.

[10] Filteau, *Histoire des Patriotes*, I, 129.

[11] H.-J.-J.-B. Chouinard, *Annales de la Société Saint-Jean-Baptiste de Québec* (vol. IV, Quebec, 1902), La Cie d'Imprimerie du 'Soleil' (1903), pp. 307–10.

[12] Speech by the Honourable J.-H. Chapleau, Montreal, June 15, 1884, reproduced in *Grand Cinquantenaire de la Saint-Jean-Baptiste, 1834–84*, compilé d'après les rapports de 'L'Étendard', présenté par H. Giroux (Montreal, 1884), p. 35.

[13] Quoted by Amédée Robitaille, 'La Société Saint-Jean-Baptiste', in H.-J.-J.-B.

Chouinard (ed.), *Fête Nationale des Canadiens-Français célébrée à Québec, 1881–84* (Quebec, 1890), p. 435.

[14] Quoted by Filteau, *Histoire des Patriotes*, III, 244–5.

[15] See J. Huston (ed.), *Le Répertoire national ou Recueil de littérature canadienne* (4 vols.; Montreal, 1848); also *La Littérature canadienne de 1850 à 1860, publiée par la Direction du 'Foyer Canadien'* (2 vols.; Quebec, 1863).

[16] Among some typical historical text-books see: *Histoire abrégé du Canada* (Montreal, 1865); the Abbé C. H. Laverdière, *Histoire du Canada* (Quebec, 1877); Hubert LaRue, *Histoire populaire du Canada* (Quebec, 1875); the Abbé Provencher, *Histoire du Canada, Le premier cours* (Quebec, 1884); the Abbé David Gosselin, *Tablettes chronologiques et alphabétiques des principaux événements de l'histoire du Canada* (Quebec, 1887). Also the pioneering pedagogical essay, *Guide de l'instituteur*, by F. X. Valade, first published in Montreal in 1843 and re-edited many times.

[17] For an elaborate analysis of the influence of European intellectual liberalism in French Canada, see Marcel Trudel, *L'Influence de Voltaire au Canada* (2 vols.; Montreal, 1945).

[18] H. Mason Wade, *The French-Canadian Outlook: A Brief Account of the Unknown North Americans* (New York, 1946).

[19] See Robert Rumilly, *Mgr Laflèche et son temps* (Montreal, 1938), ch. II, III, *passim*.

[20] See *Discours prononcé par l'Honorable M. Mercier à l'Assemblée Législative de Québec, 7 mai 1886, sur la question Riel* (Quebec, 1886), pp. 15 ff.

[21] *Ibid.*, pp. 40 ff.

[22] See, for example, a speech made at the Windsor Hotel on April 10, 1888, where Mercier said: 'The situation is serious; we are facing the greatest danger ever faced by our political structure; we are asked to participate in a regime which cannot but bear the most disastrous consequences for us. So far, we have lived a colonial life; today, we are forced against our will to assume the responsibilities and dangers of a sovereign state which will not be ours, to expose ourselves to the vicissitudes of peace and war between the world's great powers and to the demanding necessities of military service as it exists in Europe; a political regime is imposed upon us which, through conscription, could scatter our sons from the Polar icelands to the burning sands of the Sahara, – a regime which would condemn us to the compulsory tribute of blood and money and would tear from us our sons, the hope of our country and the consolation of our old days, to precipitate them into far-away and bloody wars which we could neither prevent nor stop. . . .' J. O. Pelland (ed.), *Biographie, Discours, Conférences* etc. de l'Hon. Honoré Mercier (Montreal, 1890).

[23] Chouinard, *Fête Nationale des Canadiens-Français*.

[24] *Ibid.*, p. 292.

[25] See the following: the Abbé Bauer, 'Discours prononcé dans l'église de Windsor, Ontario, le 25 juin 1883', reported by H.-J.-J.-B. Chouinard, *Fête Nationale des Canadiens-Français*, p. 20; the Abbé Rouleau, sermon on June 24, 1884, in Montreal, reported in *Grand Cinquantenaire de la Saint-Jean-Baptiste, 1834–84, compilé d'après les rapports de 'L'Étendard'*, p. 5; the Abbé Odilon Paradis, 'Sermon de la Saint-Jean-Baptiste prêché à Québec le 24 juin 1887', in *Fête Nationale des Canadiens-Français*, pp. 122 ff.

[26] Mgr L.-A. Pâquet, *Discours et Allocutions* (Quebec, 1915).

[27] *Ibid.*, pp. 181 ff. A special edition for college use with analytical notes and comments has been made of this sermon by Canon Émile Chartier, under the title of *Bréviaire du patriote canadien-français* (Montreal, 1925).

[28] See Armand Lavergne, *Trente Ans de vie nationale* (Montreal, 1934), ch. VII.

²⁹ See a speech delivered by Armand Lavergne in Montreal at the fifth anniversary banquet of *Le Devoir*. Lavergne, after having evoked 1837–8, Mercier, and Riel, goes on to say: 'But we were determined to persist, for, in this Nationalist League, we were studying a little of the history of our country; we had remembered the schools of New Brunswick, the Riel affair, the Manitoba schools, the abolition of the French language in Manitoba and in the North West territories, the settlement of the Manitoba question, the sending of troops to South Africa, the intensive immigration intended to drown us . . .' *Cinquième Anniversaire du Devoir* (Montreal, 1915), p. 15.

³⁰ *Ibid.*, p. 196.

³¹ Tardivel published in 1895 a 'prophetic' novel entitled *Pour la patrie* in which are described political events taking place in 1946 and leading to the establishment of a French state in North America. In one of his last articles before his death Tardivel wrote: 'It is true that we thought seriously of asking the British Crown, which guaranteed us the practice of our religion and our national liberty, to safeguard us effectively against the fanatic element of this country. . . . But perhaps we could be given the permission to suggest a solution to the problem, that is, to reshape the Dominion on a new basis and to subdivide it into two or more Confederations. The province of Quebec, plus the French parts of Ontario and New Brunswick, could form one Confederation; the rest of the Maritime Provinces, another one; the English part of Ontario and the West, a third one. Quebec and the Eastern provinces could perhaps even constitute a single Confederation, their material interest being identical enough. . . ' *La Vérité*, April 15, 1905.

³² Henri Bourassa, *La Convention douanière entre le Canada et les États-Unis, sa nature, ses conséquences* (Montreal, 1911). See also the booklet advertising the concern *La Publicité* which was to publish *Le Devoir*, and containing a program of which one article emphasized 'the most complete autonomy for Canada compatible with the faithfulness to the British Crown'. Also, *La Politique de l'Angleterre avant et après la guerre* (Montreal, 1914).

³³ *L'Accord avec les Anglo-Canadiens*, reproduced in *Le Cinquième Anniversaire du Devoir* (Montreal, 1915), p. 59.

³⁴ Lionel Curtis, *Independence or Imperial Partnership? A Study of 'The problem of the Commonwealth'* (Montreal, 1916), p. 54. See also *Le Patriotisme canadien-français, ce qu'il est, ce qu'il doit être* (Montreal, 1902).

³⁵ In Quebec City at that time, an Ultramontane priest, the Abbé David Gosselin, published a weekly called *La Semaine Religieuse*. Many of its articles for the years 1899–1900 express attitudes strikingly anti-British and sympathetic to the Boers. A long serial article published anonymously in *La Semaine Religieuse* in 1900, under the title of 'L'Anglomanie au Canada: Quelques conjectures sur l'issue de la lutte entre les deux races', was particularly bitter, and hopeful for the humiliation of the 'English race'. English-Canadian newspapers protested. Mgr Bruchési, Archbishop of Montreal, wrote a letter to the *Herald* denouncing the articles of *La Semaine Religieuse* (*Herald*, January 12, 1900). Three days later the Archbishop of Quebec, Cardinal Bégin, congratulated Mgr Bruchési for his letter to the *Herald* and took the opportunity of expressing his unalterable loyalty to the British Crown.

³⁶ Henri Bourassa's speech at the Fifth Anniversary banquet of *Le Devoir*, pp. 68 ff.

³⁷ See Ferdinand Roy, *L'Appel aux armes et la réponse canadienne-française* (Quebec, 1917).

³⁸ Elizabeth Armstrong, *The Crisis of Quebec 1914–18* (New York, 1937).

³⁹ The Abbé d'Amours, in a series of letters published in *La Presse* of Montreal, vigorously denounced Bourassa, nationalism, and the lack of loyalty to England (cf.

Où allons-nous? Le Nationalisme canadien. Lettres de 'Un patriote' publiées dans le journal 'La Presse', augmentées d'une introduction, d'additions et d'appendices documentaires (Montreal, 1916)). To this, the Jesuit Hermas Lalande answered in a sour and heavily serious booklet which resumed the whole nationalist argumentation (cf. Jean Vindex, *Halte-Là! Patriote. Que penser de notre école politico-théologique? De l'impérialisme qu'elle professe? Du nationalisme qu'elle censure?* (Rimouski, 1917)).

[40] As soon as the South African war began, collective protests started coming from rural parishes and small centres. For example, in a then small Eastern Township community which seems to be not very far from the contemporary Cantonville described in Everett C. Hughes's *French Canada in Transition*, at a mass meeting held on June 19, 1902, some 5,000 French Canadians representing ninety-three townships who were addressed by Bourassa voted a collective motion 'inviting the citizens of all the parishes of Nicolet to protest against the Imperial campaign and to adopt resolutions approving the position taken by Sir Wilfrid Laurier in his reply to the Secretary of the Colonies, that is to say, no contribution to the wars of England.' *The Canadian Annual Review of Public Affairs* (Toronto, 1902), p. 140.

[41] This motion stated 'That this House is of opinion that the Province of Quebec would be disposed to accept the breaking of the Confederation Pact of 1867 if, in the other provinces, it is believed that she is an obstacle to the union, progress and development of Canada.'

Trudeau
Quebec on the Eve of the Asbestos Strike

[1] Marcel Rioux, 'Remarques sur l'éducation secondaire et la culture canadienne-française', *Cité Libre* (Montreal), No. 8, p. 35.

[2] R. Rumilly, *Histoire de la Province de Québec*, Éditions Valiquette, Vol. VIII, p. 63.

[3] It will be recalled that the technique of synchronously engineering common lines of thought was perfected under an authoritarian system of not so long ago.

[4] *Le Citoyen canadien-français*, Éditions Fides (1946), Vol I, p. 101. Abbé Groulx had also blamed us for 'not protesting with enough perseverance or enough *unanimity*'. (*L'Action nationale*, September 1934, p. 46).

[5] This expression was used by Edouard Montpetit in a speech quoted in Maurice Tremblay, *Essais sur le Québec contemporain*, p. 207.

[6] *Action française* (Montreal), 1927, p. 319.

[7] Éditions Albert Lévesque, A.C.F., p. 121.

[8] *Action française*, January 1921, p. 21.

[9] *Ibid.*, March, p. 133.

[10] *Op. cit.*, p. 17.

[11] *Op. cit.*, p. 151.

[12] In a talk reported in *Le Canada*, May 30, 1934.

[13] *Notre Question nationale*, Éditions Action Nationale (Montreal, 1945), Vol. I, pp. 145 ff.

[14] To bring out the surprising element in this view, it may be compared with the more generous outlook of an expert. 'In all ages and areas, from ancient Egypt to modern America, the highest development of human mentality, initiative and achievement has been in urban communities. So long as men remained in the pastoral or agricultural stages there was little stimulus to the differentiation of economic functions; the entire energies of men were absorbed in the task of raising the food supply. But with the city came the division of labor and possibilities for economic surplus, hence wealth, leisure, education, intellectual advance and the development of the arts and sciences . . .

The city is bound to be a controlling factor in the national life . . . Its population supplies most of the national leadership . . . He who makes the city makes the nation, and
indeed it is the cities of the future that will determine the character of the world.'
W. B. Munro, 'City', *Encyclopedia of the Social Sciences*, Macmillan.

[15] *Notre Milieu*, Éditions Fides (1942), p. 135. The *Canada Year Book*, 1954, p. 20,
refers to 12 per cent arable land, of which some 40 per cent is already under cultivation.

[16] *Op. cit.*, p. 105.

[17] *Faites-nous des hommes*, Éditions J.I.C. (1938), p. 17.

[18] Éditions à la cité des livres (Paris), p. 218.

[19] *La Législation ouvrière et le régime social dans la province de Québec*, a study prepared
for the Rowell-Sirois Commission (Ottawa, 1939), p. 85. Italics added.

[20] Esdras Minville, *op. cit.*, p. 98. Italics added.

[21] *L'Organisation corporative au service de la démocratie*, École Sociale Populaire
(Montreal, 1942), p. 18. Italics added.

[22] *Ibid.*, p. 24.

[23] Extracts from *L'Action catholique*, distributed by the Jesuit Fathers to their pupils
in the form of leaflets, dated December 1, 1938. The same pupils also had the advantage
of receiving, through their schools' Catholic Youth groups, the text of Cardinal
Villeneuve's speech, dated October 31, 1937, where he said: 'I am in favour of the
opposition with which communist meetings have met in this city [these were meetings
concerning the Spanish Civil War, which Malraux had attempted to address] . . . I call
on you, should the need arise, not to relent. If it is argued that such action is against the
law, my answer is that natural rights overrule the law . . . Under the pretence of
respecting a tottering democracy, the imaginary nightmare of fascism is brandished
before our eyes. . . .' Along the same lines, see also the Cardinal's address to the
Cercle Universitaire de Montréal on January 25, 1938, concerning 'liberty and freedom'. In it the Cardinal outlines his political beliefs, where 'tolerance' takes on a
singularly totalitarian stance.

[24] *L'Action nationale* (Montreal), September 1934, p. 61.

[25] *Ibid.*, January 1935, p. 4.

[26] Preface to Athanase David, *En Marge de la politique* (1934).

[27] *L'Avenir de notre bourgeoisie*, Éditions J.I.C., Valiquette (1939), p. 34. Italics added.

[28] On the lack of realism in our culture, see Pierre Vadeboncoeur's searching articles
in *Cité Libre* (Montreal), Nos. 5, 6, and 8. See also Guy Cormier's articles, *ibid.*, No. 1,
and Maurice Blain, *ibid.*, No. 5 (Vol. II, Nos. 1–2).

[29] These three quotes are from Abbé Groulx, *Pourquoi nous sommes divisés*, Éditions
Action Nationale (November 1943).

[30] *L'Action nationale*, January 1943, p. 26.

[31] Éditions Action Nationale (1941), pp. 15 and 26.

[32] The expression 'agriculturalism' was popularized by Professor Michel Brunet
who – quite correctly – qualified it as one of the 'three illusions in French-Canadian
thinking' (lecture reported in *Le Devoir*, June 2, 1954), the other two illusions being
anti-imperialism and Canadianism. I shall deal neither with these nor with other
subjects that have caused many throats to be parched, such as bilingualism, separate
schools in the West, etc. For the purposes of this chapter, I consider them as so many
aspects of our political nationalism, rather than of specifically socio-economic thinking.
For the same reasons, I shall not refer at any length to the champions of our political
nationalism, such as Bourassa, Lavergne, etc.

[33] See also R. Parenteau, 'Les idées économiques et sociales de Bourassa', *L'Action*

nationale, January 1954, pp. 166 ff. Bourassa is here 'hostile to the establishment of industry' and full of encouragement for colonization.

[34] *Op. cit.*, p. 97. Italics added.

[35] Quoted by J. H. Marcotte, *Osons* (Montreal, 1936), p. 28. The Laureys quotations also come from this source.

[36] *La Corporation professionnelle*, École Sociale Populaire (1939), p. 17.

[37] E. C. Hughes, *French Canada in Transition* (Kegan Paul, 1946), p. 151.

[38] *L'Action nationale*, January 1943, p. 23.

[39] Cf. Mason Wade, *The French Canadians 1760–1945* (Macmillan, 1955), p. 1098.

[40] Gaudrault, o.p., *Neutralité, non-confessionnalité et l'École sociale populaire*, Éditions du Lévrier (1946), p. 56.

[41] J. Papin Archambault, S.J., *Deuxième Semaine sociale du Canada* (1921), p. 17. Italics added.

[42] *Ibid.*, p. 388.

[43] Charpentier, *Ma Conversion au syndicalisme catholique*, Éditions Fides (1946), p. 77.

[44] *Ibid.*, p. 47.

On this period, I also wish to quote the following paragraph from an unpublished work by Fernand Dumont:

The Chief Chaplain of the Catholic trade-union movement, Abbé Maxime Fortin, wrote on April 3, 1916, in *L'Action catholique* of Quebec (under the pseudonym Aubert du Lac): 'These workers' associations [the international unions] are a fruit of the early nineteenth century social revolution which, like a daughter who follows her mother, followed in the footsteps of the earlier political upheaval, the French Revolution. They were born out of hatred against God, against the Church, against religion, against order and authority, especially the authority of employers. . . .' A rather surprising summary of the workers' struggle in the nineteenth century! The Revolution allegedly lay at the root of it all, the workers' misery having had nothing to do with their unrest; apparently Villermé must have been dreaming. Steadfast in his principles, Abbé Fortin continues: 'The Church is today committed to the frightening task of rebuilding the workers' world, here in Quebec, as well as elsewhere. And you may be sure that your co-operation, if it is properly enlightened, duly obedient, and as generous as you promise, will serve a cause which is not only your own but also ours, and even that of God.' Thus, after this rapid glance at the labour movement, the author entrusts the workers with the sole noble function of obedience. The chaplains, only familiar with the workers' lives from the outside, will be responsible for all the rest. No doubt with our good employers' kind assistance.

[45] See the article by Eugene Forsey, *Canadian Forum*, June 1937.

[46] *La Législation ouvrière et le régime social dans la province de Québec*, pp. 19–21.

[47] *Deuxième Semaine sociale*, p. 387.

[48] *Ibid.*, p. 15. Italics added.

[49] *Le Devoir*, May 7, 1919.

[50] *Semaine sociale de 1920*, p. 171.

[51] *Op cit.*, pp. 54, 134.

[52] *Pour nous grandir*, printed by *Le Devoir* presses (1937), p. 232.

[53] Pierre Harvey, *Actualité économique*, (Montreal, April–June 1954), p. 62. See also

the letter of F.-A. Angers, secretary of *L'Action corporative* in *Le Devoir* of November 22, 1954, dealing with proposed legislation 'contemplated for the past 17 years'.

Ouellet
The Historical Background of Separatism in Quebec

[1] F. Ouellet, 'M. Michel Brunet et le problème de la conquête', *Bulletin des Recherches historiques* LXII, No. 2 (April–May–June 1956), 92–101. J. Hamelin, *Économie et société en Nouvelle-France* (Quebec, 1960).

[2] Quoted by Bruno Lafleur in a review of notes in 'Essais sur le Québec contemporain', *Revue de l'Université de Laval* VIII, No. 7 (March 1954), 9.

[3] *Le Magazine Maclean*, January 1962, p. 3.

Part Two
The Exponents

4 François-Xavier Garneau (1809-1866) Preliminary Discourse to *History of Canada*

History has become, dating from a half century back, a rigorously analytic science. Not only the facts narrated, but their causes also, have now to be indicated with precision and discernment, in order that the former may be judged by the latter. A severe criticism will throw aside all that bears not the impress of truth. That which presents itself without critical acceptance, and without having been discussed and approved before the tribunal of sound judgment, is treated as being of fabulous nature, and dismissed into the region of figments. In this perfect day of close scrutiny and applied common sense, disappear marvels, prodigies, and all those phantasmagoria in presence of which nations in a state of mental childhood are stricken with a secret fear or are rapt in puerile admiration; such phantasmagoria, we would observe, as of old animated the sombre forests of Canada in the brooding fancy of their first inhabitants, those warlike and barbarous tribes, of which the remnants now remaining are so few.

The historical revolution adverted to above, in the mode of appreciating events, is incontestably due to the progress of mind and to the increase of political liberty, and is in itself the greatest proof that could be adduced of the gradual perfecting of social institutions. The clouds of mystery which enveloped the early annals of Greece and Rome,[1] have now lost their awe-inspiring aspects; keenly scrutinizing eyes have pierced the veil that hid them from ordinary inspection; and if we closely scan the true origin of those nations, the clouds of historical marvel disperse, even as light morning vapours are scattered by the rays of the sun. It is a notable fact too, that while to mythological heroes and early kings a celestial origin was assigned; while the adulation of the adorers of personal might and rude regality enveloped their origin with portents and prodigy, nothing super- or infra-human preceded or attended the existence of the dominated commonalty; the prosaic life of the masses held 'the even tenor

Reprinted from *History of Canada*, 1845; translated by Andrew Bell, Montreal, 1860, pp. xxiv–xxxiii.

of its way,' in the memorials regarding *them* even in the earliest annals of pseudo-history.

No farther back than three centuries ago, superstitious ignorance everywhere dimmed and paralysed popular intelligence. Three quarters of the habitable globe were unknown to the majority; who were equally ignorant of most of those unusual phenomena of nature which raised admiration or called up fear; the sciences were wrapped in mystery by their professors; an alchemist passed for a diviner or a wizard, and often finished by becoming the dupe of his own deceptions, and believed that he did or could hold converse with the spiritual world.

The invention of Printing, and the discovery of the New World, at length began to make an impression on the thick mental darkness of the Middle Ages. And when Columbus suddenly rendered America to astounded Europe, unveiling, as by a magic touch, so great a domain of the thitherto Unknown, he dealt a brain-blow, by that very disclosure, to the sway of ignorance and superstition.

Freedom of mind also, though all but lost during prevalent barbarism, was not quite extinct in some high places, and powerfully contributed to the new movement of the human faculties. In fact, we may say, that liberty first inspired that movement, and afterwards sustained it with an ever-growing potency.

From this time, THE PEOPLE began to appear in history. Hitherto they who ought to have occupied the fore-ground, were thrown into the remote distance by the word-pictures which passed for histories of the nations; the canvas being taken up with the gigantic and lowering shadowy outlines depicted of their masters. All the figures discernible are those of absolute chiefs, holding in one hand a sword, in the other a diploma of their pretended divinity: the rest of mankind, passive plebeians, an inert and suffering mass of living, breathing humanity, has no recognised condition of existence apart from that of obedience. [In a word, the 'court-and-battle historians'[2] made small account or none of THE PEOPLE during a long series of ages.] But in proportion as the bulk of mankind resume manhood's rights, the current of history begins to change, yet slowly: that science, even when modified, long seemed subjected to the influence of prejudices and errors, surely destined to pass away; it is only in our own times that national annalists have become faithful to their true mission. Have their words thereby lost their interest or ceased to attract? We trow not. What more sublime spectacle is there, than that of a thinking people in action! We note their wants, we are pained with their sufferings, we mark and judge of their aspirations; we joy in their joys, we participate by sympathy in their sorrows. The great ocean of enfranchised humanity, when stirred to its depths by great thoughts, whether of love or hate, manifests a power capable of producing far greater effects than all the wondrous material works erected by the submissive hordes of Egypt or Asia. But it needed four revolutions, that of Batavia, those of Great Britain, and that again of the United States, [before the Lion of the Tribe of the People could be firmly set up on his pedestal.]

The epoch of national revolts, so famous in European annals, is that wherein appeared the first essays of American historians of any repute. It is no wonder if America, inhabited as it is but by one class of men only, namely 'the people' –

using the term in the ignoble sense given to it by the privileged orders, or 'the swinish multitude' (*la canaille*) as Napoleon phrased it – should adopt in their entirety the principles of the Modern School of history, which regards the Nation as the source of all lawful power.

The first individuals who set themselves to exorcise the phantoms which guarded the sanctuary of absolute monarchy against the assaults of the 'sacrilegious' masses, were an Italian and a Swiss, two men who, consequently, were born in the freest countries in Europe in their day. Lawrence Valla gave the signal of self-enfranchisement to the 12th century. Glareanus, so called as being a native of the canton of Glaris, followed in Valla's steps. 'Switzerland is a land of reasoners,' says Michelet. 'Despite the gigantic poetry of nature among the Alps, the spiritual breeze that comes from their glaciers, is prosaic; it wafts us to Doubt, chiefly.'[3]

The history of the origin of Rome exercised their critical powers. Erasmus, Scaliger, and other learned Dutchmen followed in their wake. Louis de Beaufort, a Frenchman, finished the work of demolition; but he destroyed only, he did not reconstruct. The ground being thus cleared, the celebrated Neapolitan, Vico, appeared; and gave the world, in 1725, his vast system of the metaphysics of history;[4] among which may be found, in embryo at least, all the labors of modern science. The Germans seized the plant and it fructified in their hands; Niebuhr became the most illustrious of Vico's disciples.

Meanwhile the voice of all those profound thinkers was heard among certain nations, whose people proclaimed, as we have remarked, each in due succession, the dogma of Liberty for all. From the schools of doubters issued Bacon; thence resulted the discovery of the New World, the metaphysics of Descartes, the immortal *Esprit des Lois*, the labors of Guizot, and, finally, the works of Sismondi, every line in which contains a plea in favor of the poor people, long crushed under the heel of feudalism; an institution once so powerful, but which now shows but withered or seared remnants of what it once was; even as are those trees, in our forests, when doomed to perish by steel and fire, which may be seen in many a newly gained field, clearing for tillage.

An observation we call to mind here, which seems to us to have the gloss of novelty, so pregnant is it with too-little-remembered truth. It is this; How glorious for Christianity, to be able to say for itself, that the progressiveness of modern civilization is in part due to the spirit of that most famous and sublimest of all books, the BIBLE; that continually speaking object of the meditations of the scholastics and the learned. The Regenerator-God took birth among the people, he preached only to the people; and he selected, by a preference too marked not to have its special significance, his disciples from among the lowest ranks of Hebrew unfortunates, enslaved by those Romans who were about to bring to ruin their antique Jerusalem. This fact, more than any other, explains the tendencies of Christianity, and accounts for the indelible imprint it has put on modern civilization.[5] And it was under its influence, too, and in the spirit of Christian precepts, that America was peopled by Europeans.

A new phasis turned up in the world's history; namely, that resulting from the second overflowing of population, after the Christian era began. The first, we need not say, was that which precipitated the fall of the Roman empire; the next was the immigration from Europe to America, which hastened, in its turn, the departure of barbarism.

If the spectacle presented by olden civilization, corrupted by sensuality and falling before the steel and firebrands of barbarians, is calculated to excite deep feelings of horror and pity; that offered by the discovery and colonization of the New World, despite a few gloomy shadings, inspires sentiments of hopefulness, and evokes perceptions of grandeur elevating for the soul. Touching it is to see setting forth, from different regions of Europe, those long trains of humble but industrious colonists, with countenances steadfastly fixed on our Occident. Up to that time, men of the sword had been the precursors of all combined emigrations. 'War alone,' says one author, 'opened up the olden world to general observation.' Intelligence, and impulses towards labor, accompanied, among the moderns, those who came and yet come to seek and to secure a foothold in America. The rapidly attained successes of the former proved the advantages attending a state of peace with freedom to toil, over a reign of violence, amid the tumult of arms, for founding rich and powerful empires.

The establishment of Canada, as a French dependency, dates from the times of the great movement of European populations towards the West; a consideration of which movement, as to its general causes, is of interest to this country as well as to the rest of America. We ought not to allow ourselves to form erroneous conceptions as to the direction taken by American civilization. The study of such matters is necessary for all the inhabitants of this continent who are heedful of the future.

Such is, we repeat, the character of that civilization, and the colonization begun and maintained under its all-powerful influence. Canada, though originally founded under religious auspices, is one of those colonies which has been least affected by their influence, for reasons which the reader will be able to understand as he proceeds in the perusal of this work. In a young colony, each forward step is full of import for the future. We should grossly mistake, if we regarded the early pioneer, with hatchet in hand, levelling the trees in his way in the Laurentian valley, as a mere woodman, toiling only to satisfy the daily wants of his body. The work he was then engaged in, humble as it might seem, drew after it results far more vast and infinitely more durable than the contemporary feats of arms stricken in his own country, the report of which rang through Europe. The history of the discovery and foundation of French Canada has general interests as great as the recorded origin of any other colonial empire on this continent. The boldness of a Cartier, the first who set up a tent at the mountain foot of Hochelaga, amidst unknown tribes of wild men, inhabitants of a region well nigh 300 leagues inland; the perseverance of a Champlain, contending, not merely with material obstacles but also with the apathy which denied him means to overcome them, yet succeeding at last in founding a colony yet to become an empire; the sufferings of its first inhabitants, and their sanguinary wars with the famous Iroquois tribes, confederated against them; the exploration of nearly the whole interior of North America, from Hudson's Bay to the Mexican Gulf on one traversing line, from Acadia to the Rocky Mountains on another; the military expeditions of Canadians in the North, in Newfoundland, towards Virginia, and into Louisiana; the foundation, by seculars or missionaries, of the earliest European settlements in Michigan, Wisconsin, Louisiana, and eastern Texas: here is surely a striking amount of operations of import high enough to arrest our attention and win the admiration of our posterity. The recorded incidents attending these impart to our early history a variety, a richness of coloring, constantly affecting the imagination and interesting the mind of those who read it.

When we contemplate the history of Canada as a whole, from the time of Champlain till our own day, we first remark its two great divisions – the period of French supremacy, and that of British domination. The annals of the former are replete with the incidents of wars against the savages and the people of the conterminous British colonies, since become the United States; the other portion is signalised by parliamentary antagonism of the colonists to all infractions of their nationality and designs against their religion. The difference of the arms defensively used during these two periods, shows the Canadian nation under two very distinct aspects; but it is the second epoch which, naturally enough, may most interest the existing generation. There is something at once noble and touching in the spectacle of a people defending the nationality of their ancestors; that sacred heritage which no race, how degraded soever, has ever yet repudiated. Never did cause of a loftier character or more holy nature inspire a heart rightly placed, or better merit the sympathies of all generous minds.

If Canadian valor has shone brightly in fields of war, the oratorical, argumentative, and administrative ability manifested by our leading statesmen, have been no less conspicuous in the Senate and Cabinet. The Papineaus, the Bédards, the Vallières, the Stuarts, will, in those regards, take a distinguished place in the history of the country, as they already have in the remembrance of their grateful contemporaries.

From the circumstance that Canada has had to undergo many evil vicissitudes, and not through her own fault but arising out of her colonial dependence, what progress she did make was effected amidst obstacles and social shocks; obstructions which have been aggravated, in the present day, by the antagonism of two races confronted with each other; as also by the hates, the prejudices, the ignorance, and the errors of governments, – sometimes, too, through the faults of the government. The authors of the Union of the two Canadian provinces, projected in 1822 and realised in 1840, have adduced in favor of that measure divers specious reasons to cover, as with a veil, its manifest injustice. Great Britain, prone to regard the French Canadians only as turbulent colonials, as ill-disposed aliens, feigns to mistake for indubitable insurrectionary symptoms (an artifice unworthy of a great nation), their inquietude and their firm attachment to menaced institutions and habitudes. Britain's general conduct, however, proves too well that while she believes not what is advanced against them, no regard for treaties nor official acts, drawn up for the protection of her Canadian subjects, has prevented her agents from violating concessions, which ought to have been all the more carefully respected for being regarded as forming an aegis to protect the weak against the oppression of the strong. But whatever may betide, the perdition of a people is not so easily effected as its enemies may imagine.

While we are far from believing that our nationality is secured against all further risks, like many more we have had our illusions on this subject. Still, the existence of the Canadians as a distinct people, is not more doubtful than it was a century ago. At that time, we were a population of 60,000; we now exceed a million souls.

What characterises the Gaulish race above all others, is 'that occult force of cohesion and of resistance, which maintains their material unity amidst the most cruel vicissitudes, and makes it rise superior to every attempt to depress it.' The olden Gallic heedlessness (*étourderie*), says a French author,[6] has outlived the unchangeable theocracies of Egypt and Asia, the political combinations of the Greeks, the civic wisdom and military discipline of the Romans. Endowed with a less flexible genius, more confiding and less calculating, this people, of antique blood but ever young in heart, when the appeal of a noble conception or the call of a great man inspires them, – this people would have disappeared as other races, more sage in seeming than it, had done before; and why? because they comprehend only one mission (*rôle*), one interest, and one idea.

All things concur to prove, that the French settled in America retain these characteristics of their ancestors, near and remote; that they possess a strong yet undefinable buoyancy of mind, peculiar to themselves, which, invulnerable as mind itself, eludes political guile, as spirit is unassailable by the sword. The type of the race remains, even when all seems to forebode its extinction. Is the nucleus of a French community found amid alien races? it grows apace, but always in isolation from others with whom it is possible to live, but never to incorporate. Germans, Dutch, Swedes, who came in groups into the United States, and lived apart for a while, have insensibly been fused in the general mass of population, and left no trace of their origin.[7] On the contrary, two sections of the Gallic race, one at each extremity of this continent, not only maintain their footing in two countries so wide apart, of contrasted climate and under diverse political constitutions; but, as if by instinct, concur in repelling all infractions of their nationality. Is its sacrifice called for? they serry their ranks the closer. The nationality of the great people from whom they are descended, animating them under menaces, causes the rejection of all capitulations offered to them; their Gallic nature, while separating them from phlegmatic races, sustains them in circumstances hopeless for others. In fine, that cohesive force, peculiar to their moral temperament, develops itself in proportion to the efforts made to overcome it.

The eminent statesmen who guided the destiny of Great Britain after the acquisition of Canada in 1763, well comprehended that the position of its people, relatively to the neighboring Colonists of English origin, would be confirmatory of their fidelity to the British crown; and their expectations, wisely conceived, were not disappointed.

Nevertheless, left to ponder on their position, after the prolonged and sanguinary struggles they had erewhile to sustain, and in which they had shown so much devotedness to France, the Canadians regarded the future with inquietude. Abandoned by the most opulent and intelligent of their compatriots, who, in quitting the country, carried with them that experience which would have been so useful had they remained; so few in number, and put helplessly, for a season, at the discretion of the populous British Provinces near by, whose overbearingness they had resisted for a century and a half with so much spirit, they yet did not mistrust their fortune. They advertised the new government of their wants, and reclaimed the rights guaranteed to them by treaties; they represented, with admirable tact, that the discrepancies existing between them and their neighbors over the lines, the diversity of races and interests, would attach them rather to the British monarchy, than induce them to make common cause with democratic denizens of the English plantations. They had divined, in fact, the Revolution soon to ensue.

Chance has brought to light, in the Secretary's Department at Quebec, a memoir on this subject, the author of which has traced, with great perspicuity, the wants likely to arise at such a crisis, and his predictions were not slow of realization. Thus anticipating the future independence of the thirteen provinces, he observes that 'If there subsists not between Canada and Britain prescriptive ties and mutual interestedness, of a nature such as New England could not possibly extend to the Canadians, the British could no more trust to the continued fidelity of the former than to the Provincials of New England. Will it be thought paradoxical if I add, that this union of all the parts of colonized North America, based on the principle of a universal franchise, will bring about a time when Europe shall have no American colonies, except those which America chooses to leave her? for a hostile expedition, got up in New England, might reduce the British West India possessions, before it could be known in London to have left port. If there be a means for preventing or postponing such a revolution, so far as we are concerned in the matter, it is to be done by maintaining and respecting the diversity of language, opinions, habitudes, and interests which now exists between the inhabitants of Canada and the people of New England.'

The Government of Great Britain, influenced by such considerations as the foregoing, left undisturbed the Canadian language, laws, and religion, at a crisis when it would have been comparatively easy to compass the abolition of all three; for at that time the British possessed a moiety of North America. They had soon cause for rejoicing at their wise forbearance. Two years had scarcely elapsed after the promulgation of the law of 1774 when all the Anglo-American colonies were up in arms against the mother country; and during the contest ensuing, the people of the former wasted a considerable part of their resources in vain attempts to wrench from her that Canada which they had helped to conquer for her special glorification!

The Canadians, called on to defend their institutions and laws, guaranteed to them by that same law of 1774, which the Congress of the insurrectionary provinces had so injudiciously denounced, just before, as 'unjust, unconstitutional, very dangerous, and subversive of American rights,' – the Canadians, we say, promptly ranged themselves under the banner of their new Protectress, who now profited more than she had ventured to hope for, by the effects of the wise, because liberal, policy of her general Government. That policy was sanctioned and extended on two memorable occasions afterwards; namely, in 1791, when the British Parliament accorded a representative Constitution to the Province; and again, in 1828, when the Imperial Parliament enacted that Canadians of French origin should never be disturbed in the enjoyment of their laws, their religion, or those privileges which had already been assured to them.

If this polity, which twice became the means of saving Canada to Great Britain, was virtually repudiated by the Union Act, it is not improbable that it will be found expedient to revert to it; for the time that has elapsed since 1840, has manifested that Canada has become anything rather than *anglified*: and nothing indicates that the future will differ from the present or past in this respect. A return to that policy may become inevitable, if only through the continued expansion of the colonies still remaining to Britain on this continent; and by the prospects of a new revolution, similar to that which paved the way to independence for the United States. Were it otherwise, we should opine that the people of Great Britain, coinciding in sentiment with some of their statesmen, [that 'Canada is a suction and not a feeding pipe,' as such] ought to be left to herself; the British nation not caring to expend its resources in keeping much longer an uneasy foothold on the nearer parts of the North American continent.

5 Etienne Parent (1801-1874)
Industry as a Means of Survival for the French-Canadian Nationality

Gentlemen: This Institute, as I understand it, is completely nationalistic in its aims. It was established in the new capital as a meeting-place, a centre of activity, for dynamic and intelligent men of our common stock, and for the benefit of the French-Canadian nationality as, for lack of a better term, we are wont to call our nationality.

Therefore, while I crave your indulgence for my treatment of the subject, I feel it should interest you to hear something of the means whereby this nationality can be strengthened and preserved; a nationality that is so dear to us, as indeed it should be, not only for reasons of sentiment and honour but also because of the vital interests of our race.

I know – and I say this with bitterness in my heart – that there are some who have lost faith in the cause of preservation of our nationality, either from fear of what the struggle will involve or from failing to appreciate to the full our chances of survival; or again because the entire affair goes against the grain in so far as their political inclinations are concerned. Like the Romans of old, despairing of their country's salvation, they are sitting back in their curule chairs, waiting stoically – indeed, indifferently – for the conquering foe to violate their Lares and Penates and desecrate the altars of the fatherland. My words today are not for their benefit, but for those firm believers who, I sincerely feel, constitute the majority of our people. If I did not believe this to be true, I would simply say nothing and would merely weep in silence over the shattered hope that brought me joy in happier days, comfort in times of sadness, and guidance in difficult and stormy periods. For what sacrifices, what devotion can be asked of the unbelieving? Surrounded as we are, under pressure from all sides, even overwhelmed in certain key areas by the adulterating

Translated from 'L'Industrie considérée comme moyen de conserver la nationalité canadienne-française', a speech given at the Institut Canadien in 1846 and reprinted in *Le Répertoire National*, IV, Montreal, 1893, 1-19.

encroachment of an alien influence, we cannot expect to conserve our nationality without some measure of sacrifice and devotion.

To avoid any misunderstanding, gentlemen, we should at this point emphasize that we do not nurture any feeling of ill-will or jealousy with regard to this alien element, which would include not only the Anglo-Saxon population of Canada but also that of our neighbours which, to my mind, constitutes an even more serious threat than the former. It is through a providential course of events that these two nationalities were thrown together in this sector of the globe. It is equally in the order of things providential and human that both should do their utmost to ensure their respective survival and the spreading of their influence. We cannot reproach one another for this, since each of us is a tool in the hands of God. It is up to every one of us to do what duty, honour, and legitimate interest dictate, while constantly obeying the sacred laws of public ethics. It is up to each and every one to do his best in the part that the Supreme Author has given him to play, and to await with confidence and charity toward his fellow-actors the outcome of the plot, the secret nature of which the future will reveal. And if anyone were to think that our attachment to our nationality undermines our loyalty to the mother country, the facts of the past, the symptoms of the present, and the signs of the future are there to convince him that the best guarantee of continuing British rule in this sector of the American continent lies in the survival of the French-Canadian nationality. Besides, our nationality is ours to hold, and we are merely exercising our right in trying to keep it – a right bestowed upon us by the Creator: *Dieu et mon droit* and *Honi soit qui mal y pense.*

And now, getting down to our subject: methods for maintaining our nationality can be divided into three categories: religious, political, and social. Religious and political, in so far as they are used by religious or political leaders and belong to the religious or political order of things; social, when applied outside political movements or religious action by individual members of the community.

It is not my intention to speak of the religious or political methods; such a task would be too lengthy and perhaps too delicate. Moreover, our clergy have generally been so responsible, so devoted, so nationalistic, and have already done so much for the common cause, that we may rest assured they will not hesitate to face their future responsibilities as they always have done in the past. The same can be said of our political leaders, whatever their leanings: they have never spared their devotion, efforts, and sacrifices. It may have been felt, at times, that they might have done better; but never, I believe, could they be rightly accused of acting with bad intent. They may have made mistakes, as have all great politicians the world over; but this should not tarnish their reputation as good patriots. Let us simply hope that they and their successors will continue in their efforts and devotion to the common cause. Above all, they should be urged not to hesitate in sacrificing their pride to the cause. Personal pride, perhaps, is what should most be sacrificed in our present situation; yet it is the most difficult sacrifice to make. The reason for this is simple: the stronger their convictions, the more politicians are likely to identify themselves with the common cause, and the greater their tendency to confuse their personal aspirations with those of the country. It then becomes very difficult for them to distinguish between personal sacrifice – which they would be willing to make – and the sacrificing of political principles – which they know cannot be done. The history of all peoples is full of such dilemmas and the untold misery they have brought about.

Only recently, France has recovered all that remained of the treasures she lost, and from the bloodshed she suffered during the twenty years when she followed the lead of a man who was the greatest politician and the greatest leader of our times: a coffin and ashes – crowned in glory, granted – yet nothing but a coffin and a handful of ashes. Events would have taken quite a different turn if this genius had less frequently mistaken his own thirst for glory for that of the glory and good of France. Thus, in all of our perilous political pursuits, we should always be conscious of our nationality. It should symbolize our means of salvation, as did the bronze serpent for the Hebrews; we should never let it out of sight, lest on our return we find that it has vanished and we are left without so much as a glorious tomb on which to shed our tears.

Once more, let us urge our leaders – whether or not they hold political power – to beware of this sort of illusion: for if, as someone pointed out, we need to be doubly righteous in order to have justice on our side, so shall we always be doubly to blame whenever we are in the wrong.

If we are determined to be mistaken as seldom as possible, our national consciousness must constantly be our beacon, our compass, our guiding star, as we pick our way through the stumbling-blocks of politics. We should realize that the greatest threat of all is directed not against our political freedom (a quality more or less inherent in this continent), but against our nationality. It is therefore our nationality that needs the most protection. Whenever there is anything clearly to be gained from any move, any step on behalf of our nationality, we can forsake almost everything else. Our nationality should be our prime concern, then all the rest will automatically fall into place. Once we have gained national or social strength, then we are bound to acquire political strength. Conversely, if we neglect our nationality and fail to seek opportunities of strengthening it, then we can rest assured that no one will lend us a helping hand in time of need or of danger.

We can hardly expect assistance from the outside; whence the need – nay, the duty – for us to avoid unwonted bitterness or ill-feeling when discussions arise in our midst, or, I would even say, between us and those of the other origin. For no cause is ever aided by passion. Our animosity, our quarrels, will automatically be turned to profit by that rival element, while weakening our own position. We may indeed embark on animated, even heated discussion; but let us never dip our pen in gall or poison. And, once our fellow-citizens' opinion has sided fairly with one party or the other, may the loser react like that Spartan citizen who, on returning home after a general election where he was defeated, exclaimed: Let us give thanks to the gods, for in Sparta there are three hundred citizens who are more worthy than I!

But I said I did not intend to talk about the political methods of safeguarding our nationality. Forgive this little digression, and please attribute it to a certain fear that has often crept into my mind in the middle of political discussions: the fear that if our nationality were one day to be lost, politics with their unbridled, passion-releasing effect will have been the main cause of such a disaster.

Now for the so-called social methods; that is, methods that can be used outside religious or political action, by individuals acting as members of the community.

If we wish to keep our national identity, our social strength must become at least equal to that of our opponents. It is no use relying on treaties; it is no use sheltering behind a fortress of principles involving public morals, natural rights, or the rights of man. In the world, and especially between nations, there is only one right that has invariably ranked above all others: the right of the strongest, or, what nearly always amounts to the same thing, the right of the shrewdest. Now, if we have the means of increasing our social influence or maintaining our social status, we try to use them. And if prejudice should stand in our way, we try to break it down, either by individual or by collective action. That is precisely what I am asking you to do when I urge you to heighten the prestige of a career in industry, by crowning it with a national aura; and this for a purely nationalistic purpose: it could be a powerful tool for keeping alive our nationality and spreading its influence. I come to beg you to respect industry; to respect it not so much with words as through action, by adopting a completely different attitude from the one we have had heretofore, and which explains the backward condition of our race in its own country.

No, gentlemen, industry is not sufficiently honoured in our midst. It does not receive the degree of consideration it deserves in the interest of our nationality. Yes, we are still suffering from the old prejudice against manual labour, even against labour or work of any kind, that prevailed in our country of origin when a nobleman hid his signet-ring from sight if he had to engage in some business activity, when even members of the legal profession had difficulty in finding acceptance. Nowadays, in our country, thank heavens we no longer aspire to nobility. But we yearn for membership in the professions: once again, a love of sedentary occupations. We may as well confess that we despise industry. Otherwise why should our successful industrialists spend so much time and energy in turning their children into mediocre professional men, instead of putting them to work in their shops and factories and making skilled craftsmen or businessmen out of them? Why else should our upper classes prefer to keep their children vegetating in professions for which they are not suited, or – what is worse – prepare them for an idle life of leisure, useless to themselves and to their country, rather than train them in some honest and useful craft? And where has this mad passion for the professions led us? It has led to a supply greatly exceeding the demand, with a consequent loss of prestige for the learned professions. Thus, the purpose is defeated through too much popularity. This may finally remedy the evil, in which case we need have no regrets. But where else does this harmful prejudice lead us, when it makes us ashamed of good, sound industry? Gentlemen, it leads to a general situation – and this is what is harmful to us as a nation – where those whom we relegate, so to speak, to industry, to this powerful asset of modern nations, are invariably much inferior to English Canadians.

This should not be construed as meaning that I consider our race as inferior to any other in the world – far from it – not to mention the old country, France, which has been leading civilization for centuries, at the helm of creative thinking, and the recognized authority on matters of good taste for all civilized people. But if we limit our discussion to France's offspring who were left derelict in this remote corner of the earth, we can state with pride that this little people, with barely half a century behind them, have produced professional men of the calibre of the Papineaus – both father and son – the Bédards – father and son again – Viger, Rolland, Vallières, Moquin, Plamondon, Quesnel, Caron, Cherrier, Morin, Duval, Girouard, numerous other such men of distinction, and many more to come when they have had time and opportunity to prove their worth, including those who have won distinction in other fields. So, despite all the obstacles that have stood in our way, we can pride ourselves on not being inferior to any others as far as intelligence is concerned. That our position is inferior in business and industry is mainly due to a prejudice that it is my purpose to destroy this evening. It is in our own interest as a people to root out this prejudice from our midst: the future of our nationality is at stake, gentlemen.

In order to survive, a nationality must be supported by men in its society whose social power is at least equal to any de-nationalizing force at work from within or without. And what is the source of social strength, especially in America? Industry, without a doubt. It could not be anything else in this so-called new world of ours, where the greatest challenge that the Europeans met with on landing was the taming of a hostile virgin land. What need was there then for feudal conquerors such as once subjected Europe to their rule? There was no need for warriors, but for peaceful and industrious workers. The true conquest of America was made, not by the sword, but by the hatchet. Thus it was industry that founded the civilized communities of America. Whereas those who founded the European communities and their descendants were – and still are – the European nobility, here in America it is the industrialists, those who toil with their hands, guided by intelligence, who are the American nobility.

Prejudice against manual labour and industry generally, unreasonable though it may seem, may well be justified in a European society, though even there it is gradually losing ground. It might be justified in communities originally founded under the feudal system or the feudal sword. But in America it is more than unreasonable, it is unnatural; and in Lower Canada it is suicidal. Unnatural, because it implies a denial of our origins, since our fathers were all industrialists; suicidal, because it tends to undermine our strength as a people and to subject us readily to the rule of another race. I should like to develop this point a little further.

Intelligence, no doubt, means power, yet only in so far as it generates power. You might be the most intelligent people in the world but with no definite goal your intelligence will be as useless to you as a shot in the dark. What use is intellect if it is not nurtured, or if you embark on an already overcrowded profession where the chances of success are obviously greatly reduced, and where most of us are therefore doomed to failure and ruin? But I should like to look at it from a nationalistic standpoint. Can we possibly acquire – let alone maintain – any social power if we continue to waste our energies on barren disputes, while leaving the fruitful field of industry open to people of a different origin? Of course, we do have our unskilled workers and hired craftsmen; but do we have our own leaders of industry, our own workshops, our own factories? Are we as fully represented in big business as we might be? And where are our large agricultural concerns? We allow ourselves to be exploited in all of these sectors. Our natural resources – the main ingredient for social power – are everywhere allowed to fall into alien hands. This is due to the fact that those of our people who must meet the challenge of outside competition are the least fitted for it, both in training and in capital-investment capability. But those of us who could take up such a challenge successfully would not stoop to tackle any branch of industry, and prefer to vegetate with a paltry diploma in their pocket, or to squander in a life of leisure the inheritance they might otherwise have invested to good advantage both for themselves and for their country.

I should now like to tell you an anecdote about people who are still alive today, and whom I could name. A wealthy Quebec industrialist had given his son a complete education, and spoke to him in the following terms about the choice of a career: 'Well, son, it's time you chose a career. I can afford to let you pick and choose and to meet any expense involved. But before you decide, study this statement of my accounts for the year, and see what my profits amount to. See if you think that, after all your years of work and study, you will ever be able to boast of doing half so well in whatever profession you choose. You might also consider whether you believe you can attain the social status I pride myself on having.'

His son thought it over, and made the sort of decision I wish more of our young people would make upon graduating from college: he started from the bottom in his father's business, and is now the director of one of our leading establishments in Quebec. This good man and his worthy son are of British stock. They have kept up the family business as a source of wealth, and have been for the British a source of social influence. Tell me, do not these two men deserve the respect of their compatriots?

The story I have just told you leads me to another perfectly relevant matter. Generally, as French Canadians, we are too neglectful of perpetuating in our business or other enterprises the sort of family tradition that some of our bright and active fellow-countrymen sometimes succeed in establishing. Only those who have had the task of developing a prosperous concern can say how much it has cost them in terms of hard work, worry, vigilance, and thrift; how much intelligence and perseverance it has meant. And yet, inconceivable though this may seem, we witness every day some of our people closing down without regret – I was about to say, without a feeling of guilt – a business that could readily serve as the instrument for the accumulation of a considerable fortune for someone else. It takes years to establish a large clientele, valuable contacts, reliable correspondents, good credit. Yet this is all sacrificed as if it meant nothing. Perhaps there are no children, no relatives; but are there not any friends who might be spared years of sweat and labour struggling on the lower rungs of the industrial ladder? And during those same years, some foreigners with advantages over us (they often have, as we know from experience), may set themselves up next door in desperate, unfair, and ruinous competition.

Gentlemen, may this Institute speak as one man in proclaiming, in a voice loud enough for the echo to be heard throughout the Laurentians, that the best citizens, the most civic-minded among us, are those who, through good management, have built up a successful commercial enterprise and who, out of patriotism, and even at the cost of a few sacrifices, will bequeath it in due course to some other industrious French Canadian. With time, this will help to create a French-Canadian industry that can measure up in every way to English-Canadian industry, while winning its respect. Then the competition will be noble and stimulating, making for a better development of the endless resources of this vast and beautiful territory.

This applies mainly to the French-Canadian merchants who, it should be noted to their credit, have lately taken an increasing lead that is most encouraging to other branches of industry. Until quite recently, however, we must admit that our merchants generally acted merely as intermediaries for the distribution of British goods to the consumers. But lately they have shown an eagerness to free themselves from a tutelage that has been neither a source of pride nor a means of profit to them. A number are establishing direct relations with British merchants and manufacturers. Their efforts and competence deserve to be crowned with success, and some are already showing encouraging signs of prosperity. It is to be hoped that their good example will be emulated. But those who succeed should remember the cost of building up their enterprise, and they should make arrangements for its transfer before retiring, or as soon as they become less active. This will be a way of guaranteeing fairly rapid financial success for some of our younger people. It will also guarantee that our own race has its rightful share in the country's wealth and industry, together with the resulting social power without which we could not hope to safeguard our nationality.

Were it not likely to be a strain on your patience, I could present a multitude of additional considerations concerning other points closely connected with our subject. For instance, a great deal could be said about how to promote different sectors of French-Canadian industry, especially the most important – agriculture. Yes, gentlemen, agriculture, whose old farm establishments are pathetically sunk in a rut of outdated techniques and which, for that very reason, *inter alia*, is only making slow and timid progress toward the conquest of our virgin territories. I ask you, what has been done to promote our agriculture? It is true that substantial credits have been voted to help agricultural societies grant awards. But to whom are these awards granted? To people who only know hackneyed old techniques. It is like awarding prizes to sixth-grade schoolboys for a thesis on philosophy. Make farmers out of them first, and then you can encourage them by granting awards to the most deserving.

Again, what has been done to turn to our advantage the exploitation of our vast stretches of uncultivated land? What organizations do we have for making access to such land easier for our surplus rural population in their old farm-houses, and for helping them to expand and settle there, as is done for the English-Canadian settlers? Some things have been neglected, others have been left to chance in this field as in so many others. But gentlemen, can anything be neglected, can anything be left to chance in this country of ours? We live in a world where everything is in constant motion, everything is changing. We shall be crushed in the process unless we start moving too. Forty years or so ago, a captain navigating his ship along our beautiful St. Lawrence relied solely on the winds and currents – he left things to chance. Today, ships equipped with several hundred horsepower surge forward, cutting through wind and weather, chasing before them the chugging old coasters. There, gentlemen, is your symbol of industrial change. We cannot ignore this revolution that has taken place in our lifetime, before our very eyes; may it teach us that command of this modern era comes from movement and activity, from the lively and continual action of man on matter.

But I repeat that I do not want to overtax your indulgence, and I must leave it to your imagination to fill the gaps in this lecture, just as I leave it to you to correct any shortcomings in its context. Before closing, however, I beg your attention for a few more minutes while I add some words of fully relevant explanation that I omitted in their proper context for fear of breaking the main thread of my thoughts.

Earlier in my talk, I deplored the fact that biassed parents in all walks of life are in the habit of forcing their children into the professions. Through using vague or general language, I may have given you the impression that a career in industry demands less intelligence than the practice of the professions. Nothing could be further from my mind and, in my opinion, nothing could be further from the truth. In fact, a higher degree of intelligence is often required for a really successful career in industry than is needed for proficiency in the professions. Of course, each field of activity calls into play its own different intellectual faculties, but the sum total of necessary intellectual effort may be just as great in one case as in the other. And who are we to judge the subtle shades of difference that can exist between one man's intellectual ability and another's?

Any great industrialist should therefore consider himself as privileged as any brilliant professional. Let our industrialists realize their right to this privilege and avail themselves of it if need be. Let them not be afraid to hold their heads high, for they are the fathers of civilized America. Without them we would be nothing. And it is particularly up to you, you country people, to hold up your heads proudly before all the others, for yours is the hand that feeds the nation! Rome's greatest poet has sung the praises of your labour; the world's greatest Monarch gives the signal every year for your work to begin and joins in it, thus proclaiming to some three hundred million men that your status is the highest of all. What is more, though we are still amazed at Egypt's timeless wonders, and although Greece and Rome reached artistic heights that have never since been equalled; though they have had all kinds of men whose greatness we are still forced to recognize, in spite of our own great achievements, they were never able to produce a great farmer. It is only since the advent of modern science that we have learned to consider agriculture as the foremost of sciences. And, since the advent of the industrial era, it has ranked as the first of our industries. The human brain has therefore had to labour for four thousand years before it could mould great farmers. With such a background, agriculture's rank and credentials are surely worth as much as the degrees and diplomas that some of our people are so proud of possessing.

Shall I give you a brief outline of the early history of agriculture? I might point out that the first agronomist whose name is recorded in history was Cato the Elder, who lived in the third century B.C., and left a slim treatise on agriculture. In the following century there was Carthage-born Magon, who wrote twenty-eight volumes on agriculture; and Varron, in the first century B.C., left a treatise on the same subject. These are the only names in ancient history associated with the study of agriculture. In the first century A.D. there was Columelus, the greatest authority on agriculture of that era. Following him, it is not until the fifth century that we find another agronomist, Palladius. Then, it seems that agriculture as a science remained dormant throughout Europe until the thirteenth century, when Crescenti, a native of Bologna, won through his research the title of patron of agriculture. But those who know what an important role the very recent progress in chemistry has played in the field of agronomy will agree that, in all respects, modern agricultural experts have left their predecessors far behind them. The very number of famed agronomists since the beginning of the last century – more than a hundred – is enough to show how much remained to be done since the days of the elders. I might mention in passing that Chaptal in France, and Sir Humphry Davy in England (the former died in 1832, the latter in 1839), two of the most famous chemists of that period, have left, each in his own language, an excellent treatise on chemistry as applied to agriculture. To the best of my knowledge, these are the first two works ever to be published on this subject.

But, gentlemen, it is time to sum up. Earlier I said – and proved, I hope – that the industrialists are the lords of America; and their claim to nobility is better justified and more enduring than that of your noblemen in the old world. Neither misfortune nor revolution can destroy them. It is through industry's struggle against hostile elements that countless cities and empires have been conquered, not with sword and bloodshed, but with spade and sweat. For this, gentlemen, industry must be honoured, not just through words and gestures, but through action. If we have children who seem to be gifted for any type of industry, we must encourage them to enter it. In their interest, we shall give industry a place of honour in our ranks, and thus ensure that our nationality is given the strongest possible chance of survival. Opportunities for education have been quite rare among us. But if those who can afford to give their children a good education despise industry, it will inevitably pass into other hands, and we shall reach a point of no return where the bulk of our population is dominated, body and soul, by people of another race. This is not my own theory; it emanates from those other people. That is what they meant when, as the result of our contempt for industry as a career, they sarcastically predicted that we were inevitably destined to be hewers of wood and drawers of water for them. That is also what an American author meant when he kindly warned us of our fate, saying: 'We will reform them out of the face of the earth.' Those were his very words, if my memory serves me right.

Gentlemen, we must turn such prophecies into lies! We must not allow the descendants of our heroic pioneers in the St. Lawrence Valley to become outcasts. We must not allow history to have to record some day that: 'Lower Canada, being part of what was originally called New France, was first colonized by settlers from France. This population was able to survive, through strength of numbers, for some time after the territory was ceded to England. Whether intentionally or not, the people's education was long neglected following this event, with the result that the British immigrants, with their better training and inborn gift for industry, succeeded in time in taking over all the country's natural resources. The new racial group, having acquired a marked influence on society, finally stamped it with its own special characteristics; so that today, the French element in French-Canadian society has been either smothered or absorbed. In certain remote areas of the country, there is barely a handful of direct descendants left of a people noted for their fighting qualities, their adventurous expeditions to the North-West, as well as for their graciousness of manner that earned them the name of "the gentlemanly people". If we are to believe the chronicles of the day, the decline of such an outstanding people was due to a total lack of interest in any branch of industry by the wealthy (the only ones who could then afford proper education). And indeed, this is quite conceivable in a country where industry was the only source of wealth, and where material wealth was the greatest, if not the only means of acquiring social status. The majority of the people must have been subjected to the de-nationalizing action of the rival racial group's industrial leaders and, with time, lost their own national characteristics.'

That, gentlemen, is what history will have to say (much better than I can, of course), unless the wealthy among us urgently realize the importance of their mission, unless they are ready to meet the requirements of our society. But I feel sure that each and every one of you will want to follow the dictates of country and posterity. And perhaps my words to you today have been spoken not so much in provocation, but rather as an expression of a feeling that is already growing and fermenting in the hearts of our people, and will soon come to full fruition. May our nationality feed on its life-giving product, so that we may hand down, intact, to our children, the most valuable heritage bequeathed to us by our ancestors.

6 Mgr L.-F.-R. Laflèche (1818-1898) *The Providential Mission of the French Canadians*

> Every nation must fulfil its own destiny, as set by Providence. It must understand its mission fully and strive constantly towards the goal Divine Providence has assigned it.

Why is it that God has allotted to the descendants of certain families a particular territory wherein to grow and develop as a national entity? Why did he wish such families to have their own particular language, laws, mores, and customs, so different from those of others that they create a barrier between them? We shall see why right away.

First of all, it should be noted that the subdivision of Adam's offspring into national groups scattered over different parts of the earth only happened after the Deluge. The Holy Bible definitely says that, up to the time when language confusion set in, men formed one single people, speaking the same language. The only dividing line it points to before that memorable period consists in a difference in customs. These had divided men into children of God or children of man, according to whether they had followed in the footsteps of Seth the Just or Cain the Fratricide. There was no barrier separating these two human races, apart from a strict injunction upon the descendants of Seth not to enter into any alliance with the children of Cain. Violations of this very wise rule were doubtless indirectly responsible for the Flood – that terrible punishment, vestiges of which are found to this day in the geological discoveries of bones and fragments littering the face of the earth. It was this self-same violation that brought about the very corruption Moses refers to when he talks of the flesh having so corrupted its own passage on earth that God, upon seeing the malice and iniquity of men, sentenced them to extermination.

It is quite remarkable that the first men were not charged with the crime of

Translated from *Quelques Considérations sur les rapports de la société civile avec la religion et la famille*, Trois Rivières, 1866, pp. 37–62.

idolatry. They seem, on the contrary, to have constantly cherished the knowledge of God and his Truth as revealed to their ancestors. It was through *unity of faith* that they were able to maintain *unity of language* and therefore *national unity*.

Among Noah's descendants, events took quite a different turn. There we see a diversity of creeds and the worship of mammon emerging at about the same time as the babel of languages. Careful study of the Holy Texts in which these events are recorded leads us to the safe assumption that a confusion of ideas and creeds must have heralded the coming language division, thus acting as an omen of impending doom. The fact that this portent was ignored probably further provoked divine intervention. God, who chastises always as a father, wished to stem the dissemination of errors that brought about the monstrous idolatries, while crushing the pride of men by punishment. But Providence must have planned the division of Noah's children into various nations for many reasons, several of which are mentioned in the Scriptures. 'By introducing an element of diversity of tongue among Noah's descendants,' says the learned author of the *Histoire universelle de l'Eglise catholique*, 'God thus forced them to separate into family units and linguistic groups who ventured abroad to found a homeland elsewhere. Hence it came about, in the second era of the world, that God himself created different nationalities: thus did he send them across the earth to inhabit and cultivate it.'

There are no breaks in the pattern of God's work and nothing is done at random. Everything fits perfectly into an infinitely wise, heavenly scheme, designed to reflect the glory of God and express his divine attributes, notably his power, goodness, mercy, and justice. All mankind contributes in implementing this scheme. Every individual in a family, every family within a nation, every nation in the human race has therefore been entrusted with its own special mission, its own predetermined goal. God, in the wonderful ways of his Providence, does not deny any person, individual, family, or nation the means to its end. So will he also severely punish any abuse of these means, or will even shatter like a useless tool the people or nations who have not understood their mission, or have refused to fulfil their destiny by turning away from the path God had traced out for them. *Reges eos in virga ferrea et tanquam vas figuli confringes eos.* 'Thou shalt rule them with a sceptre of iron,' God tells The Word; 'thou shalt break them like a vase of clay.'

This is an elementary truth in the Catholic catechism that might usefully be recalled here, since too many Christians have forgotten it. They think of a blind force as presiding over all earthly events. They imagine that the victories of war, the conquest of kingdoms, the growth of empires, are due, in the final analysis, to the skill of generals, the courage of soldiers, or the shrewd politics of statesmen. They no longer remember Bossuet's inspiring words: 'Man restlessly plots and strives, but it is God who leads him.'

The teachings of the sacred texts and of secular history on this subject

Now if a nation is to achieve its purpose, it must have its own territory. If we trace nations back to their origin and follow the pattern of migrations of various people, we shall find that every family was motivated by a special compelling force, as if led by an invisible hand toward the country it was meant to inhabit. The Holy Scriptures, in particular, point to this fact in describing Abraham's vocation.

And the Lord said to Abram: Go forth out of thy country, and from thy kindred, and out of thy father's house, and come into the land which I shall shew thee. And I will make of thee a great nation . . . So Abram went out as the Lord had commanded him . . . into the land of Canaan . . . And the Lord appeared to Abram and said to him: To thy seed will I give this land . . . Lift up thine eyes, and look from the place wherein thou now art, to the north and to the south, to the east and to the west. All the land which thou seest, I will give to thee, and to thy seed for ever. And I will make thy seed as the dust of the earth; if any man be able to number the dust of the earth, he shall be able to number thy seed also.

This passage from the Old Testament is remarkable in many respects, but it is of particular interest in the present context. It tells us how Providence itself judges prevaricating races, and at the same time the merciful means it evolves to spare them the blows of its justice. The land God promised to Abraham belonged at the time to the Canaanites. This depraved people had defiled it to such an extent that God decided to destroy them. Before carrying out his decision, he set before them the deeds of the Father of the Faithful, as examples of virtue and piety. For many years, this righteous man lived in their midst and visited in turn the various parts of their country. But the most eloquent signs of his saintliness and the most obvious protection afforded him by God went unnoticed, which only compounded this guilty nation's crime, while they continued treading the path of perversity. God then tried another way of shepherding them back to the path of duty. He brandished the whip. And the Holy Scriptures describe the war, the fire from heaven, the famine that lashed out in succession against this wretched country, until the hour of their extermination struck at last. Meanwhile Abraham, with heaven-bestowed blessings and after many peregrinations and long and trying tribulations, finally reached the height of prosperity. He ranked as an equal to kings. Laden with merit and the burden of years, he died in this promised land with the comforting prospect of bequeathing to his descendants a fatherland that God would place in their final possession on the day chosen by his Providence. He gave his son careful instructions for his burial in the grave he had already acquired as a respectful repository for the mortal remains of his previously departed wife. He particularly enjoined his descendants never to return to the place whence their Eternal God had taken them, but to cling for ever to this land where they were to become a great nation.

Secular history teaches the same lesson. An attentive review of the history of different peoples clearly reveals the hand of Providence which guided the footsteps of their first families, and assigned to each their own territory and a goal to achieve. Whenever their mission is faithfully carried out, peace among them leads to abundance, prosperity, and happiness. If, on the contrary, they should stray from the right course, then does the sword hang at their thresholds and over their heads. They are plagued in succession with war and slavery, pestilence and famine, until finally they are brought back to the path of duty. Should they persist, they are then doomed to destruction through invasions, division of their lands, deportations, and mass extermination. Such are the teachings to be reaped from a close study of secular history, as to the ways of Providence with nations.

But we thought it most fitting to draw this lesson from the history of God's people, since their background is relatively well known, and since there is more than one point of resemblance between the ancient history of this people and our own, as we shall see later. Besides, God chose the Hebrews as a lesson to the world.

It is therefore a constant truth, as clearly taught by revelation as it is firmly demonstrated by the salutary teachings of history, that *Providence has allotted each and every nation its own mission to fulfil, its own predetermined goal to attain.* Every nation is bound to succeed, so long as it faithfully answers God's calling: for God, in his power and his wisdom, always apportions the necessary means to a given end. As a result, whatever a nation's weakness, however restricted its territory, it need never fear while it remains dutifully true to God and to its mission. Though it may be surrounded by powerful and ambitious nations, equally endowed with brilliant statesmen, with artful generals and valorous armies, God will protect it and even take up its defence, as in the days of Sennacherib and Judas Maccabeus.

Conversely, no amount of land, wealth, or power will ever save a prevaricating people from deep humiliation, from being dismembered and possibly wiped off the map of nations, should they seem beyond redemption: witness the powerful empires whose bloody revolutions and miserable end are described in history.

This truth is both edifying and encouraging to a little people like ours in French Canada. Our fate as a nation lies in our own hands. If the few families who left the France of yore to come and settle on the banks of the St. Lawrence some two hundred years ago have now become a nation of a million souls, this is not due to mere chance or to any blind force, but simply to the merciful designs of Providence. Providence it was that used our fathers to bring the enlightenment of the Scriptures and the principles of Christian revival to those wretched communities that, for centuries, had been floundering in an abyss of ignorance and brooding in the shadow of death in this beautiful, fertile valley.

Our forebears' wonderful mission was nobly accomplished, as is convincingly shown by their history's heroic and glorious accounts. The zeal, devotion, and faithfulness with which their task was performed is etched in blood from the mouth of the St. Lawrence right up to the banks of the Great Lakes whence it flows.

Let us be *intelligent, brave, and virtuous as they were,* and fully confident in our future.

French Canadians truly make up a nation; the valley of the St. Lawrence is their fatherland.

Our statement on the basic prerequisites for fashioning a nationality and on the territory that moulded it leads us to say without hesitation that French

Canadians in this country are a real *nation*, and that the vast expanse of territory irrigated by the majestic St. Lawrence is their own legitimate *homeland*.

For here we have a population of close to one million rising up as one man upon hearing their name called out, speaking the same language, confessing the same faith. We see them adhering whole-heartedly to the laws and institutions inherited from their ancestors, and working untiringly at developing the land acquired at the cost of their blood, watered and fertilized by the sweat of their brows. We realize, with the supporting evidence of history, that this million people are but the natural growth of these few French families who came over to settle here barely two hundred and fifty years ago, to preach the gospel to the primitive and infidel natives of the area. So, once the meaning of all this has been thoroughly penetrated, all one can say is: '*Digitus Dei est hic*: The finger of God is here.' Such an astonishing result in the face of so many pitfalls and difficulties is well and truly stamped with the seal of God's work. This handful of families was obviously of a mettle on which Divine Providence could well confer the privilege of being the seed-bed of a *nation*. They were selected for this high task with such care and discernment that the words addressed in the Bible to Abraham the Patriarch could well apply to them also: 'Go out of your country and come to the land I shall show you; I shall turn you into a great nation; there, I shall make your posterity multiply like the stars in the skies, so that the number of your descendants may equal that of the sands on the sea-shore.'

Rejoicing in the past and confident of our future, we may indeed repeat once again that we, the descendants of noble families who sacrificed martyrs to the Church and heroes to our beloved country, we French Canadians have become a *nation*. The earth that these martyrs' blood cleansed and sanctified, the land that these heroes' deserving courage conquered, the soil that was defended and husbanded through so many sacrifices, is our own *fatherland*.

Any French Canadian who is not proud of his origin and happy with his native land would surely seem hard to please. There are very few nations whose emergence into history is crowned with such a shining halo. On the contrary, many of them have to be content with a territory whose fertility, climate, and natural resources are greatly inferior to what the magnificent, spectacular valley of the St. Lawrence has to offer. We should therefore, as French Canadians, be thankful to Divine Providence for endowing us so well. We must remain inextricably linked to the land where the ashes of our devout ancestors are buried, and where there is not a shadow of a doubt that a great future awaits us.

> It is important that French Canadians should
> clearly understand the mission Providence entrusted
> to their forebears – their future as a nation depends
> on their unswerving allegiance to this mission.

As a nation we have a mission to fulfil, and as a people a goal to attain. For, as has already been stated, the pattern of God's work is unbroken. Every individual in a family, every family in a nation, every nation in mankind – each has a special predestination. From then on, it is up to each member to play his part according to the ways opened to him by Providence, and subject to the worst possible punishment in case of prevarication. The penalty of destruction and death awaits individuals, families, or nations who stubbornly refuse to pursue their goal and accomplish their mission.

But what is the French-Canadian people's mission? What is this goal they should constantly strive to reach? It is of paramount importance that they should be clearly aware of this and should grasp its full meaning.

We shall not be trespassing beyond our framework in broadening somewhat the scope of our research to look for an answer to such questions. In fact, these marginal investigations are the best possible opportunity to throw light upon the constant relationship between civic and political society and the religious order. There is no better way to prove the absurdity of these short-sighted theories whereby social organization is considered as a mere matter-exploiting device and wealth-producing machine. Those who hold such theories are incapable of viewing things with enough perspective to see that a being endowed with an immortal soul has a destiny other than that of dominating his fellow-men and, through them, accumulating the means of satisfying his pride and greed. Was ever a theory more soundly refuted by the history of the downfall of nations? One need only take the trouble to re-examine the history of Asia's ancient monarchies, or of the famous Greek and Roman republics, in order to discover the overwhelming logic of events. The growth and prosperity of these nations of old only lasted as long as, to the extent of their enlightenment, they kept to the paths of justice and righteousness; and as long as, within the limitations of their religious ignorance and blindness, they remained willing to serve God with adoration and obedience. The same logic of events also goes on to show how their downfall always coincided with the onslaught of greed, an unruly love of riches, an unquenchable thirst for material pleasure or for domination. Now, these social plagues have ever been the result of false doctrines. Among them we find these arbitrary, immoral theories, the best-known of which nowadays go so far as to banish God from society, advocating complete separation of civil and political order from religious order, and proclaiming full independence of the former from the latter.

These communities then became so depraved as to close their eyes to the mysterious light of nature's law, and to follow the doctors who pointed the way to supreme and ultimate bliss through material pleasure, through absolute self-supremacy above all else. At this juncture, social bonds slackened, national virtues declined, and, when the limit had been reached, that invisible hand that guides all our worldly events suddenly appeared and wrote these awesome words across the palace walls of every Babylon: *Mane, Thekel, Phares*: 'I numbered, I weighed, I divided.' It mattered little whether the Babylon in question was the capital of one of the vast Nimrod- or Romulus-founded empires that served as a scourge to nations or as a crushing weapon against criminals, or whether it was merely one of those infamous cities nestled on the shores of the Dead Sea; or again, one of those hardened infidel townships Jacques Cartier found scattered all along the St. Lawrence: the fact remains that empires and populations alike are subject to the same laws of Providence. Their days were numbered by the same master, their actions weighed by the same judge, their sentence written by the same hand. It was also the same avenging arm that smote them and made them vanish from the land they had been granted as their own.

Such is the great and terrible lesson history teaches nations and populations. Such is the solemn denial, by the irresistible logic of facts, of those ridiculous theories that profess to consign God to his heaven and relinquish into the hands of blind force the management of human affairs, whose secrets and control are said to be a prerogative of *intellectuals* and of *skilled politicians*.

As for us French Canadians, whom Catholic teachings have made the fortunate possessors of all-encompassing truth, let us strengthen our faith in the great consolation of our holy religion's dogma, with its reassuring presages as to our national future. So long as we remain faithful to the mission entrusted to our forebears, so long as we continue steadily, straight toward the goal assigned us by Providence, we shall have nothing to fear. No power, no human devices will ever succeed in checking our progress or prevent us from fulfilling our destiny here as a people.

Even if religious teaching were not as explicit as it is about this assertion, a careful review of our history would more than suffice to prove it. It therefore behoves us to seek, in the history of our country, the judicious lessons that can show us the way in times of crisis such as we are experiencing today, while instilling us with unwavering trust in our national future. The obvious intervention of Providence when it kept such careful watch over this colony's cradle; its wonderful protection in moments of dread battle; the deep peace enjoyed under the shelter of the British flag while the violent storm of the French Revolution was raging; the wisdom that inspired our fathers into declining the advances and solicitations of our powerful republican neighbour – all these facts are like so many beacons leading us on our way and like comforting testimonies of the gentle presence of Providence constantly watching over us.

Once again may we ask: what is our destiny as a nation, and what is this mission Providence gave our fathers? We shall attempt to answer that in another article.

> The mission with which Providence entrusted
> French Canadians is basically religious in nature:
> it is, namely, to convert the unfortunate infidel
> local population to Catholicism, and to expand the
> Kingdom of God by developing a predominantly
> Catholic nationality.

It may readily be shown that this was, indeed, our ancestors' mission. It is the *first lesson* in our history and a *prevailing factor* at the most significant stages of our national development. If we study the annals of our country, we shall first of all learn what Providence-instilled incentive led the French kings to colonize these parts. They only knew of the coastal regions through the reports of fishermen who sailed there every year from the main French harbours, to provide all of Europe with their catch, mostly of cod. Then we should examine the aims and reasoning of the great, good men whom the kings of France charged with this great venture. Here is what the learned Abbé Faillon has to say about the French kings' motives in colonizing Canada:

> It should not be difficult to ascertain the primary reason that prompted François I and several of his successors to found a colony in Canada, since they themselves made it quite clear in their letters patent to the navigators they sent to the area. These rulers proudly boasted their titles of *Very Christian Kings* and *Elder Sons of the Church*.... And even to this day, there is no doubt but that their great expenditures were mainly motivated by their hope of making the Redeemer known in Canada, and of bringing it within the realm of the Catholic Church. They knew that, in ordering his apostles and their successors to preach to all nations and baptize them in the name of the Father, the Son and the Holy Ghost, our divine Redeemer was indirectly inviting Christian Sovereigns, as custodians of his power, to pave the way for the Scriptures. They were to introduce them in as yet unexplored, remote countries. And this was actually what the French kings were striving to do, in their several attempts to set up colonies in Canada.
>
> How could they have put their power to better use than by acting, not as plundering conquerors, but as heaven-sent bearers of the only true values that could turn even life on earth into a source of happiness for the most destitute of men?

Another of our country's learned historians, whose writing career was cut short by death, was the pious and regretted Abbé Ferland. He is no less explicit on this point in an introduction to his *Cours d'Histoire du Canada*:

> *Faith and Honour!* With these two words on their lips and in their hearts, French missionaries carried the torch of Christianity and civilization to tribes lost in the slumber and darkness of infidelity. *Faith and Honour!* Such was the pledge of loyalty and love between France and her children, when she sent them forth to found a new fatherland in the forests of the West, on the banks of the great American rivers. And history tells us that they followed the teachings of their mother-country ...
>
> Our country's history cannot fail in its fascination as a dramatic stage-setting for the sufferings, ordeals, and great achievements of our ancestors. It retraces the footsteps of their journeys to establish a *Catholic* colony on the banks of the St. Lawrence, *while pointing to the path that must be followed if French Canadians are to preserve the heritage of their fathers' faith, language, and institutions....* Our history, moreover, particularly in its early days, has that distinct, classically heroic flavour imparted by our people's religion and background.
>
> For religion always played a predominant role, ever since the earliest days of settlement. It was on behalf of religion that the French kings commissioned Jacques Cartier and Champlain to explore new countries *for civilization and conversion to Christianity*. The same religion was later to bless the founding of French towns on the great river. It sent its priests to bear the torch of faith among the primitive tribes of the hinterland, and it was through these few humble missionaries' distant expeditions that most of the western regions were discovered. The tireless apostles of the Society of Jesus had already explored the whole of Lake Huron, while the New England settlers were only barely familiar with the forests bordering the Atlantic coast. The first families coming to people the country followed in the wake of the missionary fathers, who guided parents in their activities and gave their children the benefit of a Christian education.

Religion therefore had a powerful and healthy influence on the organization of Canada's French colony. It was enriched by different elements from the various French Provinces. These were blended together and SHAPED INTO A STRONG, UNITED PEOPLE, *who will continue to grow as long as they maintain their allegiance to their* INHERITED TRADITIONS.

Such are our two foremost historians' opening remarks on the aims and intentions of our nation's founding fathers. Both authors were outstandingly perceptive students and writers of our country's history, and worked untiringly to clarify and rectify what had remained obscure or incorrect in their predecessors' earlier attempts. It might even be said that their work is the fullest possible demonstration of this truth *whereby our fathers' mission was to convert and civilize the country's primitive inhabitants*, while the *goal* Providence set for them was none other than to *establish a deeply Catholic* nation on this land *they were granted as their heritage.*

Further evidence of the French-Canadian people's sacred mission

We might rest content with the above two lengthy quotations as sufficient evidence that our national destiny is basically religious. But we should like to point to a few additional historical incidents where the intervention of Providence is especially apparent, and where its intentions regarding our nation are particularly clearly revealed.

We shall start by following Jacques Cartier on his expeditions. When he reached the mouth of the great river, a storm forced him to shelter in the Bay of Gaspé. That was when he first set foot on Canadian territory. What was his first deed when he landed on these shores to which Providence had guided his ship? It was an act of piety. For on the headland at the entrance to the harbour he erected a great cross, thirty feet high. What was his second deed? It was a political one. For on the cross he carved these words: 'LONG LIVE THE KING OF FRANCE!'.

Speaking through the Prophet, the Lord God had told the Redeemer: '*Dabo tibi gentes in hereditatem*: I shall give you nations as your heritage'. Thus it was in his capacity as a Very Christian King and, so to speak, as his Master's bailiff that the head of the glorious 'Eldest Daughter of the Church' took possession of this territory. This he did, not in order to treat its inhabitants as a conquered people, nor to exploit them like slaves by robbing them of the fruit of their labours or tearing the riches out of their soil. He did it to provide them with the tremendous benefit of a truly Catholic civilization, and to lay in their midst the foundations of a new kingdom, with Christ as its prime ruler. That is what was meant by Jacques Cartier when he vested French kings, through the very Cross, with power and authority over this vast expanse of territory.

Cartier sailed up the Gulf and reached the Ile-aux-Coudres. He tells us that the first thing he did on landing was to build an altar and have the Sacrifice of the Mass offered up to God by one of the priests on board. This happened to fall on the Christian holy-day of the nativity of the Virgin Mary, Mother of God. It was also the first time that the Holy Eucharist was consecrated in the inland areas of Canada. After that he went ashore at the foot of the Cape that was to bear the banner of Christ and Country, where a tributary flows into the great river. And here his immediate concern was to endow the country with a Christian name; so he called this tributary the 'Sainte-Croix'.

Upon reaching Hochelaga, Jacques Cartier did something worthy of the most zealous, devout missionary: 'Since he could not speak of God to these people whose language was not known to him,' says the learned Abbé Faillon, 'it was to God that he addressed his prayers on their behalf; and he started reciting the Gospel according to St. John: *In principio erat verbum . . .*' He then made the sign of the Cross over all the sick that were shown to him, 'asking God to give them the knowledge of our Holy Faith and of our Saviour's passion, and to grant them the grace of embracing Christianity and receiving baptism'. But since these acts of charity and piety seemed to apply to the sick only, Cartier next thought of asking God for the same privilege for all these people. As he had a prayer-book, he read aloud all of Our Lord's passion so that, although he could not fill their minds with the knowledge of this sacred mystery, that source of all human hopes, he might at least be able to penetrate their ears with its account. He tells us that while he was reading, there was complete silence among these poor people, 'as they listened with wondrous attention, looking up to the heavens and copying our ritual gestures'.

Having performed this rite, Jacques Cartier climbed the hill at whose foot lay Hochelaga and, arriving at the top, he gazed with exalted admiration at the spectacular view below. It was that particular time of the year when the first winds of autumn, sweeping through our forests, tinge them with these varied and strikingly beautiful hues of red, yellow, and green. Everywhere he turned – north, south, east, or west – he saw gigantic forests spreading their luxuriant growth right up to the horizon. The waters of the great river, up which he had just sailed, formed into scattered lakes several leagues wide, and divided into two main streams flowing around both sides of the hill on which he stood.

Imagine the thoughts and feelings that must have filled such a dauntless explorer's generous and eminently Christian soul, at the sight of this impressive scene, enhanced by the memory of all his recent impressions during the latter, inland part of his journey, covering over three hundred leagues! What he saw then must have been a revelation of the shape of things to come, and a secret voice must have told him that he stood well and truly at the centre of a territory destined to become the home of a great Christian people. So convinced was he of this fact, that he already visualized a leader of this people choosing this very spot as the seat of his Empire. This significantly prompted him to call the mountain *Mont-Royal* or, as it was then pronounced, *Montréal*.

The striking resemblance between Jacques Cartier and the Father of the Faithful

Once we become familiar with these momentous events, as recounted by Jacques Cartier himself in the detailed chronicles of his journey, we cannot help being struck by the similarity between this great man and Abraham the Patriarch.

The Holy Scriptures tell us about God's command to the Father of the Faithful: 'Leave your country and come to the land I shall show you, and I shall make you into a great nation.' Upon reaching this land where God guided his footsteps and which was then inhabited by Canaan's children, what did Abraham do? He set up an altar at the very spot where our Lord had just appeared to him to tell him: 'I shall give this country to your descendants . . .'. Moving on from there to a mountain east of Bethel . . . there again he built another altar to God and invoked his name. After Lot had left Abraham, the Lord told him: 'Raise your eyes and look from where you stand, out to north and south, east and west. I shall make yours forever all the land that you can see, for you and your posterity. Look well at all this broad expanse of land, for I shall make it yours . . .'. And at that place (near the Vale of Manabree), Abraham set up an altar to the Lord.

What Christian, believing in the dogma of an all-wise Providence controlling every event on earth, could fail to be struck by the resemblance between Abraham's behaviour when he took possession of the land God promised his descendants, and that of Jacques Cartier as he took possession of this Canadian territory to which, through his king's mandate, the same Providence had guided his footsteps? Canada, like the country of Canaan, was inhabited by a sinful race, and God in his justice had sentenced them to destruction. But, in his bounty, he wished to give them the opportunity of averting the terrible sentence that loomed over their heads. Jacques Cartier therefore appeared in their midst as if heaven-sent with his following of pious priests, like Abraham among the guilty Canaanites. Neither was welcomed by these pernicious people; and both had to leave the land where God had led them, in order to give its inhabitants time to mend their ways during the period God had, in his mercy, decided to grant them as their last chance of atonement. The Old Testament tells us how, during that period, Providence castigated Canaan's children, with a view to reforming and saving them. War, famine, fire from heaven smote them in turn, but all to no avail; for they had reached the limit.

Canadian history gives no account of what happened to the inhabitants of Stadacona and Hochelaga after Jacques Cartier's departure. But we do know that, upon the return of those for whom he had opened the way, these tribes had disappeared, while others, equally depraved, had taken their place.

Thus, the lesson embodied in the first chapter of our history is a twofold one. It teaches us both our mission and our destiny as a people, and also indicates the fate of wayward races who persistently wander off the true course.

O Canadian people, may you thoroughly memorize your history's first lesson where it tells you of your noble destiny, and beware of blind and dissolute men who might offer you to bargain it away for a mess of pottage!

More evidence of the French-Canadian people's sacred mission

All that we have previously said about the origins of the French colony in Canada, together with our two most learned historians' weighty statements, from which we quoted in order to highlight the reasons behind the French kings' great enterprise, are more than ample proof of our national mission's religious nature. No less obvious a proof is to be found in the words and actions of the outstanding men Providence placed at the disposal of the Very Christian Kings for the fulfilment of their glorious task.

This evidence may seem conclusive enough for us to close, at this stage, our inquiry into our common destiny. Yet, convinced as we are that the point is of capital importance for us French Canadians, and that our national future hinges on a full awareness and understanding of its meaning, we feel enough can never be said on the subject. It is our firm belief that we should be doing our country-men a great service by helping to strengthen their faith in our nationality and their trust in its future. We might further contribute toward encouraging us all to realize, as needs we must, that the SAVING OF OUR NATION depends, no less than that of our souls, on our constant, unyielding adherence to CATHOLICISM.

This is doubtless our most powerful bond as a national entity, and one that will always be strongly effective in protecting us from the many dangers around us, the most fearful of which is unquestionably the threat of division.

We shall therefore go on to analyse the striking purport of a few salient, relevant events recorded in our history. Providence seems to have placed them there to shine for us like beacons in these dark and critical times, or to guide us like signposts, showing us our proper future path.

The reasons why Providence caused the failure of the first attempts at establishing settlements in Canada

Jacques Cartier's first winter in the neighbourhood of Stadacona had had such a disastrous effect on his men, owing to the excessive cold and the onslaught of disease, that France came to believe that the country must be well-nigh unin-habitable. Small wonder then that, when attempts were made to find volunteers who might go and settle there permanently, virtually no one proved willing to abandon his beautiful France for the deep, dense Canadian forests; and it thus became practically necessary to resort to coercion.

As a result, François I authorized Roberval and Jacques Cartier to recruit suitable men among the convicts in certain state prisons. This strange resolve, that men destined for the gallows partly make up the retinue of recruits who would start a Canadian colony, might indicate the sovereign's kind-heartedness. It might be construed as a way of rescuing these wretched people from the avenging hand of justice, by giving them a heaven-sent opportunity to reform their ways, in gratitude to God. But you will agree that this choice of method was hardly likely to achieve the King's purpose and convert barbarians. It therefore ended in failure. The fulfilment of God's plan called for more worthy tools.

During the reign of Henry III, a similar expedition led by the Marquis de La Roche also ended in failure.

Henry IV who, like his predecessors, wanted to found a basically CATHOLIC colony on the banks of the St. Lawrence, also set about it in a singular way: he charged the Calvinist Chauvin with this task. A man of this great ruler's high intellect should, it would seem, have known better than to ignore the fact that one of the main pillars of the success of such an enterprise must rest upon the strength of group unity, especially religious unity. Surely this monarch was in a better position than any other to see in such unity a basic prerequisite for the peace and happiness of any society. For he could observe with his own eyes the horrible misfortunes that religious division had brought about in the mightiest of nations. No wonder, then, that this new attempt at colonization should have suffered the same fate as previous ones. How could a new-born country possibly withstand those seeds of destruction that had already brought even the most flourishing of nations to the brink of disaster?

We shall not dwell upon the secondary causes of the failure of so many efforts and sacrifices directed at laying the foundations of a prosperous colony in this country. Let us rather look back directly at the original cause: Providence was there, earnestly watching over the beginnings of a nation that was to enjoy the highest and holiest of destinies. And it doomed to failure all attempts at colonization that were not in harmony with God's scheme (constantly seconded by the kings of France) of establishing a *primarily Catholic* colony.

This was without doubt the first real cause of the failure of the earliest attempts to settle a land where the blood of martyrs was to be shed.

Providence selects the first settlers.

When the time came at last to found a real colony in this country, God chose Champlain to this end – just as he had chosen Jacques Cartier as its first explorer. This great man had all the requisite qualifications for such a momentous undertaking. His faith and piety helped him realize how careful he must be in selecting those who were to form the colony's nucleus.

And it should surely be a source of legitimate pride for us French Canadians to know that this colony's first families, who, for the most part, were our own ancestors, were chosen among the mother country's best, in a moral and religious sense.

From these élite families we inherited the ardent faith and gentle manners that have always been typically French-Canadian; as well as our deep respect for authority, be it religious or civil; and also this strict observance of the Church's teachings that has made us strong and has always been our salvation in times of danger, while keeping us united as one body. Our noble and pious ancestors sowed the seed of kindness in the hearts of our countrymen, along with their generous, gracious hospitality and proverbial politeness which foreigners find so attractive. And yet another part of that precious legacy is our frankly and sincerely liberal attitude for which we are liked and trusted by our co-citizens of different origin.

Now we shall put a question to all who believe in a Providence so wise and watchful that it has counted every hair on our heads, not permitting even a single one to fall out without a reason: should the absolute failure of the first attempts at Canadian colonization be attributed to ill-luck or to blind, brute, uncontrolled force? These first attempts used convicts or renegades, men divided by the deepest religious hatred. Is it not likely, therefore, that they were considered unworthy instruments for the task of spreading civilization, to which Providence had originally prompted the Very Christian Kings? Needless to say, no worse choice could have been made to bring religion to infidels and to establish a solid basis for a religiously united nationality. Hence, since the means were not fitted to the end, God was not ready to bless them, and so thrust them aside like ineffectual tools.

That is no doubt the fateful reason why the earliest efforts and sacrifices to start a Canadian colony remained barren.

Then came Champlain. Inspired by faith and piety, his intelligent mind was aware of this truth. He therefore recruited suitable followers. Despite ever-recurring difficulties, his courage, strengthened by virtue, overcame all obstacles. And his achievement has stood the test of over two centuries, to reach today's prodigious stage of development.

Once more may we wonder is this mere good fortune? And is there a French Canadian among us who does not interpret this second chapter in our history as a lesson written by the hand of Providence for our edification, saying: 'It was through Catholicism that you were given life and growth as a nation. It is through Catholicism that you will continue to thrive and will reach your highest destiny as a people.'

The inspired influence of missionaries at the inception of our nation

The third chapter in our history is even more explicit about the intents of divine Providence. It tells us, first of all, about missions among the barbarians and the Recollet and Jesuit Fathers' endeavours to impart some knowledge of the faith and of true civilization among these poor wretches. It then gives a new account of these missionaries' invaluable assistance to the first settlers, especially while there was still no established Church hierarchy in Canada.

Several of them bore the palm of martyrdom that crowned our rising nation with a bright and glorious halo.

The blood of these martyrs was truly a source of countless blessings on us. It was the price they paid for our country, for this land on which they were the first to set foot, thus sweeping it clean of the horrors spread by centuries of faithlessness.

The blood of these Heaven-sent messengers of peace and charity, shed by the savage barbarians' infamous doing, put a seal to God's reprobation of these wayward tribes who refused to see the light. God judged them, and barely a handful are now left in witness to their past existence.

This terrible outcome unconsciously brings to mind the words that Moses heard when God sought revenge against his enemies: '*Dixi!* ... *ubinam sunt?* I have spoken! ... and now where are they? ... I shall erase even the memory of their name.' Such is the immediate association that comes into Christian minds upon seeing the fate of the area's wretched infidels.

But our fathers' blood, shed for their faith, has become our most glorious and legitimate title of ownership to this land. Once its first inhabitants, who were to become our brothers, had disappeared, Providence put us in its rightful possession as legitimately as ever a people have been able to claim a country as their own.

These wonderful missions in the wilderness, started during the Canadian colony's first days on the banks of the St. Lawrence, are still alive today. Our missionaries reached the heart of the continent, and from there proceeded westward and northward, bearing the banner of the Cross to the Pacific coast and right up to the polar regions where the sun never sets in the summer and never rises in winter.

One of the Christian heroes who began the barbarians' conversion stands out as one of the greatest figures in our history, along with Jacques Cartier and Samuel de Champlain. His name was Father Jean de Brébeuf. He and his companions personify the most terrible period in our past, as also the most glorious of missions.

Church hierarchy in Canada has always been fundamental to our life as a nation.

We now come to another chapter in our history that is even more edifying than any of the things mentioned above. It tells us about the organization of the Church and about its institutions in Canada. There will be an opportunity, a little further on, to explore the work of Bishop Laval. We shall see what his foundations have meant for our nation, how they have been our salvation in times of crisis, and have become a traditional part of our people's lives. The providential survival of these institutions is yet further proof of the powerful, vitalizing life-blood that religion confers upon whatever it influences.

Champlain's political achievements perished, despite the talent of French generals, the courage of French soldiers, and our ancestors' heroic integrity. And the sacred banner of the French kings blazoning over old Cape Stadacona was, over a century ago, replaced by the British flag. But throughout this tragedy – foreshadowing the French Revolution's terrible storms, which overthrew a fourteen-century-old monarchy – the Church of Canada stood firm, like a sacred ark ready to rescue our nation's survivors and take them to shelter in its convents or colleges. Mgr Laval's religious institutions came through this terrible ordeal unscathed. They emerged from it greater and stronger than before. And it is particularly since then that, as the need arose, Providence used our Canadian bishops as guiding instruments to safeguard, protect, and defend our national interests. The regretted Abbé Ferland's *Vie de l'Illustre Evêque Plessis* clearly illustrates this point.

These then, in a few words, are some of the teachings of our national history regarding the Canadian people's mission and destiny. They can be summed up in four names, which in themselves are the best reminder that *our future as a nation depends on our faithful adherence to Catholicism.* And these four names are: JACQUES CARTIER, SAMUEL DE CHAMPLAIN, JEAN DE BRÉBEUF, and J. F. LAVAL.

7 Gonzalve Doutre (1842-1880)
The Principle of Nationalities

Mr. President and members of the Institute:

By putting my name down for tonight it was more for the purpose of talking with you than of delivering a lecture. My young predecessor on this platform suggested a subject in the essay he read to us at our last meeting.

He came to speak to you about French-Canadian nationality in terms that forced me to take pen in hand and to refute them and to place it back in the realm of humanity, which he has put a little to one side.

Please do not accuse me of exaggerated liberalism or of quixotic ideas. If you want a fanatical, biased, self-centred opinion, read our Canadian newspapers, which are no more concerned than they were in the year forty with the principles on which society in general is based. The writers, and very often their enthusiastic readers, see in the wheels of popular government and the events that take place before their eyes little more than the greater or lesser possibility of satisfying their ambitions. And so I can confidently say that the paper that talks the most about nationality is little better than the one that talks least about it.

Journalism in Canada does not hold the broad, progressive, and humanitarian position that the press occupies in other countries, notably in France and England.

Therefore I shall not turn to Canadian journalism for arguments and principles.

I intend to talk of the principle of nationalities, so peculiarly put forward by my predecessor, a liberal and powerfully humanitarian principle that he wanted to restrict to wretched selfishness and misleading declamations.

The principle of nationalities is far from being divisible, it is indissoluble and indestructible. In order to understand it fully, it is necessary to have followed the onward march of humanity through all of its phases, pagan and Christian, republican, monarchical, or democratic; it is necessary to have followed it step by step, viewing not only the great but also the little men, the generality of men.

If one looks seriously at this humanity plagued by selfishness and personal interests instead of general interests, one will see that the principle of nationalities was unknown, or rather, disregarded.

Translated from 'Le Principe des Nationalités', a public lecture delivered at the Institut Canadien, December 1, 1864, and published as a pamphlet, Typographie du Journal 'Le Pays', Montreal, 1864, pp. 34–73.

In discussing this great principle, people have wanted to talk about birth, ancestors, and special history. They have allowed themselves to be deluded by the false, illogical, and unreasonable theories of so-called patriots. The principle of nationalities does not stop at birth, ancestors, and special history. It takes in all of humanity, linked by the common interests and aspirations that apply to all men and intelligent people who live on this planet. And this is the only true, logical, and natural way to view this great principle.

People have wanted to talk of treason, and call those who prefer real nationality to false nationality traitors.

To justify this expression they try to extract great glory from the name of French Canadian. They seem to forget that because of this name we are forced to carry on our shoulders the sad burden of the shameful and unjust actions of France in 1760. Note that the advocates of French-Canadian nationality are unwilling to accept modern France, but rather the France of the time of the Conquest. If you ask them to accept the laws as well as the customs and habits of present-day France, they shout blasphemy and infamy. And the reign of Louis XV and Pompadour is for them a sacred cult they offer up for the edification of all.

Is the France of Louis XV and the Regency really so beautiful, so noble, so great, so humanitarian, so national that such hardened hearts can be attracted towards it with so much enthusiasm? Surely the history of modern France offers more glorious times than that.

I think people forget the circumstances in which Canada was separated from France. If gratitude is an obligatory feeling for a son towards his loyal mother, dislike and even abandonment is permissible towards a cruel mother who lets her children be massacred and laughs at their existence. I do not see what logical link can exist between the France of Louis XV and present-day Canada, when the abandonment of the former was so odious and the devotion of the latter so constant. Let us be men and not allow ourselves to be blinded in this matter by such words as motherland and attachment.

The reason given by those who wish for the preponderance of French-Canadian nationality as an explanation of their strange attachment to the France of Louis XV is that we were French at that time and descendants of Frenchmen.

If they had to start from this false pretext no people in the world could lay claim to a modern nationality.

The immigration that took place on this continent since its discovery has not had a distinctive character. All the countries of the world sent their surplus population. It is true the majority of those who came to Canada were French, but a majority is not a lasting fact, since it may turn against us today. If there is any people whose veins are swollen with different kinds of blood it is surely the people of the New World, opened and colonized by universal immigration. Therefore they give only one reason for this claim: we are French because we belong to France. As you can see, these advocates cannot boast of a very solid nationality, and therefore not a very lasting one.

Let us put aside this childish and vulgar way of seeing the great principle of nationalities and follow the straight line traced by humanity and by the interest of all peoples who cover the globe.

If I had the time, I could prove with books in hand and history spread out before me that the different peoples in their various peregrinations since the most distant times have changed blood and origins following the different phases of their itinerant existence, if I may express myself this way.

The crossing of the Red Sea is not an isolated historical fact. Many such crossings have taken place since then. Humanity has not chased the waters before them simply to grant to all peoples the freedom to live in every corner of the globe. We must not believe that peoples live sedentary and isolated lives: they are pushed forward by progress, discoveries, and civilization.

Do not believe that by discovering the New World Christopher Columbus transplanted a unique and homogeneous people there. Far from that, it was like a new crossing of the Red Sea, newly opened up for the progress of all peoples, who experienced new demands and needs because of the diversity of their habits, traditions, and interests. And these needs made them rally round their mother countries. They also gave birth to very special habits and customs.

After facts so obvious even to the youngest observer, could one believe that a people must live as it was born?

But look! in the course of your existence each of you changes your ideas, behaviour, customs, and principles according to age, climate, and circumstance – and you would not want peoples to undergo these same progressive transform-ations! And you would dare call nationality the gathering of some hundred individuals of similar origins who came to mix in with another population and build a new nation strengthened by union and harmony!

You must admit then that with this system the number of nationalities is infinite and indeterminate.

Let us move outside this narrow circle, since it is smothering us; and let us not be seduced by ideas so narrow that they will make us believe in the decadence of human intelligence rather than in its progress.

When I speak of the principle of nationalities please understand me correctly. I see nationalities as a natural and even a social necessity. I believe that all these masses of men that are known under the name of nationalities contribute to the public good, while preserving special traditions and inclinations.

Nationality, in the generic meaning of the word, is the national character of a people.

A nation is the grouping of all the inhabitants of one country.

Therefore a nation is not a portion of the inhabitants of one country, and it is a distortion of the word to define it this way. There would no longer be a nation: there would be a tribal, fragmented nation. And would you give one of these fragments the right to create a nationality for itself?

What makes up the people of Canada, what makes up the nation, is not a portion of the inhabitants, but all of them together. The English Canadians no more form a nation than do the Scottish, Irish, or French Canadians. To say that any one portion of a people may claim a nationality distinct from the others is to be drawn into obvious inconsistencies.

The fundamental principle of all nationality is the enlightened self-interest that links all the inhabitants of one country; it is the basic incentive for acquiring the greatest ease in moral and social relations; it is the logical calculation that proves everyone is interested in preserving domestic harmony and in cultivating like sentiments for preservation and common prosperity.

If you study the application of this principle on a small scale you will immediately recognize it on a large one. For example:

A man marries; this marriage forces him to live amidst a large new family to whom he is a complete stranger. This man's first thought will be to look for ways to live harmoniously with the ideas, habits, and whims, if you will, of his new family connections. The purpose of this instinctive response which will bind their existence to his, so to speak, will be simply to assure the tranquillity, personal happiness and satisfaction, individual advantage and good understanding that he will seek in his new family. This good understanding will give them identical interests, and if this man and this family proceed according to the rules of brotherliness, we can be sure that they will walk the straight road that will bring them well-being, tranquillity, and mutual esteem.

Please do not accuse me of materialism. The principles of enlightened self-interest are a high morality and an unbending fairness. In the above example the man's enlightened self-interest that allies him to his new family guides him in all his conduct; it throws flowers on the often thorny road of life; it makes material interest subservient to moral interest; and it destroys all unpleasantness of heart and mind that is caused by selfishness.

Well, can this small-scale application not work on a larger scale?

A people, a nation, is condemned to live in the same land with common interests: do you think the principle of its own nationality does not become general and universal?

Would the enlightened self-interest that guides two families thus joined along the road to happiness, tranquillity, and prosperity not also guide a people, a nation, with more profitable results since they would be larger and more universal?

The principle of this nationality, its basic principle, is then enlightened self-interest. Language and blood are not everything in real nationality, since this is a selfish idea, and there is real selfishness in these two words *language* and *blood*, to be entirely honest.

The sole material reason for there being such a diversity of languages is the Tower of Babel.

Babel certainly did not cause the separation of peoples, since they understood one another. Then why try to construct barriers between peoples under the pretext that their language is not the same? Is it not a question of form that takes precedence over a larger and more important question, the basic question?

As far as its material results are concerned the Tower of Babel is nothing more than a legend that to my mind does not even have romantic appeal.

But since the most distant centuries peoples have worked at the construction of another Tower of Babel that will certainly not have the unhappy result of separating men. We know the primitive goal of the biblical Tower of Babel.

The builders wanted to raise a monument that would allow them to bridge the distance that separated them from God. The peoples knew the positive side of this metaphor. They are building a tower of granite to which each century is adding a stone.

Sooner or later you will see it rise to the heights of science, where human intelligence tends to mount. No cloud will hide the view, the eye will cross space, and language will no longer be an obstacle, since each idea will have its universal interpreter.

This is not a dream on my part: nothing is surer. Modern civilization has given a strong hand to the brave workers who are building this monument.

Come with me through all countries and you will see that all scientific developments are becoming common to all civilized peoples. If a discovery is made, or a book is published, that is the fruit of great intelligence, even if it all takes place in China, the universe soon knows about it. A spark that flies from the intellectual worker's mallet sets the world aflame and lights it up. Intelligence knows no distances. Universal nationality unites the minds of all peoples. Ideas are common, they pass from one country to another, take root and blossom. Their interpreter is language, and how easy its task is today! In the sciences as in politics peoples agree and understand each other. Notice also how trifling a matter it is, since it changes with the times and circumstances.

We cannot find one single useful language that has crossed the centuries from the beginning of the world until now and remained intact. This is an important point in support of my ideas, for it is ridiculous to become attached to a language in order to protect the eternal existence of nationalities. Language is only an agent of human thought and one should cling to it only because of the services it renders to this thought. One can never think of a people's language as an element of a nationality. Blood even less so, since it changes continually in modern times. There are no longer insurmountable obstacles to prevent the mixing of races. Look at France, where all kinds of marriages are allowed, and every day the blood of individual families is mixed. France is only one example of something that is happening in almost all the countries of the world.

I think I can successfully refute the argument that uses religion as the basis of nationality by proving that religious tolerance exists everywhere.

Rome flounders in intolerance, and is far from supplying present or future times with a flattering example.

No matter how Catholic France appears, she places all existing religions under her protective care. She is no less national, or rather it would be more accurate to say that by acting this way she better understands the principle of nationalities. Religions are beginning to fraternize in an indirect way, it is true, and this tends to become an obvious fact. The Mortara affair provoked the indignation of all religious men in the world. Compare this indignation to the intolerance of the last centuries and ask yourselves if religions are not tending towards a harmonious existence side by side. There is only one God in Heaven and all the divergent opinions refer only to the manner of worshipping Him.

Therefore to attempt to form distinct nationalities based on an individual religion would be to oppose the progress of religious brotherhood. But one does not oppose the march of progress without suffering and being threatened. The revolutions that have excited the world have always been caused by obstacles that blocked the way of progress.

And so is it possible in Canada to hope for a nationality that is entirely composed of Catholics on one hand and Protestants on the other? Especially in Lower Canada we are condemned to live side by side with all kinds of different religious groups. Will we give a stronger, more legal, and more favoured existence to Protestants in preference to Catholics or vice versa? Surely this would be the height of injustice. So this is not feasible. There is also the danger of establishing a Canadian nationality in Lower Canada based exclusively on the Catholic religion and the French language. You will not force the Protestants to submit to the supremacy of Catholics, any more than you will force the French to bend under the arrogance of the English. People talk about the French-Canadian majority in Lower Canada, and it is an undeniable fact, not specifically from the standpoint of numbers, but from the standpoint of strength. If we try to humiliate the Protestant minority in Lower Canada, is this not forgetting the protests we made to Upper Canada when it came into conflict with the religious opinion of its Catholic inhabitants? It would be selfish to claim for ourselves what we refused others.

There is, then, more harmony, tranquillity, and happiness to be expected from the union of Protestants and Catholics. By union I do not mean similar opinions and beliefs, but simply tolerance. I do not mean that the one must make concessions to the other, but that they mutually recognize the other's right to exist.

It is a shameful ambition for us French-Canadian Catholics to try to form a separate nationality to the detriment of the Protestants, Jews, etc., who also have the same rights to form a distinct nationality.

We were not placed here by virtue of a preconceived idea, but by the force of circumstances, or rather, destiny. God did not want the New World to be made up of tribes divided one from the other and doomed to eternal weakness by living eternally separated.

I find it rather brazen for a newspaper to tell us unblushingly that Providence has been preparing in a way more obvious every day the reign of the monarchy in the New World, meaning by this to lay down the principle that sooner or later the New World will divide itself up in order to give some royal scraps to a few princely loafers from Europe.

We are far from agreeing with this line of thought; on the contrary we believe that the New World is becoming more and more democratic.

Mexico only accepted Maximilian under force and not by choice. It is strange to see in France the only European power trying to forcefully impose not a humanitarian regime but the most despotic – the regime of the Austrian family. Austria, which has the stigma of shame and infamy on its brow! Austria, which every Frenchman must hate in his heart!

France has also been rash in many circumstances: the Italian War, the Treaty of Villafranca, the treaty of last September 15, its neutrality in the Polish War, and its war in Mexico are just so many contradictions.

Gentlemen, forgive me this almost obligatory digression. It is impossible to calm this legitimate but often misguided enthusiasm for France that nowadays gives the example of a nation where thought is not free.

I was saying a moment ago that we had not been placed on this soil by virtue of a preconceived idea. The New World was opened up for all peoples; and the proof of this is that you will find traces of numerous nationalities from all over the globe. I firmly believe that the Frenchman who leaves France to live in another country ceases to be French and becomes a member of the new nation he adopts. Now, the inhabitants of Canada must accept the name of the country they live in and not of the country they came from. For the goal of nationality is the union of all the inhabitants of one country.

Canada must form one single nationality, bound by common interests. Our close relations with the British provinces will one day necessitate the enlarging of this nationality.

I shall go even further. A universal nationality is neither a Utopia nor a meaningless word. Ambassadors from every country give proof of this every day. They constitute an advance towards universal union. Every nation feels the need to be represented everywhere. There is not a single country that does not contain several members of a foreign country. You will find both Englishmen and Frenchmen in China or Japan. These various peregrinations will help break down differences in languages and nationalities. And the day must come some time when these scattered parts, that are of no great consequence because they are scattered, will melt into one whole. One can see proof of this in ambassadorial functions that consist not of upholding national rights at the expense of other nations but of endeavouring to reconcile these rights with those of other nations.

Moreover, I maintain that many wars have no other cause than the error committed by those who wanted to separate nationalities once and for all.

However, the principle of nationalities profits from all wars, since wars make us see that these small groups of different peoples are not lasting. They weaken the vitality of peoples for a while, but they make them stronger and more lasting afterwards. War is only a transition, a physical as well as a moral purge. We have only to look at history to show that war only destroys to reconstruct. Most often modern inventions are made during war.

The American war will have an immense effect and it is already beginning to be felt. There is no doubt about the outcome of the struggle. The war has shaken and overthrown the most iniquitous of institutions, slavery. The millions of slaves, who formed a distinct body of men, will become part of the American nationality, if they have not already. The odious principle of colour discrimination will be annihilated by universal condemnation. A half-century from now our children will be surprised that it required so much blood and disaster to blot out from the universe the shameful word of slavery.

I make no distinction between a slave-owner and a false patriot.

The one bases separation on colour, the other on language: black, red, and white are all humans, and in the same way the various languages are no more than the organs of thought.

Let us consider further the beneficial effect of wars. See how the Polish war gave birth to a new era. The best proof that a nation does not die is that Poland is still alive after several decades of persecution.

Poland is not dying at this time: she is struggling, and will bring to light the repulsive conduct of the Russians and Austrians in such a way that in future they will be forced to retreat before the frightening consequences of their conduct.

The war in Denmark will only show the small amount of interest one should give to questions of territories and possessions.

We will see in this that the odious principle of *killing men in order to preserve shreds of royalty for kings* has lasted only as long as peoples have wanted to remain divided and be ruled.

Far be it from me to give encouragement to wars. I am only observing their results. The illness is not to be desired, but sometimes it regenerates. War is a social necessity. The human body undergoes regular and necessary transformations in its development; it is the same with nations.

Treaties between nations are also a step towards universal union. Every day we feel the need of joining our special interests so that they will become general interests. From postal agreements to commercial treaties you will see the beginnings of universal union that will join the interests of different countries. Therefore it would be dangerous for us to do our utmost to establish a nationality separate from other nationalities.

Human relations need the understanding of every man, and it is the exchange of understanding and service that makes the union of men so useful, desirable, and beneficial. If nations are to remain friends they must demand the same exchanges of understanding and service.

A nationality cannot be self-sufficient; it is absolutely necessary for other nationalities to come to its aid.

No matter how hard we tried to establish a French-Canadian nationality based on blood, language, and traditions, we would only cause a progressive separation from the nationalities formed by the different parts of the peoples on the American continent. This is a common error and the real danger. Strength does not come from separation, but rather from union. Now, of what use will all these nationalities be that lead only to internal splits and not to the centralization of power and strength?

I call for the union of all people who live on the American continent. I want this because they are all guided by similar interests. I have expressed my opinion on enlightened self-interest, which forms the basis of the principle of nationalities: this interest is far from flattering or favouring selfishness and the supremacy of one nationality over another, since it is a general and universal interest.

To all those who want to base a nationality on the majority of inhabitants who make it up, let me say that majorities, like minorities, are seesaws that are dependent on time and circumstances. It is a moving base on which everything shifts and changes.

Therefore the principle of majorities is false. The proof of this is that in 1841 we were the majority in Upper Canada and in 1864 we are the minority. Another proof is that Upper Canada seems to have finished increasing its population. I am not mistaken; all one has to do is look at parliamentary reports. Immigration is finished in Upper Canada, while vast territories are still open to immigration in Lower Canada.

Could this be an argument in favour of ending the union? No, certainly not, for if there is a possibility of increase, we get the advantage. I say this for the benefit of those who tend solely towards supremacy based on numbers.

I say this especially for the benefit of those who are opposed to Confederation, since they are mistaken about their own existence. They believe their destiny is to live separate, while their moral and material interests bind them to all the people of the New World.

We have everything to gain from immigration. And so there is union. But union has caused us to spin in a small circle for more than twenty-three years. We still are what we were in 1841, and we will always be the same, if we do not hand over our resources for foreigners to develop, since they are now being wasted owing to our lack of manpower.

My predecessor came to tell you with a profusion of words and old refrains that we have nothing to gain by associating with the English.

I ask him to note that on the contrary we would gain from it as much as from associating with all the other nationalities.

If you look at this from the commercial point of view, you will see that commerce is almost entirely in the hands of English Canadians and not French Canadians.

Whether we take commerce on a large scale or a small one – jewellery, dry goods, foodstuffs, hardware, books, in fact almost all branches of commerce – we come to the conclusion that we are of almost no importance in all this.

Why? Because we have always attempted to live apart from the nationalities that surround us, and because we have endeavoured to remain strangers to our neighbours' progress, since we did not originate it.

Among French Canadians there is a strange self-love, a regrettable feeling of jealousy. It is rare for a plan to succeed, and often when it is about to be put into effect, you watch it disintegrate owing to the rivalries that spring up all the time. The salient feature of the French Canadian is, as it were, his separation.

You will not see one single French society that does not have this mania for disunity. The Canadian Institute experienced the sad result of this illness in 1858. Alone among all the institutions of the country it lives on through the union of all beliefs and ideas.

By its name and statutes the Canadian Institute sums up in itself the principle that I am defending with sincerity and conviction.

Since Canadian soil is open to everyone, may all nationalities come here and form a mixture that will be a general one and the result of climate, interests, and a common destiny!

It is a childish fear not to support the union of Upper and Lower Canada, and on the other hand of all the British provinces. People complain of Upper Canada's supremacy over Lower Canada, but I maintain that we have the same opportunities to progress and to increase in number.

And if we have been inactive for twenty-three years, to the point of becoming a minority when we were a majority, should we complain about this seesaw that we could have manoeuvred to our advantage as well as Upper Canada did?

Come now, Mr. National Separatist, forget your declamations and comparisons. Do not search in antiquity for examples that may be beautiful memories but that are far from being useful now.

The world moves like the Wandering Jew, without stopping. But what it has that is preferable to the Jew is that its movement is less the consequence of punishment than the result of progress.

Progress is a perpetually turning wheel. Whoever throws himself in front of it to hinder its movement is crushed. It knows no obstacles; in its so-to-speak calculated course, progress hurls the world towards a civilization that takes in the universe.

Nothing stops it. Everywhere it passes it leaves marks, signs of the future universal union that will come true, you can be sure. You have proof of it here on the American continent, and elsewhere.

Canada has a bright future. She lacks nothing. Mines, land, industry, factories, everything is here. But a kind of fatalism seems to bring her to a standstill. Division seems to hound her into inactivity. Instead of uniting internally, Canadians amuse themselves, with fatal complacency, by making up nationalities of every colour and description.

Every inhabitant praises the church steeple that witnessed the birth of his ancestors. No one is willing to admit that Canada is a new homeland where foreign nationalities must mix.

We forget that our life, our future, and our resources are here.

We seem to think of ourselves as prisoners whose gaze is constantly turned towards our native soil, whereas we are purely and simply in our own homeland and on our own property.

We do not take account of all the time wasted in these separations and divisions. The French Canadians waste energy and achieve nothing, while the English, who know time is money and progress, work restlessly and waste not a minute.

All one has to say is that a business has been set up by the English to know that it will succeed.

Please do not reproach me for being unfair to my fellow-countrymen. The time for blindness to the danger that threatens us is past. The time for bawling is past; now it is time for determined men to see the danger with cool composure and to remedy it.

Past history has shown us often enough what becomes of similarly useless declamations. The present proves to us all too well that we must not count on these lazy cry-babies who rant and rave without moving an inch. Is the present not striking evidence of the bad course we have followed? Can it not be used as a lesson for the future and make us understand that we were wrong in persisting to want a separate nationality?

And so the future will allow us to make up for such uselessly lost time. Canadians will know that their salvation is in union and in concentration on common interests. Once they are united, all ideas and activity will blend into a whole; the powerful force of enlightened self-interest will propel them along the road of progress; and friendly relations will only improve our ways.

Once rid of its narrow point of view, journalism will leave its orbit and flood the four corners of Canada with the light it has for so long kept hidden.

Education, which makes children out of our men instead of men out of our children, will spread afar its bountiful branches. The settler, relegated to the depths of the forest, will see the long-forgotten sun of learning shine again.

Our inhabitants will profit from this progress in education to such an extent that they will become important factors in the destiny of the homeland. They will no longer be sheep to be fleeced by our public men, but people who really count in the affairs of the state.

Men will realize that they have the right to choose the form of government they want and the kind of representatives they need.

Finally, the future will bring forth universal union that will regenerate the world by banishing selfishness and division.

The future will make of Canada a powerful addition to the New World. If Canada is linked with the other British provinces, before long you will see her rival the United States in influence as well as importance. And, who knows, once we have taken the first step, perhaps we will feel the need to spread wide this concentration of general interests, and thereby the New World may become one nation.

Then the Tower of Granite, which intellectual workers have worked on for several centuries, will rise.

And at its summit you will see brave and energetic men draw near God to ask him to come view this magnificent achievement of humanity: UNIVERSAL UNION.

8 Henri Bourassa (1868-1952)
French-Canadian Patriotism: What It Is, and What It Ought To Be

The singular situation of French Canadians

The French-Canadian people, few in number, are in a singularly difficult position.

We are subjects of a power that was the long-standing enemy of our mother country. Our political allegiance belongs to a nation we can respect, with whom we could have made a marriage of convenience, but which it is impossible for us to love with the spontaneous love that makes a common life and mutual sacrifices easy: the call of the blood and our own traditions stand in the way.

Our patrimony, the old Lower Canada, is only part of a huge territory that lacks the essential elements making up the native lands of most other peoples. It has been said that Italy, before unification, was only a geographical expression. It could be said with even more truth that Canada is a geographical absurdity. One needs only cross the country once from Atlantic to Pacific in order to note that the union of this huge territory was accomplished contrary to nature's plan. The steep Rocky Mountain chain and the sterile plateau that stretches from Lake Superior to Hudson Bay cut our national domain into three distinct regions. Each of these regions maintains much closer relations with the adjacent states of the American Republic than with the neighbouring areas of Canada. Joined together but yesterday, after a series of political transformations, these dissimilar areas already feel conflicts of interest arising among them, pulling them toward nature and against the cohesion necessary for national unity.

We are surrounded by the descendants, more numerous than we are, of a race that is foreign to us in origin, language, religion, laws, and customs. This serious disadvantage is noticeably reinforced by a lack of close contact, the result of the scattering of the Canadian people over too large a territory, by the difference and even the antagonism of material interests, and especially by the

---

Translated from 'Le Patriotisme canadien-français, ce qu'il est, ce qu'il doit être', a speech delivered at the Monument National, April 27, 1902, and published as a pamphlet, La Cie de Publication de la Revue Canadienne, 1902.

baneful work of politicians and journalists who play up the divergence in our national aspirations instead of toning it down.

This complicated situation makes active patriotism very difficult. Love of the land, of its institutions, of its nationality, which in other people is focused in a simple and strong patriotism, is divided in us and gives us three separate duties to fulfil: our duty toward England, our sovereign power; toward Canada and our fellow-citizens of a foreign origin; toward ourselves and our nationality.

This situation is full of perils; but it is not impossible to cope with, provided we bring to it goodwill, intelligence, steadfastness, tolerance, dignity, and a true Christian charity – which is as opposed to weakness and to cowardice as it is to violence.

Duties to England

In the present state of the world, it would be easy for me to garner applause by denouncing the British people, their rulers, and their policies. I will not do this, and for two reasons. First, I have no belief whatsoever in the efficacy of appeals to popular passion in order to enlighten the national conscience. It would seem to me cowardly to ignite the anger of an exclusively French audience when I come to preach the message of mutual understanding between our two Canadian races. Further, it would seem to me supremely unjust to make the entire English people responsible for the mad and criminal politics of those who govern them today.

I believe I have earned the right to mete out justice to England. I denounced her activities and her propensities at a time when there was some inconvenience in opposing the jingoist current that was sweeping our country. These tendencies I loathe, and I shall always fight against them. We French Canadians have a special duty to keep up a tireless resistance against this policy of expansion and military domination. But I repeat today what I never stopped saying in the worst of the turmoil: this policy is contrary to the best traditions of the English nation. There still exists an England that is truly liberal: she detests this delirium of brute force; she has constantly fought against it, and soon, I hope, she will overcome the misguided men who today dominate the British Empire. This England I love and admire; and so long as we are British subjects, it is to her we must look. In organizing resistance to the attacks of imperialist England, we must always take into account the existence and feelings of sane liberal England.

Our obligations to Great Britain have been, and still are, the theme of numerous ardent controversies. To understand these obligations better and to fulfil them, we need only read our history carefully. Let us read the past in order to determine our present duties and our future relations. This study will help us ascertain that England has done us much harm and much good. Men who prefer peace to honour find that the good outweighs the harm, and that in giving us political liberty Great Britain has generously redeemed the wrongs she has done to us. These men forget that liberty has been the fruit of a difficult and protracted struggle, and that if England had refused it to us any longer, there would not now remain an inch of British territory on the American continent.

In short, if done without meanness and passion, this historical review will lead us to the conclusion that we owe to England neither grudge nor gratitude. A detailed calculation of the good and the bad deeds of the mother country would balance out perhaps slightly to the detriment of British justice. Our English compatriots readily assert that we are not 'business-like'. I should like us to give them new proof of this by offering to close for ever the account books of the past. However, I attach one important condition to this: that no new accounts be opened, and that neither England nor citizens of English origin seek to impose on us any new obligation. Nothing in our past, the present, or the future obliges us to take on any new burden on England's behalf. And when I say nothing, I mean from the standpoint of moral obligations equally as much as of material interests. Let us honestly accept the situation we have been put into; let us remain in it peacefully; but if we are forced to move, let it be forward and not backward.

A word on what we call, in season and out, 'loyalty' to England. We owe allegiance to the British Crown. Let that allegiance be genuine – I want it to be and I adjure you to do so too, but, in the name of our dignity, let us stop saying so endlessly, and using it as the insipid and trite seasoning in all our public and private demonstrations. The English who know us and who have read our history know that the French Canadians' allegiance is not an empty word, and that we have proved this by strong and steadfast deeds. Those who are too narrow or too partisan to accept this tangible evidence will not any the more readily believe in the sincerity of our words.

Our allegiance to England can be and should be only a matter of reason. To make it the refrain of constantly repeated protestations, to adopt toward England the postures of bashful lovers – this is to make ourselves, at the least, needlessly ridiculous.

Duties to Canada and English Canadians

First, our duties in the political sphere.

Our line of conduct seems to me to be completely laid down by the system established for us by the Act of Confederation. The benefits and the drawbacks of our constitution are numerous. It is not within the scope of this study to examine them in detail, nor to decide whether we should have rejected the federal idea.

Taking our situation as I find it, I assert that we ought to make the best possible use of it. Let us avoid living in or falling into an over-narrow provincialism; let us resist the encroachments of an over-absorbing federalism. Let us keep under provincial jurisdiction everything necessary to the maintenance of our national character: education, civil laws, municipal organization. Equally, let us work for the good functioning of the federal system; let us take the place that belongs to us in federal affairs, and let us gain our neighbours' confidence by showing ourselves worthy of sharing with them in our common government.

Let us be generous without being weak where we are the majority. Let us not give up the least of our rights wherever we are the minority. Let us not forget that we are not hired servants, even less parasites tolerated at a rich man's table: we are associates with equal rights. The strength and the extent of our rights in the Canadian confederation are measured neither by the number of our nationals, nor by the size of our fortunes: this is something we are perhaps too often inclined to forget, in a century and on a continent where the power of numbers and the even more brutal power of wealth tend to become the supreme arbiters of justice.

The imperial statute that gave us the present system is only the sanction of a double contract: one, made between the French and the English of the former province of Canada; the other, which had as a goal the union of the scattered colonies of British North America. We are therefore a contracting party to two compacts, one national and the other political; and we ought to watch over the integrity of these treaties with a jealous eye. How can we demand the fulfilment of this contract without observing scrupulously all the obligations it lays on us?

By maintaining the federal nature of our constitution, we can resist most successfully those who want to impose on us a closer link with England and to make us take on new duties on behalf of the Empire. We are told that Canada is a British possession and that her citizens cannot divest themselves of the responsibilities of their allegiance. Yes, we can reply, Canada is a British country; but why and how? Because the British Crown gave us, the Canadians of French origin, a constitution and certain privileges, we refused to join her rebelling subjects who deprived her of half of North America. Without the compact she concluded with us, English power would no longer exist in America. Because of that pact and those who were party to it, we promised to defend the British flag in Canada, on condition that we should not be called on to contribute to its defence outside our territory. The English colonists who come to settle in Canada have a strict duty to help us respect the conditions of that treaty and have not the right to use their present majority in order to break it – we always respected it when we were more numerous than they.

Let us speak now of our individual and social duties toward our neighbours.

The two dangers we should avoid are merging and isolation. We should seek every common ground where it is possible for us to give our hand to our English fellow-citizens without lessening our dignity and without altering our national individuality.

On the question of language, I do not believe it possible or desirable for the mass of our people to learn and to speak English. A man of the people can generally make use of only one language. The spread of the English language on the popular level would take place at the expense of the national idiom, and would not be long in reaching the very fibres of our ethnic temperament. This would be the surest way toward the annihilation of our nationality. But this is not true of our leading classes, of those who because of their wealth, their intellectual culture, and their political and social situation must guide our people and uphold the union between us and our neighbours. For the latter there is a duty to learn English, to draw close to the leading classes of the English majority, to study thoroughly the temperament, ambitions, and traits of English Canadians. Further, the same duty is incumbent on the leading classes of English Canada. If the most influential and educated groups of the two races endeavoured to associate more with each other, and to know each other better, our national future would be less precarious. We should observe that there exists among English Canadians, and particularly in the great province of Ontario, much less fanaticism than we generally believe. On the other hand, our neighbours would find that we are not the inferior race that a great many of them scoff at with such silly arrogance. They would realize that having money does not constitute the only superiority, and that, if they know better than we how to obtain large dividends, we have superior talents in other areas.

To make this contact fruitful and this study useful, we must bring to them certain essential qualities: sincerity, honesty, leniency, and a strong dose of altruism, so as to put ourselves in the other's place before we condemn what we call race prejudices. On our side, as we are fewer in number and poorer, it is particularly necessary for us to avoid debasement when we speak politely to the English face to face but insult them behind their backs. This is a valet's task, or to speak more accurately, the wretched task of a bad valet. Let us do our utmost to avoid making ourselves contemptible!

Duties towards ourselves

These are the most important; for by being faithful to our national responsibilities, we draw the strength and understanding that we need to fulfil all the others.

The first problem which comes to mind is this: should we be more French than Canadian or more Canadian than French? In other words, should we be Frenchmen in Canada, or Canadians of French origin?

I cannot imagine anyone hesitating a moment before answering that we should stay essentially Canadians.

Far be it from me to wish to stifle in my compatriots the call of our blood. Our love for France is legitimate and natural: it can and should be genuine, deep, and lasting; but it should remain platonic; and, especially, it should never make us forget our responsibilities toward ourselves, and those laid on us by events in our history and by our present situation. To understand and decide what is the nature of our feelings about France, the same method must be used that I indicated above, when I spoke of our obligations to England: study our history coolly and without making a legend of it.

This study will demonstrate to us that the separation of old and new France was plainly part of providential design. Not only did our mother country very willingly agree to break the bond; the governing classes also worked very effectively to bring about this rupture. I make an exception of the very short regime of Colbert; and if the range of my subject permitted, I should insert a parenthesis in praise of this man of so unassuming and profound a genius, to whom history has not yet done justice. Colbert was not only a financier and statesman of the first order; he conceived a great and true colonial policy more than a century before circumstances forced one on England. With Colbert gone, separation became unavoidable.

Long before the Treaty of Paris, Canadians had begun to form a distinct group of the French nationality. Montcalm already complained of the spirit of independence among the colonists: a perpetual preoccupation of this last hero of French arms in America was to keep peace between the officers and soldiers of the occupation army, and the militiamen of the colony. One of the remarkable aspects of the articles of capitulation of Montreal is the invariable distinction that M. de Vaudreuil draws between the French and the Canadians, even when he speaks of those who are going to stay in Canada and become British subjects. Reading this document demonstrates to us that the governor was much more concerned with encouraging the departure of the soldiers and officials of the King of France, and retaining the wealth of the fur companies, than in seeing to the fate of the colonists. The authenticity of Voltaire's remark about Canada's acres of snow is disputed today; but if the cynical old man did not make the remark, it was certainly the sentiment of most Frenchmen of his time. And this outlook was crudely manifested when the French government allowed the colony's debts to go into bankruptcy, and refused to pay the bills of her intendancy – an intendancy that had plundered, then abandoned, us when we were starving and exhausted by half a century of war against the Iroquois, the New England colonists, and the armies of Great Britain.

If the Treaty of Paris had saved us for France, what would have become of us? Assuming we would have escaped the bloody Reign of Terror, it is more than probable that Napoleon would have sold us to the Americans without even consulting us, as he did with Louisiana. If we had survived the Empire, how would we fit into France's present regime? Much more than our overseas brothers, we have kept our character as Normans and as French of the North: we instinctively detest centralization, administrative organization, legal militarism, and all that makes up the essentially imperialist regime that Bonaparte gave to modern France and that the Third Republic has retained untouched.

I sum up all these historical facts without hatred and without rancour; I do not even undertake to pass judgment on them. If I were obliged, as a Frenchman, to appraise the conduct toward us of monarchical France, and the policy of modern France, I should point to a throng of extenuating circumstances and uncontrollable causes. But, as a Canadian, I say that it is foolish to waste our time in expressing fruitless regrets and unattainable desires.

We ought to be French as the Americans are English. We ought to preserve and foster the instincts, traditions, and manner of thinking that our origin has bequeathed us; but we ought to centre our political loyalty and our national hopes on the land of Canada.

Some of our compatriots contemplate with joy the day when we shall reestablish in America, in law and in fact, a new France, a free state where our race will prevail entirely. This is surely a justifiable and alluring dream; and the work of centuries can bring it about more quickly than appearances indicate. But it is still a dream; and what must be done now is the duty of the moment.

The best way of keeping our national traditions and preparing our future, whatever it may be, is not to live among the memories of yesterday and the desires of tomorrow, but to perform faithfully each day's task.

We are the neighbours and associates of an English majority. We do not want our fellow-citizens to tighten the links that bind us to England, nor to upset, to their own advantage, the balance between the two races in Canada. On our side, we ought not to wound their national feeling and their rightful sensitivity by wanting to be closer to France politically or to break up the Canadian confederation. Let us remain firm on the ground where historical events have placed us. Let us steadily resist the political absorption of Canada into the Empire, and the extinction of our nationality in Canada. Let us abide by the faith that we have sworn to England and to the English-Canadian majority: it is the best way to make them, in turn, keep their own word.

It is necessary to our security to persuade English Canadians of one further undeniable fact: that it is not as Frenchmen but as Canadians that we desire not to draw closer to England and to take on new responsibilities in her Empire.

Moreover, in the area of nationality may be observed the dangerous extremes I pointed out above: grovelling when face to face with the English, but hating and insulting them behind their backs. Race instinct is, like all natural instincts, a powerful means of individual and social action; but, like other instincts, it must be checked and tempered by reason. Otherwise it can lead to deadly folly and become the most effective agent of our national break-up.

It is to race instinct that politicians appeal in order to blind us when they have to choose between duty and power. It is the same instinct that is called on when someone wants to compel people to put their trust in men of their own blood – even when they betray their national interests, or when they dishonour their positions by indulging in corruption, dissolution, and malpractices of all kinds. In a word, speculation on this instinct is often used to prompt us to unpardonable leniency for the renegades and gamblers of our race. It is this kind of patriotism that Doctor Johnson, if I am not mistaken, characterized so well when he described it as the last refuge of a scoundrel.

Speeches of June 24

I insert here a digression on speeches of Saint-Jean-Baptiste Day.

Far be it from me to condemn these regular displays of our national existence. They are fine and legitimate; they ought to be profitable. But to attain this last aim, it is essential that our patriotism is not dispersed altogether in processions, flag shows, floats, the din of trumpets and fireworks, banquets, and speeches.

Permit me to make a short analysis of the sonorous harangues whose perpetual themes are: Our Ancestors, Our Language, Our Institutions, Our Laws, Our Religion, and Our Nationality.

It is doubtless very fine to give a eulogy on our ancestors; but what matters above all is to work to make ourselves worthy of them. And if their ashes ought to tremble with joy in their humble and glorious tombs, let it be from seeing us continue the work they began so well; let it not be from hearing a pompous panegyric issuing annually from lips that are not ashamed of dishonouring the memory of our fathers and selling for a mess of pottage the birthright they preserved for us with so much trouble.

Let us extol the beauties of our language; but the best evidence we can give of this is to learn it well and to speak it well. Let us remember that it is fundamentally the tongue of honesty, valour, and regard for the word of honour. Let us not demean it by making it the instrument of falsehood, meanness, vulgar passions, and treachery.

Let us exalt our institutions; but let us not merely sing their praises. If we want them to continue to be good, let us keep making them better, and more and more able to serve our country and our race. In these times of keen competition, whoever stands still is trampled under foot.

Let us be proud of our laws: they show the intelligence and skill of those who made them; they unite the best qualities of the French laws we inherited and the English laws that our change of allegiance gave us. But let us watch especially that those who make them do not betray them, that the judges who interpret them do not make them despised.

Let us bless God who has preserved for us the faith of our fathers. But just as we must not be content to be patriots only on June 24, so let us take care not to be Catholics only on Sundays and holy days. Let us not forget that a minority is held to a certain degree of moral superiority over those around it, who are richer and more numerous. We glorify ourselves readily as the apostles of the true faith and of French traditions in America; let us preach by our acts more than by our words.

Being Catholics, let us be upright, austere in our habits; may our conduct not be the condemnation of our faith. And especially, let us not be Catholics solely in the governing of our private lives, but let us witness to our faith by the evidence of our social and national life. Let us prove to our Protestant fellow-citizens the truth of the saying of Guizot, himself a Protestant: that the Catholic Church is a great school of respect, not only of the respect owed to others, but also of the respect we owe to ourselves. Let us set that respect against the satirical spirit that splinters old societies; let us set true charity against the egotism that assails us, disinterest against the cult of money, true honesty, which is the daughter of honour, against mere fear of the laws, which is the mother of compromise, of shady deals, and of all the byways of a bad conscience.

French in origin, let us make our nationality and our traditions respected; let us make France loved by reproducing her better qualities rather than by seeking an impossible political *rapprochement*.

Let us renew or let us develop in ourselves the characteristic traits of the French race: the profound sense of individual and national honour; precision and honesty rather than boldness in commercial affairs; the spirit of economy, perseverance, and perfection in work; deep and varied culture in the diverse workings of the intelligence.

We cannot contemplate dominating by force – and certainly, I am far from regretting it: let us try to stabilize our situation by qualities of character and superiority of mind.

Among the dangers that threaten us in this world, I would call attention to the love of money. This passion is seen just as much among our neighbours; but with them, it takes on a certain strength, which removes from it something of its brutalizing materialism. For the Anglo-Saxon, having money is the best means of dominating: it is a tool of action and of power. As his faculties naturally incline him to financial affairs, wealth does not inhibit his activity and his appetite for work. Being less grasping, we do not get as far as he along the road to riches. Being more quickly satisfied, we find in wealth nothing but a means of enjoyment: it fosters in us conceit, egotism, and the love of ease and idleness. Intellectualism is blamed for having bred social indifference among modern Frenchmen; the wish for material enjoyment is well on the way to causing the same affliction in us, without giving us in compensation the intellectual superiority that our overseas cousins can claim; moreover, it forces us to compete with our Anglo-Saxon neighbours on ground – that of business – where they will always be our superiors.

It is unnecessary to emphasize the dangers of the indifference I have just mentioned. In all democratic countries its immediate result is the delivery of the public domain into the hands of schemers and wire-pullers. Placed as we are, and surrounded as we are by perils from without, this pernicious tendency also deprives us of elements invaluable for national organization. I shall return to this below.

Ways of action and particular duties

Let us look for a moment at the means of assuring that our national life works well, and of protecting it from dangers jeopardizing it from within and without.

I could condense my ideas into one sentence: Let us love Duty! The fulfilment of national duty is only the result of the fulfilment of the individual duty of each of us. But I wish to say a word about the particular duties that belong to certain leading classes in our society.

The role of the clergy

If there is a ruling class here, it is certainly the clergy. We have allowed our viewpoint to be permeated by such a curious pettiness that it has become nearly impossible to talk about the French-Canadian clergy, its history, and its social role, without being charged either with toadyism or with sacrilegious insolence. This derives, no doubt, from the unique role that the French-Canadian clergy has played.

To study the history of our country is to understand the significance and the beauty of this role. When we were left abandoned to the conqueror, more than ruined, starved, deprived of the elementary necessities of life, the clergy had to cope with an almost hopeless situation. When all our civil servants and a great number of our professional men, merchants, and nobles left us, the priests remained. I know very well that it has been shown that the exodus of the ruling classes, at the time of the Conquest, was not as complete as is generally believed. It is none the less true that the nobles and bourgeois remaining in Canada made up only a small group of people, whose wealth had been more or less exhausted by the wars. They certainly did not make up a social class that could guide the people in their new course. Only the clergy retained its position and its influence, collective as much as individual. It is only just to say that the clergy was equal to its task and that it admirably steered our poor, disabled ship. It knew how to make people accept the situation that the change of allegiance had created for them. It kept alive in us loyalty to the faith, language, and traditions, love of the land, and the spirit of unity and of passive resistance – the only kind then possible. At the same time, it succeeded in softening the bitterness and hatred left in people's hearts by the Conquest's bloody wars. It is possible to discuss the clergy's attitude on various difficult occasions: in the wars of the Empire, in the 1837 Rebellion; but unless our history is ignored or is read idly or in a sectarian way, it cannot be disputed that the clergy's role was at once firm, reconciling, well-informed, and deeply patriotic.

This role was necessarily altered by events. For a long time, our priests had to assume social and even political functions that did not belong to their priestly office. Little by little the growth of the nation and of social forces and the spread of education created leading men and classes to whom the exercise of functions that the clergy had had to perform for many years rightly returned. This displacement was not achieved without some chafing and even, sometimes, painful crises. But, all in all, the transformation took place smoothly.

What in my eyes remains valid through this evolution is that the clergy is yet and ought to remain our supreme leading class. It forms among us a genuine moral and intellectual aristocracy, whose titles, carved in the people's hearts, are stronger than the titles of nobility of any crown. I am among those who wish to continue this aristocracy; for nothing in the world would I have our priests become good middle-class citizens, more concerned with the affluence of their homes and their carriages than with priestly and patriotic grandeur.

I noted above the dangers of the love of comfort, of easy circumstances, and of leisure. It is above all the job of our priests to denounce this trend toward moral laxity that threatens us, and to set against this the example of self-sacrifice, intellectual liveliness, simplicity of habits, urbanity of manners.

The teaching body

To speak of the teaching body is to remain within the clergy's sphere of action, at least with respect to higher education. While materialism, and what I may be allowed to call moral snobbery, have penetrated the study programs of most civilized countries, our great educational establishments have remained essentially independent and religious. This is a superiority that must be kept. But if we want to withstand the levelling process, the heads of our universities, our colleges, and our high schools must make them beyond reproach from the standpoint of the ability of the teaching staff, and they must adapt their pedagogical methods and programs to today's needs, and even to tomorrow's.

I set no value on hidebound criticisms, and on all automatic reflexes that attack any enterprise of which the Church and her priests retain the direction. It is one of the glorious privileges of the Catholic faith to be exposed not only to fierce persecution, but even to the pinpricks that have demolished more human works and doctrines than have sword and cannon. But just because of this continually jealous watch, it is essential that the educational establishments remaining under the Church's authority secure themselves against any well-founded censure.

I shall not linger over the question of technical teaching. But I wish to say a word about the moral shaping of our student youth. It seems to me that our educators are too apprehensive about allowing newspapers, politics, questions of administration and finance, and even scandals in public life, to penetrate their institutions. I understand that they are reluctant to put the young, innocent souls entrusted to them in contact with the gutter's mud and filth. But these young people, whom they strive to make men of, will have to step down into the road tomorrow. If no one has taught them that they must keep from walking in that mud, how will they know to follow the straight path?

The transition from college to public life is too abrupt. From a regular, well-ordered life, where all the pitfalls are concealed or carefully bounded by strong paternalistic railings, our young people move suddenly to complete liberty, which possesses them, intoxicates them, and leads them astray. In the realm of political ideas, they fall back into the narrow mould, Liberal or Conservative, where their fathers and grandfathers have gone before them. And for particular guidance in practising their profession or trade and in performing their civic duties, they imitate instinctively the behaviour of those around them: a group of highly placed men – mayors, magistrates, or churchwardens – who guard themselves carefully against committing the least personal misdemeanour, but who have no scruple about being the authors or accomplices of all manner of public malpractice. Thus there is produced in our society that strange, I might even say monstrous, phenomenon of a deeply Christian education, the nearly universal practice of religion – and of a most decided corruption of conscience and moral depravity in the government of the public domain. An evil and a peril exist in such matters that it would be criminal not to expose.

Let the colleges be invaded at least by the newspapers, the noises and meanness of the street! And all the while a young man's character and intelligence are being shaped, let him also be taught to distinguish, in the light of the religious principles and intellectual truths instilled in him, all that is sham, shabby, and dishonouring in society's dealings. Let it be impressed on his mind, at the same time, that he has duties to fulfil toward the social community which are as important as those laid on him by his family and by himself. He would thus be better prepared to keep himself from corruption and to play his role in reforming this society, of whom he will tomorrow be a leader.

I shall say only a word about primary and secondary education. We are sometimes too carried away, as others have been before us, by the desire to overload our program of studies. It is less important to teach a lot of things than to teach the necessary things and to teach them well. In the country, especially, studies ought to be reduced to essential matters. It is pointless and harmful to keep too long in school the child who will have to make his living by agricultural labour. For those of unusual intelligence and character – and they are very often discovered in the country – there should be founded several good secondary teaching establishments, to serve as steps between primary school and college. These schools would be able to train the young man early for business or a trade; and if circumstances allowed him to advance his education, he could go from here to higher teaching establishments, where the number of students and courses would accordingly be fewer.

Duties of our public men

I shall not make the section on the duties of our public men a long one. This is my own trade; and I would perhaps speak under the influence of too lively a feeling of disgust to be entirely fair. But I do not know how I can pass over a weakness that is the result of the moral state I spoke of above – I mean that selfishness, that intellectual laziness, and that craving for pleasure that cripple so many characters and dull so many minds!

I often hear about 'practical politics'. By that is understood the possession of power and the advantages this entails. I do not quarrel with those who like power: it would be impossible to form a political party without letting it glimpse the way to the highest honours as recompense for its battles. But I could wish a greater diligence to deserve this success; let moral strength be valued more highly than power, and honour more than honours. I claim that in the long run, even from the viewpoint of success, this policy is best; and it is decidedly the most practical way of guaranteeing the good government of a country and the honest administration of public funds.

From the national point of view, the duties of our public men are of two kinds, because of the particular form of our constitution.

In Ottawa the situation is difficult. There, as everywhere that we are in touch with the English element, we have two dangers to avoid: letting ourselves be paralysed, serving as tools for cliques, playing the role of recruiters of French votes for the benefit of our political allies while they pull the strings, and sacrificing the rights of our nationality to party interests; – and isolating ourselves, exposing our race to the hatred or mistrust of those who do not know us well. Our representatives in the federal Parliament have the task of inspiring trust and respect, of speaking and acting bravely, sensibly, and firmly. I leave it to you to judge whether this is at present being done.

In Quebec the situation is at once more easy and more dangerous. It is easier because we are at home, because we are the masters of our laws and our administration. It is more dangerous precisely because we are at home, and, having in our grasp the government of the only French province in Canada, we are judged by our actions and our behaviour. Are our provincial legislators well aware of this moral responsibility? Do they consider that each bad law they vote for, each administrative error they commit, can become a nail in the coffin in which our legislative independence may be buried? Let us hope we shall be delivered from the evil of one day having to strip ourselves of our prerogatives and our provincial autonomy, because we have no other way of freeing ourselves from a corrupt or powerless Parliament!

The leading class

I shall appeal here to all who can form a leading class outside political parties, to all who, by their wealth, intelligence, and social position, can influence public opinion and make or break parliaments.

What has made the great political strength of England, what will perhaps enable her to raise herself from her present decline, is not so much her statesmen and her Parliament as the political strength and activity of her middle class. It is to be hoped a class of this sort will be formed among us and will make its influence felt in political struggles and especially in the editorial policies of our large newspapers.

It is unbelievable how many of us are convinced that politics belongs to the politicians, as the law belongs to lawyers and medicine to doctors. In a democracy, politics belongs to everyone; the rulers are only the representatives of the ruled, and if the rulers are corrupt or impotent, the fault lies with those who are ruled. The greater your social influence, the more you are called upon to watch over the conduct of those who administer the public domain – federal, provincial, or municipal. Do not say that the people are foolish or corrupt, that they give their votes to schemers or fixers. If, being wealthy, influential, or educated, you have neglected to enlighten and direct the people, not only have you lost the right to accuse them; but you also are guilty.

I know many respectable and prosperous people, full of income and virtue, who raise their arms to heaven and pour waves of scorn on politics and politicians, on councils and aldermen. They are careful, however, not to ask the least personal sacrifice of themselves in order to reform custom; without scruple, they deliver the public treasury over to rogues, and the nation's business over to renegades. These people pride themselves on being model fathers and husbands, and in making themselves worthy of the triumph of the title 'bourgeois' – all in vain; I say to them that they are social evil-doers. It is this race of virtuous and satisfied egotists, of whom the Pharisee in the Gospel is the supreme type, that makes me often say, without paradox, that honest men are responsible for most social crimes.

Canadian women

Shall I dare to speak a word about the social action which the Canadian woman could and should practise? I do not know whether you realize, *Mesdames*, everything you can do for the good of your country. It is you who imprint on the child, at an age when his heart and brain are only soft wax in your hands, those indelible traits that make him what he will be all his life. It is you who form the heart and the character; and since people are governed, grow great, or decline through the expression of their temperament much more than through the exercise of their intelligence, it is in your hands that the future of our nationality really lies. We shall be steadfast, brave, honest, and generous; we shall have all the essentials for battle and for victory, if you know how to teach these small creatures you love so much something more than eating and drinking; if you make them understand early that people are not created and put in the world first to feed themselves well, then to dress well, and then to have a fine job and make money.

Outside the family home, but within the circle of your social relations, however large or small it may be, you can exert a healthy influence on the moral condition of those around you. I do not ask that you become involved in politics, finance, or municipal administration; that you hold meetings and launch programs; but in the simple welcome you give to men of your acquaintance who are concerned with all these matters, you can play a very important role. Make it known that to please you, to open the doors to your salon, and to aspire to the hand of your daughter, they must first have integrity and honour; they must not mix themselves up with dubious intriguers, nor cultivate in politics or elsewhere counterfeit popularity and success. You will thus help to cleanse public life and society, and to stop this shameful and indiscriminate mixing of honest men and rascals that is all too characteristic of our salons.

The young

A word to you young people still full of the purifying zeal of youth. Stay young long; do not listen too soon to the chilly words of those who tell you everything is but calculation, and patriotism is good only to inflate the resounding sentences of 24th-of-June speeches. Keep your enthusiasm, keep it long, keep it for ever! But in order to make it last, control it: temper it with reason; do not spread it thin at every turn; do not lose it in sterile work; do not soil it through contact with corrupt work. Make enthusiasm penetrate your being so that it inspires you at the time of conflict, when the faith or the homeland needs you. Be serious; cultivate your intelligence; put dignity into your private life and your public appearances. You have already proved you know how to meet insults, and to set firm, dignified resistance against crude injuries. Prepare for the battles of tomorrow by doing joyfully the work of today!

9 Henri Bourassa
The French Language and the Future of Our Race

Mr. President, Honourable Members, Ladies and Gentlemen,

It is difficult for me to believe that the organization of this magnificent congress did not have a discreet ulterior motive in giving me a topic that deals with the realm of the future. However, since I lay no claim to the gift of prophecy, I trust you will allow me to proceed with the forecasting of the future, relying on the teachings of the past and the lessons of the present day.

I have been asked to speak to you about the French language and its influence on the future of the race. If you will bear with me, we shall study the question from two points of view.

First of all we shall consider what the influence of the language may be on the future of the race itself; then we shall study the role of the language in the relations that must exist between the French race and the races that live with it on the American continent.

Is it necessary to speak to you at length about the necessity of conserving the language in order to conserve the race? In the realm of diplomacy and politics perhaps Talleyrand was right in saying that speech was given to man so that he could disguise his thought. But when it concerns the life of nations, thanks be to God, His gift has not failed: nations and races possess the gift of speech so that they can express all that is most noble and generous among them; and they have ceased living when they have lost their language.

Perhaps you will rightly raise as an objection the example of a race of which I intend to speak kindly this evening (maybe because this is no time to do it): I mean the Irish race, which has continued to exist and preserve its ethnic character, although it lost its language a long time ago. This evening there is no reason for relating the circumstances that brought on this loss. I only want to remind you that if the Irish race was able to preserve its own special character through three centuries of persecution and disruption, it is precisely because of

---

Translated from 'La Langue française et l'avenir de notre race', a speech given before the first Congrès de la Langue Française au Canada, June 28, 1912, and published as a pamphlet, Imprimerie de L'Action Sociale Limitée, Quebec, 1913.

this persecution, it is through fighting for its very life and the preservation of its faith, that this race has kept its identity.

But take a look at the position of the Irish race in the United States. To the men concerned it certainly is an astonishing situation. The Irish in the United States have exercised a considerable influence, one that our compatriots sometimes complain about; but maybe they would do better to follow their example in everything they do well and not content themselves with senseless denunciations or feed on hate that has never brought forth anything of use.

But if the Irish have become the leading political group in the United States, the race has drowned in the vast Anglo-Saxon melting-pot that is the American people.

Now consider the Scottish people, who are so remarkable in their talents, their energy, and the diversity of their intellectual and moral powers. By losing their language and being intellectually assimilated into the Anglo-Saxon race, the Scots have furnished England and the British Empire with a moral and intellectual factor of undeniable value; but the Scottish race has disappeared as a race and become simply one of the constituent elements of the British people.

When a race ceases to express its thought and feelings in its own language, the language that has grown with it and been formed along with its ethnic temperament, it is lost as a race. The preservation of language is absolutely necessary for the preservation of a race, its spirit, character, and temperament.

Is there any advantage in preserving our language?

One day in a private conversation an eminent French Canadian expressed regret that his fellow countrymen had wasted so many years fighting for the preservation of their language; for, he said, it is very difficult to imagine that they will have permanent success. In the end they will adopt the language of the majority – and so why not resolve themselves to it right now? Either that or they will remain isolated, like the Hebrews in the land of Egypt; they will be deprived of many advantages they might enjoy if they were to fuse with the other races in language, customs, and habits of everyday life. Moreover, he added, by preserving their own qualities and acquiring those of the Anglo-Saxons they would exercise a commanding influence.

Indeed, if we disregard all national pride, this opinion seen in a narrow perspective is tenable. But, gentlemen, do our pride and our instincts not tell us that when we have lost our language we will have lost precisely this individual character and these special faculties that can make of us a desirable element in the building of the Canadian nation and the development of the American nation? When we have lost our language, we would likely be mediocre Englishmen, passable Scots, or bad Irishmen; we would certainly no longer be real Canadians.

Remember the polished words you applauded a short time ago, spoken by the distinguished representative from the French Academy, M. Lamy: 'Each language solicits, reveals, and consecrates the individual spirit of a race.' In fact it is the language that gives to works of the mind that indelible mark which constitutes all its value, just as a country's art is worthless in itself unless the works it inspires reflect the special spirit of the nation.

Do we have the right to preserve our language?

If it is necessary for us to preserve our language, and if this preservation is to our advantage, do we have the right to it?

This is a question that merits being viewed from several angles. No one denies the natural right to it. If I may be permitted to quote the words of M. Lamy again: 'The advantage of weapons and the size of the population give no people the right or the means to impose its language.'

Beside the word 'means' I would likely put a question-mark, and the history of Ireland is sufficient to justify my doubt; but as far as 'right' goes, surely there can be no hesitation, at least not from anyone who is level-headed and good-hearted.

In Canada do we have the *legal* right, the *constitutional* right, to demand the preservation and the spreading of the French language throughout the length and breadth of the Canadian Confederation? I know that the Treaty of Paris contained no stipulation about this; I also know that it was not mentioned at the surrender of Quebec and Montreal; I am aware that the constitutions of 1774 and 1791 were mute on this subject; and I know that the constitution of 1841, discussing for the first time the use of the French language in Canada, forbade it in all official spheres.

In the very interesting work the Honourable M. Belcourt presented to you, he treated this subject intelligently and clearly, and it was helpful. It certainly is good that we be well-informed about our legal rights so that they will not be denied. M. Belcourt examined the question especially from the viewpoint of a legal man. Allow me to prevail upon you to go beyond the strict limits of the wording of treaties and constitutions, and to return to the fundamental principles of the English constitution, to these broad principles of acquired but unwritten right that are the most glorious prerogatives of all British subjects.

What is the English constitution itself if not a series of principles of private, social, and political right practised for centuries and recorded from time to time in the letter of the Statutes of Great Britain? If one were obliged to follow the Statutes to the letter, what moral, political, or social right would be in any way solidly based in all the British Empire?

Our entire history proves that beyond the letter of treaties and laws we have a definite right to preserve and spread the French language throughout the length and breadth of the Canadian Confederation.

1775

Twelve years after the Treaty of Paris there was still only a handful of English merchants on the old rock of Quebec, but several thousand French colonists were abandoned there – inevitably I like to think – by the mother country. An army of Anglo-Saxon rebels besieged the city. Communications with Montreal were disrupted by General Amherst's army. Seeing that he could count on neither the power of his cannon nor on the English army to defend the city, Sir Guy Carleton appealed to the people of Quebec. He urged all citizens old enough to carry a gun to enlist voluntarily, and he ordered all those who did not have enough courage or conviction to take up arms to leave the city. The twenty-five or thirty English merchants left and went to the Ile d'Orléans to await the outcome of the battle, under cover. Who would win? The King or the League? But the 'pea-soupers' took up arms and ran to defend the ramparts, where fifteen years before the English cannon had peppered them. Loyal to the oath they had sworn and to the voice of the clergy that had advised them to accept the new regime, they saved the city of Quebec from the American attack; and all during the war they defended the colony and the British flag against the colonial weapons of New England and Lafayette's soldiers. This was the first spring of their moral right. It has not been recorded in the Statutes; but it seems that it will never be erased from the hearts and memories of those who boast today of living in Canada, and with just cause. They live under the flag of Great Britain, but they seem often to forget that there was a day when, without the loyalty of French Canadians, there would not have been an inch of land in America where the staff of an English standard could be planted.

1812

When the danger had passed, another representative of the Crown, less broad-minded than Sir Guy Carleton, and with a shorter memory, undertook a campaign to assimilate the French colonists. Panet and Bédard, whom even in these days of 'conciliation' we will certainly not call agitators or demagogues, were imprisoned because they claimed for their fellow countrymen the right to live as free British subjects. But a new cloud hung over the horizon. War broke out between England and the United States. Then, still remembering the dangers of 1774, the English authorities found once again that it was good policy to extend the range of the French Canadians' freedoms and rights, since they still made up the majority of the population. The colonists took up arms again to defend England; for the second time they helped to save Canada from the invasion of Anglo-Saxon Protestants from the south. It was at Chateauguay that the unwritten second amendment was voted into the Canadian constitution.

The Rebellion of 1837

Perhaps you will raise the rebellion of 1837 as an objection? I shall not speak now of the causes of this uprising. Today is not the time to pass any judgement on the taking up of arms. But during the entire heroic struggle that preceded it, which lasted half a century and made not only French Canadians but Canadians of all origins realize what their rights as British subjects were, I maintain that not only did our fellow countrymen commit no act of rebellion, but they continued the worthy struggle against absolute power that the British people had kept up for three centuries. By mounting the scaffolds that Colborne erected, the 'rebels' of 1837 won the same debt of gratitude from the English democracy as did the heroes of the great battles for freedom in England, Scotland, and Ireland.

Lafontaine breaks the law

Then came the union of the two Canadas and the constitution of 1841, which was the first one to mention the French language – but just to forbid its use. Even with its injustices and falsely reckoned rules, this constitution was accepted loyally and generously by the majority of French Canadians and, among others, by a statesman who is readily designated as the father and leading spirit of the policy of conciliation. But what was the first public act of Louis-Hippolyte Lafontaine, deputy and Minister of the Crown, in the first Parliament set up under the rule and authority of the 1841 constitution? It was to break the law by speaking French. He appealed against an unjust written law by calling on an unwritten but eternally just right.

A few years later, the Draper-Viger government, an even more conservative one than Lafontaine's, had the Legislative Assembly of Quebec adopt an address calling for the reinstatement of the French language. At that time no one was afraid to appeal to the spirit of justice of the English against their deepest prejudices. And the English and the French united to vote for the unanimous condemnation of this unjust and vexatious law. After another delay of a few years, the British Parliament joined its voice to the unanimous one of the Canadian Parliament and repealed this iniquitous law. Finally in 1867 the principle of equality between the two languages was written into the constitution itself.

The 1867 Constitution and the language

What are the exact terms of the Act of 1867? We do not need to discuss this tonight. All that it is helpful to recall to those who have forgotten and to impress more strongly on their minds is that as far as federal laws and administration are concerned, the principle of absolute equality between the two languages is recognized to the letter; and that is enough. In fact if the law recognizes the principle, common sense as well as justice says that this principle must receive the sanction of all the means that are necessary to assure its application. In other words to suggest that under the authority of the 1867 constitution the rights of the French language exist only for Quebec is to say that the pact of 1867 was a trap, that Cartier, Macdonald, Brown, Howe, and all the authors of this magnificent constitution were in league to deceive the people of Lower Canada!

As for me, I do not believe it; I think the true interpretation of the constitutional law that governs us is the one given it twenty-four years later by its chief author, Sir John A. Macdonald, in the memorable words the President of the Senate quoted the other day. I shall simply recall their content. It was that since 1867 in Canada there has no longer been a conquered race or a triumphant race, a ruling race or a subject race, but that on the contrary there is complete equality under the authority of the law itself for all that concerns the political, social, and moral rights of the two races, particularly for the public and private use of the two languages.

If French and English make up the double vocabulary of the Canadian people as a whole, how is it that there are narrow provincialists who affirm that any one of the legislatures of the Dominion of Canada can deprive the French-speaking citizens of any province of the means of giving their children knowledge and complete possession of this language in all the schools where their money is accepted just the same as the money of English-speaking people?

If the two languages are official, according to the very terms of the constitution, these languages have the right to coexist everywhere that the Canadian people leads a public life: at church, at school, in Parliament, in court, and in all public services.

If they have the right to exist, each of them has the right to demand from the State, whether it be federal, provincial, or municipal, which are all nothing more than segments of the State as a whole, that is to say, of the power that comes from all the races and individuals that make up the Canadian nation – each of the two languages has the right to demand from the State, in whatever form it exists and under whatever legal authority it possesses, that it use its power to ensure that the coexistence and equality of the two languages is completely and absolutely recognized.

Means of preserving the language – the schools

I wish to speak to you this evening of only two means of assuring the permanence, life, and fruitfulness of the French language in Canada.

The first and most important of all is teaching, that is, the schools. In 1875, eight years after the inauguration of the constitution, Edward Blake – another great statesman who was not afraid of the truth, even when it was dangerous for him – proclaimed on the floor of the Commons that the principle of separate schools should be adopted all across Western Canada, so that the two races and two religious beliefs could teach as they chose, but with state aid; because, he said, this is the very principle on which the federal pact was arranged between Upper and Lower Canada. Between the French Canadians and the English Canadians, and between the Canadian Protestants and the Canadian Catholics; and if this principle is good for the Canada of old, it should be equally good for the Canada of the future.

Those in the English provinces who are opposed to the teaching of French in public and separate schools are really the violators of the fundamental spirit of the Canadian constitution; and those of our fellow countrymen who preach to us a doctrine of subservience and who say that it is monstrous to claim for the French language equal rights with the English language are violating the spirit of the constitution just as much. No, the pact drawn up by those two great statesmen Sir John A. Macdonald and Sir George Etienne Cartier was not a pact of subservience; quite the opposite, it was a straightforward and honourable treaty, signed by the sons of two great nations that wished to join forces in order to end past divisions and hatreds for ever, so that from this fruitful union a great people might be born, conceived in justice.

Those in the English provinces who preach the exclusion of French and those in our French province who teach a lesson of subservience are both betraying the constitution and the faith sworn in it.

They are both traitors to our forefathers and traitors to the national spirit – and by the national spirit I do not mean only ours, but the great Canadian spirit that is composed of the most noble elements of the English race as well as the French race, the Irish, and the Scots.

We will preserve the French language and spread it only in so far as we fight for its preservation and growth, but not by going to beg for the favour of living according to our spirit and traditions. That would be a contemptible act unworthy of a free people.

Towards French sources

The second element necessary for the preservation of the language is to nourish it continually at the source from which it springs, at the only source that can assure its vitality and purity, that is, France.

You have all heard many eloquent speeches and well-prepared studies on this subject, so I shall not linger over the matter. In passing may I just touch on this question so often debated, perhaps more in the discreet surroundings of halls of learning than among the public. It is the question of the risk we are taking with our faith and morality by reading licentious contemporary French literature. I shall raise a first objection to this fear, that is admittedly not philosophical, but that is perhaps not lacking in common sense; it is that if one stops eating through fears of being poisoned, one dies of hunger, which is just as straight a road to the cemetery as the other. If we allow the language to waste away due to lack of nourishment from its true source, it will disappear; and if the language dies, the national spirit will die; and if the national spirit dies, our faith will die too.

Moreover, is the danger of poisoning so great? If in contemporary French literature there is no lack of poison, is it necessary to add that there is an abundance of antidote? Instead of trying to close our doors to French literary works, to prevent bad works from coming in, let us open them wide to all that is worthy, generous, idealistic, strong, and great in this eternal production of the French genius, since it seems that God wanted to make it intellectually the continuation of the Greek genius and morally the family home of Christian thought and all the noble apostolates.

But you will say that there is danger to our national unity. This nourishing at the sources of French thought can give rise to mental reservations and feelings of regret among the French Canadians; can isolate them from the British Empire and even from the Canadian Confederation. Those who talk like this show that they do not know the first thing about American history and are also ignorant of the human heart.

To think that by drawing intellectual light from the source that is France, or by seeking the nourishment the language needs, the French Canadian is going to become more French or less British or less Canadian is almost as sensible as believing that the cultured American wonders if he should not return to the Crown of England simply because he continues to read Shakespeare or Thackeray instead of nourishing his mind with the literature of the dime novels that fill the railway trains of the United States. The educated American is intellectually more English today than he was twenty-five years ago. He has learned that if he is to make gigantic material accomplishments by himself, to develop his territory, industry, and commerce in a really astonishing way, and to amaze the world with his political, industrial, and commercial vitality, he cannot ignore fifteen centuries of British civilization, from which he has drawn the best part of his blood and thought. But is he therefore less American, less devoted to his splendid homeland?

In the same way the French Canadian knows that if his language is not to become a dead language or a patois, as they call it in the 'Parisian French' shops in Toronto, it must continue to find its nourishment in the homeland where it was formed.

A Canadian literature

But if our language must become more and more French in form, it must become even more Canadian in content.

It must give birth to a Canadian literature, it must help us to write and read Canadian history, it must teach us to write well and to plead in favour of Canadian laws, and it must make us understand the spirit and the letter of the Canadian laws and constitution. And *Canadian* is not meant here in the narrow sense of our province or of our race, but in the complete and national meaning of this name that belongs to all the races that inhabit Canada. With the aid of this French language in an improved and living form we must seek out the origins of the English and American civilization; we must study the history of England and the United States; we must come to know the English and the Celts better and make ourselves better known to them.

Neither isolation nor amalgamation

And this brings me to the second part of this study. I said that for the preservation and growth of the language we must bring ourselves closer to the intellectual life of France and at the same time *nationalize* our language along with all the other elements of our national life. Likewise when we define the scope of our claims we must keep in mind our situation with regard to the other races that share this land with us. We must be as wary of isolation as of assimilation. We cannot allow ourselves to be absorbed by any other race in Canada; but also we should not live like the Hebrews in Egypt, accepting the offer of seductive flesh-pots as compensation for their slavery. In Canada we must play the role of allies, brothers, associates. Therefore our duty forces us to investigate the ideas of those who fear and fight against the preservation and growth of the French language. Some see in this a danger to the unity of our faith and moral discipline; others an obstacle to national unity.

I shall not discuss the religious question this evening, not because I fear opinions, but because you have heard authorities more qualified on this subject than I. Also, I have already had an opportunity to express the feelings of most of my fellow countrymen on this question.

For those of the venerable leaders of the Church in Canada and America who believe that the keeping of the French language poses serious dangers from the standpoint of customs or religious unity, let me respectfully submit that if there are bad French works, there are also bad English ones; that the most immoral French books are read in English translations perhaps more than in the original French; that if there is an unhealthy literature in France, capable of weakening the family spirit, and if the French language is in some of its works the language of sensual pleasures and looseness of morals, English is still to a large extent the language of Protestantism, materialism, and especially in the United States the language of the most enthusiastic worshippers of the golden calf. Has the resistance of the English-speaking Catholics and even several of their priests been stronger to the influence of this mentality than has that of the French Canadians to the infiltration of unhealthy French literature?

In politics D'Alton McCarthy was the public man who expressed most forcefully, logically, and sincerely the fear of the disintegrating influence of our bilingual culture. He left behind him a large and fanatical group of followers. Is it necessary to repeat after so many others that the preservation of the French language does not constitute a danger to national unity? That on the contrary French Canadians are never more faithful, or to use the English term, 'loyal', to British institutions or to their new home in America than when all their national privileges, and particularly their language, are respected?

The other day M. Lamy told you that 'it is by knowing enough to leave us to ourselves that England conquered us.' Undoubtedly England took a rather long time to learn this and she did not practise it immediately in its entirety; several external circumstances and a long evolution were necessary to make her understand that this was not only the just way but also the only means of assuring herself secure rule. However, let us not regret the century-long struggle we had to make in order to ensure the recognition of our language. For there are two things that make the foundations of the English race stable: first of all, slow advancement, and secondly the combination of two feelings specially developed in the English people: the spirit of justice and interest in the race. Let us not reproach them for what we might consider to be the least noble of these two feelings, for it is precisely this duality of instincts that makes for the power and greatness of this people. For when they have exhausted their desire for ruling through energetic resistance and persevering affirmation of a right, there is no more generous or honest people in the observance of a truce or respect for sworn faith.

More French than Catholic

We are surprised sometimes that of all our privileges the one we demand most insistently and the one most often disputed is the principle of language. When this point arises we are accused of being more French than Catholic.

If the superficial observer judges by certain external signs he can easily believe this is the case.

The explanation is very simple. First, we believe that the preservation and development of the language is to us the human element that is most necessary to the preservation of our faith; and second, due to the simplicity of our minds and hearts in this 'medieval' province, we have held on to the Catholic faith as it was taught long ago, and we believe that in all the dealings of the Church, the first guiding steps must be taken by those in whom we see the authority that was invested in the apostles by Jesus Christ and passed on by them to the bishops and clergy of the succeeding centuries – whereas the language is our own possession: and if we do not defend it, no one will save it for us.

Our language received no divine promise of preservation, except the one that

God made to all the peoples and men who have enough heart and energy to defend their soul, their body, and their national and family heritage; but this promise holds nothing for those whose hearts are so base that they would swap their birthright for a mess of pottage or beg the favour that they should demand as their right.

The French language and the upholding of Confederation

Not only does the maintaining of the French language offer no danger to the religious and national unity of the country, but I am sure that the preservation and expansion of the French language in each of the English provinces of Canada is the only positive moral guarantee of both the unity of the Canadian Confederation and the maintaining of the British institutions in Canada.

Human institutions are preserved only by the survival of the vital principles that fostered these institutions. I have proved that the Canadian Confederation is the result of a contract between the two races in Canada, French and English, based on equality and recognizing equal rights and reciprocal duties. Canadian Confederation will last only as long as this equality of rights is recognized as the basis of the public right in Canada, from Halifax to Vancouver.

At first glance it is difficult to explain the blindness of those who – and they are numerous – honestly want to bring about the gradual destruction of the French language, or the blindness of those more moderate people who agree to allow it to live on in the Province of Quebec, but strive to prevent its penetration elsewhere. However, this mentality is easily explained.

First of all their ignorance of history and the absence of any philosophy deprive the English-Canadian statesmen and journalists of really knowing the depths of the human soul and the concept of distant repercussions of events in the history of nations. They do not know the past, or they forget about it; and consequently their vision of the future is short-sighted and limited.

In the second place the habit of colonial servitude hampers them from seeing beyond the borders of the country they live in. Most Anglo-Canadians know only two countries, England and Canada; and many of them are hesitant to decide which of these two is their real homeland.

Finally, the absence of an intellectual culture and the intense pursuit for wealth that permeates Canadian society as well as American society very often make us disregard the immense superiority of the latent moral forces that brood under the conspicuous brutal force. This is particularly true of politicians who seek driving powers of immediate interest.

There are some Anglo-Canadians who honestly believe that since the English language is the language of the mother country, it should also be the colony's. They seem to forget this very important fact: that the English language is the language not only of England, but also of the United States.

Our relations with the United States

Please allow me a digression. The remarks I wish to make on this subject are not dictated by a feeling of animosity toward the great Republic. No, these racial hatreds, this habit of criticizing foreign peoples, are among the most obvious proofs of the limits of our public mentality and of our 'colonialism'. I admire the American people. They came at the appointed time in the design of Providence to offer their contribution to the harmony of nations. But I sincerely believe that in the true interests of America and the human race the United States and Canada must remain two separate nations. I am sure that the honest American opinion that does not fall prey to the temptations of greed in continually enlarging national territory is identical in this matter to the feelings of the Canadian people.

Now if Canada is to remain separate from the United States it is high time our fellow English Canadians opened their eyes and ears and broadened their outlook to realize that a real danger threatens the unity of the Canadian people and the preservation of its political existence. This danger is the slow but sure infiltration of Americanism that creeps into all the phases of our national, political, and social life.

Perhaps this will surprise you, but in reality Quebec, Champlain's old city, so French in character, is more Canadian and more British than Montreal. Montreal is more Canadian and more British than Toronto. Toronto is more Canadian and more British than Winnipeg. Why? Because thanks to the predominance to the French language in Quebec City you have protected yourselves better from the American invasion than Montreal. Not only to the traveller passing through but also to the careful observer, that particularly 'loyalist' city Toronto seems half won over to American ideas, to the American mentality, to American customs, to American speech, and to the American way of life; and this dangerous situation is to be feared far more than any commercial treaty or attack on the constitution, since it is the moral and personal winning over of the individuals who make up the nation.

As a result of our common idiom there is a more immediate contact between Canada and the United States than between Canada and England. What is more, between the Maritime Provinces, Quebec, and New England, between Ontario and the state of New York, between Manitoba and Minnesota, and between British Columbia and Oregon or Washington communication is much more frequent and personal than between the different provinces of the Canadian Confederation. If we do not unify all our vital forces and if we do not make all the efforts that the men of goodwill from the two races can, American thinking will have not only separated us from England, but will also have disunited the Canadian Confederation, before the peasant invasion from 'medieval' Quebec has been successfully pushed back from Ontario and Manitoba.

What have we French Canadians been fighting against in the field of education during the last twenty years? Against the English way of thinking, against English traditions? No.

What principle must form the basis of the so-called 'national' school, as opposed to the separate or bilingual school in Ontario, the Maritime Provinces, and Manitoba as well as the new provinces of the north-west? The American ideal is to shape all intelligence and all individual will in the same mould by means of the same intellectual training, whereas public education in England is based on the principle of personal freedom and on the training of individuals and groups according to their aspirations and abilities.

If the plans of the anglicizers were to succeed, we could make a prediction tomorrow that would undoubtedly come true: it is that if they succeeded in anglicizing the French Canadians, they would not make Englishmen of them, but Americans.

There is no use deluding ourselves about this in the least. We have been detached from Europe for one hundred and fifty years. We love England out of respect, and if I may add my personal feeling, I wish to say that I love England out of admiration. But it is not only with respect and admiration that a race's temperament is formed. It has been said for ages that men are governed much more by instinct than by laws and intelligence. When the French-Canadian people have learned through a long succession of humiliations that their rights are respected only where they are the strongest element, and that their rights are violated everywhere where they are in the minority; when they have finally realized that only in Quebec can they speak their own language, and that in Manitoba, Saskatchewan, Alberta, and even Ontario their rights are not recognized or are reduced to ones similar to those of the Italians, Greeks, or Doukhobors, at that time the French-Canadian people will have become American, since they would then see no advantage in remaining British.

French groups and Canadian unity

However, the biggest obstacle that could be thrown up against the slow but sure conquest of the English provinces by American thinking – especially in the western provinces – would be the implanting in each of these provinces of French-Canadian groups that were as strong as possible. They could be given their own schools and French-speaking priests so that they could set up their own parishes and they would be like so many small Provinces of Quebec. In this way there would be men everywhere for whom the American ideal, the cult of the golden calf, the profits of commerce and industry, would not be the principal objective. There would also be people in all parts of Canada who were behind the times, *dumb* enough – forgive me this word, gentlemen – to hold on to an ideal above that of wealth and success; people who would continue to do outside the Province of Quebec what they have done in the Province of Quebec for the last one hundred and fifty years: that is, keep the British institutions intact while at the same time claiming the right everywhere to express freely their thoughts on all political matters that concern Canada and the Empire.

A few weeks ago I was reading a letter, in one of the leading newspapers in Ontario, written by an Anglican missionary. This letter was calling the attention of the 'loyal' Ontario people to the French-Canadian invasion of Ontario: 'Ontario,' he said, 'does not want the France of Louis XIV imported from Quebec.'

What is he saying? The France of Louis XIV? Fifty years ago the Province of Quebec adopted the civil code, while the English provinces still cling to the old English common law and to the most out-of-date laws of the old English procedure.

The France of Louis XIV? For more than a century we have had complete freedom of all cults and all religions, while in England it is still being discussed whether the Welsh dissenters are going to stop filling the already well-lined purses of the prelates in the Church of England.

The France of Louis XIV? Sixty years ago we settled the problem of seigniorial tenure peacefully, without plundering or revolution, whereas one-third of the English people are dying of hunger because their Parliament does not know how to handle the rights of the Duke of Westminster or of other large landowners who hold half the territory.

The France of Louis XIV? Even before we had responsible government, the Province of Quebec was the only part of the British Empire where the Jews were freed from all political hindrance, whereas in England the Catholics were excluded from all important political offices and the English people resorted to riot because the Catholic Church, that 'prostitute of the seven hills', dared to re-establish her hierarchy in the United Kingdom.

And while they fight off this imaginary peril and fear the invasion of 'medieval' French Canadians, they are allowing Canada, in habits, language, and mentality, much more surely than by any fiscal measures, to become 'an adjunct of the United States'.

Probably there still exists in the back of some people's minds the narrow instinct that prompted a Scottish merchant in Montreal to utter these instructive words, reported in Lord Durham's biography. The Governor was asserting how necessary it was for the maintaining of the British institutions to reconcile the French Canadians, especially in what seemed to be dearest to their hearts: the preservation of their language. And the Scot replied with brutal frankness : 'My lord, Canada must be English, even if it should cease to be British.' In other words: 'Let us make the French language disappear, even at the risk of seeing Canada become American.'

I repeat that those who seek the destruction of the French language are the worst violators of the Canadian constitution; those who hinder the spreading of the language from one end of Canada to the other are, some subconsciously and some consciously, the surest agents of destruction for British institutions and the unity of Confederation, as well as the most effective instruments Americans could use to gradually absorb the Canadian Confederation.

The French revenge

Gentlemen, there is one point left for me to discuss. Looking further ahead into the future, I dare to hope – and I think you share this justifiable ambition with me – that one day Canada will become a civilized country. If this is the case, we must look beyond our borders and ask ourselves if the time will not come when we will have to become more and more involved in important matters of foreign relations, whether as an independent country or as a colony of Great Britain.

Indeed, if you read the bulletins published by the Department of Trade and Commerce in Ottawa you will note that many Canadian commercial agents abroad add this to the information given to the Canadian merchants: 'Here you must correspond in Spanish and French; there in Italian and French; elsewhere in Portuguese and French.'

This gives an early indication to Canadian commerce and industry that when we have more extensive commercial relations not only with England and the United States but with other countries as well, the French language will become an absolutely necessary tool. The merchants and industrialists of Toronto, London, and Winnipeg will agree that it is of greater advantage and in their own interest to have their letters written by French Canadians who speak the Quebec 'patois' than to venture into the linguistic acrobatics they naïvely think is Parisian French.

Let us go even further. Undoubtedly the day will come when we will rise above our narrow interests and petty local politics and seek the supreme ideal that a nation must achieve in order to merit being called a nation. Let us hope the day will come when we, Americans as well as Canadians, will enter the sphere of activity M. Lamy defined the other day as the sphere where 'the great concerns of the human race' move. The time will come when Canada and the United States will be intent upon displaying to the entire world a civilization as mature as Europe's; and the time will come when Canadians and Americans will feel more and more that man cannot live by bread alone but also by the word of God; that man does not only need street-cars, electric lights, railways, steamships, and limited companies, but that he especially needs to give expression to his soul in the most lofty spheres of human thought; I hope the time will come when we French Canadians as well as English Canadians will want to have a distinctly Canadian art and literature and will want the Canadian spirit to make its contribution to world science.

When all this comes about the French language will resume its position and have its revenge. It will be triumphant because of its universal character, which M. Lamy analysed so well; the Americans and Anglo-Saxons in Canada will endeavour to learn this language which will be as indispensable to the moral and intellectual life of the modern world as Greek was to the Roman civilization. The legislators in Washington and Ottawa will do what the Romans did after they had conquered Greece and reduced it to the size of one of the smallest and weakest provinces of the empire. They bowed before the intellectual superiority of the Greeks, they entrusted their schools to pedagogues from Athens, they studied Greek philosophy, they admired Greek painting and imitated Greek statuary, and finally they wrote the laws of the empire in the Greek language on the very gates of the Forum. And at this time the Anglo-Saxons in Canada will bless us for having preserved the French language, the immortal seed of modern Christian civilization, through so many mishaps and struggles that often occurred because of their ill will.

The memory of Joan of Arc

A few days ago I had the pleasure of being present at the splendid and touching festival in Rouen where the beatification of Joan of Arc was celebrated. I heard one of the most eloquent speakers of the French pulpit. Allow me to summarize part of this orator's magnificent speech, although, alas, I do so in colourless language. After telling the story of the heroine's long, cruel suffering, he recounted the moment of horror, the instant of amazement when hate and remorse tore at Winchester's and Bedford's hearts. At the foot of the stake a handful of ashes had been found, along with the martyr's heart which was still bright red. 'What are we to do?' said the executioners to themselves. 'If we do not get rid of these, the people will make relics of them and the dead Joan of Arc will still fight us.'

They threw them into the Seine, thus giving all that remained on earth of the heroic maid the only fitting tomb. And her still-beating heart made its way to the source of the river and went to the very heart of France where it revived the national spirit and completed the task of redemption. Then, coming down the flood and crossing the sea, Joan's heart landed on the shores of England where it forgave her executioners and planted in English soil the seed of future harmony that the work of the centuries was to germinate, finally uniting in friendly agreement these two great nations who had sought for so many years to snatch from each other the rule of the world.

Allow me to extend this very touching image. Let us take pleasure in thinking that this French saint's heart has crossed the Atlantic and come to Canadian soil, where the cross of Christ and the French way of thinking were the first to push back the barbarians, where the French spirit cast the first seeds of Christian civilization, where for one hundred and fifty years the sons of two identical races quarrelled with armed force over the banks of the St. Lawrence, but where Providence has willed that these races be finally united under one flag. Let us ask Joan of Arc to accomplish the alliance between the defeated and the conquerors of old. Let us ask her to allow that her so beautiful and clear language, which thwarted the casuist subtleties and repelled treason and cowardice, that this, the French language, preserved by us American Frenchmen, become not an instrument of discord between the two great races, but on the contrary the vehicle for the most beautiful and lofty thoughts, generous designs, and hopes for union, by means of which Anglo-Canadians and French Canadians, Saxons and Celts, will be able to win victory in the northern part of the American continent for the best traditions of the two great nations that gave birth to the Canadian homeland.

10 J.-P. Tardivel (1851-1905) and Henri Bourassa
A Controversy

Le Nationaliste and Nationalism

[This article was published anonymously in *La Vérité*, April 1, 1904, p. 5, but everyone recognized the author as J.-P. Tardivel, the editor of the paper.]

We do not want there to be the least misunderstanding about the Nationalist League and its mouthpiece *Le Nationaliste*.

We are labouring under no delusion: the nationalism of the League is not our brand of nationalism. We have already stated this quite clearly by publishing the program of the new organization last January.

Our own brand of nationalism is French-Canadian nationalism. We have been working for the last twenty-three years toward the development of a French-Canadian national feeling: what we want to see flourish is French-Canadian patriotism; our people are the French-Canadian people; we will not say that our homeland is limited to the Province of Quebec, but it is French Canada; the nation we wish to see founded at the time appointed by Providence is the French-Canadian nation.

The gentlemen of the League seem to see things from a different viewpoint. One would say that they wish to work toward the development of a Canadian feeling that is not concerned with questions of origin, language, or religion.

We consider our job as French Canadians to be the defence and development of our own nationality. The other elements that make up the population of Canada are in a good position to defend and develop themselves without our help.

In a welcome inconsistency in the first issue of *Le Nationaliste*, Mr. J.-A. Chicoyne seemed to lean toward our brand of nationalism.

In fact his article on 'Our Daily Bread' is an eloquent plea in favour of the growing of wheat in the Province of Quebec so that our province might be self-sufficient and not be obliged to ask for its daily bread from the other provinces of the Dominion.

Translated from the texts as quoted in André Laurendeau, 'Sur une polémique entre Bourassa et Tardivel', *L'Action nationale*, XLIII, 2, February 1954, pp. 248-59.

We agree with this idea completely; but as *La Presse* remarked, this is not Canadian nationalism.

Really, from the Canadian point of view, it is of little importance whether the Province of Quebec grows the wheat she needs or buys it from the other provinces and territories of the Dominion.

From the French-Canadian point of view it is quite a different matter.

In the views on French-Canadian nationalism put forth in the columns of *Le Nationaliste* does Mr. Chicoyne represent the ideas of the League or is he simply giving free rein to his own feelings? Only time will tell.

In the meantime the chief point of contact between *Le Nationaliste* and *La Vérité* is the struggle against party spirit.

The new mouthpiece promises to deal with these questions publicly, looking beyond the narrow horizons of the political organizations, and to banish from its columns the petty quarrels between the *bleus* and the *rouges* that have done immeasurable harm to our nationality. It was because of this article in its program that we congratulated it and wished it success.

We would have liked to hail *Le Nationaliste* as a new champion of clearly Catholic ideas. It would have pleased us to state that its program is as broad as that of *La Vérité*, including the defence of material interests as well as religious ones. We regret to say that this is not the case: *Le Nationaliste* seems to be nothing more than a strictly political mouthpiece. Moreover, let us say that the tone of some of the less important writers for *Le Nationaliste* is not up to the level expected in a serious organ. And is this the place for caricatures?

To be fair we must add that the wretched things that have happened and are still happening in this country to those who indulge in fundamentally Catholic and really serious journalism are not of a kind to invite the new contemporary to cultivate a land so rich in rebuffs!

A Friendly Reply to *La Vérité*

[An article published in *Le Nationaliste*, April 3, 1904, p. 2, signed by Henri Bourassa.]

In the day before yesterday's *La Vérité* Mr. Tardivel traces the line of demarcation that in his eyes separates (*sic*) his nationalism from the League's.

'Our own brand of nationalism,' he says, 'is French-Canadian nationalism. We have been working for the last twenty-three years toward the development of a French-Canadian national feeling: what we want to see flourish is French-Canadian patriotism; our people are the French-Canadian people; we will not say that our homeland is limited to the Province of Quebec, but it is French Canada; the nation we wish to see founded at the time appointed by Providence is the French-Canadian nation.

'The gentlemen of the League seem to see things from a different viewpoint. One would say that they wish to work toward the development of a Canadian feeling that is not concerned with questions of origin, language, or religion.'

The Nationalist League has entrusted me several times with the task of spreading knowledge of its cause and its principles. Please allow me here to be its interpreter once again.

From the outset I would like to express all the esteem and admiration the editor of *La Vérité* inspires in me. One could not over-estimate with what courage and perseverance he has waged war on numerous occasions to defend the French-Canadian nationality against the undertakings of those who want to make Canada more English or more French, and of the fusionists and the isolationists. But this prolonged struggle has developed in him an exaggerated mistrust of those who see patriotism and national feeling other than he does.

The Nationalist League and its organ wish undeniably to 'work toward the development of a Canadian feeling'; but far from wishing this feeling to develop 'unconcerned with questions of origin, language, or religion', the League proclaims loudly that the Canadian people's duality of origin, language, and religion must be recognized and preserved. This is, in fact, the subject of one of the articles in its program:

'Complete observance of the rights guaranteed to the provinces by the constitution of 1867 according to the intention of those who drafted it. Respect for the principle of the duality of the languages and for the right of minorities to separate schools.'

Mr. Tardivel goes on to say:

'We consider our job as French Canadians to be the defence and development of our own nationality. The other elements that make up the population of Canada are in a good position to defend and develop themselves without our help.'

We also want to 'defend and develop our own nationality'; but we think that is only part of our job; we believe that this special development can and must come about in conjunction with the development of a more general patriotism that unifies us, without fusing us, to 'the other elements that make up the population of Canada'. We do not believe, as Mr. Tardivel seems to suggest, that the other elements need us to develop. But we feel that all of Canada is our homeland and that it belongs to us for the same reason it belongs to the other races. We want to play our part in it, add our contribution to the national edifice, and fill the place that is ours by right; we do not believe that in order to achieve this goal we must look for land that is shared by the 'other elements'.

Borrowing the energetic and concise language of *La Vérité*'s distinguished editor, I would like to summarize the League's beliefs this way.

Our own brand of nationalism is Canadian nationalism, based on the duality of the races and the special traditions this duality imposes. We are working toward the development of Canadian patriotism, which in our eyes is the best guarantee of the existence of two races and of the mutual respect they owe each other. Our people, as for Mr. Tardivel, are the French Canadians; but the Anglo-Canadians are not foreigners, and we view as allies all of them who respect us and desire, as we do, the full maintenance of Canadian autonomy. Our homeland is all of Canada, that is, a federation of distinct races and autonomous provinces. The nation we want to see develop is the Canadian nation, made up of French Canadians and English Canadians, that is, two elements separated by their language and religion as well as by the legal arrangements necessary for the preservation of their respective traditions, but united by brotherly affection and a common love for a common homeland.

Henri Bourassa

Concerning Nationalism

[Extracts from an article published in *La Vérité*, May 15, 1904, p. 2, with the subtitle 'A Friendly Reply to Mr. Bourassa'.]

Those who cherish the idea of creating a great, unified Canada, homogeneous, stretching from Atlantic to Pacific, and taking in all the British possessions in North America, are also proposing an aim that has attractive aspects. However, this plan frightens and terrifies us, because, as we see all too clearly, it will come about only to the detriment of the French-Canadian nationality.

Mr. Bourassa distrusts colonial ties because the imperialists make use of them to build up the empire they dream of. We agree with this distrust, but does he agree with the distrust we feel for the interprovincial ties that serve as instruments in the hands of those who dream of creating a great, unified Canada by slowly strangling the autonomy of the French-Canadian nationality? We dare not answer this question, but we do feel the need of clearly defining our position and feelings. . . .

We are neither revolutionaries nor dreamers. We do not want to resort to violence in any way to break these interprovincial ties; the danger that we see for our nationality in the existence of these ties is very real; we wish these ties had never been formed, yet we know they exist and we must take them into account in all our dealings.

But it is only to prevent them from harming us French Canadians that we must take them into account. And we must know how to proclaim at the top of our voices: may these interprovincial ties perish rather than allow the French-Canadian nationality to be injured by them! . . .

'Our brand of nationalism is Canadian nationalism, based on the duality of the races and the special traditions this duality imposes. We are working towards the development of Canadian patriotism, which in our eyes is the best guarantee of the existence of two races and of the mutual respect they owe each other.'

This plan – or should we say this dream? – could have perhaps been put into effect if we had confined ourselves to the original plan of federation; that is, if we had been content to unite the four provinces of Quebec, Ontario, New Brunswick, and Nova Scotia under one federal government. Such a confederation would have had a certain geographical symmetry and sufficient uniformity of general material interests to keep itself going. Moreover, the two races would have been sufficiently equal in power to preserve the desired equilibrium and keep the governmental machine in good working order, based on 'the duality of the races and the special traditions this duality imposes'.

But from the beginning, megalomania and the mania for constant growth have laid hold of our politicians, and they introduced Prince Edward Island into the confederation – which could have been tolerated if really necessary – and then British Columbia and all the Northwest.

This was obviously too much; and wishing to erect a colossal edifice, we sinned against the laws of stability.

Concerning the Geography of a Great, Unified Canada

[An extract from an article published in *La Vérité*, June 1, 1904.]

Canadian nationalism 'based on the duality of the races and the special traditions this duality imposes' is a beautiful theory, but it is nothing but a theory. In embroidering on this theme, people have made and will continue to make lovely speeches that have not been and will never be turned into action.

In practice Canadian nationalism is based on an entirely different idea. The partisans of a great, unified Canada, whatever their political affiliation, Liberal or Tory, want to make the Dominion of Canada an exclusively English-speaking country with English customs and English traditions; and all their actions aim toward this goal. Some people can certainly talk about different views; but, when they act, it is always with a view toward the anglicizing of the great whole.

We admit that this is quite natural, but what is unfortunate is that French-Canadian politicians do not notice it and they do not know how to react strongly against the current that is carrying us toward the abyss of national annihilation.

We believe this is much more important than beguiling ourselves with the illusion that someone among the English in Canada seriously dreams of erecting a political edifice 'based on the duality of the races and the special traditions this duality imposes'.

II Mgr L.-A. Pâquet (1859-1942)
A Sermon on the Vocation of the French Race in America

> *Populum istum formavi mihi; laudem meam*
> *narrabit.*
> This people have I formed for myself;
> they shall shew forth my praise.
>
> Isaiah, xliii. 21

Your Excellency,
   Your Grace, the Archbishop of Quebec,
      Your Graces,
         My Brothers,

On the twenty-fifth of June, sixteen hundred and fifteen, a few steps from here on the tongue of land that projects out from the base of this cliff on which we are now standing into the deep water of our mighty river, a scene unfolded which was to that point unknown in this land. In the shade of the centuries-old trees, in a hastily constructed chapel, and in the presence of a few Frenchmen and their leader Samuel de Champlain, a humble son of Saint Francis turned toward a modest altar and lowered onto this rustic table the Everlasting Son of God. In the Lord's name he sanctified the first step in the founding of a city and the cradle of a people by the most holy rite of our religion.

Since then this people has grown. This city has prospered; and now, approximately three centuries later, this nation, born of this fertile seed, has gathered, not at the base of the cliff but on its heights, to renew its act of consecration and to dip its life once more in the blood of the Lamb of God.

What transformations and contrasts! All around, despite the immutability of the great lines that make up the frame of the picture, nature has received the imprint of man's mind and hand; the desert has come to life; the wilderness has been populated. Near at hand the eye falls on massive castles and artistically

---

Translated from 'Sermon sur la vocation de la race française en Amérique', an address delivered near the Champlain monument on the occasion of the Diamond Jubilee of the Saint-Jean-Baptiste Society of Quebec, June 23, 1902, and published in *Discours et Allocutions*, Quebec, 1915, pp. 181-202.

designed buildings instead of movable tents where barbarians dwelt; towers and lofty spires have replaced the tall pines; a whole mature civilization has risen; and the founder of Quebec, proud of his accomplishment and prouder still of the splendid progress made since then, can look hopefully into the future from the top of this monument, erected a short time ago as a token of public recognition, and confidently greet the approaching dawn of a new day and of a more and more glorious destiny.

My brothers, we are here this morning to contemplate this same future. The resounding horn of our patriotic festivals has rung out, and from the four corners of the province, from the farthest parts of the country, and I could almost say from all the places in America where the French race has planted its flag, you have flocked here with heads high and hearts throbbing. No people could have answered the call more unanimously or more enthusiastically.

This is a solemn occasion. Beneath this festive atmosphere and through the sounds of our mutual rejoicings I detect disquieting doubts, questioning glances, and anxious thoughts displayed on your brows; on the one hand I can hear vague and confused shouts, and on the other the echo of restrained emotions and quivering secrets that move in the soul of the nation. What does this mean?

It means, my brothers, that through the course of our history we have arrived at one of those times when a people becomes aware of itself, of its vitality, and of its power. It means that in being present at grand celebrations in honour of joyful anniversaries in our intellectual and social life, we are present at the same time, and perhaps in a more particular way, at real national assemblies. It means that in these assemblies it is our duty to study thoroughly the question of our destiny, and to declare once and for all, not impudently or weakly, but discreetly and wisely, what we have been, what we are, and what we must and will become.

This is why I quoted to you above the words of our Holy Scriptures: *Populum istum formavi mihi; laudem meam narrabit.* 'This people have I formed for myself; they shall shew forth my praise.' In this language of such lofty meaning and in these inspired words I see indications of the noble mission entrusted to our nationality; I think I discern in this light the exalted vocation of the French race in America.

I

Is there then, my brothers, a vocation for peoples?

Only those who separate the hand of Providence from the events of this world and who abandon men and things to a blind fatality could doubt this. As for those of us who believe in God, in a wise, good, and powerful God, we know how this wisdom, goodness, and power are revealed in the government of nations; how the Maker of All Things has created different races with varied tastes and aptitudes; and also how, within the hierarchy of societies and empires, He has assigned to each one of these races a distinct role of its own. Certainly a nation can fall from the heights of its destiny. But this does not imply powerlessness or lack of foresight on the part of God; the fault is that of the nations who, once they have lost sight of their mission, misuse their freedom and run madly towards the abyss.

I will go even further and dare to assert that not only is there a vocation for peoples but in addition some of these peoples have the honour of being called to a kind of priesthood. Open the Bible, my brothers, glance at these moving pages which overflow with the Divine Spirit, from Abraham to Moses, from Moses to David, from David to the Messiah who was imagined by the patriarchs, announced by the prophets, and who sprang like a flower from the Jewish stem, and tell me if the Hebrew people did not fulfil a priestly mission on the earth despite shame, failure, and disbelief.

It is the same under the new law. All peoples are called to a true religion, but not all have received a religious mission. History both ancient and modern proves this: there are peoples dedicated to the soil, there are industrial peoples, merchant races, conquerors, there are peoples versed in the arts and the sciences, and there are also races of apostles. And who are these races of apostles? Ah! recognize them by their radiating genius and by their generous souls: they are the ones who under the guidance of the Church have done the work and spread the blessings of the Christian civilization; who have put their hand to all the beauty, greatness, and divinity that we see in the world; who with the pen or the point of a sword have engraved the name of God into history; who have treasured and kept alive and undying the love of truth and goodness. They are the ones whom all noble causes preoccupy and instinctively impassion; whom we see quivering with indignation at the sight of the downtrodden and weak; whom we see devoting themselves in the most numerous ways to the triumph of truth, charity, justice, honesty, and freedom. In a word they are the ones who have merited and who still merit the glorious name of champions of Christ and soldiers of Providence.

Now, my brothers, – why should I hesitate to say it? – we have the privilege of being entrusted with this social priesthood granted only to select peoples. I cannot doubt that this religious and civilizing mission is the true vocation and the special vocation of the French race in America. Yes, let us not forget, we are not only a civilized race, we are pioneers of a civilization; we are not only a religious people, we are messengers of the spirit of religion; we are not only dutiful sons of the Church, we are, or we should be, numbered among its zealots, its defenders, and its apostles. Our mission is less to handle capital than to stimulate ideas; less to light the furnaces of factories than to maintain and spread the glowing fires of religion and thought, and to help them cast their light into the distance.

Is it necessary for me to produce proofs of this honoured vocation? My brothers, the task is easy: we carry the marks of this vocation on our foreheads, we carry them on our lips, we carry them in our hearts!

In order to judge the nature of a work or of any foundation, all one need do in most cases is look back to the beginnings of this work, to the builder of this foundation. The life of a tree is in its roots; the future of a people is revealed in its origins. What then is the motherland to which we owe our existence? What was its role, its intellectual and social influence? Already your hearts, touched with emotion, have turned toward France; and in naming this homeland of our souls the entire history of Christianity is evoked and brought back to life in your hearts. Here is the race of apostles in the highest sense of the word, a race of whom Pope Leo XIII could say in a memorable document:[1] 'Through the great deeds that she has accomplished in peace and in war the most noble French nation has won for the Catholic Church merits and titles which will always be recognized and whose glory will never fade.' These highly flattering words may call forth a hesitant smile on the lips of those who think France is self-centred and unfaithful. But let us quickly add that ten, twenty, even one hundred years of desertions, especially when these desertions were made up for by the heroism of sacrifice and the martyrdom of exile, could not wipe out thirteen centuries of generous faith and unparalleled devotion to the cause of Christian honesty.

When one descends from such a race, when one counts among his ancestors such people as Clovis, Charlemagne, Louis IX, Joan of Arc, Vincent de Paul, and Bossuet, is one not justified in laying claim to a special role and to a superior mission? Through a happy and providential combination we have French blood and Christian blood circulating in our veins. French blood alone leads quickly to corruption, perhaps more quickly than any other; but mixed with Christian blood it produces heroes, disseminators of fruitful spiritual doctrines, glorious craftsmen of the most beautiful and divine works.

This is what explains the admirable sentiments of deep religious devotion and active faith that animated the founders of our nationality on this American continent, and in this very sentiment I find another proof of our civilizing and religious mission.

My brothers, who would not recognize this mission, knowing that the highest personages whom our early history honours made the extension of the Kingdom of Jesus Christ the sole goal of their undertakings and, so to speak, marked each of their actions with a religious stamp? Who would not acknowledge and admire this vocation, knowing, for example, that (with a pious hand on the heads of poor savages) Jacques Cartier unrolled the beneficent pages of the Scriptures;[2] knowing that Champlain and Maisonneuve put the most sacred part of religion at the basis of their establishments; knowing too that as soon as Marie de l'Incarnation and her brave companions had landed on the shore, they prostrated themselves[3] and ecstatically kissed the soil of their adopted homeland, which later they were to make famous by their heroic virtues? Is it by chance then that so many saintly women, so many prominent Christians, and so many devoted religious men came together in common thought and laid, as if on bended knees, the first stones of our national structure? Is it by chance that these stones, cut by such unsullied hands under the gaze of the Lord, were soaked and cemented in the blood of martyrs? Could the establishment of the French race in these regions have been an historical error, and could the wave that set us on the banks of the St. Lawrence have brought to the shore nothing but shapeless debris, incapable of serving and accomplishing the designs of Heaven in a lasting work?

No, my brothers, and what proves this even better than anything else is the growing influence that French America exercises all around her on the progress of the faith and of the true civilization.

There is also something worth mentioning that throws considerable light on the mission of a people: each time that our ancestors came in contact with the primitive forest people during their voyages of exploration, and even in war, it was to civilize them rather than to dominate them; it was to convert them, not to annihilate them. Why do I not have time to call to mind the labours of our bishops, in particular those of the immortal Laval, of our priests, of our missionaries, of our discoverers, of all our apostles? From them came the religious concept, which is today spread over a large part of North America. From them sprang the fountains of doctrine, of virtue, of devotion, and these waters have been spread from one ocean to another, out-distancing our mighty railroads and carrying to foreign races the treasures of Christianity of which our race is the trustee.

And is this very powerful and beneficial influence, which was so widespread earlier, now in danger of decreasing? Because of the presence of rival influences will it lose at least its special character and the stamp of spirituality which has made it so outstanding in the past? Oh! my brothers, ask this of the venerable prelates whose presence among us adds so much lustre to these celebrations and whose staffs, like Moses' rod, have brought forth innumerable parishes and flourishing dioceses, as if by a miracle, from the wild bush and the thick forest. Ask this of the University, the pride of our homeland, whose brilliant beam of learning is cast by a double hearth. Now after fifty years of existence this University sees thousands of former students, its joy and its crown, gathering here from different parts of the continent.[4] Ask this of all our people who have been scattered far from us by the breeze of emigration, either to other provinces or to the territory of the vast American republic, where these compact groups, still Catholic and still French, are gathered closely around the Church and the parish school, emerging here and there like solid rocks in a foaming and angry sea. Finally, ask this of our brothers in Acadia, whose patriotism, adherence to the faith, love of their language, and unconquerable steadfastness have been equalled only by their misfortune, and whom God has rewarded for such faithfulness with constant increase in their numbers and influence.

Populum istum formavi mihi; laudem meam narrabit. It is I, said the Lord, who formed this people; I created it for my glory, in the interest of religion and for the good of my Church; I wish it to persevere in its noble mission and to continue proclaiming my praise.

Yes, to spread knowledge of God, to proclaim His name, to propagate and to defend all that makes up the precious heritage of Christian traditions, surely this is our vocation. We have seen obvious and unquestionable signs of this. The France of America must be for the New World what the France of Europe was for the Old World. But in the present social situation at what price, my brothers, and by what means will we effectively fulfil this mission? What are the rights that it includes? What are the duties it imposes? This is what remains for me to talk to you about.

II

In order to perform the role among nations that suits its nature and that Providence has assigned to it, a people must remain true to itself: this is a primary and absolute condition that nothing can replace. Now, a people remains true to itself only through the freedom of its life, the use of its language, and the cultivation of its characteristic spirit.

It is not fitting for me to discuss here the political future of my country. But what I am anxious to say, what I wish to proclaim loudly before this patriotic gathering, is that French Canada will accomplish God's purposes and respond to its sublime calling only to the extent that it maintains its own way of life, its individual character, and its truly national traditions.

And what then is the life of a people? To live is to exist, to breathe, to move, and to be one's own master in genuine freedom. The life of a people consists of the temperament it inherited from its fathers, and the heritage it received from them, the history with which it nourishes its mind, the autonomy it enjoys, which protects it against all assimilating forces and all corrupting intermixture.

Let us not be mistaken: the greatness, the real importance of a country, depends less on the number of its inhabitants or on the strength of its armies than on the effulgence of its social accomplishments and the free expansion of its life. What was Greece in its most splendid days? Simply a strip of land, as it is today, cut into small parts, bordering on the Mediterranean, and populated by scarcely a few million citizens. However, everyone knows that of all the peoples of antiquity not one climbed as high on the ladder of glory; not one extended so far the dominion of its characteristic spirit or made a stronger mark on ancient civilization. I shall dare to state this: it is more important for our race, for the prestige of its name, and for the power of its actions, to keep the free movement of its organism and of its life in a small sphere than to revolve in the orbit of vast planetary systems.

Moreover, individual life scarcely persists without language; and the blessed language of our fathers, who have passed on to us their faith, their examples, their virtues, their strifes, and their hopes, is so closely related to the question of our mission that it cannot be separated from it. The language of a people is always a sacred possession; but when this language is French, when it has the honour of carrying along with it, as in a jewel-case, the treasures of human thought enriched by all the traditions of the great Catholic centuries, then to mutilate it would be a crime, to be contemptuous of it, or even to neglect it, would be apostasy. It is with this language which is in a way so Christian, it is with this instrument which is so well constructed to spread resplendent truth and magnificent beauty to all minds, to bring to light all that is ennobling, all that enlightens, and all that gives embellishment and perfection to humanity, that we will be able to play a role more and more useful to the Church, and more and more honourable to ourselves.

And this role will grow and increase in influence as the level of our knowledge becomes greater and as lofty intellectual culture makes greater and surer strides among us. For, my brothers, there is no need to say it, it is science that rules the world. It is true that abstract ideas, hidden behind the veil of senses or the thick curtain of matter, are invisible; however, they are similar to the motivating force that no one sees but that distributes light and movement everywhere with such marvellous precision, since they inspire all advice, determine resolutions, and set all energy in motion. This is why the importance of the universities is so great, and why the rejoicing that will take place tomorrow is so closely bound up with our great national celebration. It forms, so to speak, the necessary complement.

Oh! I am sure you will tell me that we must be practical, that in order to withstand the competition of modern peoples it is of paramount importance to augment public wealth and to concentrate all our efforts on this. Indeed everyone agrees that we are entering an era of progress: industry is awakening; a growing wave of comfort, activity, and prosperity is sweeping the countryside; on the docks of our cities smiling Fortune is lining up her store-house of abundance, and commerce becomes more venturesome every day, sending to our ports its peaceful fleet of giant ships.

God forbid that I should scorn the natural benefits of Providence, my brothers, or that I should go so far as to preach a renunciation to my fellow citizens that would be fatal to the economic interests that concern them so greatly. Wealth is not forbidden to any people or race; it is indeed the reward of fruitful initiative, intelligent effort, and persevering labour.

But let us be careful; we must not turn what is only a means into the very goal of our social behaviour. Let us not step down from the pedestal, where God has placed us, to walk commonly among those generations who thirst for gold and pleasure. We must leave to other nations, less inspired with the ideal, the kind of feverish mercantilism and vulgar bestiality that rivets them to material things. Our own ambition must aim higher; our thoughts and aspirations must be loftier.

A distinguished journalist once wrote: 'Materialism has never created anything great or lasting.'[5] These words are surely a truism. My brothers, do we want to remain faithful to ourselves and to the superior civilizing mission that emerges from our entire history and that has made up the honour of our race until now? Let us make use of material goods, not for themselves, but for the more valuable benefits they can give us; let us make use of wealth, not to multiply the base pleasures of the senses, but to encourage the more noble and elevated pleasures of the soul; let us make use of progress, not to sicken ourselves in the dullness of mind that too often results from opulence, but to give our minds freer range and our hearts more vigorous drive.

Our mission demands this. And the more we convince ourselves of this mission the more we will grasp its true character and its powerfully edifying religious significance. Also we will find more readily in our patriotism the kind of ardent and passionate zeal and the enlightened and generous courage that shrink from no sacrifice in the attempt to give victory to a principle. Knowledge of our destiny will forbid us soft complacency, cowardly surrender, easy resignations.

Let us be patriotic, my brothers: certainly in ambition and word, but also, what is more important, in action. It is unified action, the grouping of forces, the rallying of thoughts and desires around a single flag that wins battles. And when must this action commence? When is the time to close ranks? Oh! each time that freedom suffers, that justice is overthrown, that what is sacred receives an impious blow; each time the nation sees a menacing cloud rise over the horizon or its heart bleeds from some wound inflicted on its dearest feelings.

Let us not forget either that all the groups in which a single national sap runs are interdependent. It is right and timely that this interdependence be asserted; that all those to whom Providence has given the same blood, the same language, the same beliefs, the same concern for spiritual and immortal matters, tighten these sacred bonds among themselves, and push the spirit of union and social brotherhood as far as their duties of political loyalty will permit. The feelings of brotherhood within a race are like the notions of justice and honour: they know no boundaries.

Finally, my brothers, in order to preserve and consolidate the moral unity, without which all our efforts would be in vain, the most essential things are a filial obedience to the teachings of the Church and a complete submission to the authority of the leaders who represent among us the power of the Church. This obedience and submission are absolutely necessary in all Christian nations; they are even more necessary to a people like ours who were first fed and, so to speak, rocked on the knees of the Church, who lived solely under her aegis, grew only through her holy care, and now undertake a mission that is inseparable from the progress of religion on this continent. The more evidence or respect a society shows, the more esteem, confidence, and deference it gives to religious power. Also it receives more rights because of this protection, which, although some-times secret, is always effective, and with which God shields the faithful peoples. What a guarantee for our future! and how appropriate is today's ceremony to affirm our faith and uphold our wildest expectations! Church and State, clergy and laymen, all societies, all classes, all orders, all professions have joined hands and come to the foot of the altar, face to face with Him who makes and breaks empires, so that they could renew the close alliance between fatherland and God that was drawn up not far from here on the occasion of the birth of this city. And so that there might be no lack in the solemnity of this public act, Providence willed that a personal representative of His Holiness Pope Leo XIII, illustrious visitors, distinguished sons of our ancient motherland might heighten the splendour and beauty of this ceremony by their presence.

Now, my brothers, may this social pact at whose making you have been present with moved hearts be, and may it remain sacred for ever, since it seems that each of you is happy to subscribe in mind and heart to this national pledge! May it be attached to the forehead of our race as a Heavenly sign! From now on it must be the Magna Carta that governs us. May this charter, which states all rights and recognizes all sacred freedoms, be posted everywhere, on the gates of our cities, on the walls of our temples, inside our parliaments and public buildings! May it guide our legislators, enlighten our magistrates, and inspire all our writers! May it be the law of the family, the school, the workshop, and the hospital! In a word may it govern all of Canadian society!

In this way our nationality although still young, but rich in Heavenly gifts, will move confidently towards the fullness of its power and glory. While all around us other peoples are placing their stamp on material things, our spirit will blaze its trail of light higher up in the realm of Christian letters and science. While other races, including Catholic ones, use their time to enhance the exterior framework of the Church, our race will prepare what constitutes her life, heart, and soul, with more intimate work and finer care. While our rivals are, no doubt, in polite struggles contending for the power that stems from industry and finance, our aspirations shall be, above all, to uphold the honour of our doctrine and to gain the palms of apostleship.

On the heights we will hold the flag of ancient beliefs, of truth, justice, and this eternal philosophy, which never becomes outdated; we will hold it high, proudly and securely, against all winds and through all storms; we will show it to all of America as the glorious emblem, the symbol, the living ideal of social perfection and of true greatness among nations.

And so, some day in the future even better than today, these prophetic words that a mysterious echo brings to my ear, and that, although spoken many centuries ago, resume very well the import of this celebration, will come true: *Eritis mihi in populum, et ego ero vobis in Deum.*[6] 'And ye shall be my people, and I will be your God.'

So be it, with the blessing of His Grace the Archbishop!

12 Errol Bouchette (1863-1912)
Economic Development in the Province of Quebec

We are led to believe that we are on the brink of economic changes that will have a great influence on Canada and on the Province of Quebec. We shall likely experience the industrial revolution that Prince Bismarck foresaw and predicted. Whether this revolution is beneficial or harmful in its effects, it will undoubtedly have as widespread significance as the revolution 'in which', to use Sir Walter Besant's words, 'France overthrew the old order of things for ever and gave life to the spirit of freedom for the benefit of all races and all nations'. We may approve or disapprove of such movements, but no people could ignore them; it is impossible to stop them.

In our time everything else is relegated to the background by the incessant and ever more desperate industrial struggle that is taking place among nations, and, within each nation, among the parts of which it is made up. The unusual interest of these struggles is due as much to the new methods they produce as to the unexpected results that often follow. Thus the United States of America has gathered together on its territory the population surplus of the world, somewhat as ancient Rome did, and has watched its industrial strength grow in hitherto unparalleled proportions. It has become too enormous even for its vast territory, and the overflowing population of the Republic seems to aspire to ruling the world, as Rome did. Capital and industrial power are held by powerful and daring men who conceived the idea of making the entire world their tributary.

Europe is distant, wealthy, and powerful, and she takes this all very seriously. It is unlikely that the Italian Admiral Canavaro spoke lightly, when he said in an official statement from Toulon: 'I am convinced that the Triple and Dual Alliances together will guarantee peace in Europe for the next thirty years, and this will perhaps lead the European nations to consider *the possibility and the necessity of uniting against America*, Africa, and Asia, in the interest of civilization.' 'Europe is arming against America,' said the London newspapers in summing up the situation.

Translated from 'L'Evolution économique dans la Province de Québec', *Proceedings and Transactions of the Royal Society of Canada*, 1901, Section I, pp. 117-43.

However serious may be the question this brings up, the social and economic problem within each nation seems much more serious still. If in the United States, for example, a few individuals have been able to lay hold of almost all the nation's industrial assets, oil, steel, petroleum, railways, telegraphs, shipping, insurance, what will become of the other citizens? Will they resign themselves to economic slavery? This seems hard to believe. Consequently every day we see many signs of revolt. Various expedient moves could slow up the inevitable, but it will happen. An order of things different from the one that exists today will be set up, in which the capital and labour monopolies will give way to new conditions. If these conditions are not more favourable to the general well-being than present-day ones, should we conclude that while believing they were arming themselves for the defence of their rights, the people were being given only toy guns; or that the fault was the soldier's and not his sword's? Only time will tell.

Because of its geographical position, Canada is more interested than any other country in a prompt and peaceful solution to these great problems that disturb the United States. We too will have to put our institutions to the test. It will be helpful for us not to lose sight of what is happening elsewhere. Since the trusts can no longer find new fields to conquer at home, they are already preparing to invade us, bringing along with them all the economic problems that are waiting to be solved. Upon their arrival a new industrial population will spring up beside our agricultural population. It will not be centred almost entirely on the large cities, as in other countries, but will quite naturally follow the industries, which will tend to move closer to the raw materials – timber and water-power. And so this new population will be scattered about the countryside, among the farmers and settlers, from whom it will be in part recruited, and will thereby slowly change customs and ideas.

What should our attitude be, especially in the Province of Quebec, toward the new changes that are happening to us? Should we try to avoid them? Indeed could we, since we are far from believing that it would be the most advantageous course of action to follow or the right position to take? Instead, listen to what Lord Strathcona says:

> I am glad that some of these energetic and ingenious Americans who have dotted the plains of the United States with prosperous cities are concerned with the development of Canada. I am told that several of them are in London to bring about the investing of British capital in the British possessions of North America. We applaud their efforts, and we invite American capitalists to go ahead, if they can, with the development of Canada's resources. The words 'Morgan' and 'trusts' do not frighten us. We do not fear the combination of capital. On the contrary we welcome enterprising spirit and money, no matter where they come from.

It seems to us that this is the right attitude to take. Lord Strathcona is talking to Americans; but his words also contain prudent advice for his fellow-Canadians. We must welcome the forces that may come to us from across our borders, but we must wait for them in a good strategic position, in order to remain in control when they arrive.

It seems to us that we could put ourselves in a position to take advantage of these new forces. The economic troubles that exist elsewhere have not yet reached us. Here lies a precious advantage. Most peoples have been taken by surprise in these matters. They have had to examine new problems while struggling amid new conditions. This is not so with Canadians. We have been able to see and reflect before being called upon to act. Thus, in the past, new ideas in matters of the science of government that in France and Europe gave rise to violent upheavals were more wisely and gradually applied in Canada and produced better results without any trouble. Likewise, at the present time we are enjoying a period of relative calm, whereas the economic crisis is at an acute stage in almost all civilized countries. It is clearly our duty to profit from this respite by looking for a solution in advance, and to act in such a way that when large industry takes root in our country, it will not enslave our people or make them lose the character we cherish in them, but, while enlarging their field of action, will leave them free to accomplish their destinies by means of the institutions they have set up at the cost of long and patient efforts.

It is easy to say that only in ourselves will we find the balancing checks and forces that we need; forgetting to assert that we will obtain them only through widespread industrial training and wise laws that will regulate industry and help develop this training in conditions that will be favourable to us. These propositions are self-evident. But here in Canada everything remains to be done, and there are numerous obstacles to overcome before we can arrive at true reforms. Who then will strike the first blow; who will do for us what was done for the Magyars; who will organize industrial training; who will endow us with wise and effective laws to solve the economic problem? Public apathy and the problem of disbursements seem at first sight to be insurmountable difficulties. However, we hope that in fact they are not. We believe that our fellow-countrymen will want to take action as soon as they have understood. Therefore we must give these questions as much publicity as possible. This is the sole goal of this work, just as sincerity is its only merit. But if it is discussed, disputed even, especially by enlightened and authoritative men, it will be like the flint-stone, which is cold and powerless in itself, but which produces a spark when struck with steel.

The Aptitude of French Canadians for Industry

Before going further, perhaps it would be of some use to briefly examine this question: Have French Canadians an aptitude for big business and large industry? Not that the answer is doubtful for those who really know our fellow-countrymen of French origin. But many people have repeatedly said that we are unfit for commercial and industrial business; and this opinion, although unconfessed, has gained ground in several of our classical colleges – a very unfortunate thing. In comparing ourselves to businessmen of other origins, whose long-established prosperity has made our painful beginnings seem even more pitiful, too many of us have said: 'Oh, let's give it up, obviously it's not our vocation.' We ourselves have heard men who were supposed to be enlightened argue this way, and quite recently.

Circumstances have caused even scholarship to look as if it is conspiring to support this false idea. By providing material for lovers of folklore, Parkman has become, perhaps unwittingly, the source of more and more surprising stories, so surprising in fact that we are now little more than an interesting phenomenon of fossilization in the eyes of many Americans. 'Parkman discovered French Canada,' people cry, and they weave novels around it, just as one could around the ruins of Pompeii or Babylon. Others make discoveries on our behalf in matters of social economy. 'You are French,' they say, 'of Celtic and Latin origin, with a communal background; do not think you can do what we can; many long years will pass before you are capable of large industrial undertakings.' This is all the more serious because social science, which is new, has dazzled the world with brilliant theories based on accurate, but obviously not yet complete, observations. The eminent founder of the school admitted himself that he was unable to complete his study of contemporary social phenomena. His followers have not either. It is long, slow work that often has to be redone. This science will certainly be called upon to give important service, especially when the observations that make up its basis are completed. But in the meantime, we can see by what happens on this continent before our very eyes that some studies must be revised; those concerning the Celtic race in America, for example. Certain writers record that the pure Celtic Highlanders described by Sir Walter Scott, living in clans, unwilling to work, despising commerce and industry, and valuing only the professions of soldiers and thieves, have become brave fighters in the arena of commerce and industry in the new countries where they were forced to go by the collapse of their old social organization. The Irish Celt, like his Scottish brother a proletarian and unsophisticated emigrant, underwent a surprising transformation when he reached America. Whoever has travelled in the United States will realize this easily. But if we think carefully about it, we will be forced to conclude that the Irish and Scottish Celt's transformation is less surprising than that of the handful of French peasants, so home-loving and given to routine in their native land, who could open up the new continent to other peoples, and, all alone, axe in hand in the virgin forest, could set up lasting institutions, protect their freedoms, and assimilate the British constitution while contributing to its improvement.

The explanation is not difficult. In anthropology there is a factor not found in the other sciences. Here physical laws are dominated by another law. In the study of man and of human aptitudes one cannot proceed in the same way one does in the study of animal habits and instincts. Certainly man has physical characteristics and instincts, but these are only accessories. The splendour of Homer shines from beneath the rags of a travelling bard. Maimon's thought lives in this base drunkard's body, in this beggar and thief. Every man has an immortal soul; enlighten him and his soul can reach incalculable heights. And so, in studying humanity, no absolute rule is possible, if it is not that man is essentially capable of improvement. If some Caucasian races seem to be inferior, it is not because of their inherent inferiority, but is due to unfavourable circumstances that surround them, which their ignorance or weakness keeps them from controlling. And in this lies the usefulness of social science. By pointing out the

real causes of inferiority in certain groups of men, it shows at the same time
how they can be fought and eradicated.

Social science seen in this way will help support our thesis. It will prove that
the bush transplanted in new soil has improved its fruit: that we have preserved
the good qualities of our ancestors while acquiring others that are our own; that
we are in fact a primitive people, somewhat like those men who left the forests
of Germany a long time ago to take the place of Roman power. We have their
intelligence, their independence, their courage. We have already accomplished
a great deal. Notably in commercial matters, despite our apparent inferiority,
history will say that we achieved a real success by holding firmly to our small
part, although we were hindered and discouraged by a group of men who
wanted to keep a lucrative monopoly for themselves, and who succeeded in this
for a while, thanks to powerful influences they had in England, for a long time
our only market, and today our principal one. If these facts were known they
would be kept in the background. There is something of the reasoning of the
fox in the well-known fable, in the following argument put forth by a former
teacher of mine. Commerce and industry, he said, are material occupations; we
French Canadians are made for something more noble; let us be farmers like
Cincinnatus, orators like Cicero and Bossuet; the plough, the rostrum, and the
pulpit call us; let us leave material gain to more vulgar natures. Perhaps there
was a time when this sophism could get by, but that time is past. Ideas and
circumstances have certainly changed, and it is essential now to illuminate the
real causes for the apparent industrial and commercial inferiority of our fellow-
countrymen. This will be one of the jobs for the future, a task calling for much
research and analysis, but a useful task since it will make short work of certain
common errors. We will understand then that no race is more fit for the producing of industrial wealth than we are. An agricultural race in a country that
possesses natural industrial resources can develop these resources with the
most intelligence and to the greatest advantage of the country. Agriculture is the
first stage in the production of wealth, and industry is the second. Imperceptible
gradations bring together these two professions, especially in our time. In
support of this proposition economists point to Hungary's transformation. A
few years ago it was exclusively agricultural, but it now possesses a considerable
industrial population. In Hungary more than half a million dollars is spent on
industrial training, aside from the encouragements lavished on industries. (See
Economiste français.) This is a noble goal without equal, since to work today for
the industrial development of French Canadians is to work for the salvation of
an entire people, it is to continue the mission of our forefathers, it is to achieve
something that is not only useful, but so essential and necessary that to fail in it
would be being anti-patriotic.

The limits imposed on this paper do not permit us to study this question at
length. It is all to the good if we can outline it; if we can say a few words about
why we believe our fellow-countrymen in the Province of Quebec have all they
need to succeed in any industrial undertaking that is reasonably and wisely
conceived. Up to now circumstances have forced the largest part of their energies
to be directed into other paths. Now that economic evolution pushes them toward

careers in large industry, why would they be less fit for them than the Anglo-Saxons, the Scots, or the Irish? History teaches us that large industry was born in France and first developed there, later being spread through Europe by groups of Frenchmen who had left their country.[1] We believe Frenchmen were the first to think of large companies for colonial trade, which in England contributed so highly to the greatness of the British Empire. For, like the Romans, the English have known how to understand and appropriate the great ideas that change the world. Economists tell us that French laws still form the basis of international commercial law. 'Colbert's genius,' said Luigi Cossa,[2] 'thought of a grand undertaking, and he had the strong will to complete it. He was not satisfied with the petty expedients of his predecessors. . . . It is easy to see why Walpole and Pitt (the elder) in England, Frederick-William I and Frederick II of Prussia, Joseph II of Austria, and Peter the Great in Russia tried to follow Colbert's path, rarely with the same skill and consequently with varied success.' And in the last century, despite the Revolution, wars, and incessant political upheavals, although France was weakened, she did not give in. On the contrary, she is moving toward a recovery, despite the causes of national weakness that we all know, but that do not exist in French Canada.

We possess the germ of the dominant qualities of two peoples: the one we came from and the one under whose flag we have grown. Sometimes we are unambitious country-folk much like the farmers in England. But when we have been shown how we can improve our farming methods, we have launched ourselves bravely along the new way pointed out to us. For a long time we have shown an all too prevalent tendency to follow the liberal professions and politics. This is caused by a habit acquired in the course of our long constitutional struggles, when the titles of 'lawyer' or 'political leader' were not vain trimmings but implied a real patriotic mission. Today that is only a prejudice that is slowly disappearing, and the lawyer is no longer the demigod he used to be. At present we seem too inclined toward inferior positions in paid labour. That should not surprise us, if we remember the numerous obstacles caused by colonization and the almost complete absence of technical training in our country. 'For a long time,' says the late Arthur Buies in his work *La Province de Québec*, 'the lack of schools for the professions and applied science has kept French Canadians from knowing and appreciating the real value of the astonishing resources in their country; if they finally succeed in obtaining schools of this kind, and if they can finally open the great book of applied sciences, since the French Canadians are so singularly well-gifted and so ingenious in matters of intelligence and in the use of natural forces and mechanical inventions, one can be sure that they would make and keep for themselves a prominent place in the future of the North American peoples.' Those who have been able to see our fellow-countrymen in the industrial centres know how true this is. There is a job yet to be done of collecting in one place a multitude of facts to help prove how fit our fellow-countrymen are for large industry; it is a relatively easy job, since there are abundant facts, and it would really open the eyes of a great many people.

Already the day Buies named is beginning to dawn. Open the newspapers, those reflections of the public spirit, and you will find clear signs of an awakened ambition, of a new force that we must not be slow in channelling and directing. But in what direction? Here we find ground already prepared where only the seed has to be planted. For many generations these men have cleared land in the forests, and they know better than anyone else the nature of the forests and living conditions in the woods. Therefore we must direct them toward forest industries and related activities. They know these industries in part already. If we put them in a position to exploit the forests scientifically and to develop large industries from them, we will not be violating nature but helping in the completion of evolution. Perhaps this evolution would come about naturally by itself, but it would be relatively slow. Unfortunately, in our times, and situated as we are, we scarcely have time to wait. We must be quick unless we want to be left behind. We know there is still much to be done to complete the evolution.

But now we are coming to another part of our topic. For the moment let us be content to examine these considerations in the light of common sense. We believe the inevitable conclusion is that our fellow-countrymen in the Province of Quebec are no less fit for industry than the other races on the continent, and that if well trained and guided they will obtain results that will astonish everyone, and themselves most of all.

Industrial Training

May we say from the beginning that this chapter will borrow nothing from the pedagogical viewpoint; we are more concerned with the social aspect of the subject. General interest is the guide to follow here. It is not only a question of the interests of industrialists or of young people who have a taste for industry. If the question ended there, one could very reasonably maintain – and this doctrine has prevailed in England for a long time – that everyone must manage as best he can, improve himself at his own expense, and yield to the law of supply and demand. We will still find many people who go no further in their thinking. This kind of industrialist says that for his factory he must have workers with a certain technical training; but he knows that not far from his establishment there are schools where this training can be had free. 'What more do you want?' he cries. And from his standpoint he is right. From our standpoint, which is different from his, he is as terribly wrong as those who, at the time when Canadians were trying to obtain responsible government, would have said: 'But why all this upset? We have an honest and good sovereign, represented by a well-arranged government.' No doubt these things are good and desirable, but a people wants other guarantees. It organizes its army in order to defend its borders, and when it is a question of constitutional freedom it organizes its parliament. This is what we did. Now it is a matter of protecting our economic existence, upon which our national existence depends. Are we going to give ourselves over to chance or even to the goodwill of industrial magnates? 'The man whose protection against injustice rests entirely upon the good-will of another man or a group of men is a slave – a man without rights,' said Benjamin Harrison, one-time president of the United States. Instead are we not going to *organize* the industrial training of our people so that they will be in a position to understand their interests and rights in the new era that is coming, to protect them with wise laws, and to put themselves in a position to partake of the advantages of industry? This is the question.

But the organization of industrial training in the Province of Quebec is not a small undertaking. It is very difficult to imagine a system that would answer the need and at the same time be within the limits of our financial resources. What we are venturing here is only an outline, but it is based on the highest European authorities.

Sir G. W. Kekewick, K.C.B., Secretary of the Board of Education in England, and Mr. Michael E. Sadler, Director of Special Research and Reports, gave a number of specialists the task of studying the systems of industrial training in the different countries of Europe. Thanks to the graciousness of Lord Strathcona, Canadian High Commissioner in London, we have been able to obtain several of these reports, which, coming from such distinguished sources, will form an excellent basis for this chapter. They are a *Report on Technical and Commercial Education in East Prussia, Poland, Galicia, Silesia, and Bohemia,* by James Baker, F.R.G.S.; *The Realschulen in Berlin,* by Michael E. Sadler; *Higher Commercial Education at Antwerp, Leipzig, Paris, and Havre,* by the same author; *The Continuation Schools (Fortbildungsschulen) in Saxony,* by F. H. Dale; *The French System of Higher Primary Schools,* by R. L. Morant. We also thought it would be interesting to make a very complete list of the reference works on this same question provided by the Board of Education. We have also consulted other American and English authorities. These studies show clearly that in the last twenty years continental Europe has been transformed as a result of universal education directed toward the technical branches of learning. According to this report the United States and especially England and Canada are very far behind France and Germany. What characterizes the achievement of industrial training in these countries is the *organization,* the *system,* under central guidance but with sufficient elasticity to allow for local needs. The results are not yet entirely complete, especially in France, but they are already astonishing. In 1886 in France nineteen per cent of the graduates from higher primary schools, which one could call preparatory schools for industry, began an industrial career instead of remaining simple day-labourers as they would have been otherwise. In 1887 the proportion rose to twenty-three per cent, in 1889 to twenty-six per cent, and in 1892 to twenty-seven per cent. The percentage increases every year, says Mr. Morant. And why, we may ask? Because in these higher primary schools, which are the continuation of elementary schools and which require a minimum age of eleven, an attempt is made not only to give the child general and indispensable knowledge about industrial development, but also to inspire in him a taste for the occupation he will enter and in which he will spend his life and earn his living. Here is an example. In young girls who are destined to become farmers' or workers' wives one inspires a taste for domestic chores, which is so important and so often ignored in certain countries, notably in the Province of Quebec where these chores are slowly disappearing. This beneficial influence spreads to all levels of workers. As Mr. Morant remarks, we must not confuse this with the purely utilitarian tendency that is predominant in most current educational efforts. Industrial training is distinct from technical training in several respects. According to the French legislator, industrial training must precede and facilitate technical training, just as a classical course facilitates the study of a liberal profession. This is a very important point, and we will return to it.

M. Cohendy, the director of higher primary schools in France and one of the European authorities on professional and technical education, will explain to us the economic conditions for which people are prepared nowadays.

As Arago already said in 1836, beet sugar is not made with fine words; soda is not extracted from sea-salt with alexandrines. Neither is it, we will add, with a purely classical education that the farmer will be able to make his land more fertile, the industrialist produce goods more cheaply, or the businessman open new outlets.

This large population, linked to commerce and industry, demands a new form of education. It wants education that will best answer its needs, that will prepare it the most directly for the professions it follows, and that will produce merchants and industrialists as a classical education produces learned men and scholars. Technical training is called for as a necessary consequence of the transformation of our social state; and this necessity seems all the more urgent when one examines the new situation of our foreign relations. Struggle between peoples, which was formerly the exception, has now become the rule, and forms the normal state of international relations. It is true this struggle is not fought with cannon-shot and it takes place more and more in the realm of production and trade; but although one has qualified it, ironically no doubt, as peaceful, in reality it is just as deadly for the vanquished as bloody defeats are. Now, one can assert without fear of contradiction that victory, here as elsewhere, will fall to the one who has best prepared his weapons, that is, to the one who is best educated. Therefore the organization of technical training is not a simple pedagogical matter; it is an essential and vital question for our country.[3]

It is not necessary to go very far to realize that M. Cohendy's point of view is the true one, recognized as such by the thinkers of the entire world as well as by most educational systems. Now let us examine, as extensively as space permits, what measures different countries have taken to arm their citizens for the industrial struggle. We shall base our discussion on the official data given to us by the British government. We will be concerned particularly with the French system because it seems to us to be the best organized. In fact, in France, the legislator has profited from experience gathered in other countries and has been able to avoid certain dangers. The results of this are not yet as visible as they are in Germany, since the system was put into effect more recently.

The professional schools in France, better known in our country under the name of technical schools, are the naval school, the military school of Saint-Cyr, the school of the Ponts et Chaussées, the polytechnical school, the agricultural school; next the higher commercial schools, the higher primary professional schools, the higher primary schools, the practical schools, the technical schools of arts and trades. For the time being we are not concerned with the large scientific schools that make up the first category.

We can prove that the basis of the French system of industrial training is the

higher primary schools or their equivalent, the idea of which was conceived by
Guizot but only finally adopted quite recently. They are the basis first of all
because their influence is general, in the sense that their influence is exerted
on all the children of a certain level of intelligence. This influence is even more
general than that of the primary schools, since they also accept the graduates
of the denominational primary schools and from the religious point of view
do not have the same drawbacks as the primary schools; as well, they can
provide freedom, variety, and elasticity of approach. Freedom: the syllabus of
study is not fixed by law, which in this case is content to give some advice as
guidance for the professors. Variety and elasticity in a program that can be
changed to suit local needs. In these schools the student's intelligence is shaped
so that it can respond readily to new ideas and methods.

These schools are day schools and on quite a different level from the night
schools set up for workers. Obviously they are destined not for the great mass
of workers, who most often enter workshops when they leave primary school,
but for the *members of the élite*, those who will become foremen or managers
of agricultural or manufacturing industry and often rise much higher than this.
To be accepted, they must be at least eleven years old and have a certificate of
primary education obtained in a competitive examination, or, in the case of
students from private or denominational schools, they must write an examination. These limitations are set to exclude the children who are incapable of
profiting intellectually from the instruction given there, and who, by studying
there, would be uselessly spending public funds. Since it often happens that the
qualified children are from poor families who could not afford to keep them
during their stay in a higher primary school, a general system of scholarships
has been set up by the government and often by the *département* or the *commune*.
These scholarships are awarded to the candidates who, after writing a serious
aptitude test, prove that their financial situation is such that without the help
of a scholarship they will not be able to continue their education; and when
one of the problems is distance, the scholarship will pay for room and board.
In this way nearly a quarter of the student population has the advantage of
continuing its education in the best imaginable schools and of acquiring, as we
said, not only general knowledge, but a specialty and a taste for the occupation
they choose. The number of students in higher primary schools increases
considerably every year, although the number of students in primary schools
remains the same.

These schools are run partly by the State and partly by the *départements*
or municipalities. The government's contribution covers about five-sevenths of
the amount needed to run the institutions and does not depend on the number
of students or the results obtained. The municipality that provides the rest of
the funds is free to determine the details of the program, within certain limits.
Here in Canada most of us believe the French system is rigid and uniform,
that all children are put through the same mill, so to speak. But this is certainly
not the case in the higher primary schools. What the government requires is
free education, then a program that fills the needs of the locality and at the
same time provides a certain amount of indispensable basic knowledge.

You must read Mr. Morant's work to understand how rapidly this admirable system of higher primary schools prepares the entire nation for industrial jobs. They train excellent foremen and shop managers for all industries and they send some students to the large technical and scientific schools. Please notice that all this applies to the *élite drawn from the masses*. This system provides a very good answer to the serious and often-made objection that everyone cannot hold an important position in society and that it is unfair to those who do not have the ability to give them aspirations that they will never be able to fulfil. There is nothing more interesting than following the thinking of these illustrious men, Guizot, Duruy, Duplan, Buisson, Gérard, Cohendy, and others, through their experiences and the applications made from them. One is present at a kind of artificial incubation that the entire nation experiences and one sees results forming that will affect the destiny of the world.

If the more recent French system of generalized industrial training seems to us better conceived, this is not to say that the German system is not admirable. In the large scientific schools in Germany there is probably more attention given to practical application than in France. It is true one does not find the preparatory schools for industrial professions that form the basis of the French system, but great efforts are made to give technical training to the worker. To understand this we can do no better than listen to Mr. F. H. Dale, one of the Board of Education members sent to Germany, who in his report talks mainly about Saxony and its system of continuation schools (*Fortbildungs-schulen*). The era of German development dates from the war of 1870; it is also from this time that the continuation schools were developed, since they had existed previously only in an embryonic state. Imperial German law decrees the following:

> Employers in all branches of industry are required to give to those of their workers who are under the age of eighteen, and who attend an institution recognized as a continuation school by the local or state authorities the amount of time necessary to attend this institution as it is fixed for this institution by the authorities.
>
> By an order of council from the district or locality, attendance at the continuation school can be made obligatory for all male workers under eighteen years of age. Measures will be taken to insure that this order is enforced and that students attend regularly.

The principal object of these schools is to establish a certain minimum of culture for all the inhabitants of the country; and as M. Pache, director of continuation schools in Saxony, says, 'Since children from the poor class, at the age of fourteen when they leave elementary schools, cannot understand the need for continuing and improving their studies, we must force them to do so.' In Saxony this is so not only for young workers, but for all young people leaving elementary schools. An attempt is made to make the studies as pertinent as possible to the special branch of industry in which the young worker is employed. Here there are some difficulties. First of all, in the cities there are always various kinds of industries, and consequently they necessitate different studies. How then will the employer view the enforced absence of his worker? This has been managed in an ingenious way. The workers are divided into classes according to their occupations, and with the employers it is determined what day would be best for each class: Monday for weavers, Tuesday for founders, Wednesday for butchers, and so on. They go even further. The employers are consulted not only about the best day for them, but also about the kind of studies to promote. They are put on school commissions, they are present at examinations, and naturally they end up becoming greatly interested in the schools and the students, often so interested that they offer prizes or other encouragement. Besides the knowledge they acquire, the young workers on their part become accustomed to the idea of solidarity between them and their employers. And this way everyone receives real advantages.

We must not forget that this set-up of industrial instruction in Europe also includes the technical schools, properly speaking, and the apprenticeship schools, which in many cases are factories that produce marketable goods. These schools are the natural consequence of the system and they are greatly needed to prepare these kinds of workers. If we do not make special mention of them, you will readily see the reason. It is that such institutions can yield results only from prepared ground. One must dig a garden before planting seeds. However essential this second operation may be, it is no less difficult when the ground is prepared. For a description of some good technical schools in Europe see Mr. Jules Helbronner's report on the social economy section of the 1889 Paris Exposition. Also the report from the Department of Agriculture in Washington, 1892.

In Germany and France, contrary to what has been practised up to now in England and Canada, one can see that, in principle, the education of the young on all levels, not only the elementary, is a public duty that must not be left to the mercy of changes in supply and demand. This is the fundamental difference. In these countries industrial training has been scientifically organized, given uniform guidance, and then, beyond industrial schools of every kind, large higher State schools have been set up, centres from which radiate pure science, the producer of all wealth, all over the country. Mr. James Baker's work and Mr. E. E. Williams' book *Made in Germany* are worth reading on this subject.

We have really mentioned only a few of the authorities one should consult on the question of industrial training. The most we have tried to do is extract some general principles that might be useful to those who would like to use these studies in setting up a system of technical training in the Province of Quebec. It has seemed noteworthy to us that in closely examining the problems of adaptation, they do not appear as insurmountable as one might think at first. Without touching our system of primary, secondary, and higher education as it now exists, we have within reach the elements we need to set up a system of industrial training, not cheaply – if we remember how meagre our resources are – but not with excessive expense. Think about it. Our universities are the supposed locations of schools of science and higher industrial research, but not as they operate at present. As Thiers would say, to broaden their scope in a greater country should be our ambition as well as our duty. Let our authorities be generous in the installation of the most complete and modern laboratories, and let them be sure of the co-operation of distinguished scholars and professors so that a real centre for industrial education may be created in the Province of Quebec. Then they will have accomplished a great thing, without having overburdened the budget. However, in order to gather the fruit of the sacrifices these things will cause, we must do still more. To have a lamp is all very good, but if we want it to light our way, we must find oil to fill it.

Whoever speaks of 'system' and 'organization' implies a completed thing where everything fits and stands firm. Without this all efforts are fruitless or lead to a great waste of effort at the very least. Why is our polytechnical school in Montreal wasting away for want of students? It is a sign of a vice that is deeply rooted in the lower levels of education. It is the lamp going out for want of fuel. The head suffers because the body is sick. A railway company would lose money if, after building a line, it did not go about finding travellers and traffic to nourish it. Sometimes these travellers, in our case the student population, come by themselves, if the line crosses an already rich and populated region. In a new country the railway often precedes the colonizing movement and because of this becomes an agent in the development of the nation. In this last case it is not sufficient for it to choose its route carefully; it must put forth the greatest efforts to attract people and trade to it. It is up to us to open a way in the undeveloped area of industry. The flow of traffic remains to be created, and to do this we have an absolute and basic need not only for great universities, but also for higher primary schools or something similar. Our young people are wonderfully gifted, and all we have to do to interest them in industrial matters is to make them aware of them. Then they would want to ride to the end of the line. It seems to us that in our model schools and academies we have a precious resource. In a way they are already higher primary schools, but to make them truly useful to the goal we have in view, they must be modified considerably. First, the programs of study must be changed to make them into real preparatory schools for industry; second, there must be completely free education at least for the members of the élite chosen from the competition; and last, a certain number of scholarships must be created for the members of the élite who, owing to lack of financial means, could not otherwise continue their studies. We believe that such a system, guided by competent and enthusiastic men with sympathetic minds, would cause a need for technical schools of all kinds in a few years, and would eventually assure us of superiority in matters of industrial training. To continue our image, we in fact would have two central stations: preparatory schools for industry at one end of the line, and schools of advanced science at the other. Between these two points the stations would be placed at intervals: schools of arts and trades, technical schools, continuation schools for young workers and farmers, all of which would come along as they were needed. Once the flow was established, no school would want for students, as long as there was organization from top to bottom and free education all the way through. Since our railway will be running through a new country where the advantages it brings are unknown, it will be necessary to prepare facilities for the public traveller as well as to accustom him to using them. In some countries adjustment would be made quickly, and people would willingly get aboard. Here such a radical move would be a little too surprising; perhaps it would be better to turn to publicity and advertising. Also it would require the active and enthusiastic participation of all the leading men in our country, ecclesiastics as well as laymen. We believe this participation is absolutely assured.

Industrial Loans

We have seen how the principle of organization is applied to the industrial training of the people in other countries; and we have outlined a plan for adapting this organization to the needs of the Province of Quebec while still remembering our financial limitations. But as we have tried to show in a previous study, in order to guide our fellow-countrymen toward industrial development we need something more than schools. How do we reach this goal then? Several peoples have successfully made experiments in this area, especially the Hungarians, who have undergone a quite recent transformation and who offer more than one point of comparison with French Canadians. These examples are useful in showing that peoples, like economists, recognize the need for industrial development, and that it can be greatly encouraged by our public authorities. Nevertheless, we are not deluded into thinking that radical reforms can be adopted in our country. No doubt it is better to stick to a more gradual modification of things that is more suitable to the character of our people. Therefore, it is not a question of encouraging the construction of large and costly factories, and still less of blindly rushing into risky undertakings.

We have watched the spreading of farmers' unions for the manufacture of butter and cheese in our old parishes. This alone has been enough to bring back affluence in the farmlands. Then why should settlers' unions not be set up for the making of wood pulp and its products in the new parishes? We would like this idea to become more widespread and this kind of industrial development to extend throughout all the parts of our territory, not limited to only one sort of industry, but, on the contrary, including the greatest possible exploitation of our countryside and forests. There in a few words is our opinion on industrial development in the Province of Quebec; and this could be easily accomplished by industrial loans.

The benefits of such a system are quite clear when you think about it. The value of large factories is the cheapness of the goods they produce. Here we could have a host of small factories with similar results. Supposing a settlers' union could, through the intervention of the government, get a loan at the same rate of interest as that paid on the public debt, to pay for materials and the cost of installation; and also supposing this industry were conducted according to scientific data and by a knowledgeable person, it can readily be seen that the expenses would be much less than in a factory controlled by one man. The private manufacturer's main concern and his means of livelihood come from his products; he has to pay the full price for raw materials and labour. On the other hand, for the settler who manufactures goods, production would be important but it would not be essential – a second string on his bow, on which his livelihood would not depend. This would be a parochial industry, a family one, so to speak, run somewhat like domestic industries. He would cut wood himself either on wooded homesteads granted to the union to which he belongs or on his own land, and with this wood he would make pulp, thus simultaneously clearing land for farming and nourishing industry. His family would contribute manpower to the co-operative factory. He would thereby be able to sell his manufactured products very cheaply and still make a good profit. Especially in our new northern parishes such a move would inevitably spread far and wide. Once invaded by our men, our forests would no longer shelter nomadic speculators. Once the land was cleared and colonized, with the aid of the industrial exploitation of our forests, there would be a great expansion of intensive farming, the only remunerative undertaking in our time, and one that prosperity and training would have made possible.

In this way we could become an industrial people without ceasing to be an agricultural people. We would take advantage of all our resources and be in a secure position. At the present time we are not, since a people is never in a secure position when it neglects to exploit the resources of its country. If it does not exploit them itself, others will, and will thereby acquire a pretext for interfering in its affairs. Or they may even form an industrial oligarchy in the country, and this is to be feared just as much. History provides us with examples on every page. Either one of these eventualities causes the inevitable punishment of a people for its lack of vigilance and initiative. Now, let us read what Mr. Poultney Bigelow says about those who threaten us with industrial servitude unless we quickly put ourselves in a position to combat their influence. It is not an attractive picture he paints.

Mercantilism is running wild in the United States. The Yankees convert all their ideas and energy into gold, and the trust builders do the rest. Of course these financial kings exert a corrupting influence on the civil servants; they create all kinds of temptations and carry on many underhand dealings. In Washington I have noticed a cynical contempt for the constitution. Corruption riddles the government and disgraces the Houses of Congress, which are now only gambling rooms where permission to rob the people is sold. Legislators and civil servants do not miss a single chance to turn official prerogative to their profit. I knew of several cases of blatant intrigue, especially concerning the war in the Philippines, where a thousand civil servants stole both large and small amounts . . . Public awareness must be awakened in America. To free themselves from the slavery of capitalism they need men and women of quality like those who earlier freed human beings from slavery.

The protection of our country against such a calamity seems to us to be an absolutely necessary task. 'These examples of a humanity bent on conquest that have reappeared in such modern situations as industrial warfare and in this contrasting setting where the most refined civilization is basking in open barbarism' – as M. Paul Bourget describes them – are certainly not elements we can want to see take root in our country. However, we will not escape it if we do not exploit the industrial resources of our country. If, on the contrary, we increase this exploitation, then, once resolutely at our tasks, we shall be able to await the invaders without fear, since they cannot breathe in countries where good economic conditions prevail.

A system of industrial loans is a financial project destined to release and make available a large enough proportion of the natural resources in the Province of Quebec that capital can be raised to help in the industrial development of the province by Canadians, as far as this is possible.

Every sound financial venture must be based on real values of absolute solidity. Industrial loans would be based on the natural resources of the province, whose carefully calculated balance-sheet would be known to the entire world. In passing, let us note that some American governments are at present drawing up this account of our resources for their own purposes.

Here we find ourselves faced with a double operation: to borrow on the guarantee of undeveloped real capital; to lend to those who will undertake to develop this same capital.

Consequently, the first thing we must do is to restrict loans to those industries for which the province supplies the raw materials; the second, to have a guarantee that these industries will be managed with sufficient wisdom and according to scientific methods. Without these two conditions, the operation would lack stability. And so, while respecting the flexibility necessary in such matters, we must determine legally, in advance, what industries would be allowed to benefit from industrial loans, and under what economic and financial conditions these loans would be made.

Which industries would be allowed to benefit from them? Surely they would be the ones deemed most advantageously exploitable in the judgment of the bureau of scientific and industrial research. And this bureau would be part of the system of technical training in the province and would be attached to the organization of the central polytechnical school. As far as the conditions of the loans are concerned, they would have to be determined by statute. I hope these loans would be made available to all, individuals or companies, who were willing to obey the law. However, for this law to have the most beneficial effect, it must not be forgotten when we are drawing it up that it is meant for settlers' unions that want to exploit the woods and other potential industries that are within their reach. Moreover, it seems to us there is a very important distinction to be made concerning the guarantees of repayment in both cases. In the case of the individual industrialist, this guarantee would not be absolute, since it would be at the mercy of common commercial vicissitudes. In the case of the settlers' union, it would be more stable. At first their undertakings would be more easily controlled, since in most cases a municipal guarantee could be obtained for interest charges. And so, as much from the standpoint of public interest as of a good financial guarantee, it seems that, all other things being equal, we should give preference to the settlers' unions.

By this means, without touching the existing budgets, we could find assets that would allow the State to borrow and lend, or to guarantee loans for industrial purposes. This brings us to a serious difficulty. Since the permanence of industrial lands in the Province of Quebec is the base of the system we are studying here, it follows that we must exploit this land without alienating it, except for the lots given to colonizers. In fact, by founding a lasting settlement, the honest colonizer gives more to the State than he receives from it. Sometimes one can increase the value of public property by wise land-grants. Until now we have ignored this principle of the permanence of our industrial land. We have rather carelessly followed the general procedure of civilized nations, one that tends to alienate rather than to increase the national domain. This rule prevails not only in Europe but also in America, despite the different situation in which American nations find themselves. Nevertheless, in the last while, we have begun to suspect that the opposite method might be the right one, for the setting up of large national parks is an important step toward the preservation of public lands.

The rule made here by economists seems to be a wise one. In countries where cultivation is advanced and the population is dense, they say, it is not advantageous for the State to preserve vast areas of public lands, although it is always wise for a government to preserve and acquire forests.[4] On the other hand, in countries where the population is still sparse, the State can profitably preserve and increase public property. Please note that in speaking about the alienation of public lands, I do not mean, and especially for our province, only the selling of land. We know well that by putting up for bid the 'limits' for the cutting of commercial wood,[5] the government does not sell the land, and the land is often worth little or nothing. What it is in our interest to treat carefully, since it is real capital and often the most important, is that which this land produces. This does not stop at the value of the trees; no matter how valuable they may be, there are other things of equal value. We know that forests regularize the run-off of water and consequently supply the water power necessary for their exploitation, not to mention protecting farmland against floods and other problems that follow deforestation. And so, from an industrial as well as an agricultural point of view, we must alienate only the usufruct of our forests. To permit people to ravage them is to sell, indeed to give, our industrial capital to people who themselves do not even exploit it; it is to close the door to colonization and industry and, at the same time, to open wide the doors to speculation and stock-jobbing.

A modification in the principle as well as in the framing of our laws in these matters would, therefore, be the necessary consequence of the system we are putting forth here. It is important for these laws to decree the permanence of our industrial lands and to provide for protection against all waste. Such laws combined with other industrial reforms would not remain a dead letter as so many others have. Attempts to annul the effects would be in vain. By finally giving the settler the advantages of which he has been deprived for so long, and by placing our people in possession of its heritage, we would be creating that many more vigilant and interested guardians of national industrial capital. By exploiting the resources themselves, they would finally learn all their value, and besides their self-interest, their customs, and the law, they would have the basic patriotic instinct to make use of their national property with some restraint. This last observation will perhaps make the sceptics smile, but this feeling is more widespread than you imagine.

This method, which consists of retaining the ownership, and maintaining the value, of our public industrial property, offers obvious advantages that every thinking man admits. However, it is doubtful if the public grasps all its importance. A large number of economists and specialists in commerce and finance, among them Emile de Laveleye in France, and Rau and Wagner in Germany, go so far as to say that we should not alienate any part of our public property, but only grant land on long leases of ninety-nine or one hundred and fifty years. Obviously these ideas are not very practical, at least in our province, and it cannot be a question of applying them to the land grants for colonization, which, moreover, are small compared to our vast industrial property. But we can apply the principle in such a way as to produce all its effects while assuring the permanent preservation in the hands of the State, and the progressive growth, of our industrial resources, by all the means that science, experience, and common sense can suggest. 'We do not hesitate,' says M. Leroy-Beaulieu, 'to declare ourselves in favour of this method for countries where a large part of the territory is still unoccupied. The United States and Australia (and Canada) could avoid for generations to come all the financial difficulties and economic obstacles against which contemporary peoples struggle.'[6] It is true, he adds, that the realization of this would take a long time. It would not take so long with the system of industrial loans that would make possible the development of a sizable portion of our currently unproductive natural resources.

When M. Leroy-Beaulieu wrote the preceding lines, perhaps he himself did not realize the great importance of the question, especially for our country. Specialists agree that fifty years from now there will be a catastrophe due to the scarcity of wood. The only world resources they see are Norway and Canada. (See *Congrès de Sylviculture, Exposition de Paris, 1900*, speech of M. Mélard, Inspector of Forests in France.) This is almost to say, in this respect, that we hold the fate of the universe in our hands. We would therefore be quite guilty if in such circumstances we neglected our duty and our interests by remaining inactive.

For the purposes of this study, it would be of little importance if the government made loans directly to industries, or indirectly through the intermediary of a bank, as is done in some countries. However, we do admit that given the customary slowness and lack of flexibility of all official procedures, it seems to us it would be much more preferable to have the State give guarantees to a financial institution, with wise laws making the loans sufficiently easy to get but well safeguarded. Loans made under such conditions, at the rate of interest paid on the public debt, plus a small additional interest to cover service charges, depreciation, and industrial tax, would bring about the desired goal, we think.

This, then, is the outline of our idea. We submit it knowing that a considerable number of practical difficulties make its application complicated, but also with the conviction that the basic principle is right and that its adoption would be advantageous. Some of the people to whom we have talked about it were enthusiastic. To listen to them, one would think that by applying the system we had found the remedy for many evils. The success of such a measure would give rise to a considerable increase in revenue; it would inspire greater confidence, proportional to the public wealth thus acquired; it would create Canadian capital that would be used to buy up government bonds, thus permitting in time a decrease in interest being paid on the public debt and an increase of a similar amount in the tax on industrial loans without harming industry. In fact, if we suppose, for the purpose of demonstration, that the average interest on the provincial debt is three per cent and that the industrial loans rise to ten million (about twenty million less than the province gave as a subsidy to the railways) lent at five per cent, the interest on these loans will be a half-million dollars, of which $300,000 will be given to pay the interest on the public debt, and the rest, $200,000, will be an increase in revenue. They tell us this is how a new state can extract important and permanent resources from its public resources without sacrificing them or diminishing them; this is how the ghost of direct taxation that has haunted our populations so much and for so long will finally be relegated to oblivion and give way to a financial system that will strengthen our provincial institutions. But these considerations are not part of our topic and we do not want to linger over them.

We have also found many people who disapprove, starting with the one who sees rising behind our modest study the hydra of socialism in the form of Louis Blanc. Others have pointed out to us, and their objection is well founded, that we would expose ourselves to great risks by lending, on the guarantee of the State, to inexperienced industrialists. In fact there is no doubt that the lack of technical and industrial experience of our people would be the cause of many errors and failures at first. It is precisely because of this that we insisted on the importance not only of a central polytechnical school, but also of a bureau of industrial research that would help guide the government in its encouragement of industry. Moreover, the state of things people fear would be only temporary. Competence comes quickly when theoretical learning and practical application march abreast. Three or four years are enough to prepare a man for a liberal profession. Why should it take more to prepare young people for a career in industry? Turn public awareness to the side of industry and you will soon have an industrial generation, just as a warrior generation sprang up in Italy after the French victories.

Perhaps the most plausible and also most dangerous objection, since many people make it, and which, if it were true, would topple the edifice we have tried to erect like a house of cards, is this: your idea of industrial loans is useless, and dangerous because it is useless. All ideas and all undertakings that are worth while find capital to support them. If you do not find someone to lend you money, the reason is that your business is of no value or that you yourself are incapable of making it prosper. If we reduce this objection to a syllogism, this is what we will have:

All ideas and all undertakings that are worth while find capital to support them.
Your idea and your undertaking find no capital.
Therefore they are worthless.

Or even:

Every man truly capable of guiding an industrial undertaking finds capital.
You find no capital.
Therefore you are incapable of guiding an industrial undertaking.

This is how a crowd of people reason. These are sophisms that could not stand up to serious examination. If many people repeat them, it is because in all times sophists have been more numerous than philosophers. One of the logical consequences one can draw from similar reasoning is this other syllogism:

Every industrial undertaking needs capital.
Capital distrusts all new experience.
Therefore you may not undertake anything new in industry.

As soon as one persists, especially in a new country like Canada, in defending and proclaiming that the only acceptable and even respectable state of things is one that relies on idly waiting for free capital to be presented or refused, one falls into absurdities such as these. Capital, in the more restricted meaning economists give it, has not always existed. It is not very difficult to return to the origins of industrial capital in each country. Those who would like to do this research will be convinced that, excepting the differences in time and circumstances, there is an analogy between what we are proposing here and what has happened in other countries. By the very nature of things, all countries without exception have been forced to resort to some form of direct or disguised national credit in order to begin the development of their industrial resources. And so our project is not revolutionary; it is as old as industry, because without it, or something similar, the creation of a national industry is impossible.

Without our going too far back in history, Germany provides us with the example of an agricultural people that became an industrial one thanks to the assistance of the authorities. More recently, Hungary has entered the same path. There, by the laws of 1890 and 1899, the favours of the State were granted to a whole group of industrialists, but especially 'to the unions of small industrialists or farmers, who produce goods the raw material for which is found in the country, as well as to all enterprise founded with the goal of raising the domestic industry of a region to a higher level'. These favours consist of tax exemptions, temporary financial aid, and training. This is the system we propose for the Province of Quebec, with this difference: financial aid in Hungary is in the form of subsidies and not loans. A whole group of industries are profiting from it, and in the list we see the making of paper, pulp, wallpaper, and many other products for which we could have almost the monopoly in our country. The Hungarians, who, according to Jean Frollo in a recent article, count for only seven million in a population of twenty million, have thus acquired, in a few years through their own efforts, wealth and influence that have made them the undisputed masters of their country, and even assure them of preponderance in the Austrian Empire. We have already pointed out that Hungary offers more than one analogy with the Province of Quebec. The great reform brought about by this farming people should be a meaningful example to us.

Now, is it true that any idea, any man, or any undertaking with industrial value will find capital to support it? The proposition is false, even for countries where large industry has been established for a long time. The opposite is the general rule, and exceptions are quoted with surprise; and this does not take into account the fate of the great inventors who, for the most part, died in penury, but whose work enriched nations. As far as Canada in particular is concerned, if it were necessary to prove the complete falsehood of this proposition, we could provide even official proofs. All we would need to do would be to quote the works published in the reports of the Bureau of Industries in Ontario, especially the report of 1897. Mr. J. W. Patterson, the author of a series of articles on labour problems published in the *Ottawa Journal*, but with whose ideas we are far from agreeing, describes in an amusing way in his article of August 31 the disappointments of an unfortunate young man who obtained by chance in Canada a loan for industrial purposes. We know that this portrayal of the impossibility of his succeeding in the given situation is not exaggerated, for we ourselves have witnessed similar situations.

But why should we hesitate any longer in refuting what is obviously false? We must view the question from a loftier viewpoint. When it is a matter of creating an industrial movement among a people that up until that time has not devoted itself to industry; when it is a matter of making available and productive one of the greatest industrial resources of the world, which is our heritage, let us be careful not to listen to those who advise us to dispose of it for the mess of pottage that is wage-labour in the service of foreigners. Let us arm ourselves so that we can exploit it ourselves for ourselves and our children. In outlining a system of technical training and industrial loans as the means of reaching this goal, we believe unquestionably that we are right, but our ideas are not unshakeable. We are quite ready to discuss them and defend them, or even to give in to the arguments of better-inspired men. On one point everyone will agree. We must take an active and energetic part in the great industrial struggle that men of experience predict is due shortly, and that will surely come.

13 Olivar Asselin (1874-1937)
Industry in the Economy of French Canada

I was asked to deal with the subject of industry; I trust it will not be contrary to the spirit of this meeting if I do so primarily from a French-Canadian standpoint.

The subject covers various points, some of which, of course, are of common interest to both French and English Canadians, as you will doubtless be aware without my having to stress the fact. But since the economic situation of the two different groups is likely to affect their respective destinies differently, so must there be a difference in their respective economic points of view, as in their history, their political tendencies, their intellectual and moral needs. Besides, I am sure our English fellow-countrymen will tolerate this one-sided approach, if only because such an approach is even more widespread with them; and they may also find, in certain respects, a useful source of emulation in the social content of our particular standpoint. We do not feel, for instance, that they could hold it against us if we, for our part, were to deem it appropriate to adopt – within limitations and after certain necessary adjustments – their own hydro-electric-power policy.

For the past few years, our economic situation has been a source of some concern to most French Canadians. We realize that, although it is not given top priority and must come after certain other matters such as, for example, a certain moral order of things based on religious thinking, its satisfactory solution will none the less have a considerable influence on our political, social, intellectual, and even religious development. That such a solution has not yet been found should certainly be blamed in part on our basic character defect: an inborn individualism that is aggravated by a more or less open, more or less conscious disloyalism encouraged by daily contact with Englishmen and Americans. But there is another reason, namely the shocking lack of public information on the matter. It is easy enough to say 'Let's get rich'. It is no great strain on the intellect and, in this century, it does not require much moral courage

Translated from 'L'Industrie dans l'économie du Canada français', *Semaine sociale du Canada*: 8ème session, St. Hyacinthe, 1928, les Editions Bellarmin, Montreal, 1929, pp. 47-64.

to shout, even from the house-tops, and let our fellow-countrymen know that there is power in well-administered wealth. What we would like to know is: how, by what method? By what method, because the methods we have applied until now have not been too successful, at least collectively speaking. How, because it would be quite easy to prove that certain procedures for acquiring material wealth can very well run parallel to, and even contribute to, a weakening of the noblest sentiments.

So long as our economic organization lacks a general direction capable of crushing individual resistance or of neutralizing its harmful effects, the consequences of the present system can only get worse. But such a general direction will never be followed as long as our leaders continue to hesitate between various incompatible courses of action, and as long as the economic factor is not given its rightful place and is not viewed in proper perspective. And by 'proper perspective' I mean once more from the standpoint of our own interests, subject to their fitting in with the country's over-all interests. It is nonsense to try to subject the whole world to the same laws of economics. It is nonsense again constantly to apply the same economic policies throughout a given country, without taking varying conditions into account. Canada, of all countries, should beware of stereotypes and panaceas in this respect. My contribution to the goodwill shown during the *Semaines sociales* will be a modest one. Yet it may not be altogether futile if all it achieves is to persuade our educators to look elsewhere than in the outmoded manuals of the old liberal school for economic principles for French Canada.

First of all, what is economic independence? Is there any single possible – not to say desirable – ideal? There was a time, perhaps, when frugal habits and unsophisticated material wants enabled certain peoples to remain self-sufficient. Such times are a thing of the past. Nowadays, interdependence is the inevitable rule, and, in order to realize how true this is, we need only look around us: without foreign trade, how could we survive? And since clarity of language is all-important in such matters, allow me to suggest the word 'equality' instead of 'independence'.

Yet whether we call it independence or equality, we all know what we mean. In a survey published by *L'Action canadienne-française* (then called *L'Action française*) on the occasion of the sixtieth anniversary of Confederation – the first survey of its kind to be made in French Canada, to the best of my knowledge – I established the fact that the total wealth of French Canada could not be estimated at more than one-seventh of the country's wealth. Our ancestors, after the Conquest, were not wealthy people; this has been repeated often enough for us to know it. But were the majority of English emigrants any richer when they first came to Canada? And, as compared to them, did we not have the great advantage of a longer history of land ownership to compensate for our lack of funds? I know full well that, carried beyond certain limits, wealth does not make for happiness. I also agree that a more equitable distribution of wealth among its members might be a consolation to a community for its relative poverty. But are we so sure that French Canada enjoys or is trying to establish such a fair distribution? Industrial development in

Quebec, for example, has only just started, and yet it already seems the established rule that we should always have to do the donkey's work and let the English or the Americans rake in the profits. We felt that trade and commerce could wait, while industry could not. And, at the same time as we set up a College of Commerce – and an excellent one at that – we also rushed into selling, and sometimes even giving, to foreigners those of our natural resources that were the easiest to develop, for fear that there be something left of them, perhaps, for the sons of the land to use for themselves by the time they acquired the necessary technical skill and financial means. Should we put this down to simple lack of foresight on the part of democratic governments? Or to a self-interested pursuit of plutocratic goals on the part of members of government?

Anyway, it is difficult to believe that we might ever enjoy economic equality at home, when any group of foreign capitalists that comes along can obtain the legal right, upon payment of a few thousand dollars, to have the map of traditionally French areas dotted all over with names like 'Shawinigan Falls' and 'Riverbend'. The truth of the matter is that, in spite of the undeniable success of certain individuals, we are becoming poorer every day in comparison with English Canada. One of my fellow-countrymen, who is not bereft of culture nor, in many respects, of common sense, but who unfortunately is apt to see no farther than his own immediate interests, was recently heard to state proudly in my presence that the Banque Canadienne Nationale's assets today were equal to those of the Bank of Montreal thirty years ago. He would have been less boastful had he taken the trouble to find out that the total assets of the Bank of Montreal, the Royal Bank, and the Canadian Bank of Commerce are today, in 1928, fifteen times as great as the combined assets of the Banque Canadienne and the Banque Provinciale. Of course we have progressed, for how could we have remained completely stationary? But meanwhile the others were progressing twice as fast. Is this to say that we should give up the struggle? Is it all we can do, if we want at least to save face, to lick our wounds like the wounded wolf

> *that silently suffers his death-pangs*
> *And snaps at the knife with bleeding fangs?*

Quebec is the only place in America where concessions for public utilities – public transportation, gas, and electricity, etc. – are granted by a French-speaking government or French-speaking municipalities. It is, therefore, the only province where we might have tried to take over the management of such utilities ourselves. Yet, in spite of certain notable achievements such as the organization of public transportation in Montreal, we were left out for several reasons. The rapid growth of big cities – at a time when we had only enough capital for the trams of Detroit! – required financial resources and technical skills that we then lacked. We could have obtained foreign loans, but it so happens that enterprise – that prime quality of a great contractor, which had guaranteed the success of the Canadian Pacific Company – seemed in those days to be the almost exclusive prerogative of crooks. Our failure can also be partly blamed on a government whose members, through personal interest, sheer stupidity, or otherwise, seem to have done their utmost to avoid having these utilities come under our management, with the result that today, short of a miracle such as is never likely to happen under democratic (not to say plutocratic) governments, the public utilities in French Canada are definitely outside our control – apart from some small benefits some of the shrewdest among us might be able to draw through political or personal connections. There is no question of confiscation: the only respectable thing left for one to do after one has sold one's land – that is, the use of one's roads, streets, and public property – for a mess of pottage is to honour the contract. But we still have the right to set the rates so as not to become the victims of our own concessions. The chief English users, who, like us, pay as much as thirty-five and forty dollars per horsepower of industrial energy produced for twenty and twenty-five dollars in Ontario, would be the first to acknowledge this right. The indifference of our government or of its so-called control commissions to the orgies of over-capitalization that have prevailed in recent years is a downright betrayal of public interest.

As joint owners of the State railway system, it is mainly to our second-class-citizen apathy that we owe the fact that, even in our own province, we are practically excluded from sharing in the profits of its management and operation. We would therefore do well to think carefully before allowing this invaluable asset to be given over to a company that tomorrow is likely to be run on American capital, if it is not already. State monopoly certainly has its serious drawbacks. But are these worse than the corruption that the railway companies have been fostering in the legislative branch of government since 1870? Apart from such ethical considerations, we should be twice as eager for national independence if the latter were to coincide with the economic interests of French Canada.

Is there ever likely to be any economic equality among us as long as in our own Province of Quebec the very sources of industrial energy fall completely outside our influence? One cannot call the meagre shareholdings of the small fry that merely serve to back up the financial speculations of a handful of powerful profiteers joint ownership. We just get our two per cent. The others periodically collect their millions through the creation and resale of branch companies, the purchase and sale of independent firms, the conversion of bonds needlessly issued to the detriment of the public patrimony. Our public servants, who until about 1906 permanently and quasi-gratuitously alienated our water-power resources, must have been either stupid fools or sordid rascals. Those who have since farmed out the left-overs to the same holders without demanding, in just return, a time limitation on the previously conceded rights have not shown much more national pride than their predecessors. Must we continue eternally to suffer the consequences of such mistakes, or should we say such crimes? Possibly not. At one fell swoop the Shawinigan concessions on the St. Maurice were more than doubled. But Carillon, if it is to be retained as provincial property, would give us a trump card. The total amount of power to be produced within fifty years' time, as it is estimated today, will prove insufficient in the next twenty-five years.

We should make the most of our right to levy taxes and control rates; set a higher price on government concessions that are sold to those hydro-power companies, which are needed practically everywhere; and prevent artificial increases in capitalization. We should curtail all new concessions so long as the original concessionnaires do not urgently require them, and then turn round and tell them: 'Gentlemen, we wish to be fair with you; but we ask in return that you be just and fair toward the people whose property has made you fabulously rich. If you surrender all of your concessions to the Crown, you will be granted a new one for seventy-five years, or a century; moreover, on condition that we have strict control over your financial operations, your accounts, your rates, we shall extend this new concession to all still-available power-sites. At the end of the lease, everything will be returned to the State, according to the percentage of capital remaining to be amortized, under special conditions to be determined by a board of auditors to be set up as an integral part of the new plan as soon as the latter comes into force.' This may sound utopian. Upon reflection, however, it is not, since, first of all, no board of directors' planning in private enterprise ever extends over more than a century; second, in order to amortize, over seventy-five or one hundred years, capital bearing interest at five per cent, a total annuity of only 0·05132161 or 0·05038314 would be necessary; finally, people would be only too happy to wait a century to come into the sort of fortune that was unheard of in the past, except in legendary El Dorados. To be our own masters in a hundred years' time or to remain perpetual slaves: such is the choice to be made. There is no alternative.

Summing up: as landowners, there are hundreds of ways in which we can make our land more productive, and only indolence, inconsistency, physical and mental laziness can deter us from our purpose. Home industries can improve the comfort and well-being of thousands of homes. Deep-sea fishing, like agriculture, could be made much more profitable. With more advanced technology and a gradual expansion of our sources of credit we could, if we wanted, raise ourselves to the same standard as our English countrymen in light and medium industry. In heavy industries, with some strenuous efforts and expert planning, we could conquer, if not outstanding, at least satisfactory positions in every field – except perhaps in metallurgy, shipping, the automobile industry, and probably (alas!) the aircraft industry.

But it goes without saying and need not be over-emphasized that such results will necessitate a deep transformation in our public spirit, a general pooling of all our energies, a loyal and intelligent devotion on the part of government to the cause of the governed. It is not through slavish imitation of our English colleagues that we shall make good the tremendous lead they have over us, but through a proper use of those means that are best suited to our purpose. We should, if necessary, change our banking system. Should the processing of crops require special long-term credits, we should be the ones to administer such credits for ourselves. Should agencies be needed for the granting of special funds for our fisheries, we should create them. If they were properly run, our credit unions could be a tremendous asset: instead of letting them survive as best they can under the jealous and not always benevolent patronage of the discount banks, we should try to secure competent management for them. Our commercial schools keep on producing, year in and year out, hundreds of would-be book-keepers, all of them built on the same English standard: it would require only a very few additions to the curriculum for those graduates to come out with a better training. We should organize special courses on agriculture. Elementary schools should be equipped with separate primers for the fisherman's son or the farmer's son. The teaching of economics in our universities should be more nationally orientated and better centred on our own interests. On a political level, those who find that it pays to betray the nation, whether their purpose is calculated or not, should not be allowed to falsify their statements in order to disguise their shady deals. Whatever the dangers of nationalization, it should be applied without hesitation if no other measure can break the bonds of slavery. If it has proved possible to nationalize that most corruptible of trades, the liquor trade, and the measure, though not really indispensable, was found to be generally acceptable, one cannot very well pretend that the government control of hydro-electric power could not, without causing too great a stir, be beneficial to the majority, as has been the highly successful experience in Ontario. It has been aptly advocated that a high commission for economic research be set up by the State: but why should not some millionaire make us a present of such an institution, in the sort of altruistic spirit in which our national problems should be tackled? We should be able to blend strong idealism with strong realism. In a word, there should be less talk and more action. After one hundred and seventy-five years of gradual and sometimes imperceptible slipping back into an inferior position, with the risk of reaching a point of no return if we relinquish all our natural resources into foreign hands, we should now be able to show the world that there is at least one thing we have acquired that we so sadly lacked in the past: the instinct of preservation.

14 Canon Lionel Groulx (1878-1967)
If Dollard Were Alive Today

Ladies and Gentlemen:
You all know this beautiful tale of heroic youth.

For over twenty years a savage terror has paralysed New France. The foremost power in Europe allows itself to be insulted and held in check by a handful of Indians. Tribe after tribe the Huron nation, ally to the French, has been destroyed by these barbarians; they have murdered fur-traders, blocked trade routes, martyred missionaries: and still France has not moved. They have even pursued the fugitive Hurons as far as the Ile d'Orléans and, in defiance of the Fort's cannons, paraded their human trophies right in front of Quebec. Surreptitiously their small bands spread throughout the colony's lands: women and children are kidnapped, men are scalped in their fields or taken away to a fiery death in distant villages. And still France does not move.

In vain the colony appeals for help in its distress. A series of over ten embassies produces no result. In 1642 and later in 1644, Richelieu and the Queen Regent condescend to send forty, then sixty soldiers.

We are now in the year 1659. Emboldened by the weakness of a colony that seems unable to defend itself, the Iroquois nation has resolved on a final attack. In the spring of 1660 an army of twelve hundred warriors is to assemble at *la Roche-Fendue*, near Ville-Marie, move quickly from there to destroy the post at Quebec, and then fall back upon Trois-Rivières and Ville-Marie.[1]

The colony, when it hears the news, is gripped by panic. In Quebec the Blessed Sacrament is exposed and processions are organized. On May 19 Mgr de Laval has the Eucharistic species removed from the parish church and monastery chapels. On the bishop's orders Ursulines and Nursing Sisters evacuate their convents to take refuge in the stronger Jesuit House. Terrified settlers arrive from the surrounding region and from as far afield as Ste-Anne-de-Beaupré to seek refuge with the Jesuits or within the Fort. In the terror-

---

Translated from 'Si Dollard Revenait...', an address delivered at the Monument National (Montreal), January 31, 1919, and published in *Dix Ans d'Action Française*, Bibliothèque de l'Action Française, Montreal, 1926, pp. 89–122.

stricken little town, sentries patrol endlessly back and forth, and the nights are filled with their solemn challenge: 'Who goes there?'

No longer does any doubt seem possible. For the majority this is the end of New France. The bravest are exhausted, can no longer bear the horrible nightmare. They talk of sending for French ships to take all the settlers home. Others wonder in anguish whether there will be any survivors to carry the sad news to the Old Country. Only a small group of confident men still believe, in spite of everything, in the future of the colony and look to heaven for a saviour to appear.

The saviour appeared.

He was twenty-five years old. He was the commanding officer of the garrison at Fort Ville-Marie. A precocious hero, marked early for greatness. Having arrived in Canada at the age of twenty-two in 1657 it seems, he had taken up his post at Ville-Marie, the colony's western outpost and most dangerous point. And there, at the Fort, he acquired the confidence of his superior, a hero and saint called Chomedey de Maisonneuve, and the intimate friendship of another such man, called Lambert Closse.

In the mystic and military colony of Mont-Royal, the exaltation of generosity spread contagiously. Of those men, who prayed while clearing the land with their muskets always within reach, who took communion every day, and who volunteered their services as soldiers of the Virgin in constant expectation of death, not one was beneath heroism. One day, when one of them was reproached for exposing himself too much, Major Closse (for it was he) replied in his characteristic, impatient way: 'Sirs: the only reason I have come here is to die for God, in the service of arms; and were I to be assured that I should not die for Him, I should leave this country and serve against the Turks, so as not to be deprived of that glory.'

In this atmosphere Dollard[2] lived for three years, and within him there occurred a mysterious, supernatural germination: each day the spirit of heroism grew stronger and purer in his soul. The enthusiasm of his youth made him dream of ever more daring exploits, of ever more sublime sacrifices. He was in the full grip of these exalting sentiments when he heard the news of the Iroquois invasion. Around him everyone was wondering how to dispel the terrible threat. The time of half-measures and half-sacrifices was past. Now was the decisive moment. The men at Ville-Marie, far-flung sentries, soldiers at the foremost front, had no right to hesitate. They had to strike boldly to stop the invader, or lie down to die amid the ruins of their colony.

During his tour of inspection around the Fort at night, when the danger was always greatest, the young Dollard no doubt meditated over this tragic alternative. He was the commanding officer of the Ville-Marie garrison. As a leader he had to set an example; more than others he was obliged to give of his own person: and he fully understood the extent of a soldier's sacrifice. But was it worth it – this embryonic colony, this nation still at its very beginnings – was it worth such a holocaust? And Dollard listened to the murmur of nature, the unbounded nature that surrounded him. Beyond the bastions of Pointe-à-Callières he could hear the solemn crash of the Saint-Louis Falls and the rustling of the virgin forest. What appealed to the hero was the mysterious, throbbing life of a world still latent. Beyond the mountain that hid the setting sun every evening, the young man scanned in his mind the immensity of this country waiting to be awakened from its sleep. Farther still, past the 'fresh water seas', there arose above the smouldering ruins of devastated Indian villages the ghosts of the martyrs. They too called out to the hero. He could hear them saying: 'Come, child of our race and faith; here we lie down that others might live. Come, in blood are prayer and redemption: ever since Calvary this rosy dew has been the essential source of all great futures.' Then the young man turned inward once more, and heard the voice of his soul, the soul of a volunteer for the Holy Virgin, a soul inhabited in his daily communions by Christ, the sublime recruiter of sacrifice. Dollard's dream came to an end, his martyr's determination firmly established. From the depths of his soul and from the heart of the great virgin forest an urgent, mingled voice arose, crying out to him: 'Go, young commander of Ville-Marie, be the hero of our delivery, if necessary, its martyr.'

He needed companions: he started to recruit them. He had only to show himself and to speak in order to gain followers. Sixteen heroes volunteered. So as to be free to give their lives, some of them made their wills and gave away their goods. Then, one morning in April 1660, in the humble chapel of the Hôtel-Dieu, a vigil of arms came to an end. The sixteen, with Dollard as their leader, attended their last mass, received communion, and left.

They had hardly left the shore when a first misfortune befell them. Three of their number were killed in an ambush. They returned to Ville-Marie. Very simply they buried their dead; new recruits filled the vacancies; and the company of heroes set off again on their way to sacrifice.

Their plan was a very simple one. A large number of Iroquois who had spent the winter hunting north of the Ottawa would soon be returning along this route. Their plan was to go out, meet the invaders, block their way for a time, and inflict such staggering losses on them that the enemy would be terror-stricken and turn back. You know how they carried out this plan. On the first of May they were at the foot of Long Sault. The invaders arrived. Three hundred Iroquois decided that their number was not great enough to do battle with the pious defenders of the little fort. In all haste messengers were dispatched to the Richelieu Islands to summon the advance guard of the invading forces gathering there. Soon there were eight hundred barbarians attacking the Frenchmen's palisades. The siege lasted eight days. The besieged fought and prayed; a few Hurons came to their help only to betray them later. During the last supreme assault, the Frenchmen fought with both hands, with swords and pistols, 'a sword in the right hand and a knife in the left', as Dollier de Casson tells us. Dollard was one of the last to succumb, and after his death the three or four survivors kept to the end, like their leader and like all sixteen, the heroic resolve to ask no quarter.

You know the rest. At the end of the struggle the Iroquois counted their dead. They were filled with stupefaction. Horrified, they said to themselves, according to the report of the deserting Hurons: 'If seventeen Frenchmen, with a miserable hut found by chance as their only defence, have managed to kill so many of our warriors, how should we fare if we went to attack men of such courage when they were gathered in stone houses fortified especially for their defence? It would be pure folly: we should all perish. Therefore, let us withdraw and make our way back to our villages.'

The colony was saved. There was astonishment in Quebec. Everyone wondered what had happened to the army of invaders. Meanwhile, on the wild shores of the Ottawa, the wind scattered the ashes of their saviours, and with the thunder of Long Sault was mingled the hymn of a new epic.

'We must give glory,' the *Relation* said soon afterward, 'to these seventeen Frenchmen of Montreal, and honour their ashes with the praise that is their just due.... Everything would have been lost had they not perished: their tragedy saved the country.'

The Option

If Dollard were alive today. . . . What a scandal, what a startling anachronism the man would be, a knight of holy courage and sacrifice, in our age of fear and pragmatism! And yet it is a hypothesis worth considering for the timely and important lessons we can gain from it.

It seems to me that if Dollard were alive today and wishing to use his life, as he did long ago, in the most noble and perfect way, he would begin by accommodating himself to the realities of his environment. His first action would then be to choose his homeland, and he would opt for Canada, his natural country. Have you ever thought that at the very beginning of his sacrifice, he was obliged to face this initial option? Nothing forced him to go as far as death. And no one does so without a motive strong enough to dictate such devotion. If Dollard chose to die for New France, it was doubtless because it appeared to him to be an extension of the old France; and because, too, he already loved it as much as a native country; because he saw in it the country his ardent youth had elected, a country that would claim his thought and his work and be the perpetual resting-place of his bones. Recent documents appear to confirm this: the hero had decided to settle here; he had taken a grant of land and had even started to clear it. There can be no doubt that the reason for Dollard's sacrifice was his love for New France and his precise, definite decision to choose it for his country.

Does not this view of the hero's psychology explain why devotion to one's country is so rare among us? To devote oneself to a country requires a belief in it, an option for it. And how can we fail to think of all those who have not yet made their choice, even among us, the oldest inhabitants of this country? How many go through their entire lives without ever having acted for patriotic reasons? Alas! We could almost believe our minds and hearts radically emptied of those thoughts and sentiments to which men usually cling until the very end. In the weary and sceptical Old World, men who have rejected the old rules of Christianity develop an unshakeable conviction in the idea of the mother country and the morality of patriotism: it is the standard by which they scrupulously judge all their acts; in our young country and in our society of French Catholics who posit the morality of the Gospels as a sovereign and universal way of life, we can lead a life in which we are unaware of, or quietly ignore, the most natural duties!

An imprudent break with history and the past, the nefarious influence of those who wish to uproot our entire nation, and, above all, political and moral colonialism: these are the causes for the almost complete annihilation of national feeling in our people. And once uprooted, we have certainly had our share of artificial countries foisted upon us. In less than a hundred years, how many attempts have been made to attach us through political or sentimental ties either to our southern neighbours or to the two nations of Europe so devoutly called 'our two mother-countries'. And with what paltry results! These absurd attempts may have prompted some ephemeral enthusiasms, or inspired a few pseudo-expatriates, who elevate love of exotic things to the level of a religion, who prefer other countries to their own and strangers to their brothers. But a closer look shows that, on the whole, our people have found no response in their souls for these chimerical appeals: they have not been strengthened in the only patriotism that is natural and logical for them, the love of Canada. And the reason for it is that no patriotism can be formed against geography and against history; nor is it within the power of politics to change either a people's history or the land beneath their feet.

Such a mutilation of our conscience nevertheless contains grave dangers. It severs us from a whole group of superior motives. It allows collaboration in public life to be governed solely by selfish interests. Perhaps it would also help to explain the easy substitution of loyalty to a party for loyalty to a country, and the substitution of a political, for a national, spirit.

Our generation, because it has to bear it, can judge how heavy is the heritage of these misguided policies. The most generous effort, the most urgent initiative, can barely find support in the popular conscience. Worse still: at times it almost seems as if our nation has lost its instinct for preservation. Despite all the work done in recent years, and the new awakening, are there not still many signs to warn us that the fraternity of patriotism is not yet strong enough to unite us or to force upon us a liberating decisiveness?

If Dollard were alive, how ardently, how forcefully, how convincingly he would argue for the patriotic option! He who needed only three years in New France to adopt it as his country, would he not plead with us in the most eloquent and urgent terms? Willing to give the same devotion as in the past, he would justify his actions on the basis of his friendship for the country and his analysis of the past.

This Dollard of 1919, a patriot by instinct and conviction, would have more or less these words to say to us:

'Yes, we have a country, and, indeed, only one. Mgr Pâquet has said, following Saint Thomas, that one's country is the land where one is born and grows up. And the land where we were born and grew up is, until further notice, Canada. Three hundred years of residence in this part of North America; the right that falls to the first occupant, the first missionary, the first settler; a strong settlement in all provinces: these are the reasons for which the French race can rightly claim to consider the whole of Canada as its country.'

But in the large country, we in Quebec have a smaller country, our French province. The land between Montreal and Tadoussac was, for a long time, the cradle and hearthstone of our race. And in this space, more or less, we were confined after the Conquest; on this territory we lived, suffered, grew, we developed our institutions and our ethnic character. Here, in a word, we placed for ever our French imprint. And it is the autonomy of this State as well as its national particularism that was recognized in the federal pact of 1867. What is there still lacking for us to feel attached to this land and to determine to stay here at home?

Dollard would then turn, and with no vain fears, to an examination of our past. 'True patriotism,' Fustel de Coulanges once wrote, 'is not love of the land, it is love of the past, respect for the generations that have preceded us.' I have no doubt that, in this respect as well, Dollard would find enough reasons for pride to confound the uprooted. He would be unimpressed by those misunderstandings that are caused by ignorance of our national heritage.

Because we cannot claim to have twenty centuries of history behind us, because, having been pioneers and labourers, we have written no epic but that of the plough, because on our foreheads shines the stamp of virtue rather than the immortal laurels, there are many aesthetes and *parvenus* who turn with immense condescension from our people, considering it merely an inferior branch of the French family.

Dollard would not let himself be dismayed by such superficial views. The first task he would undertake would be to look for himself at this history that is so often despised through sheer ignorance. There would be no need for him to delve into all the branches or corners of history: general impressions and main outlines would soon be enough to reassure his patriotism and stimulate ours. 'It is true,' he would say, 'that we are not a very ancient race, and that there are many laurels still missing from our young forehead. But, scornful expatriates, is it to be counted for nothing that a mere handful of Frenchmen were able to explore and Christianize three-quarters of a continent larger than Europe, that they were able to leave durable memories of France throughout America, and that, having been masters of this territory for a century, they left it, in the end, only as the result of an epic military struggle, wearily dropping their flags grown too heavy with victories?

'You will perhaps add to this initial merit that of having withstood a fantastic pressure for assimilation, no small merit for the 65,000 Frenchmen who made up our nation in 1760; and of having continued during the last hundred and fifty years our normal and regular development, always pushing forward, marking with steeples our conquest of the soil, seizing the rights of the conqueror and forcing him to respect ours, retaining our Christian and French qualities, our language, our faith, our customs, all the elements of our diversity, remaining, finally, in the middle of an immense Anglo-Saxon ocean, an untouchable island built of Catholic and Latin granite. And yet, this is indeed our immortal history,' Dollard would cry out, 'and let richer nations despise it if they will. But when even strangers call it a *miracle*, is that not enough to satisfy the most exacting pride? And have the founders of our race not deserved something better than repudiation by their sons?' Then Dollard would conclude, at the risk of completely offending those who would advocate uprooting our nation and adopting foreign ways: 'Were we the last branch of the French race in the world, and dependent only upon ourselves for our survival, I would still not hesitate to proclaim it: our past, our honour, our spiritual heritage, the human value represented by our ancestors, each of these by itself is sufficient motive for us not to give up our right to live.'

So Dollard would speak. And having laid this solid foundation for his new patriotic option, he would once again call for volunteers to serve the country. Is it not your duty to listen to him? And is he not already the young leader who is listened to and followed? A generation has arisen that we would call, with Barrès, 'the promotion of hope', and that carries bound to its heart the entire history of our race. Do not speak to them of those diminished men who carry nothing of the past within themselves and appear denuded simply because they are their own beginning. To this generation, it seems completely obvious that one should lead a life supported by one's ancestral land, in close contact with the race from which one has sprung, within the family of its living and its dead. These young people have not, on that account, renounced all culture or all forms of superiority. Look at some of their leaders. Their talent is an honour to the causes they serve: they represent an élite level that we have not yet reached. There is, however, a difference between them and their elders, which is, that whereas culture used to uproot people, now it strengthens their roots. Whatever may be said about them, these young men are not aspiring to intellectual independence – no one could be more willing to pay due respect to the culture of France; but they are also convinced that we must maintain a free attitude toward that country. The best kind of homage to give her, they seem to say, is to ask of her not a despotic rule that tears us away from ourselves, but generous inspiration, appropriate to the free development of our own personality. And, contrary to what certain people would strive to make us believe, this does not mean closing one's mind, refusing to see universal beauty and truth, or being fanatically enamoured of the beauty and truth of one's country and no other; but it does mean loving and serving truth and beauty *in* one's own country, seeing all things as they are reflected in one's own soul, and believing in the superiority of original work over pastiche.

This is what constitutes the strength of the present generation. Through it, traditional forces, supported and directed by the best powers of the spirit, will once more move and guide us. In this quarrel between our Ancients and our Moderns, we could have been worried that progress would not be sufficiently inspired by tradition, or that it would be the mere novelty of youth, hazardous and anarchical. Thank heavens, today it is the young who are old. It is the young who return to the past, however forgotten or hidden, who go over the heads of their fathers to renew historical continuity with their ancestors.

The Duty of the Elite

If Dollard were alive today, he would applaud this rebirth and become its prime instigator. His brief life teaches us that he believed in the special duties of the élite. If he was the first to think of the sacrifice at Long Sault, it was because *noblesse oblige*: he was the commanding officer in a garrison of soldiers. He called upon an élite to share his heroic adventure. The sixteen companions at Pointe-à-Callières were the flower of the day's youth. They were all, except two, young men not yet thirty.

For Dollard, the duty of the élite was the most complete and absolute duty possible: it went as far as total immolation of the person and his life. Of the men who pledged their devotion to New France, some gave away their goods, and one of the first seventeen, Blaise Juillet, had a wife and four children; moreover, they made an oath never to surrender, for they would choose only death or victory. 'M. Dollard,' said Sister Bourgeoys, 'is gathering sixteen or seventeen *of the most generous* men to attack the Indians, *with the intention of giving their lives if such should be the will of God.*'[3]

If Dollard were alive today, we can be sure that he would take up his role as leader of the élite and remind it of its solemn duty. No longer would he hear, as long ago on the bastions of Pointe-à-Callières, the confused appeal of a race still to be born, but the anxious, trembling voice of a people dispersed in all parts of the continent and conscious of the old barbarous coalition closing upon it once again. Dollard would also hear that other and more remote voice, the solemn, troubling voice of the innumerable dead, the voice of our country mingled with that of our racial instincts, a voice that rises within us at the most tragic moments and pursues us into the very silence of our studies to call us to the defence of our nation.

At the sound of this voice Dollard would go into the city as he did once before, calling thoughtful and ardent youths to the supreme sacrifice, for what he could call, like Péguy, 'the eternal salvation of our race'.

Could the élite escape this imperious call? Dollard would summon it, not to die, but to serve in the name of its high responsibilities. 'Dying for a cause,' he would say with Ozanam, 'is very brief. True human dignity, which is long and endures, consists in working and suffering until the very end of life.' After all, the élite is an élite only in order to devote itself. Its reputation and dignity derive solely from the nobility of that which it sacrifices. Just as, on the material level, wealth acquires through Divine Will a kind of social destiny, so, on the spiritual level, there must be a part set aside for the poor. No one is given intelligence or generosity for himself alone: those who are wealthy in their mind or heart must administer their superfluity for the profit of God and country. 'Whoever has received from Divine Providence a greater abundance either of exterior, bodily goods or of spiritual goods,' Leo XIII teaches, 'has received them for the purpose of perfecting himself and, as an agent of Providence, relieving others.' (*Rerum novarum.*)

Wherever an élite exists nowadays, it no longer has the right to conceal itself. Ollé-Laprune has written: 'There is no life in which it is not necessary, at some time and on some matter, to do more than is required by strict duty. Similarly, in the life of nations, there are more serious moments when the élite, at very least, must transcend mere duty.'

Our happiness and our hope lie in the fact that already among us mere duty has been transcended. Here I am thinking of a conquering élite: people who have been forming themselves, over the past fifteen years, into small study-groups, striving through great labour and prayer to enrich their minds and their hearts with lucid truths and great incentives. In order to be of their time and race, they closely link their will for the future with the cult of the past; in their favour they have youth, organized strength, ardent enthusiasm, the glorious promise of a radiant dawn; they call themselves L'Association Catholique de la Jeunesse Canadienne-française.

I am also thinking of that other élite in the thick of life, an élite of brave and proud crusaders whom one meets everywhere, carrying a good book or a propaganda pamphlet, valiantly spreading the words of faith, apostles of the Sacred Heart, displaying His picture in hotels, striving against alcohol and blasphemy, speaking French and making others speak it as well, an élite that originated in Ville Saint-Martin and is called L'Association des Cercles Catholiques des Voyageurs de Commerce.

And there are other élites doing similar work in other fields. Is it not true that we live at a magnificent time when there is work for everyone? If, here in our country, there ever was a time when men who wished to lead great and beautiful lives looked in vain for practical ways of doing so, for actions that would be sufficiently wide in scope to allow the personality and integrity of their dream to develop unhindered, then thank God, such a time seems irrevocably past. Today, in this French-Canadian country bursting with new inspiration, we are no longer reduced to the mere service of men or parties. Thanks to the new programs and new frameworks being constructed, the services of both humble and great are called forth by the most worthy causes of man: the soul of a race and its past, culture, and faith.

Shall I add that they call in particular upon our intellectual élite? It is to this élite, it seems to me, that Dollard, wishing to equip himself with the best means of action, would have liked to belong. He would have chosen to be among us that fine kind of Latin soldier, cultured and vibrant, that has been described somewhere by René Bazin. For this intellectual élite is the one that must, more than others, fulfil great hopes and accept great duties. 'Nowadays,' Léon Ollé-Laprune also writes, 'the great are those who *think* or claim to think, those who speak and those who write.'

'Politicians have lost their panache,' a young writer, Guy Vanier, has said. The phrase has been a great success because it corresponds to an undeniable fact. The gods are disappearing, unattended by last rites or funeral orations; and, although we have not repudiated political action because it is still necessary, we are now giving it its proper place, which is not in the first rank. A few of our political personalities still retain some influence, or even quite a lot, but this is no longer due to the mere office that they hold as deputies or ministers, to some sort of magical prestige with which the public invested Members of Parliament or speakers on the hustings; they manage to escape the general disfavour only because of their superior culture, greater dignity of character and more generous estimate of their duties and of national affairs. Others who are unwilling to rise to this level will increasingly come to represent an inferior type, overwhelmed by the magnitude of future tasks. Politicians are on their way out: only policies will remain.

But, as some of you will think, it is not enough to shake off the old servitude and stop our ears against the 'verbal mechanics'. We must give the public the enlightenment and firm guidance that it failed to receive from the degenerate descendants of our first parliamentarians. It seems to me that, at this very moment, our race awaits a word, a great word full of clarity and strength to lead us all together into a great future. Precise directions are required from our intellectuals. We ask them to give us, above all, that spirit that Auguste Comte called 'the spirit of cohesion', and that is no more than the subordination of individual problems to an over-all view. We have been so divided and subdivided by political rivalries; so little prepared for social responsibilities by our atavistic sense of history; and our energies so scattered into various anarchical directions by our long lack of leadership! More than ever, we need to use and to co-ordinate our resources, to raise our material and spiritual energies to their point of greatest production, since this is our only way of standing up to the overwhelming superiority of our rivals. Shall I be more precise? I would add: it is not enough to become all excited, today about colonization, tomorrow about public education, the day after – or yesterday – about credit unions, labour problems, or economic organization, thus dissipating our efforts on one thing and another, and sharing every enthusiasm, every passing whim. What is needed most urgently is to make a scattered and intermittent effort continuous and unanimous; to establish firmly, in our next work of construction, the relation of the parts to the whole; to ensure balance and good proportion in all things, so that the structure of our country may rise at last in solid strength and beauty.

This unification and orientation of our labours must begin without delay, for we must be saved, we can wait no longer. Post-war preoccupations press utilitarian goals strongly upon us. The desire to recapture lost ground, to move rapidly and catch up with our competitors, pushes us toward the development of technical education and toward men of hasty achievements. At the same time, restraint not being the strong point of young people, we are moving toward an ideological crisis, toward contempt for the higher speculative disciplines. And what imposes itself at this very point is once again the role that must be taken by liberal youth – by 'liberal' I mean of humanist and classical culture. It must intervene courageously to prevent what may be a disaster. Nothing is as legitimate as a desire for practical ends and prompt results; and we still have a great deal to achieve in this respect. But it would be an irreparable mistake to forget that practical things are always dependent upon theory to sustain and develop them, and that, as material research and development become more important, a country needs to provide itself with a greater fund of spiritual and idealistic values; another mistake would be to relegate moral forces to a secondary position for pragmatic reasons and thus prevent the flourishing of aesthetic faculties in a people whose superiority must, by the imperative of its destiny, be in the intellectual field. As you can see, the time is a decisive one, and the task immense. If those who keep watch for us are unable or too fearful to sound the warning, our generation may take the wrong path, with no possibility of turning back, and our race compromise for ever the very essence of its originality, the spiritual qualities deriving from the Latin race.

At what cost and with what sacrifices will these watchers fulfil their duty? Are they aware that they will have to start by imposing a kind of intellectual asceticism upon themselves? Georges Goyau reminded us of it recently in his preface to a beautiful book: 'At the root of every fruitful action there lies, indispensably, an ascetic effort.'[4] An effort that first asserts itself in the leader's long preparation. Merely by desiring it, a person cannot assume the august and formidable authority of leadership. Only he who possesses truth, absolute truth, can claim it. There is a definite interrelationship among the orders: the economic, the social, and the moral orders depend upon the intellectual. And whoever cares to examine the matter closely will see that there have been deviations in the existence of nations and catastrophes in their history simply because one day they were led into error by ignorance, or into falsehood by cynical bad faith. Is not the present spectacle of the world enough to make vigilant people take heed of the way doctrines are linked and have implacable repercussions? During the past four years nations have been crazed with mirages of unbridled democracy; they have occasionally been summoned, under the pretext of being emancipated, to extremes of revolution. These inflammable doctrines are transmitted from the highest tribunals to the masses, already in ferment and irritated by the sufferings of war; and behold: impatient, embittered nations rise up and apply them with shattering logic and rapidity. A revolutionary blaze threatens the whole of Europe, and even here across the ocean we feel its sparks falling upon us.

Let us hope that this spectacle will prove enlightening to those among us who advocate rash reform without seeing that we undermine the principle itself when we undermine the things that support it, and that we are never too cautious in protecting the sacred foundations of families and the religious potential of a country.

The leading élite must also practise intellectual asceticism in the austere choice and acceptance of its work. What cowardice it would be in this case to sacrifice the slightest thing to whim or personal preference! In these dire times it is impossible for those of the élite to fulfil their mission and at the same time look for mere aesthetic pleasure or enchanting pastimes in their studies. On the contrary, they would be summoned imperatively by Dollard to give their entire life, to give all their desire to be useful. 1660 is past, he would say, and with it the time for the adventure of a heroic moment, the hero's exalted bid for glory. We are now at 'solitary posts' for our entire existence. No mistakes, for they would be irreparable. Intermittent efforts are not enough to stem fatal trends and enlighten one's era: isolated and occasional work is not enough. The intellectual élite will fulfil its entire duty and save the future of our French race only if it accepts long periods of seclusion and indefatigable labour. Ready to assume power, it must also secure the co-operation of workers in the spiritual field; must hold itself so high as to renounce all honours, wealth, the favours of the great, in order to retain the right of serving truth; it must, in a word, love its country and the commandments of its faith to the extent of becoming, in the near future, an élite of sacrifice.

If it does so, with what great hopes will its effort be sustained! Even in this life, sacrifice multiplies devotion. See what magnetic force it lent Dollard, the young leader who summoned twenty youths to die. Only on this condition will our young masters compel followers. A cause is always attractive when its leaders have decided to put their very lives into it. And the fecundity of sacrifice greatly transcends the life of the sacrificed. When Dollard fell with his companions, it would have been possible at first to think it was a fatal decimation, the shattering of a great promise. Ville-Marie was shorn of its heroes. After the first moment of gratitude and remembrance, such a lead weight of oblivion fell upon this memory that the work must have seemed lost in the holocaust. Not a line, not a word remained of the glorious fallen. Yet a century and a half later, behold, he lives again; more alive than ever, he takes his place amongst our teachers of heroism. The young commander Dollard will soon be given his true name: one of the first masters of our youth.

Efficient Action

The fecundity of sacrifice nevertheless requires one condition. Man's sacrifice means very little if it is not infused with divine ferment and thus elevated to a supernatural level.

Dollard had understood this truth, for he wished to incorporate into his sacrifice and that of his companions the most noble of spiritual elements. You will recall the vigil of arms, the mass in the little chapel of Ville-Marie, where, under the gaze of their mothers, their sisters, their fiancées, under the gaze of their fathers and friends, amidst the sound of muffled sobs, seventeen young men who had taken communion and were going to their death allowed a prayer to form in their breast, which must have been similar to this one: 'O God of the host and of New France, O God who art in our hearts as thou art in heaven, we stand here before you, Dollard's small company, we who are going to die for our country. We have made this decision because we believe in the effectiveness of sacrifice united to yours, because with our death you will create the future. We leave everything behind us: our sisters, our mothers, grief and tears. But you have told us, O Master, that the grain dying in the earth generates a new and infinite vitality. . . .' So they prayed, these brave children; and while this prayer was springing in their hearts, the priest at the altar took their sacrifice in his trembling hands and united it with that of God. And you know how much sprang from this wonderful union.

If Dollard were alive today, he would still require from companions ready to follow him this infusion of the supernatural into their human effort. He would tell them: 'If you are sincere and want results, if you are unwilling to lose, through your own fault, through some voluntary deficit, even the smallest part of the returns from your action, then first have the loyalty to give this action all the conditions of power.'

Faith reveals to us moving realities, which we cannot afford to ignore. We need, as they say nowadays, a mystique for our actions. This mystique must not be simply a positive, exterior application, a mere show of mechanical activity. It must proceed from a powerful, interior psychological characteristic. It must be supported by a doctrine of charity and truth to give it enthusiasm and constancy, as well as the greatest possible effectiveness.

Today Dollard would urge volunteers for sacrifice to count upon this profound and fruitful mystique. 'Ultimately,' he would say, 'French heroism ends in French saintliness.' And our Catholicism would be empty if it did not substitute in us 'a way of thinking, a way of being.'

Let us consider for a moment the play of forces in which we are enmeshed. There is the world we can see, those forces that operate in front of our eyes, that we can set in motion, and the power of which can be calculated. But there is also the world we cannot see, forces that exist, but are hidden in a superior atmosphere. The dynamic forces of these two worlds constantly mingle and unite, but governed by the Power above, which is the focus of all supreme aims. 'Through a unique grace,' the good Joseph Lotte said, 'we men are at the point where spirit joins matter, at the intersection of the mortal and the immortal.' To intervene in the actions of the Superior Power: such is our honour and incredible power, if it is not, indeed, our only power. If God is the universal first cause, then man's action has value only when it is seconded by divine action. In other words, it is neither our momentary agitation, nor our little human effort that is able to accomplish great things, but whatever divine co-operation enters into it. However, to obtain this divine intervention, in favour of his country for example, what resources a patriotic Catholic has, for he can, if he wishes, obtain the intervention of the triumphant Church, whose communion includes the saints of his country! He has only to make his intentions and will supernatural through faith; adapt his activities to God's designs; call upon the legions of his glorified ancestors; and immediately, with increased dignity and power, he enters that region where the fates of nations are decided; where, by magnificent pre-ordination, and in response to human prayer, the most generous of divine plans are elaborated. The man of faith who prays as he thinks, acts, speaks, writes, or fights is no longer a man; he acquires the status of a sublime collaborator in the works of Providence.

From this you will perceive how much more elevated are the aims of life, how much more fortified the motives for our sacrifice, when into them enter the eternal, and the omnipotency of the Infinite God. The consoling aspect of this truth is that here the way lies wide open to everyone. Our faith no longer knows petty actions or petty doers when, bound as closely to Christ as the branch to its stem, we participate in the infinite dignity and power of this glorious Leader. I believe in the statement of the young Christian philosopher Jacques Maritain, professor of philosophy at Stanislas, who once wrote:

> Because of this supernatural solidarity, it is certain that not only the life and joy of the converted, but also the actual grace received by all those people, who, though not yet professing the Catholic faith, already perceive in the beauty of the Church a reflection of the eternal light and are proud of it, all these have been exactly paid for by the tears of some very humble contemplative, or by a gaze of

love upon the Holy Sacrament, or by entire lives filled with heroic penitence, in short by this unique yet innumerable mass in which Christ and all his members offer themselves each day to God.[5]

How much more strongly must the volunteer for intellectual service be impressed by these truths! He who devotes his intelligence to God serves Divine order in the highest possible way, because the vocation of a Christian, as Maritain has also said, is the vocation of a contemplative. To slowly wear the spirit in research and the struggle for truth is to use the best in man and become part of the élite.

Who could wish to lose any part of the value of such a holocaust? It makes us think, not without high and generous envy, of the supernatural forces that would act for us if one day those who speak and write and, like Dollard, want to serve their country should no longer write a line, not a word, without repeating to themselves Ernest Psichari's striking observation to Paul Bourget: 'It is a fearful experience to write in the presence of the Holy Trinity.' Who knows? We would, perhaps, even witness the disappearance of the depressing gap that always seems to insinuate itself between the best devotion and its results.

Ladies and Gentlemen:
These are the lessons and examples Dollard would relive among us were he alive today, adjusting his acts to our new realities. But why do we speak of it as merely a hypothetical case? Will the hero not live again? Is he not alive at this very moment? Has he not been among us during these last few years as we revived his memory and celebrated his immortal youth? In a few months he is to appear in a square of our great city, real and palpable, in the posture of his victorious defeat, covered with a final glory, pathetic and beautiful, as conceived in the mind of Laliberté.

O Commander of the old Fort of Ville-Marie, it is time you were among us! We have such pressing need of a young leader like you, a leader of men. Look, on the frontier where you fell a barbarous throng as menacing as the old threatens our French soul. The work we must now undertake is one of total reconstruction and restoration. Arise, Dollard, and live on your granite pedestal. Summon us, with virile charm, with a hero's accents. We lift toward you our hands quivering like palm leaves, ardent with ambition to serve. Together we shall work for the reconstruction of our family's house. And should you command it, O Dollard, O powerful leader, we are ready to follow you to the supreme holocaust for the defence of our French tongue and our Catholic faith.

15 J.-M.-R. Villeneuve, O.M.I.
(1883-1947)
And Our Dispersed Brethren....?

The Objection

That a French and Catholic State should, during the course of the present
century, be established in the St. Lawrence valley is, according to many people,
no longer a utopian dream, but a viable ideal, a hope founded in reality. That,
moreover, the French race in North America should thereby fulfil its supernatural vocation; that because of this long-awaited political independence our
nationality should be granted the majestic role long destined for it by Providence;
that its idealistic, generous civilization should thus become a flame to light the
great complex of parts that is to be fused by our American future; that it should
become, finally, a modern-day Israel in the midst of an emerging Babylon, a
France of America, an apostolic nation, a nation of light: this is a divine grace
that we would do well to request in our prayers and to become worthy of by
meditation and by that courage that makes nations great.

To achieve such an end, however, our nation must preserve its soul, shield it
from destructive contacts, escape from the pressures that could suffocate it, and
parry the blows seeking to diminish it.

Otherwise, a future French State would have no reason to exist in this northern
New World; worse still, it could never summon the kind of strength that engen-
ders heroism and the victories it needs, nor could it be assured of the extraordinary
help granted by the Almighty to those individuals or nations who are ambitious in
their dreams for His greater glory and who risk all in their attempts to secure it.

It seems to me that such are, in substance, the conclusions to which we have
been led by the inquiry into our political future conducted by *L'Action française*
since its January issue.

Shall I be blunt? I know very well that this masterly program of political reorientation that is being proposed to the French race of Canada has been a

---

Translated from 'Et nos frères de la dispersion', *Notre Avenir Politique: Enquête de l'Action
française*, 1922, Bibliothèque de l'Action Française, Montreal, 1923, pp. 113–39.

source of profound concern to certain people, and not without considerable cause. The warning but electrifying trumpet-call that has stirred the blood of Quebec's sons with enthusiasm and hope has struck a melancholy, anxious note into many a soul: into the minds of our dispersed brethren – those who have remained true to themselves, that is, in communion with us, and those who meditate, searching the future, desiring their part in the French epic and their share of Christian glory.

There are a great number of these offshoots that have been scattered throughout the land according to the whim of our fecundity or spirit of adventure: scattered in the name of an ideal that was more generous than wise, sometimes because of necessity, but more often through a kind of patriotism that was too short-sighted, and far too bohemian. They went to the United States, spreading from east to west and even to the south, usually against their better judgment, and against the advice of our leaders and most prophetic minds. They went out to western Canada, drawn by urgent appeals from men who were serious and authoritative, but who could not foresee the course of subsequent events and could still adopt an optimism that it is no longer possible for us to affect. These men could not hear, as we do, the distant rumblings that presage the more or less imminent breaking up of a certain great, ostentatious empire, nor the significant creaking of a federation for which it would definitely be foolhardy to predict a very long existence; nor had they witnessed the land overrun, almost overnight, by European immigrants who settled for good, making themselves at home with their exotic ideals and interests, immigrants solicited by politicians who were certainly devoid of the qualities required of builders of nations.

The present anxiety of these, our kin, gives us, we must admit, food for thought.

'What about us?' they ask.

'If it is indeed the case[1] that, to preserve our soul – this apostolic, exemplary soul that must be the supreme cause of the civilization we must build in the heart of America – we must be free from fatal contact with foreign influence, from the mortal pressures of a selfish, mercantile civilization: how can we achieve this if you abandon us?

'In order to realize an ideal which we share with you, must you take an axe and sever from the trunk all those branches that have sprung from your own life and spirit, branches that you yourself have nurtured? Must we suffocate so that you may be left in peace to meditate upon the uncertain hope of an independence that will be a heavy burden to carry and that may well prove to be a mere exchange of allegiance and servitude? While you prepare to sink into the quicksands of our great, neighbouring democracy, must we in the West be submerged by the rising tide of a foreign sea, like an island cut adrift from its continent?'

So will speak our French of the Diaspora. And so, I fear, will they all think.

And in fact, could we prepare our escape from the approaching storm with a dry eye and an unmoved heart before even, as families say, 'seeing to the children'? Could a shipwrecked mother seize a plank floating by or climb aboard an inviting raft if, all around her on precarious bits of wreckage or on isolated and barren crags surrounded by abysmal depths, the youngest children cried, with outstretched arms, for help?

In this inquiry into our political future are we really giving sufficiently serious consideration to the case of our brothers in the outposts, those whose fortune it is to succeed our great ancestors, the forerunners, heralds, discoverers, civilizers: Frenchmen whose taste was for vast horizons, whose gaze was bold and acute, whose ideal was ambitious; Frenchmen who cut out for us a new France larger than Europe, because it was a pleasure for them to work on such a large scale in creating both land and country?

Would not the severance of those colonial and federal ties that our own sense of loyalty does not consider unbreakable lead to more serious ruptures, much too cruel for the French family in Canada, too fatal to our permanent existence and our common mission?

Let us be precise. Some beginning of an answer has been made to the scruples of our national conscience as well as to the fears of our brothers outside our State. We need only to widen the perspective of this answer, and to analyse its elements.

'Our attitude does not imply desertion,' declared the program.[2] 'We are not seeking any kind of separation, and will accept only that which is imposed upon us by necessity or the hazard of history, against which all of us are in any case powerless.

'When we speak of separation, we do not mean closed or, even less, hostile boundaries. For a long time it will be in our interest, and it will be our duty, to maintain relationships with our former associates to whom we will continue to be attached by many bonds.

'Our compatriots are quite aware, moreover, that our loyal friendship for them, and our ardent desire to share in their life, are in no way the result of actual political ties. Such feelings spring from a more spontaneous solidarity and a more profound sense of fraternity. They also realize that this solidarity and fraternity can only be strengthened if Quebec acquires a national personality.'

This logical and complete reasoning outlines the four parts of an answer to the above objections against the great project for the future that now haunts our masters of patriotism and national dignity, men who, in the eyes of the entire race, hold high the standard of the ideal.

1. Whether we like it or not, Canada is bound to split up. We do not have to bring it about, but merely to foresee it so that we can supervise the lines of fissure; and it would be inappropriate, indeed unjust, to blame us for it.

2. In any case, the political separation that could result for various French-Canadian groups would destroy neither our *duty* nor our *interests*, neither the *sentiments* nor the *ideal* that now lead us to maintain and strengthen our ethnic links with all French centres of America, and especially with those who are most desirous of remaining faithful to what we are in the schemes of history.

3. The breaking up of our present political structures could hardly diminish our ability to help our dispersed compatriots: that is a fact against which it would surely be difficult to argue. For, putting aside rhetoric and exaggeration,

we may well ask what the fate of these compatriots has been under the federal régime during the half-century that has just elapsed, if not to be shackled, weakened, annihilated by the letter of hypocritical laws perversely turned against them each time they tried to invoke them in their just appeals?

4. Quite the contrary, a strong French State, practically homogeneous and completely free in its activities, would be the surest guarantee of the survival and integrity of our people of the Diaspora, since they would, in a sense, be protected by the zeal of a powerful French and Catholic civilization, which would command the respect of, and finally triumph over, the always ephemeral forces of those civilizations rising to surround us, which are ambitious, but divergent and materialistic, in their aims.

And that is how, even from the point of view of French groups remaining outside Quebec, a French State of smaller but more sensible proportions would still continue to be, through its superiority, the best means of serving the universal interests of the entire race.

That is what we shall now attempt to demonstrate.

The Answer

We seek no separation. We see it coming, for it is indeed coming. It can be felt, glimpsed; there are indications, and even unequivocal signs. We must give it a great deal of thought.

Let us briefly recapitulate these premonitory symptoms. We need only mention, to refresh our memory, the present upheaval in the world, particularly detrimental to Europe, but the consequences of which we will surely have to share.[3] We have greater cause to fear these fatal disturbances in Europe because the country most vulnerable to them is England, a country as proud and avid as always, but now destined, it seems, to drink deep of a vertiginous draught. Meanwhile, the Dominions, including our own, slowly progress by force of principle in their constant evolution toward self-government.[4] This separation, added to the increasingly profound fissures in the Empire, does not bode well for its continued existence.[5] 'Canada is moving toward total independence,' was the judgment of Marshal Fayolle in France last year.[6] The time is past, if it ever existed, when our sole obligation to the metropolis consisted in drinking the Queen's health.[7] Loyalty now involves us in subsidies, dreadnoughts, cannon fodder, all of which rather dampens our enthusiasm for it.

When the bonds of imperial nations are loosened, Canada, if it wishes to be a true nation, will surely not remain *one* country only. For, quite apart from the forces that undermine our bonds with the Empire, there are others at work preparing the dissolution of our federal ties. The United States has one hundred and ten million inhabitants. Canada has a total of seven or eight. Neither history nor our understanding of the psychology of our neighbours permits us to think that they never entertain the desire of Ahab for Naboth's vineyard. If, in our Canadian land, whole provinces are already Americanized, not only through the common language, but also through ideas, sentiments, and tastes; through interests, business, entertainment; through religious sects, schools, magazines and daily newspapers, the theatre; through equal licentiousness in their moral life: religious indifference, divorce, birth control, women's rights, libertarian democracy, social egalitarianism; through a similar materialism in their ideals, and an equally shameless paganism in their pleasures; in short, through a mentality tarred with the same brush, and a civilization as limited in its horizons; and if, in the four years from 1910 to 1914, over a million and a half American subjects have crossed into the Canadian West:[8] is it possible to maintain that at the crucial moment these provinces would refuse the great honour of being annexed? That at this very moment, despite a superficial British surface, they are not more or less consciously promoting this permutation of imperialism?

In the long run will anything be able to resist the ogre next door? Yes. A province that has a civilization based on Catholicism and Gallo-Latin idealism will cultivate aversion for the new alliance. The element in our country that is concerned about rights superior to those of finance or pleasure to the extent of choosing to die rather than betray them, such an element alone will be able to stand up to the Colossus when negotiations begin. It is clear that, at that point, French Canada will no longer have the choice of breaking or not breaking with the rest of the Dominion if it wishes to remain at all faithful to its ideals and not deviate from the providential path its origins have traced.

God grant that the cancellation of the federal pact at least precede the political haggling over Canada that is bound to take place in the councils of the masters of the world! The French section would then be less likely to follow suit as a simple accessory. But could the disintegration of the Dominion occur independently of Americanizing pressures? Although some are still hesitant,[9] we are not rash to consider an affirmative answer, without, of course, any need of trying to turn our predictions into reality. It would be enough to probe the Dominion in order to find, outside our own area, the symptoms of advanced dissolution.

Between the East and the West there is the great enemy, *distance*.[10] Attempts to bridge this gap by the construction of interminable and costly railways have all been futile. Their only result will be the country's bankruptcy, unless those provinces that have no need of them pay for those that do, a state hardly calculated to cement unity. In any case, the natural divisions of a territory that has been called a 'geographical absurdity' impose a neat division of interests, making free trade imperative at the other end of the country, but requiring tariff protection at this end. I know very well that 'human geography'[11] is not entirely dictated by rivers or mountains, and that the political boundaries that still exist derive from national spirit rather than survey demarcations. But only through close solidarity of interests and through a common spirit can geographical gaps be bridged. In the present case these are exactly the things we most lack.

The divergence of interests is obvious. The spiritual divergences are still more profound.

There is not the slightest meeting-point between our languages, social traditions, religious aims, habits of mind, spiritual formation, public institutions, or civil laws. The only way in which these could be closely united would be through the complete abdication of our Catholic and French personality. And these immigrants with whom it is 'criminally'[12] desired to populate the West, these thousands of immigrants arriving from all over and spreading socialism and revolution, will certainly not help to strengthen interprovincial bonds! Their lack of assimilation to an effectively Canadian ideal will long retard the growth of the generous, faithful civic spirit that they would need in order to be helpful in this way. And when will Orangeism rise above itself and judge us fairly? When will it ever contribute to the organization of the country something other than malice and bitterness?

When will the English mind ever be able to conceive of a country effectively bilingual, with mutual respect between the races instead of abuse and the subordination of one to the profit of the other? To this add the religious fanaticism characteristic of any dissidents in matters of faith; the particular narrow-mindedness of a population that is completely unenlightened, that is not bound to the tradition of the great centuries by faith, or education, or purely human philosophy; a population whose science is mere mechanics, whose logic is numerical strength, whose unique standard for judging all things is number of dollars or weight in gold. Can we forget habits that consist entirely of sectarian chauvinism, or the reserve of virulence always ready to sally forth against 'French domination', 'the priest-ridden province', and 'Roman-Popism'? Can we altogether ignore the political passions that, at each new election, stir up to a frantic pitch the ambitions of conflicting parties whose fierce persistence is equalled only by the fanaticism that they provoke throughout the organized press and that sets province against province in shattering struggles. How much longer can this kind of 'clash' continue without the weaker side being crushed by the stronger?

Some people dream of 'bridging the chasm' that separates the two races. That would, indeed, require a new mechanism, and who is to invent it? Even if, through politics or interest, we desired to do so, it would become increasingly impossible to consolidate our part in Confederation. A nation is a moral organism, the fruit of nature: mathematics does not enter into it. Well might Joseph de Maistre scoff at the thought of a group of men putting themselves to the trouble of creating a nation. Any federation is by definition precarious. How much more so when there are hidden but increasingly strong forces working toward its disintegration!

We should perhaps be quiet about these apprehensions, since they are likely to cause anxiety. But what about our partners? 'A timely suggestion,' wrote one Westerner a short time ago in the Regina *Leader* reproduced in the Montreal *Gazette*,[13] 'is that when the Prairie Provinces are conveniently grouped in their provincial Parliaments under the Progressive banner, these provinces, whose needs and development are diametrically opposed to those of the Eastern provinces, should themselves take steps to ensure their complete independence; such a demand could not easily be opposed if all the provinces were united in it. And this would open the way for reciprocal treaties with the United States.'

And so Canada will have its political hegemony. The consequence, unless it happens sooner, is almost bound to be the separation of its component parts. Even if we have, ourselves, tended to move in that direction, the separation would thus not result exclusively from our actions. We are, rather, witnesses of the trend. Our western compatriots may fear such a conclusion: they would perhaps suffer from it, particularly from a national point of view. But it would be a mistake for either of us not to think about it manfully and talk about it openly. From now on it becomes inevitable and will happen sooner or later.

For the moment it is not important to determine which of our brethren will be forced by future events to remain outside the boundaries of a broadened and liberated Quebec. In the first place, there will always be the part played by unforeseeable circumstances. But there will also be forces that can be brought freely into play and that others may need to define more precisely. The French-Canadian groups dispersed, for example, across the great prairie that constitutes the interior basin of the Canadian Northwest will inevitably be the ones most exposed to this severance from the mother province. And who is at fault? History, no doubt, for it sometimes acts without taking account of human wisdom or sentimental preferences. But Providence nevertheless weaves its mysterious designs, and its magnificent plan can be discovered later in the rise and fall of empires. We most warmly hope and wish that Quebec may hold on to all its offshoots; but we must not lull ourselves with chimerical hopes that are contradicted by the symptoms analysed above. When Canada's great skeleton is taken to pieces, French Canada will necessarily have to limit its power and territorial ambitions according to geographical indications, and especially according to the ethnic factors that are capable of being unified; otherwise the future state would lack stability: it could never last. To put it simply, it can never enter into any scheme not based upon reason.

Does this mean, however, that with no further ado we resign ourselves to abandoning our people who live, say, in provinces beyond Ontario? Not at all.

Four elements, as we have seen, combine to form a particular nationality: *origin, language, territory,* and *form of government*.[14] These elements are of unequal importance: the first two are the soul, the last two the body, of a nation. As the soul by far transcends matter, so must unity of origin and community of language be much more important than the claims of territory or political forms. A family depends upon bonds of blood rather than mere physical proximity.

If individual charity is a duty, so is national charity. And if charity is judged by unity of hearts as well as need, it obviously follows that the disruption of political unity and the division of territories do not obviate the dictates of national duty, because they do not totally destroy its foundations. They leave the best part intact, the formal and spiritual links, those that ensure that the basic moral character remains the same; and an ideal community also remains: spirits and hearts are moulded in the same way by the influence of familiar words that carry the same connotations of superior thoughts and sovereign ambition. From this it is clear that even separated by legal boundaries our blood relationship would not be broken, but would continue to dictate the obligations of an effective fraternity.

It might be objected that our response to such a duty would be no more than platonic sympathy or short-term devotion. That would be to forget recent events which have revealed to both sides what our national fraternity makes us capable of accomplishing. The Ontario question, Green Valley, Gravelbourg, to mention only a few names, are eloquent testimony to it. Moreover, consider this fact: these public-minded acts did not spring from federal unity, but from a patriotism more alert, more fully conscious of its duty. In our opinion, any independence that gave us a country more completely ours would thereby develop our public spirit so that it became more enterprising and wider in scope. The dictates of duty would, in any case, be reinforced by our own interests.

Our French State, created through historical evolution, would not, we presume, be so puerile as to desire isolation and insularity. Fences do not prevent neighbourliness. Shunning our neighbours – former associates become competitors – would immediately spell ruin. Compromise would be necessary. Our politics, our trade, our social life would have to take theirs into account, for the separation of our governments would not of itself eliminate common problems deriving from similar needs or dangers. We would still need the water from their lakes, as they would that from our rivers. Our railways would end in their territory, and theirs in ours. To make us realize that all this would mean permanent relationships as close as those of today although more independent, we need only remember our necessary, but so imprudent, relations with our powerful neighbour, the United States. In addition, what an advantage it would be in our dealings with the other Canadian States of tomorrow to have, right there in those States, minds and intelligences fashioned in the same mould as ours, politicians, newspapermen, and men of our religion capable of understanding the situation within our country and of informing us about that of theirs. Obviously there would be shades of difference between our views and theirs, but would this prevent intimate affinities and profound understanding? Especially if we all tried, through an exchange of culture and customs, to safeguard our original temperament.

Then too, what is it that inspires our people in Quebec to fly to the rescue of our distant kin if it is not a religious and patriotic ideal unhampered by meridian lines? Our main ambition is that our Catholic faith be maintained and strengthened in every soul born of our race. The treasure of religion we consider a priceless one; whatever the cost, we intend to preserve it in those who received it at baptism, as well as to carry it to strangers still in the shadows of death.[15] How much more strongly do we wish this for our brothers and nephews! I know that with time the bonds of consanguinity will be loosened. Others will be created by family alliances. And then we shall be stronger, and our distant compatriots as well. In any case they shall, if they wish it as we do, have remained our co-nationals. For since we know that language is the key to freedom and the guardian of faith;[16] that ancestral traditions are as involucres protecting the flower of religion; that a nation's soul cannot be wounded in its individual, family, or social habits without also being wounded – and often fatally – in its religious sentiment; since we know this, we shall continue, through apostolic ideals and French proselytizing, to give our people beyond the 'lines' our vigilant interest and effective sympathy.

Why should not what happened to a certain extent for Franco-Americans – albeit largely through a kind of unreflecting, excessively naïve patriotism – why should it not occur for our Diaspora, and, indeed, for all those who, though stationed outside our political sphere, are nevertheless not insensitive to our moral attraction and the blaze of our genius? Comparisons, though they always falsify to some extent, confirm our ideas in this case. We have been neglected, forgotten, even despised, by political circles in France, because they were exclusively political; we have received very little attention from intellectual, literary, or social circles in France, and that little belated and awkward, because they were on another continent, separated from us for over two centuries, at a time when distance necessarily meant ignorance. But from the religious and most traditional circles we have received innumerable priests and religious persons. Through them has France not lent us its literature, preserved the memory of its history, which was ours as well in the beginning, inspired us with its enthusiasm? And has it not in some measure contributed to the survival of our nation? It would be unfair not to recognize all this. There were some indiscretions that could have been avoided, misunderstandings that should have been cleared up; but these are, at least partly, unavoidable human miseries. We shall never be so presumptuous as to cast doubt upon the continued influence that France has exerted, even during the English régime, upon our national mentality. And, in this age when visitors and tourists move about as easily as books or magazines, what would prevent our French charity from assuming a similar role, but magnifying it, fulfilling it with more determination, more wisdom, more results, with regard to all the miniature Canadas scattered throughout America? What was accomplished for our separated brothers, even under the federal régime, by a mere sister province hobbled by superstitious respect for provincial autonomy, will surely be multiplied tenfold in a State with a population comparable to that of Belgium or Portugal! Our civilization could fill this role the more easily were it to become, through its originality, through the transcendence of its traditions and the homogeneous nature of its religious spirit, a beacon for America, a shining example for everyone to see.

Furthermore, would it be legitimate to accuse us of betraying our fraternal obligations toward Canadians who have left the valleys of Quebec and Ontario, simply because we intend to withdraw, freely, from the political association of provinces? Let us ask a categorical question: what real profit, leaving aside some presumed comfort and some constant but futile hopes, can our French-speaking brothers in English provinces have derived from the federal bond? Confederation has perhaps had the advantage of protecting us from our former bugbear, annexation. Today, as we have seen, the régime aggravates the peril for us: indeed it revives it. As for religious or national protection for French minorities outside Quebec, what assurances has Confederation really provided? At the beginning, and in the minds of the Fathers of Confederation, there were sincere, though relative, concessions of freedom. What has happened in practice? Has Orangeism faded, fanaticism waned? What about the Riel affair? And the *Ne Temere* decree? And the so-called 'troubles' in Quebec during the war? And the Despatie-Tremblay union, to mention only a few of the most unjustified crises? Was Confederation responsible for the concession of separate – that is to say Catholic – schools in Ontario, or the interests of the Protestant minority in Quebec and the excess of fanaticism in Upper Canada?

But was it not Confederation that prevented confessional schools in New Brunswick? And that also deprived us of them in Manitoba in 1896, in Alberta and Saskatchewan in 1905, in Keewatin in 1912? And was it not Confederation that refused to intervene on a federal level, and Confederation whose timid remedial bills were disdained when we tried to have recourse to them? Is it not Confederation that has always interpreted laws in the literal spirit that kills and has never understood that living, vital laws need a soul? Is it not Confederation that imposes upon us divorce, and women's suffrage, and imperial conscription, all principles of social dissolution fatal to a race? Is it not Confederation that gives us State schools, unilingual and neutral, and uniform laws in which perish the last traces of the French spirit that enlivened our civil and judicial institutions?[17] Is it not Confederation that refuses to recognize the rights of our national, liberating unions, incapable as it is of judging the true meaning of order and the advantage of safeguarding sensible freedoms? And is it not Confederation that doles out our French language in the most parsimonious amounts in the public services; that keeps it from our youth in many provinces, and ostracizes it with insult and injury?

And finally, is it not Confederation that has anglicized the entire policies of our public representatives, subordinating them to the most risky naval, military, or imperialistic forces? It is impossible to calculate to what extent our morale and our political sense have been depressed by the role we have been fulfilling since 1867.

We must face the fact that Confederation by itself, as far as our national interests are concerned, has been nothing but a miserable bankruptcy, a bitter, humiliating deception. If we have progressed at all since its inception, it has been in spite of its framework; it has been entirely due to our natural growth, our Catholic institutions, our French vigour, the progress of the times, and not to a federal protection that has not proved to be the support we hoped it would be. I shall not mention the criticism that could be made, from a political point of view, of the work Confederation has done in developing a *Canadian* spirit in the largest sense of the word.[18]

And that, in brief, is the kind of power we have received from Confederation to help our western brothers and friends in their survival and development.

Are they satisfied with it?

Let us now consider – without futile optimism, but in the light of our own hearts – the powers a State of Quebec would possess for the expansion of the French force in America.

The child who becomes a man, the teen-ager who comes of age, these constitute progress for the family and for the nation. The design of nature has reached maturity, and nature's aim, when not distorted, is good, its final result is good. The slave who is freed, the ward who is released from tutelage, the colonial who gains independence, the common man who is granted civil rights, all these, when they know the cost of freedom and the right way of using it, constitute a good for society and for human civilization. The same is true of a colony that becomes a nation or a province that becomes a State by the regular and judicial evolution of social factors; these are gains for humanity. Explicit confirmation of this was quoted recently: 'The autonomy of each adult race is not only its right and the normal condition of its proper life, but it is an advantage for all the others, since it is the most perfect form of order among humans.' (Etienne Lamy) And here is also the testimony of the great Bishop of Hippone: 'Everything would go much more smoothly in the world if all kingdoms were small ones, living side by side in joyful harmony. There would thus be many nations in the world, as there are many houses and families in a city. War and the subjugation of nations for the expansion of an empire are necessities that we bear . . .'[19]

Could it be claimed that the common advantage for human society that results from the independence of a nation would not be particularly great for those ethnic organizations similar in kind, I mean the French groups scattered outside our territory? A superficial notion, devoid of social psychology. Imagine this wonderful vision: a French race established on the shores of the Saint Lawrence, maintaining its traditions, remaining united in composition but liberal toward its temporary or permanent guests, a race that, through the crises of our contemporary age, would have gained the highest summit of freedom and there planted its banner for everyone to see, now and in future ages. It would present a model of autonomous government, steeped in wisdom because of the faith of its men and its institutions. With increased scope and brilliance, it would give examples of social responsibility and magnificent generosity, as outstanding as those that now have to be borrowed, for education, the arts and letters, religion, and public progress. Freed from its bonds, our Parliament would also shed its 'county council' atmosphere. It would inspire thinkers whose work would be elevated because Latinate, and gestures that would be civilizing because Catholic. Since it would control the main factors of the sociological problems that arise, the genius for political order and the chivalric nobility that form part of its heredity would find a field of action large enough to allow all the best instincts in our collective soul to be developed to the full. This would certainly not prove harmful to our remote brethren, and might indeed provide an ideal strong enough to strengthen resistance and eradicate weaknesses.

It may be objected that, according to many reports, our brothers in the United States are being lost to us. And what can we do for them?

Let us remember, first, that today our hands are tied; and that our people now living beyond the forty-fifth parallel left us at a time when our consciousness of nationhood was not well developed, and their own awareness of the possible alterations of a race living in a foreign nation less keen. From now on all these things could change considerably. We shall put aside modesty and ask whether all the priests we have sent them, the leaders we have trained for them, the attention and the esteem with which we have surrounded them, the fraternal friendship we have had and wish to continue having for them, the social ties they are free to keep with us, whether all these things have counted for nothing in their present French vitality? But we repeat, all this could be bettered.

There is not enough consideration given to the fact that ideas rule the world: *Mens molem agitat.* How strong our universities, our colleges, and our convents would become if their influence extended beyond our frontiers, if their doors were kept open for the sons and daughters of our brethren everywhere! They would be similar to those great schools that in past centuries formed a neo-Latin Europe and contributed so much to the extension of French influence. Would it not be possible to transplant our social institutions so that they grew and flourished under foreign skies, no doubt acquiring some native originality, but never losing any part of their own special personality? Would not the French-Canadian thought that fills our literature and our art, our customs and our experience flow outwards to fertilize our emigrated colonies? Then too, we would be a stronger country, free and independent: the exodus of our surplus population – this transfusion of new blood – would no longer present such grave risks. A glance at the geography of history, and the names of Ireland, Poland, Tyrol, Trentino, Latvia, Croatia, or the Balkans, would significantly confirm these views, which might otherwise be called over-hasty or optimistic. And this confirmation amply justifies the greatest hopes of all those who, like us, tend to believe that the day Quebec and its surrounding territories form a true State with complete mastery over its national personality, that day will see the dawning of a new era for all the French Canadians in America, those outside our State as well as those within, a dawn full of promise, heralding a beautiful day of hard work and glory in the history of nations.

And now to summarize the major conclusions to be drawn from the points we have just outlined.

In our humble opinion our distant brothers have little or no need to feel concern about the political system that links them to us at the moment, for heaven does not seem to smile upon it. What is of the foremost importance for them is to struggle along with us to preserve their soul; and what we owe them most is the Catholic faith and an authentic French civilization.

Let them not be unduly severe with those of us here who hesitate to send them new contingents: one would hesitate at less. Let them rather seek whatever will strengthen in them the desire to remain French and the awareness of belonging, in the words of Mgr Langevin, that great and blessed man of the West, to the most beautiful race in the world.

Let them import heroic priests who understand the value of the French school that stands beside the parish church. Let them train, or obtain from us if they wish, masters to teach their sons the harmony of our ancestral syllables and the lessons of enthusiastic patriotism to be derived from history.

Let them listen, as we do, to the teachings of our professors of national energy; let us all possess the uncompromising ambition always to continue our ascent toward superiority; let us remind one another that a race always has some call of duty and that, through its imminent energy and its desire to live, it weaves itself the mantle that envelops it in the gaze of human history. They, and we, will then have imposing destinies because we shall have used the ten or five talents given us. Equally, our tragedy would be to bury them in inertia or mediocrity.

16 Antonio Perrault (1880-1955)
Inquiry into Nationalism

L'Action française of Montreal has been following with intense interest the inquiry into nationalism begun in *Lettres* of Paris by M. Maurice Vaussard. Our group has been invited to contribute to this inquiry, but we prefer not to express an opinion on the main issue of this difficult question. Moreover, the writer of this article does not possess the competence required to treat this subject from a doctrinal point of view or to define accurately the agreements or disagreements modern nationalism has with the principle of nationalities and Catholicism. We will point out only the attitude of French Canadians with regard to the national problem and the solution to the problem that *Action française* wants to suggest. The study of specific cases is necessary for the understanding of the concept of 'nationalism'. 'All general theories about nationalism,' correctly wrote M. O. de Halecki, 'are nothing more than words until they are illustrated by specific examples and proved by the experiences of individual nations.'[1]

And the 4,000,000 French Canadians (about 2,000,000 in Quebec, 600,000 in the eight other Canadian provinces, 1,700,000 in the United States), how do they view the problem that gave rise to the inquiry in *Lettres*?

Their national feeling has not changed in 163 years. It is a reaction begun in 1760 and it still continues today. *Action française* wants to increase it and define its conditions, methods, and goals.

Is this feeling 'patriotism' or 'nationalism'? In reading the replies to the inquiry in *Lettres* it is not easy to find the line of demarcation between these two terms. Our people has always called its sustained effort to conserve its Catholic and French spirit 'patriotism', and its respect for the established power, its submission to the political system set up by England and to the various forms it has taken in the course of our evolution 'loyalty'. We think it is better to call the attachment our people feel to their nationality 'patriotism'.

We have special reasons for trying to avoid the ambiguous here. 'Nationalism' sometimes serves as a label for some of our political parties, and the use of this term can provoke irritated opposition to a feeling that is quite legitimate.

Translated from 'Enquête sur le nationalisme', *L'Action française*, II, February 1924, pp. 105–18.

Thus, around 1885, Honoré Mercier, the leader of the Quebec Liberal Party, taking as a motive the differences that had cropped up in the Canadian West between the English Canadians and the Métis, inaugurated a policy that was called 'national'; he succeeded in winning over the large majority of the people of Quebec and he became prime minister. In March of 1903 a 'nationalist league' was founded under the inspiration of M. Olivar Asselin. M. Henri Bourassa was the theorist of this group and he propagated 'nationalist' ideas in Parliament, in speeches, and in the press. These ideas, however, were not limited to the defence of French Canadians. In 1899 Canada began participating in the wars of the Empire; she sent troops to aid England in ruling the Boers. Asselin-Bourassa 'nationalism' was a reaction against British imperialism and it denounced the attempts of Joe Chamberlain and his ambitious friends to maintain English world-supremacy with the money and lives of the colonials. The 'nationalist league' of 1903 wanted to keep Canada out of England's wars and to increase its autonomy as an English colony until, through Confederation, it might become an independent nation. After trying to turn itself into a political party (1907–12), the league soon gave up its rigid framework and limited itself to spreading its theories by the spoken and written word. This nationalist group, much like the national party of 1885, was linked with Canadian politics, but not solely in the service of a distinct French-Canadian race. These changes in opinion – especially those sponsored by the nationalist league – contributed, nevertheless, to the reawakening of a national feeling among French Canadians. This is one of its merits that we must not forget.

Whether it be 'patriotic' or 'nationalist' this feeling is identified with the very existence of our race.

If our ancestors had remained under the rule of France in the eighteenth century, the problem never would have arisen for them. New France would have grown as a colony of the mother country, or would have become an independent country dominated by our ethnic group. We would have developed along the lines of our origins; one day we would have made up an independent State that was supported by one people, one territory, one language, and one religion. But in our history there is the year 1760.

The year 1760 placed a question mark in front of the future of our race. France renounced her colonial lands and ceded them to England. But what were the 65,000 Frenchmen whom France abandoned here to do? Were they to take flight as well? Were they to submit to all the demands of the conqueror? Were they to accept, for example, the substitution of English laws for French ones, as Governor Murray ordered in 1764? Were they to learn quickly the English language and forget their own? Since the ministers in London listened attentively to the leaders of the Anglican Church and opposed those of the Catholic Church, were our fathers to simplify the situation by becoming Protestants? An affirmative reply from our forefathers would have erased all traces of France in Canada; our ethnic and religious difficulties would not have existed. But because our ancestors refused to follow this downward route, the national problem entered into our history, and it is still with us.

Racial feeling, which without the break of 1760 would have developed and grown naturally and spontaneously, has been wilfully maintained among us through rational and disciplined incitement. This national feeling appeared in the life of our people when the Conquest injured the integrity of our spirit and when its natural energies were checked by the surrender of Canada to England. This national feeling continued to exist because the Anglo-Saxon element wished to bring about internal unity by an often brutal policy of assimilation, and because it wished to impose its ways of thinking and living on us without consideration for the special character of our French spirit.

At the very time the French in Canada were giving in to the English in London, they were showing their desire to conserve their own racial peculiarities. The surrender of Quebec (September 18, 1759) and of Montreal (September 8, 1760) attested to the fact that they wished expressly to protect their inalienable rights and, despite defeat, to conserve in this land the characteristic aspects of their nationality, their religion, language, laws, and customs. In the Treaty of Paris, February 10, 1763, the King of France provided for another ratification of this collective will to live, and England was forced to recognize the legitimacy of this in the Quebec Act of 1774.

The struggles endured since then by the French Canadians are supported at one and the same time by natural law, which assures each people the right to live, to develop, and to grow along the lines of its origin, and by positive law and the accepted understanding between conqueror and conquered.

These struggles are still going on. Our country has not regained the homogeneity it lost in 1760. Two chief nationalities make up Canada, the French and the English. Every attempt to mix them, even to unite them, has failed.

From 1760 to 1791 the bureaucratic oligarchy tried to subject 100,000 Canadians to the rule of a few English merchants. In 1791 these efforts were wrapped in a constitutional cloak that poorly concealed the underhand schemings of the executive. The Act of Union in 1840 pointed up the obvious intention of London to be done with the French-Canadian element; the province of Lower Canada (today Quebec), where the French Canadians lived, was united with Upper Canada (today Ontario), where the English Canadians lived. It was hoped that this new political system would ensure the Anglo-Saxon element complete mastery of the country. In order to make this more certain, England abolished the use of French in our Parliament, and English became the only official language. The struggle continued. In 1848 French regained its status. After twenty-five years of this régime its failure seemed certain. Another shift was tried. In 1867 the confederation of Canada was born, the union of Quebec, Ontario, Nova Scotia, New Brunswick, and five other provinces that were to join between 1867 and 1905. The new constitution took the form of an explicit treaty between two races, a charter into which each race wrote its particular rights. This federal pact was accepted by the great majority of French Canadians. Finally, they thought, they would have peace; here were the foundations of the Canadian nation. Just an illusion. The federal system was not to give better results than the one in 1840. It would be impossible to attribute this failure to our nationality, since for forty years no disagreement with Confederation had been voiced among us; loyally the French Canadians tried to obtain the best

possible advantage from the new political system. Our leaders repeated continually: 'union of races, agreement, harmony'. The English Canadians profited
from our complacence to move away from the spirit of Confederation. Confederation was made up of two elements: the French and the English who had
signed the pact in 1867 as allies and equals. In order to ensure that Confederation would last and be successful, this equality of rights had to be maintained.
Each ethnic group had to develop in conformity with its national aspirations,
according to the nature of its language and upbringing, just as it might have
done before the signing of the alliance. However, it did not happen this way.
Confederation had existed scarcely five years when the English Canadians
began to harass French thought and religious ideas everywhere outside of
Quebec. The Anglo-Saxon element preferred to assault the fortress of our
schools; abolition of the Catholic schools in New Brunswick in 1871, and in
Manitoba in 1890; in 1905 the creation of two new provinces where the French
were refused their full rights; the same procedure followed in Keewatin in
1912; for ten years now the persecution of the French in Ontario has been
carried on by English Canadians and supported by the majority of the Irish.

After 1910 the talk of harmony and goodwill began to lose its hold on the
minds of French Canadians. Everything contributed to their disillusionment –
an imperialistic movement that drew Canada into the wars of the Empire and
retarded its march toward independence, destructive federalism that hunted
down French and Catholic ideas everywhere and attacked the very soul of one
of the groups that had signed the agreement of 1867 – and they began to regret
that they had consented to Confederation. They were convinced that Confederation was a fool's market. It severely weakened our national strength; it
caused the French Canadians slowly to lose their rights; it led them step by
step toward assimilation and disappearance as a distinct race. What was there
to do?

The *Action française* group, formed about ten years ago, proposes to French
Canadians a doctrine that will keep national feeling awake and give back to our
nationality its traditional ways. *Action française* was founded with the principal
goal of restoring the French language to the position that belongs to it in the
various spheres of our activity, in particular in business and industry, but since
then it has enlarged the field of its efforts. It feels that there are excellent
reasons for the keeping of the French language in Canada. The leaders of
Action française think that it is the changing of a state of mind that will extract
our people from the indolence, weakness, and forgetfulness that often they
show with regard to the French tongue. Language is too closely linked with
other constituent elements of a nationality for it to be isolated from the over-all
national problem. Without forgetting to defend the language, *Action française*
tries to view in a comprehensive perspective the survival of our nationality.

It is preoccupied first and foremost with the fate of French Canadians. It
asks this race to fall back upon its own thoughts, to become aware of the
harmonious order in which the normal life of a people should be led, then to
tighten all the strings of its heart so it can develop and grow according to a
hierarchy of values: religious and moral, intellectual and economic progress. It

asks French Canadians to believe in the virtue of their original culture and to hasten toward superiority so that it can keep its head above the mounting waves of Anglo-Saxonism that are submerging the other Canadian provinces and the United States. *Action française* has complete confidence in the essential characteristics of our nationality and it attempts to bring back into prominence the type of man that France sent out to our shores and that indelibly marked three hundred years of life in Canada. It is this ethnic type, personified by Samuel de Champlain, his companions and followers, it is this type, modified by the Canadian *milieu* and enriched by its three centuries of struggle and sacrifice, that *Action française* wants to perpetuate here. The colonists who came in the seventeenth century from Normandy, Poitu, the Ile de France, and Anjou carried the French way of life in their hearts. They were filled with it. For a century they continued to sustain this way of life with intellectual and moral assistance from their motherland. On this background was sketched the outline of what they became since their arrival on American soil. In 1760 the moral shape of our ancestors showed signs of the characteristics of both the French race and others added by the new social environment. If 163 years of English domination have not succeeded in wiping out this ethnic type, they have nevertheless blurred the outline of some of its traits. *Action française* wants to restore this type to its original beauty, to rid it of Anglo-Saxon and American accretions, to reshape its thought, and to give it back the views that disclose the bright and clear French genius. And so *Action française* wants to keep in mind historical and traditional peculiarities that will provide an obstacle to centralization and unification. In pursuing this goal it rebinds our people to their local traditions, to the love of man and of things that concern them most personally, and to the study of our origins through a more profound knowledge of history.

Our group turns its attention to the entire French family in America, to our racial brothers scattered across the other Canadian provinces as well as the United States. It tries to maintain ties of French affection with the Acadians in the Maritime Provinces, the French Canadians in Ontario, Manitoba, Alberta, Saskatchewan, and the Franco-Americans in the United States. Quebec was the cradle of this race; it must remain the home of Catholic and French ways of life for all the scattered members of our family. And indeed we do not ignore the precious help, in this struggle for survival, that may come from the land of our ancestors. No one has better expressed the feelings of our group toward France than Abbé Lionel Groulx. On February 2, 1922, speaking in Paris to the *Publicistes chrétiens*, the director of our review said:

We love her [France] because ties of blood bind us to her; because her splendid history is the same as ours up until the eighteenth century. We love her because from her and from Rome come all our intellectual life, the best parts of our moral and Christian life; we love and admire her because, while we face another civilization that tries to beguile us, the French soul and French intelligence represent for us the highest, the most refined, the most orderly part of humanity; and we have learned that there is French thought at the root of all that is great in the Church and in the world.

But toward what final goal are all these efforts aiming? I shall tell you without more ado: toward the establishing of a French State in eastern Canada.

Canadians are at a cross roads: maintenance of Confederation with the strong possibility of a more burdensome imperial association or the distant prospect of national independence; annexation to the United States; separation of the Canadian provinces in order to regain freedom of life and action. *Action française* favours this last alternative.

We must not dream of tighter imperial solidarity. This would hasten the breaking apart of everything else; Canadians would eventually become tired of this burdensome régime; in fact they are already. If the tie with Britain were broken, could the confederation become an independent nation? There are geographical and psychological obstacles to be considered. Could one single State be formed from all the European countries? Canada, which takes up the northern half of North America, is equal in size to nine-tenths of Europe; in area Quebec is larger than France, Belgium, Holland, and Italy combined. The inhabitants of western Canada are strangers to those in the East, and between their territories there is a geographical gap; the Great Lakes form a large zone of discontinuity between them that extends to the north in the form of a deserted area. In addition to this natural division there are obstacles of a moral kind. Western Canada has been recently populated by immigrants, some coming from Central Europe and the British Isles, and a large percentage from the United States. Consequently, the American spirit is predominant. The land and differences in race and in distinct ways of life have created two peoples in Canada, Easterners and Westerners, who are separated by ideals, geography, and economic demands. The people of the East are not even unified, since Quebec and Ontario are not friendly. Instead of encouraging a spirit of brotherhood with Quebec, Ontario embitters its neighbour by the way it treats the 300,000 French Canadians living within its boundaries. It is Ontario's idea to increase federal power, to restrict the use of French in the federal administration, and to treat the French officials as servants. If Canada were to become an independent State it would be even more exposed to this racial rivalry; the principle of harmony and unity necessary for survival would be missing.

Annexation to the United States would remain a possibility. The Western provinces, where the American element is strong, would favour it, and if the United States wanted to seize this English colony by force, resistance would be impossible. Would they want to? Would they try to annex eastern Canada, since its joining the American republic would only add to their religious and educational difficulties? American statesmen reject this dangerous means of growth. One can assume, therefore, that this annexation would come about only with the consent of the interested parties.

Here is where our solution comes in. If French Canadians were strong and resolute enough, they could profit from the circumstances and establish a French State in eastern Canada. Moreover, this would be the accomplishment of the plan our forefathers conceived. *Action française* is simply recommending a return to the political system, organized by England in 1774 and completed in 1791, that lasted until the Act of Union in 1840. The State of Quebec remained a separate State, the continuation of New France, until 1840. Fifty years after the Conquest, in 1810, Governor Craig informed his superiors in London that the *Canadiens* wished to be considered as a distinct people, taking pleasure in talking of a *nation canadienne*. London wanted to check these aspirations, shatter our hopes of French unity, and suppress French Canada as a distinct political entity. In 1840 London arranged for a 'mixed marriage', as Abbé Lionel Groulx calls it. When the marriage was annulled, French Canadians should have regained their freedom, but instead we made an alliance in which we now number one in eight. Since it now appears that this new situation is not final, *Action française* urges its fellow-countrymen to cling to their former aspirations, which were formulated in a distant time when the ideas of nationality and homeland and the dream of French independence arose among us, stimulated by the awareness of our ethnic entity.

But we wish to bring this plan into being only within the limits imposed by natural and divine rights and within the sphere of our duties of justice and charity, which are imposed upon communities just as they are upon individuals. If the tie with Britain, which keeps on weakening, breaks some day, and if the confederation, which is powerless to unify its heterogeneous groups, cannot become an independent nation, then the parties concerned will regain their freedom. We ask French Canadians to prepare for this eventuality and to keep alive in their hearts the feeling of uniqueness that is three hundred years old, in the hopes of founding in eastern Canada a French State.

These aims are based on religious foundations. If we defend our French integrity against imperialism and federal assimilation, it is only to safeguard our Catholic integrity and to uphold the apostolic mission of New France. Without generalizing a theory and uniting the safeguarding of religious concepts and national thought in the human soul, we realize that things would be as follows with our people. If French Canadians do not keep Catholicism alive, they will become anglicized, and if they do not preserve their language and the intimate motives of the French spirit, they will seriously risk ending in Protestantism. Catholicism and the French spirit are the sources from which French Canadians draw the strength to overcome the obstacles against their survival as a distinct race in America.

One can see that the doctrine that *Action française* propagates embraces in a harmonious whole all the activities of our people; it binds them to the past and directs them toward a bright future. *Action française* knows that the setting up of a nation is complex, that it is the work of time, of circumstances, and of man's will, and that through the course of long labour these factors produce an original character. Since time and events do not dispense with our acts of free will, *Action française* wishes to organize them along the lines of our traditions. The national problem of French Canadians seems to it to be of vital interest to our very life, and it sees in this problem all of the elements that make up the normal life of a people: material progress, moral worth, and great culture. In order to uphold a philosophy of life, an inner rule that sustains our resolutions and develops our gifts as a Latin people, *Action française* offers the hope of a great future. It urges our nationality to develop within itself a love of life and to affirm its will to endure and prosper, in order to broaden its personality and blossom forth as a State spreading Christian and French civilization in America.

Patriotism? Nationalism? A magnificent plan that finds its justification in natural law, our history, our political and social situation, and three hundred years of effort and sacrifice.

17 Esdras Minville
Corporatism and National Concerns

We have already dealt with this subject during the *Semaine sociale* in Trois-Rivières in 1936. Therefore, we shall take up this topic again only to summarize what we said on that occasion.

Let us note immediately, in order to calm beforehand the apprehensions of certain people who are frightened or aggravated by the mere suggestion of nationalism, that the doctrine of corporatism is neither English, nor French, nor of any particular nationality. It is universal in principle, just as it is in its practice, which corporatism aims at organizing in such a way as to make it one of the main parts of the social structure.

But if there is the doctrine, there is also the *milieu* in which it must be applied. And if the principles of the doctrine are universal and unchanging, the *milieux* on the other hand are varied, as ever-changing as our material and human world. Consequently, there is unity of inspiration but diversity of action and methods. This is why His Holiness Pope Pius XI, in recommending to the world the corporate institution as a formula for social organization, refrained from laying down, or even from suggesting, methods for its application. On the contrary he asserted that these methods must spring in some way from the spirit of each people. Therefore, if one cannot conceive of national corporatism, one can very easily imagine national forms of corporatism. And it is in this sense that we shall speak of French, Belgian, or Canadian corporatism.

Having said this, let us consider the problem as it exists in Canada. We want to bring about corporatism, not in the abstract, half way between heaven and earth, but in a given *milieu*: our *milieu*. There is little need to remind ourselves that this *milieu* is geographically, economically, and ethnically diversified to a perplexing degree. And so the question arises as to what method of instituting corporatism would be both the fastest and the most reliable.

Would it be advisable to start the task in the country as a whole, or to restrict ourselves in the beginning to a territory which, although more limited in size,

Translated from 'Le Corporatisme et le national', *L'Action nationale*, XI, October 1938, pp. 131–40.

would offer ethnic, social, cultural, and, let us say, even spiritual homogeneity –
all of which are indispensable to the success of such an undertaking – and then
be ready to extend this action gradually to the rest of the country?

More precisely perhaps: would it be necessary to attempt the organization of
the Canadian population into a single block, with no consideration for cultural
and moral differences? Would it not be preferable to choose the group best
suited to embrace the idea, so that, supported by a solid nucleus, we could later
extend the reform to the rest of the population? In short, a question of method.
Let us examine this more closely.

A glance at the map convinces us that our country is too varied in its
geographical, ethnic, economic, social, and moral composition to lend itself
unanimously to a work of such magnitude and complexity. Such are the
contradictions of facts, from one end of our territory to the other, that the
federal government has been unable in seventy years of methodical effort to
draw up a policy capable of reconciling the most general economic interests of
the different parts of the country. Now to these contradictions of facts are
added others, more serious and perhaps more unyielding, that are of a moral
nature: in the Province of Quebec the great majority of the people is of French
origin, culture, and expression; the majority in the other provinces is of English
origin, culture, and expression; each group having a different way of life; an
almost unanimous adherence of the French population to Catholicism and of
the Anglo-Saxon population to Protestantism; the economic inferiority of the
French group and the financial, industrial, and commercial preponderance of
the other group; finally, the attachment of the Anglo-Saxon Protestant population to a socio-economic set-up of liberal inspiration that is closely related to,
and almost derived from, its very religious beliefs, and which has acquired for
this group economic and political supremacy in the country.

These, then, are the fundamental contradictions with which we fear we may
grapple in vain, especially in the present unsettled situation.

If, as we said above, the federal government after seventy years has not yet
been able to reconcile the purely economic and administrative interests of the
different parts of the country, how could we hope to make a reform succeed in
one sweep, a reform that brings into question particularly lofty principles, and
that goes so far as to claim to modify man's attitude toward economic, social, and
political matters?

Does this mean that the Province of Quebec, considered as a territorial entity,
would present none of the obstacles that we have just listed for Canada as a
whole? Since Quebec forms a fairly well-defined geographical and economic
unit, the contradictions of facts disappear, or almost. Is the same true of the
other provinces? Unfortunately no. They have neither ethnic, cultural, nor
religious unity; but they do have the same economic supremacy of the Protestant
Anglo-Saxon element, even when it is a minority. And, because of this
economic power, the same stubborn attachment of this element to the socio-
economic set-up to which it owes, or believes it owes, its present wealth and
power.

Whatever way we turn, it does not seem that the reorganization of our society in the form of corporatism can be undertaken on a territorial basis, to speak frankly. It is the human factor that counts first of all, and it is with men that we must work first and foremost.

And so we believe that, to ensure ourselves the best chances of success, we must begin to organize the corporative institution, not in a given territory, but with the human group that by its situation and its mentality is best suited to understand these chances and to assure the triumph of corporatism – namely the French-Canadian group.

1. Canada and the Province of Quebec, seen as a field of action, oppose many all but insurmountable obstacles to an undertaking of this kind. However, the French-Canadian population, viewed in the same perspective, offers considerable facilities for accomplishing such a project: economic and moral homogeneity; cultural unity and common aspirations; and especially, unity of religious faith, and, because of this, an adherence, which is at least tacit, to the social doctrine that must be made a living reality.

2. In the minds of French Canadians a pressing need for a nation-wide restoration is linked with the daily more evident necessity for social reform. We are greatly interested in reconciling the two movements, which can only gain power and magnitude, the one reinforcing the other. It is a fact that:

(a) No social doctrine answers our needs as a people better than that of the Catholic Church. What is surprising is that we did not notice this earlier. Since we are a minority in our country and a very small minority on the entire continent, and since we are subjected daily to influences from the four corners of this continent, we must adhere with all our strength to a national credo and plan our action carefully in all spheres, if we are to resist, to persist, and to grow in number and power.

Is this in fact what we have done? Our economic and social life has been organized haphazardly, without guiding ideas, without unified views, under the anarchical impulse of foreign power. Far from establishing a social framework based on our individual spirit, we have accepted that which a minority erected among us, and we have even done ourselves harm by entering into it. Therefore it is not surprising that, having given up all the control levers, we have been overcome, then bypassed, and finally reduced to a state akin to servitude.

At first we laid the blame on others, then upon ourselves, accusing ourselves of all manner of shortcomings. But only a relatively short time ago we opened our eyes to the true cause of our confusion, namely the lack of national social doctrine.

The disorder that is so evident everywhere prompts us today to reconstruct our economic and social life on a new basis, one that is adapted to our own temperament and to the demands of our situation. People are becoming more and more convinced that our very national survival depends to a large extent on this reorganization.

(b) Moreover, we will go so far as to say that, as a people, we would reap few benefits from the corporative institution if the reform were brought into effect, as so many others have been in the past, without consideration for the **national character** of our population. Could one in fact maintain that the social reforms carried out here in the last quarter-century have revived our national spirit and consolidated our positions?

The life of a people is something other than a succession of isolated compartments; and because we have treated our lives this way for a long time we have arrived at nothing definitive. This crisis, which is still acute, is merely the painful manifestation of an illness that exists first of all in the mind. Now we ask: is this mental deficiency among us caused solely by the weakness of our social sense, or is it caused also by the widespread absence of national feeling, extending from the top to the bottom of our society? Undoubtedly it is caused at least as much by the one as by the other. In order to be entirely effective our therapeutic action should therefore aim as much at the one as at the other. Without this we would risk losing in the sphere of national concerns, and consequently in the cultural and eventually the economic spheres, what we had tried to win in the domain of social concerns. Where would the progress lie? We must never forget this: our problem is quite special. This kind of problem among other peoples arises as a simple social problem, but in Canada it assumes the proportions of a real national problem. The abandoning of farms, the proletarianization of the masses, the education of the younger generation, etc. – all social problems for any people; but for us essentially national problems, since, due to our position, they bring into question our national existence itself. And so how do we resolve these problems if the national preoccupation does not join with, and even superimpose itself on, the social preoccupation for the purposes of enlightenment and guidance?

No. What we must implement is a combination of national education and social education, the one functioning along with the other. National education will make patriots of us, aware of the value and richness of the national culture and therefore attached to it. Social education will liberate us from the petty and destructive individualism in which we have delighted until now, while proving that there are no valuable and lasting organizations other than those that respect ethnic and cultural peculiarities, and that employ the methods imposed by these peculiarities.

(c) Furthermore, in order to convince people that no very extensive social reform could be undertaken in the Province of Quebec without consideration for the national character of the French Canadian, it would be sufficient to examine briefly, at close range, the notion of common good, as M. Maximilien Caron did in this review a short time ago. In fact we make up about eighty per cent of the population, that is, a very large majority. Under the terms of the constitution that governs us, we are entitled to lead an autonomous life and to establish the social framework that suits our spirit and temperament, as long as there is no injustice done to the minority; also, through the action of democratic institutions, we are entitled to provide ourselves with the political policy we want. We have not always taken advantage of this prerogative: is this any reason for renouncing it, especially nowadays when decades of a faulty sense of direction have placed us where we are? With regard to this point of view there is, however, a reawakening, a kind of recovery of mind and will. No one any longer believes, for example, that the next generation will endure economic dictatorship to any great extent, or that it will yield to the powerful foreign capitalists the privileged position that they have enjoyed at our expense until now. The time is coming when great Anglo-Saxon or American industrialists and powerful businessmen in all fields will have to accept the regulations that our political authorities impose on them. But our political authorities will impose only those regulations that the majority dictates. We are largest in number, and there is no reason why our influence should not predominate. The lines that the corporative reorganization of our society could follow appear quite clear from the first glance. The agricultural population, taken as a whole, and the great majority of the working-class are French Canadian. In both these cases there are professional associations and trade unions for which it would be sufficient to round out their membership and modify slightly their basic ideas in order to turn them into corporations. In the country small business belongs to us; in the cities we are still generously represented. Our participation in large industry is almost nil, but in small and middle-sized industry we still occupy a certain number of positions. Everywhere in the liberal professions we dominate completely. We own the rural property and a good part of the urban property. We have, therefore, all that is necessary to establish quite rapidly the elements of the corporative institution. A good number of pre-corporative organizations, in addition to the farmers' associations and trade unions already mentioned, exist in French Canada: the College of Physicians, the Bar, etc.

It is all too clear that we cannot leave the restoration of our economic life to the initiative of poorly informed individuals; it is just as clear that we could no longer expect everything from politics even if they were greatly improved. It is essential that we react against the tendency, which is growing stronger every year, to expect everything from the State and to rely on it to solve all problems, whether individual or collective, economic or social. What we need from now on is the careful organization of individual initiative in accordance with a well-defined doctrine, so that we can stipulate the political policy that will answer the needs of the majority, that is, our needs. Now, such a doctrine cannot avoid taking into account the cultural and national well-being of the majority of the population, since this well-being is of such importance that no people could renounce it without giving up at the same time all hopes of success in every area. The social reform that we are contemplating, even if undertaken solely with the common good in sight, cannot ignore national preoccupations. The corporative institution will not be French Canadian, since, we repeat, it is universal in principle. But what will be French Canadian and Catholic in inspiration is the social framework within which the economic activity of our province will flourish. And it is precisely this that the constitution of the country aims at establishing.

18 François-Albert Angers
Why We Shall Never *Accept Conscription for Overseas Service*

In the discussions that have centred around conscription for overseas service since the beginning of the war, a whole series of arguments was collected against such a measure. Some of these arguments should, to our mind, take precedence over others, as having the sort of common sense that might appeal to our Anglo-Saxon compatriots.

The principal argument has been, especially at the start of the war, that we must avoid conscription in order to save national unity. This was tantamount to saying: because the French Canadians do not want it. As the matter was not urgent, and as everyone remembered what happened in 1917, even the Conservative Party accepted this theory without further thought as to why – in the words of M. Lapointe – we would *never* agree to conscription. 'We shall see in due time . . .' muttered the people in fanatically pro-conscription circles.

Then, with a gradual hardening of the situation, people asked – and still continue to ask: 'What is the use of conscription, if requirements are amply met by volunteers?' Some have even gone further. Mr. King himself nearly came round to this opinion in his last speech. It has been stated that our particular role in this war does not leave room for conscription; that conscription would impede a total war-effort by depriving our agriculture and industries of the necessary manpower for supplying an England cut off from its European and Far Eastern markets; that it would prevent us from furnishing England with enough equipment and ammunition to make up for possible losses in her own factories, exposed to enemy raids. Finally, the objection was just recently raised that we needed all of our men for the defence of our own threatened Pacific coast.

This is all very well, in a way. But it also serves to confirm our English-Canadian friends in their belief that our stand against conscription is not as strong as it might seem; that our objections are purely incidental; and that we would accept conscription as readily as any English Canadian if volunteers

Translated from 'Pourquoi nous n'accepterons *jamais* la conscription pour service outre-mer', Actualités No. 8, Les Editions de l'Action Nationale, Montreal, n.d.

were lacking and it were shown that our real coastal defence lies in Singapore, in Bombay, or in London. Moreover, they have been encouraged in their conviction by certain ambiguous and dangerously subtle arguments on the part of some of our officials. And three ministers in the King Cabinet – Messrs. Ilsley, Mackenzie, and Ralston – have based all of their recent speeches on this conviction, from which comes their theory that the only mistake the Conservatives made in 1917 was in acting too bluntly, and that the Liberals will accomplish the same purpose through the use of tact and moderation. So that, with the sod barely settled over the grave of Ernest Lapointe, English Canadians are already beginning to think he was grossly exaggerating when he said that we would *never* agree to conscription.

Because of this wrong impression having been created – and wrong it is, as we shall see – I feel that, on both sides of the racial barrier, Canada is in for a great disappointment, which might be even more fatal (if that were possible) to national unity than a brutal enforcement of conscription. Disappointment on the part of the French Canadians, who have been and are still being promised there will be no conscription. Disappointment – with dangerous repercussions for us – on the side of the best-intentioned English Canadians, who will be astonished to see us protesting (if circumstances make us lose our case) against a measure we shall have given the impression of accepting, and to which they will have assumed we had been converted! Then they will no longer be ready to accept the valid reasons we shall be disclosing too late, after having concealed them for so long. They will say, once again, that we do not know what we want. They will label as treachery or sedition on the part of a few hotheads what will actually be the tacit – if not explicit – refusal of a whole people, who were never resigned to the acceptance of anything other than of keeping quiet or of hiding their true feelings under plausible excuses. For there are no two ways about it – as any French Canadian will tell you spontaneously and even bluntly – Ernest Lapointe was right: we will *never* accept conscription. Never, because our main objections are not merely incidental or, if they are, they are dependent on incidental circumstances that are much broader in scope than the present passing conflict.

In my view it is high time some light was shed upon this confused state of affairs. We should try to make our English-Canadian compatriots understand – to quote Mr. Godbout – that it would be criminal to enforce conscription. And the crime would doubtless be compounded by the irrefutable validity of some of the above-mentioned arguments against conscription, incidental indeed, but rooted deep in the fundamental reasons for our objection to conscription. The true reasons, that is; those that make it inevitable that we should say *never*, to the dismay of English Canadians, to whom very few people have ever taken the trouble of explaining the true reasons for our attitude. And now we feel we have the right to expose these basic reasons in broad daylight, for all of Canada to see. There is no other way of making ourselves understood. It is in the interest of Canada as a whole that, in the days to come, we should all do our utmost to avoid the future of our country being built on the quicksand of misunderstanding.

Our Concept of International Policy

The first and most fundamental reason for our attitude, and the least tangible of all, pertains to our concept of international policy.

Every English Canadian, however 'Canadian' he may feel, is an imperialist at heart. Having lived in the atmosphere of a world-wide Empire, he carries with him, or inherits from his parents, an imperialist concept (which, in all good faith, he calls 'international') of his new country's defence. He is not an imperialist in the sense that England any longer comes first – this reaction is no longer as common among English Canadians as one might think. Nor is he an imperialist (though such cases are rarer) when it comes to being more interested in the Empire than in Canada. But as a Canadian, he will not feel safe unless the Empire remains untouched. And if the Empire as we know it did not exist, if all his energy were concentrated on Canada, he would deem it necessary for the security of Canada that all sorts of strategic posts be equipped with the strongest possible fortifications. If he is more ideological than practical, if he is, say, a socialist, he will reason quite differently. He will criticize imperialism in all its aspects. He will preach equality and international justice. But as soon as anyone in some remote part of the world so much as points a threatening finger in the direction of these strategic posts whose very existence he originally condemned, he will instinctively want to crush the foreign intruder in the name of the defence of Canada. In other words, his interpretation of the word 'defence' is so distorted and subjective that he will demand *absolute security* for himself; the world must be so ordered that he himself will be made to feel fully protected. He will take it for granted that this theory is legitimate, since he is naturally convinced that no one has anything to fear from him. That is what I call an imperialist concept of national defence or international relations, because it implies the maintaining all over the world of outposts that the other great nations have a right to consider as being based in their own immediate security area.

It cannot be denied that there is some measure of truth in this. There is no doubt that the less its neighbours' relative strength, the greater a people's security. Factually speaking, this is true. Whether it is a *fair* and *necessary* concept of foreign policy is another matter. As far as French Canadians are concerned, if they search their conscience, they are not likely to agree with such a concept, even in the subconscious of those not trained to think about such problems.

As the descendants of a small people in whose minds the imperialist concept of the world is a long-lost memory except for the suffering it brought upon them, the French Canadians are too weak to aspire to dominating anyone, or to try to lord it over any other nation. They ask for only one thing: to be left free to live in peace. This being the case, they do not in the least wish to be mixed up in the quarrels of the great powers, whose ambition and desire to seize and maintain advanced positions are a constant source of conflict. And they do not approve of the great powers' policy of dragging all the smaller powers into their ventures and of tying them to their apron-strings. They feel that it is up to the great powers to settle their disputes among themselves – disputes in which neither party is ever as totally in the right in thought or action as each likes to pretend. French Canadians are therefore basically uncommitted. There is no doubt about that. Even M. Lapointe had to admit it, in a speech that was to become famous in recent months, when he spoke of the compromise that had been reached between the committed and the uncommitted. But, although the compromise has to some extent been consummated, it has not altered basic positions in any way.

French Canadians, of course, are no stupider than anyone else. They can grasp the meaning of world events fully as well as any English Canadian. And so they are quite ready to decide, in a case of conflict between the great powers, which side should have their sympathy. They are the first to disapprove of violence, of violations of international law, and of unchristian ethics. In a war such as this one, which is not *per se* a fight for democracy or Christianity as we are told it is, but a conflict of imperial interests, they are too shrewd not to realize that democracy and Christianity were dragged into it, to a certain degree and in a certain way, to suit circumstances. That is why they are ready to show and to prove their sympathy for those with whom they prefer to side. They would be even more willing to do so if the English Canadians were not so demanding, tactless, and obtrusive. They would be ready to prove it if they were allowed to act of their *own free will*; that is, if a majority of a different racial origin did not demand and expect so much more than the French Canadians feel, in all fairness, truly able to give.

Besides, such sympathy should have been voiced from the neutral position that Canada, to their way of thinking, should have adopted in the best interest of humanity. Not only was a neutral position warranted by Canada's geographic situation (though this, again, is purely incidental), but also by the fact that, *as a small power, its war-time mission should consist in preserving the soundest values of civilization – those values that are always threatened by that exalted brand of war-time patriotism that unleashes man's most brutal instincts*. In this respect the French Canadians are more clear-sighted than the English Canadians, whose vision of Canada is blurred by the lenses of imperial power, and who are apt to forget that, although it has become an international power, our country is only a small power and, as such, cannot share the same interests, the same responsibilities, or the same obligations as the larger powers. They are in closer agreement with a man they respect – the Pope – who, for the sake of humanity and civilization, has always tried to prevent modern conflicts from spreading, by inviting the two parties at war to abandon their goals of pride and prestige and make their peace in the name of justice and charity.

Of course, there is no point in reopening a debate on this. Nor is it our intention to do so here. But now that the matter of conscription has been officially brought up, one cannot explain the French-Canadian attitude without reference to this basic reaction of theirs. This reaction is the only reason why they will not put up with coercive imperialist measures for sending them to England, to Libya, or to India. 'If the English want to hold Singapore, that is their affair; but then, let them look after its defence themselves,' is their attitude.

And it is common sense. The thought that Singapore might be essential for the protection of *vital* (that is, neither commercial nor imperialistic) Canadian interests seems all the more ridiculous to them, for if all the powers applied the same reasoning, then Japan would be justified in having a base on Vancouver Island. They do not blame the English for wanting to keep Singapore – they prefer to mind their own business, unless unduly badgered – but they do not want to be forced into sharing the responsibility.

These are not petty reactions. They stem from our particular concept of international life, which is very different from that of the Anglo-Canadians, though it is far from being more backward or primitive, as is all too often supposed. If we take the trouble to analyse it, we shall find, on the contrary, that our concept is more civilized; perhaps *too civilized* for the so-called 'practical' world in which we live today, whose realism, however, has so far led to nothing but conflict. It cannot be dubbed isolationism. It is a perfectly sound concept of international relations, a concept that may well fall into line with certain French-Canadian isolationist aims, though no more than the policy of so-called 'collective security' for maintaining the *status quo* coincides with the aims of the great powers after winning a world war.

Given this particular outlook, French Canadians could never accept conscription for military service all over the world. They would be the first to rise up in ardent defence of their country, if attacked by foreign powers that they considered their enemies. They would fly to the aid of outposts or countries that are naturally situated within their own defence-area – Newfoundland, for instance, or Alaska (in joint action with the United States), or St. Pierre and Miquelon. They could be persuaded to serve in other parts of the world, *if they felt like it, and much more out of a spirit of adventure than for any other reason.* But to be sent there by force – never! Let every nation play the part to which it is suited. Let the smaller powers prepare their defence efficiently. Let them support friendly great powers with their sympathy, by avoiding direct or indirect collaboration with the enemy[1] and, if circumstances, situations, or resources allow, by co-operating with their friends. As for the rest, let the great powers defend and pay for the advanced positions they feel they must hold. As powerful nations they are the ones who are best equipped for the task. If not, then they should limit their ambitions to what is really *vital*, according to fair international policy, and learn to abandon old habits and adjust to new situations.

That is the true meaning of the French Canadians' 'never'. Its political and philosophical connotations are such that it really does mean never, so that in no circumstance could they possibly be made to change their mind. Their gesture of self-commitment was made with much more good grace than was to be expected. It was made only because, first of all, they were assured by people whom they trusted that they need only commit themselves moderately; and more especially, it was made because they were formally promised there would be no conscription, a definite 'never'! To persuade them to retract this 'never' would require their conversion to imperialist views on international policy or on their own security. And such a conversion is all the less likely since, with their purely Canadian outlook, they feel that Canada is not in a position to play the imperialist game, and that it would not be in its own final interest to do so. Lastly, such a conversion is made less probable still by the fact that, even if the venture were to be profitable to Canada, they, as French Canadians, would not be likely to draw the same benefits from it as the English Canadians.

Our Survival

This last statement brings us to the other reason why French Canadians will *never* accept conscription in the current conflict: our position in Canada. Granted, the reason is highly incidental, but the incidental circumstances surrounding the case are of a long-term nature and have nothing to do with the war.

It has been said time and again that we are fighting to preserve the advantages that result from our being a part of the Commonwealth. This is only a half truth. First of all, barring a few individual cases, there is practically no economic advantage to our being a part of the Commonwealth, or at least none as compared to English Canadians. For the simple reason that in all those industries that thrive on the Commonwealth connection we hold only minor positions. I imagine any conqueror would be inclined to use us as mere unskilled labour. But let us leave such minor considerations aside.

The major consideration is the one our propaganda so often likes to boast about: our freedom to develop according to our nature and in the way we ourselves determine. In this respect the propaganda is not altogether wrong, except as regards the economic aspect of this development. True, we have enjoyed a freedom we would probably never have had anywhere else. But – and this is the important point – we do not enjoy this freedom to the same extent as our English-Canadian friends do. *What freedom we do have consists merely in our being allowed to continue our 182-year-old struggle for survival and for preserving the heritage that cannot be taken away from us.* The struggle is not yet ended. The survival is not yet certain. What we already have is no doubt a great deal when compared with what many other countries have but it is still very different from the complete freedom our English-Canadian friends are eager to safeguard abroad. For, in our case, all of our forces are already so tied up on the home front, in keeping a watchful eye on a numerically stronger and more powerful competitor, that we can hardly afford to pay much attention to outside events without running the risk of our neighbours stepping in as soon as our backs are turned.

For our survival is more than ever threatened on all sides, within the very boundaries of Canada. French Canadians, conquered by military force in 1760, are still being forced today to accept the decisions of a so-called democratic Anglo-Saxon majority, after having had to fight against the political and even military (1837) coercion of a colonial oligarchy. Unfortunately, this majority force, this special brand of democratic totalitarianism whose action might otherwise be tempered by wise politics, is still stirred by unseen influences that have not yet given up the thought of anglicizing French Canadians, and that have, indeed, already partly succeeded in this task through economic development with its undermining effects on our three pillars of defence – the family, the parish, and the school[2] – in which economic factors have begun to shake our faith. Such influences are still continuing their work in war time, and are trying to consolidate the victories brought about by Ottawa centralization – as a University of Toronto professor confessed in his comments on the Rowell-Sirois Report. What is more, they are banking on conscription to help them achieve their evil purpose by the much more effective process of *elimination*. A recent article in the *Ottawa Citizen* made this quite clear when, in order better to justify the aggressive plot against our national existence, it accused us, in Nazi-like fashion, of being against conscription purely out of a spirit of aggression and domination.

Despite their being absorbed in the war effort, our opponents still do not leave us a moment's peace. It is therefore understandable that we should not be as receptive as certain Anglo-Canadians to the idea of being forced to run to the aid of a people who are fighting to preserve what we have not yet so much as acquired; namely, a well-defined status and the acknowledged right to remain as we want to be – an unconditional right, granted without any ulterior motives, in such a way that we might truly be partners in a bi-ethnic country. Far from this being the case, we find that our reasons for complaint outside Quebec are many when it comes to such elementary rights as language and religion, notably as regards the schools. Not to mention the aggressive and insulting attitude of far too many English Canadians. The extent of their aggressiveness is reflected in the English-Canadian press of whatever political persuasion. The force of their hatred is such as to prompt them to say – as a St. Thomas, Ontario, daily did – that we were done an unduly great favour in being allowed to fight for our rights, to struggle for preserving them. This same hatred even goes so far as to threaten withdrawal of such rights, and is coupled with the worst possible insults, such as were published in a paper of such high standing as the *Winnipeg Free Press*. Even inside Quebec unpleasant incidents and offensive actions are multiplying. And all this is part of one big plot under way since Confederation, with Machiavellian intentions on the part of some, and in perfect good faith on the part of others who do not know any better. The plot consists in placing the province of Quebec increasingly under the thumb of the English-Canadian majority, through centralization of taxation and economic and social control in Ottawa.[3]

Given this exhausting internal struggle and the growing dangers of our situation, how can we possibly adhere to a policy of war that would jeopardize our only chance of survival – namely, through mass passive resistance? How can we dream of joining in such a policy, knowing as we do that we have no way of making up our losses, while all the other racial groups in the country can always count on immigration to swell their depleted numbers? How can we ever submit to such a policy, knowing full well what this 'equality of sacrifice' asked for in conscription actually means? It means that for every six sons fathered for his country, a French Canadian will have to send all six to serve on the Rhine, on the Channel, or elsewhere; while an English Canadian – who has spent his income on himself instead of raising children – will have to send only one or two.

Even if he does have two sons, he can be pretty sure that one at least will find refuge in the federal civil service or in the war industry, where one French Canadian out of six will be lucky to find employment, if he does find it at all.

For if there is one grave injustice that we have always had to suffer and that I have not mentioned before, it is the fact that we are not given more opportunities in federal and industrial administration, and in higher-ranking positions generally. I need not quote the statistics; they have been published repeatedly and speak for themselves. This particular situation is due to the hatred of anything French Canadian on the part of those who hold key positions in government or industry. It is also due not so much to our over-emphasized incompetence, as to the fact that, even with the best of intentions, English Canadians cannot appreciate our concept of teaching and training, with its accent on general education rather than on specialization. English Canadians, as the lords and masters of the country as a whole, have built up our civil service and our industrial world in an English-Canadian context, without taking us into account. They cannot be bothered with training a young French Canadian as they would one of their own youth, when the former might not be as familiar with such or such a technical skill, but would be quick in acquiring it and would soon become a better colleague than any of their trained staff. It is a well-known fact, which *Maclean's* recently confirmed as far as the army is concerned, but which applies just as much to the civil service, that the entrance tests or examinations are based on Anglo-Canadian school standards that are no better than ours; they are simply totally different.

You may feel that this has nothing to do with conscription. It has. It is because of this situation that the son of an English Canadian, as I was saying before, always has a chance of escaping front-line danger. He will even be made to escape it, whether he likes it or not, because he is needed on the home front. But the French Canadians are not needed. Yet their intelligence is often far superior, so that they too might aspire to serving their country just as competently at home, while by the same token ensuring the protection of French-Canada's post-war élite. Is that what is meant by equality of sacrifice? And do we not have the right to cry out in exasperation at such a scandalous political threat? Does it not follow clearly, then, that in these circumstances and in this war, French Canadians can *never* accept conscription for military service abroad? Their indignation is indeed justified when to all this we add the previously mentioned argument that conscription would be useless anyway, since it would be harmful to the over-all war-effort even as envisaged by the most convinced, but intelligent, imperialist.

Let us leave such considerations aside for the time being. Let us suppose for a moment that the strongest motive for our objection to conscription were removed by our becoming converted to an imperialist concept of our own country's defence. Well, even so, any just and intelligent being would still understand that, given our situation in Canada, we will never, *never* accept a policy of conscription for service anywhere in the world while our rights in this country – and not just our right to defend our rights – are not fully and universally recognized. By recognized, I do not mean the general, vague sort of recognition that takes away with one hand more than it gives with the other. I mean a clearly drawn up charter that does not mince words, where the existence of a French-Canadian people is acknowledged, along with their unconditional right to their own life as a full-fledged nation. A charter wherein the bases will be laid for true co-operation in a confederation that guarantees to French Canadians everywhere their fundamental rights to education in their own language and religion, as well as the highest degree of autonomy in Quebec. A charter where clear provisions are made for granting them their share of opportunities at all levels of the civil service, even if this should require changing Canadian administrative structures and adapting general standards to fit in with our educational system, rather than expecting us to conform to the general pattern and to become anglicized if we want to hold federal positions. This is a prerequisite to any real union or national unity in this country. And the fact that it is nowhere near materializing adds weight to the strength of our 'never', at least as regards this particular war.

We must say NO!

If anyone had ever brought all this evidence to Mr. King's attention; if Mr. King had taken the trouble to understand it, setting aside his own biased opinions (he presumably has them, like everyone else); and if Mr. King is truly the honest man and the great liberal he is said to be, then I cannot help but feel that the thought of calling a plebiscite would never have crossed his mind. At any rate, it is high time that such evidence be revealed to all English Canadians who pride themselves on their sense of honour. It is high time they should learn the naked truth, as it lies deep in the soul of any French Canadian, whatever his outward attitude. Complete frankness remains the only way to put our best foot forward on the road to national unity.

As far as we are concerned, this recapitulation of the reasons behind our attitude should convince us of one thing: namely that, considering our sub-stantiated objections to conscription, and considering how adamant we are about it, no one should so much as consider himself free to go back on his word and enforce conscription. If a commitment has been made *never* to impose a given policy, then no one should ever be released from such a commitment. Mr. King has made a mistake. He was probably badly advised by people who misjudged us. The only way he can be made to realize it, there being no other alternative, is for us to say NO!

19 Canon Lionel Groulx
Why We Are Divided

I am not quite the first to deal with this subject. I know that it is full of dangers and pitfalls. Our independent and impartial C.B.C. allows only certain people to talk about it. I know that this cloth I wear requires me to be careful and discreet. But I know, too, that truth sometimes requires intelligent courage.

◁ Causes of Division of a General Nature

Why are we divided? The question is often asked, though in merely asking it one assumes a painful state of affairs. When a country's leaders are always talking about *union* and national *unity*, it shows that these things do not exist except as ideals. We are disunited, profoundly disunited. That is the hard fact. National union has never been so weak in Canada as during this war. And never before, we might add, have such clumsy attempts been made to preserve it.

But what are the causes and who are the people that have divided us? A mystery, an unanswerable question? Not unless we dodge the issue or seek the culprits where they are not to be found.

Our divisions, like all divisions between countries, peoples, or nationalities, have fundamentally the same general causes. Man turns away from man the day he turns away from God. If people do not believe themselves to be children of the same Father, then the brotherhood of man is dead. One cannot love God without loving one's neighbour. Ever since Cain, if you like, or since Adam, we've had a fratricidal tendency in our blood. We seem to have taken Cain as an example. Like him, man has not merely refused to be his brother's keeper. Men hate and kill each other. This hatred has spread from person to person, from clan to clan, from class to class, from tribe to tribe, from people to people, as human organizations have become larger and more diversified, and as they have opposed each other because of interests or differences of blood, of culture, or of ideas. In ancient and modern times alike, political or military empires and great economic forces have all failed to produce the brotherhood of man.

Reprinted from the English translation by Gordon O. Rothney, published as a pamphlet by Les Editions de l'Action Nationale, Montreal, 1943. This address was originally delivered at the Monument National (Montreal) on November 29, 1943, and published with the title 'Pourquoi nous sommes divisés'.

Internally, empires have too often bullied small peoples and thus driven them to desperation. Externally, because of covetousness, and a desire to monopolize the riches of the earth, empires and economic organizations have provoked competition, and rival organizations have precipitated savage wars.

Leagues of Nations controlled by Big Fours or Big Fives have done no better. Christianity remains the only real attempt in the world's history to re-establish human brotherhood. It reminds us of our common origin. It reminds us to say 'Our Father who art in Heaven'. It has added the further conception of a God assuming our form, giving us a brother and a leader, and establishing for us the incomparable brotherhood of the Church, a brotherhood that associates men not only in the same faith, but in the same hopes, the same love, and the same eternal happiness. But when Francis I of France, to save his country from being crushed by the Austro-Spanish forces, made an alliance with the Turks and the Protestant princes; and when the Reformation tore to pieces the seamless robe of Christianity, then the commonwealth of united Christendom accomplished by the Middle Ages was well and truly destroyed. The old causes of division, for a while mitigated by Christianity, were again let loose, with unprecedented violence. Eighteen hundred years after the death of Christ, Joseph de Maistre could make this bitter but just statement: 'The nations do not love each other.' Everywhere they are divided by frontiers which are now traditional – race, colour, language, faith, interests. One must deplore such a state of affairs. No politician, sociologist, or historian who makes any claim to a healthy realism, has any right to ignore, nor even to minimize, these deep-rooted causes of division. Moreover, we have had sad experience in Canada of how these conflicts of belief, of language, and of culture have disunited us even more, perhaps, than conflicts of interests.

To demonstrate that for ten centuries Englishmen and Frenchmen shared the same Roman Catholic faith; that their two languages have exchanged thousands of words, and that after all, to quote Clemenceau, England is only 'an old French colony gone astray', to think up beautiful ideas like these is not the way to have much effect on an Orangeman of Brockville or Toronto. There is no use trying to bring us together by showing that we are close to each other in blood and culture, otherwise the Poles would have no better friends than the Russians.

✕ Specific Causes: History?

Apart from these general causes of division, are there others that apply more specifically to our country? According to some, the chief responsibility lies with history. And the strange (I am tempted to say grotesque) idea has been put forth that the history of Canada should be taught in the same way from one ocean to the other, with a single text-book in which our history would be carefully smoothed out and written with a mixture of ink and honey and – a little soft soap. Of course I don't want a history full of hatred and passion. But two kinds of history cannot exist. I know only one – history that is objective and impartial. Once, when certain University men tried to force me to write an official history, and gave me a choice between my University chair and my freedom, I replied that I would choose my freedom. History as a means of propaganda (or official history, which amounts to the same thing) is the very negation of history. The only real history is that which says, not what could have been or should have been, but what has been, no more, no less. It must call the good, good, and the bad, bad. It takes into account, of course, the ideas, the atmosphere, and the customs of each age. But it has not the right to alter the truth in any way, and even less to pardon everything. Don't worry, such a history does not teach hatred of the English. It would teach rather to know a certain type of Englishman as he really is. It would not be the servant, I hope, of politicians, promoters of national union at all costs, nor yet of those who more or less consciously want a 'melting-pot'. It would have the invaluable merit of not teaching lies and of not sabotaging the past. And I would even add that it would do more to bring about an intelligent, genuine *bonne entente* than those apostles of concord who are either self-interested or naïve will ever accomplish. Supposing objective history did no more than to teach French Canadians not to think of the British Conquest as necessarily a 'providential benefaction', or of the expulsion of the Acadians as a somewhat hurried conducted tour, a theme for Longfellow's poetry; not to confuse a Craig with a Sherbrooke, a Sydenham with a Bagot, a Metcalfe with an Elgin; not to mistake the Durham Report for a Christmas greeting nor to put it down to a little indigestion on the part of a Lord who had overeaten; not to consider the Union of the Canadas as an outburst of brotherly affection nor the school laws of the English provinces as monuments of legislative wisdom or a unique chance to learn English; if, to put it bluntly, it taught nothing else to our compatriots than to make a distinction between justice and injustice, between right and hypocrisy – not to mistake a kick for a compliment – and finally to know in what country we live and with whom we live and to regulate our attitudes accordingly, such a history, I venture to say, would work effectively for good understanding in Canada because the way to come to terms with English Canadians is to make the French Canadians neither a naïve nor an enslaved people, but a people with their eyes open and as much backbone as the English.

Furthermore, regarding this idea of a uniform or single history, could we adopt it without betraying some of the greatest and most original aspects of our past? If there is one strong chain in this past it is Catholicism. French Canada is, more than anything else, a child of the Church. In fact, a whole epoch of her history grew out of faith and mysticism. Her fundamental social institutions, her customs, her traditions, come to her directly from the Christian spirit and her French law. If there is a constant factor in the life of our little people, it is their missionary spirit; first evangelizing the American Indians, then sending pastors to every diocese in Canada and to a considerable part of the United States; then, in recent times, a producer of apostles for the conversion of heathen continents. Now, I ask those of good faith how a uniform history to suit the taste of all sects and of agnostics, how such a history can be written and taught without the risk of altering or obscuring to our detriment some of the essential aspects, indeed the foundation, of our life? If it were possible, moreover, to write this smoothed-down and patched-up history, whom would it profit? Which of the two races has the more apologies to make? Which has, in its past, the more disagreeable acts to strike out? You find here again the old doctrine of abjection, the politicians' old tradition of unilateral and unlimited concessions. They ask us to forget our past; I am all for it, provided that they forget both sides of it, and that, for example, one group does not believe itself to be still on the Plains of Abraham or in front of the signature of the capitulation of Montreal. I accept any forgetfulness that will serve to bring us nearer to one another; but I don't want a forgetfulness that will only serve to put us to sleep. Moreover, this camouflaged history, eminently suited to make our people into a race that cheerfully receives knocks, injuries, a race resigned to any humiliation, politicians of every stripe can try if it pleases them to impose it upon our schools. For my part, I believe that I know teachers who will not teach it, and little French Canadians who will never learn it.

Moreover, apparently our English-Canadian friends do not all have a very firm confidence in the effectiveness of *bonne ententiste* history. Concerning a study by Sophy L. Elliott, *The Women Pioneers of North America*, an idealistic history that aims at cementing friendship and understanding between the races in Canada, Mr. R. M. Saunders, of the University of Toronto, protests in the *Canadian Historical Review* (March 1943) against the rise of a history in which he sees 'naïveté and a lack of realism'. 'Writers with such aspirations should realize that if greater harmony is to be cultivated between these two groups, they must meet together and study their existing contemporary problems.'

Sensible and true! A doctored history would do no good for the excellent reason that to look for the causes of our divisions in history is to look where those causes are not to be found. Just let the pact of 1864–7 be faithfully observed; just let French Canadians from one end of the country to the other be treated not as brothers (we don't ask that much) nor with generosity, but simply with the justice due to associates of equal rights, and more simply still, as a race that has a right along with all the others in the world to the four liberties prescribed so grandiloquently by the Atlantic Charter – and who would then believe that the exploits of Winslow, of Lawrence, of Wolfe, of Craig, of Dalhousie, of Colborne, of Durham, of Metcalfe, even when told and taught exactly as they were, would prevent our two people from understanding and respecting each other, would prevent especially a people that has always extended the hand of Christian pardon from extending it again in order to bury racial passions and give peace to Canada? It is not what happened yesterday that divides us. It is the injustices that are still being perpetrated.

ⅹ Extremism?

Whatever those among us who toady to the Anglo-Saxons may say, we are not extremists. And our so-called extremism is no more the cause of disunion than is history. I know of nothing stranger nor sadder in our life than this morbid propensity for belittling our spirit and for accusing us of every sin, particularly of one we have not committed. Number if you can the good souls who pester us continually with 'Watch out' and 'Be careful', as if we were warriors always ready for a campaign, or mad fanatics always wanting to devour our neighbours. I even read in a large French-Catholic newspaper, following some statistics concerning the favourable effect upon Quebec of her high birth-rate, these shameful and unbelievable lines: 'The large family is the precious monopoly of the French element in Canada. We should not abuse this monopoly'! These singular *bonne ententistes*, so sweet for others, so sour for their own, more sensitive to disunity among the races than to disunity among their compatriots, so zealous for general reconciliation that they are ready to achieve it at the price of strife among their own brothers: they would have us believe that we are the wolves in Canada, and that the others are the lambs, which leads to the paradoxical conclusion that it is the lambs who have eaten the wolves. Certainly we are in an epoch of romanticized history. In my opinion there is a very simple way of settling once and for all this question of extremism. Rights have been trampled under foot in this country, and it is known where. Laws and solemn promises have often been violated. Anyone can point out those who despise justice and those who break the constitution. Well, of those who put history into reverse and insist that we have the spirit of the wolf, I ask only one thing, that they show us our victims. Let them show us the minority or the weak whom we have crushed, the rights upon which we have trampled. Let them cite a case, only one, where national feeling has carried us beyond the limits of right and justice. And if these gentlemen have no complaining victims to produce, what less can we ask of them than that they keep quiet. They want to know what has divided us? Let them look somewhere else besides in Quebec. Let them ask in Charlottetown, in Halifax, in Fredericton, in Toronto, in Winnipeg, in Regina, in Edmonton, in Ottawa, especially in Ottawa. And if in these places there is no reply, there are other ways of finding the answer. Extremists, French Canadians! I know only one form of extremism among them: extreme candour and credulity, extremism in humbling themselves before the English. If our compatriots deserve to be reproached, it is not for holding tenaciously to a grudge, nor for being slow to pardon. It is for having too short a memory and for always ingenuously believing that each blow they receive will be the last. Surely we are a wounded, humiliated people. During the last hundred and fifty years we have often been cheated, humiliated, bullied, and betrayed. But one must add proudly, we have remained a people without hatred. Extremists that we are, we have never returned blow for blow. Thank God, we do not covet either the goods or the rights of anyone in this country. We do not nourish the slightest desire for vengeance against anyone. And if we could only be left alone and be given no more than justice, then they could demobilize all the *bonne entente* preachers and send them back to their war effort.

True Causes: Failure to Recognize the French Fact

Since they lie neither in the teaching of history nor in our alleged extremism, where shall we look for the causes of disunion? A major question which no one can evade. One can palaver indefinitely about national unity, about the need for it and the stupidity of disunity. Nothing will be changed as long as we do not get to the root of the matter and have the courage to face the facts when we find them. The first obligation that English and French Canadians owe to each other, and I would also say, the primary condition for a *bonne entente*, is frankness. I shall avoid subtlety. I say quite simply that so deep a division as that which separates the two races in Canada must have deep-lying causes, for it indicates disagreement on major issues. Let us say it: the two races do not get along well because one of them wants legal equality all right, but on condition that it keeps for itself the lion's share. I know there is nothing new about this truth. I know also that it is a crude truth. But it is true. In the final analysis one category of Englishmen cannot forgive us for existing – and for claiming to exist with the same rights as these gentlemen, the same liberty, the same dignity. In other words, what they do not wish to recognize or accept in Canada, with its juridical and political consequences, is the French fact. There does exist a category of open-minded and generous Englishmen with whom we can get along. But there exists another that cannot realize that everybody does not think and feel *à l'anglo-saxonne*, has not the same reactions as the Anglo-Saxons, as if the human race inhabited an Anglo-Saxon universe. I certainly do not deny, and none of us would dream of denying, Anglo-Saxon greatness. But can they not recognize in certain circles, as ex-President Hoover pointed out the other day, that the Anglo-Saxon race constitutes only ten per cent of the world's population, and that consequently there are on this planet several handfuls of people who believe themselves to be French, Spanish, Portuguese, German, Russian, Italian, Greek, Bulgarian, Norwegian, even Japanese, Chinese, Burmese, and Hindu, and who, after all, don't seem to mind it? Why do we have here this obstinate opposition to French, not only to its official use in the political sphere, but even to its being taught in minority schools? Why this rationing of culture, imposed on those who inherit one of the world's greatest cultures? Why this opposition to French influence in the federal civil service and even within the ministerial offices? Why this persistent effort to limit the French fact to the borders of Quebec? Why? How can such facts be explained? And if it were we who were guilty of such an attitude, what would our English-Canadian friends see at the bottom of it if not the reflexes of a still virulent racialism, the old spirit of the conqueror always thirsting for domination and knowing well how to keep a respectful distance between the races.

The historian Duncan McArthur, former professor in Canadian history at Queen's, and formerly Minister of Education in the Hepburn Cabinet, was thinking of that sort of an Englishman when he wrote, in one of his historical works: 'In French Canada, after the Conquest, as elsewhere and at other times, the greatest hindrance to the anglicizing of the community was the Englishman.'

We need wonder no further by what phenomenon the right to think, to feel, to act French Canadian became narrow provincialism and, in war time, isolationism. In this attitude, moreover, these English Canadians see eye to eye with our renegades and our big politicians. According to a good observer, the American journalist William Henry Chamberlain, 'the regional spirit is strong in the Dominion . . . Every Canadian province,' as he wrote in his book *Canada*

To-day and To-morrow, 'has a strong mark of individuality.' This does not prevent French Canadians from being regarded as the only ones sadly afflicted with a particularist spirit! Their particularism alone is a sin. And our sin of particularism is that we sometimes think of our country before thinking of other people's countries. Have they asked themselves whence comes this particularism? Since from 1604 to 1760 the French fact existed alone in Canada, I do not think we have any excuses to make. Since 1760, with whose assent and with whose complicity has the French fact been maintained and strengthened? I ask your indulgence for returning thus to matters I have recalled so many times. In 1764 we refused to become English, in the British Empire. Ten years later the Quebec Act, that is, the Imperial Parliament consecrated, and we know with what éclat, this will to isolation. This consecration the same Parliament renewed in 1791 by the forming of Lower and Upper Canada, and this at the express request of the Loyalists and the British emigrants who were to constitute Upper Canada. The deplorable result, which we cannot help, was that, for half a century, Lower Canada continued to live its life as a distinct province or State. In 1841 an attempt was made to return to the assimilation policy of 1764. We became stubborn in our isolationism. We formed a bloc around LaFontaine as for twenty years we had done around Papineau. In 1842 first Bagot and then the Imperial government bowed anew before the irreducible French fact, because they could not do without our political collaboration. The final and most solemn consecration took place in 1867. Confederation was not possible without Quebec, and we refused to enter Confederation except as an autonomous province. We thus again became an autonomous province, a French province. Once, twice, thrice, four times. How many times must the French fact be recognized and consecrated before certain people decide to accept and respect it, without undue limitation, without equivocation, without offensive bargaining? There indeed lies one of the main causes of our divisions and our quarrels, and our *bonne ententistes* would do well to recognize it. There has been an everlasting policy of hesitation, or, if you prefer, a two-faced policy – recognizing and not recognizing the French fact, recognizing it but seeking always to limit it and, if possible, to suppress it. In 1774 they seemingly bowed to the French fact. Yet, in this country which was to remain French, to whom did they give political power? To whom went the best of civil positions? To the immense French-Canadian majority? Not at all. To a handful of American Loyalists and new immigrants from the British Isles. The first movement of this infamous minority was to begin a fight against the French laws of this province and for the repeal of the Quebec Act. After 1791, in this province, which according to Pitt, Grenville, Burke, and several others was to retain its French character, who continued to govern? Did they place confidence again this time in the majority and in the original population of the province? In the face of an elective chamber three-quarters French-Canadian they raised an omnipotent governor, responsible only to London, then an Executive Council and a Legislative Council where never, during fifty years, did the French Canadians hold a majority. In other words, under a political régime supposedly representative or democratic, the minority, or rather a bureaucratic clique which at first represented less than one-tenth and toward the end less than one-quarter of the population, really possessed and exercised power. For half a century this clique governed Lower Canada as it pleased, and maintained institutions that were not only radically opposed to the national character of the province, but the very negation of democracy. And in spite of that, some people are amazed that our fathers were at times discontented and that an 1837–8 occurred in our history. Would you care to know how a historian has judged this régime?

'It was,' he wrote, 'the very obvious lack of frankness in the process of reversing the policy of the Quebec Act, while professing to respect it, which increasingly exasperated the French Canadians ... To insure the French Canadians all the essentials of their nationality, and yet to deny to them the logical and necessary consequences of a complete control of their domestic affairs and of an ultimate escape from the national humiliation of a foreign yoke, was nothing short of the refinement of racial cruelty, which, fortunately for the reputation of British humanity, the English people have repeatedly condemned when practised by other countries. To expect the French Canadians,' continues the same historian, 'to voluntarily forgo their nationality, and peacefully resign themselves to British citizenship, was the height of absurdity.'

The historian who speaks thus is not a French-Canadian historian and is not a professor of the University of Montreal. He is an English-Canadian historian, Mr. Adam Shortt.

✕Misunderstanding about Confederation

The last consecration of the French fact took place at the time of Confederation. This was its greatest consecration, completely categorical. No one can be ignorant of what this régime of 1867 was meant to be. In the minds of the Fathers of Confederation it was to be the legal expression of a free collaboration: collaboration between the races, collaboration between the provinces. They supposed that they had settled for ever, beyond dispute, the French fact, the question of races and languages. An article of the constitution proclaimed the legal and political equality of French and English. According to the statement of the most authorized leader of the English Canadians, there were no longer either conquerors or conquered in Canada, but associates possessing equal rights in all domains. The new régime asserted the idea of political decentralization. The unitary State, or what was then called legislative union, was rejected in order to form a federation of autonomous provinces, which restored to old Lower Canada its complete political and national individuality. Quebec even attained, in this federation, a privileged situation, a supplement of guarantees. Paragraph 13 of Article 92 of the constitution assured us exclusive control over property and *civil rights in the province.* According to a judgment of the Privy Council of England, this has the same meaning as Article 8 of the Quebec Act, and thus the federal Parliament should be incapable of removing anything in the domain of our civil rights. Moreover, by Article 94 of the same constitution, Parliament kept the right of unifying civil law in Ontario, Nova Scotia, and New

Brunswick, but *gave up the same right* in regard to the law of the Province of Quebec, which thus became doubly untouchable.

These were the basic ideas that gave birth to Confederation; these were the masterly stipulations of the contract of 1867. But what has been the policy, in regard to the French fact, that has generally been followed in the English-Canadian provinces and at Ottawa for the past seventy-six years? The direct opposite of what it should have been. In all the provinces the French minorities have been submitted to a rationing of their culture and to restrictions in the teaching of their religion. At Ottawa, the centre of Confederation, in the Parliament and the government that should protect minority rights, the French and Catholic minorities, one after another, have vainly implored protection against the despoilers of their rights. In the federal domain, the French language holds its position with difficulty only at the price of being constantly on the defensive. Canadians of French origin are forced to struggle with a voracious bureaucracy, without too much success, for a meagre share of positions and influence in the civil service. By its social legislation, the federal Parliament knowingly undermines our civil rights. Even in our own province, the federal bureaucracy undertakes to pervert and, at times, to demolish our type of workers' organization. What do I say? Ottawa does not respect even the fundamental principle of Confederation. The general tendency of its policy in regard to the provinces is to take over their autonomy. This policy, begun before the war, Ottawa has continued stubbornly with the war as an excuse. Wherever possible, it has tried to extend its ambitious centralization, a uniform-ism that affects particularly the most differentiated, the most original province, namely Quebec. It endangers its fundamental institutions, its liberty of action, and, consequently, its future. Penned up in the Quebec 'reserve', behold our 're-serve' itself threatened by assault. Whatever may be the opinion of a contributor to a recent issue of *Relations*, Canada does not deserve to be considered an example to the world for its liberal solution of the problem of nationalities and minority rights, so long as one nationality, ours, which is thirty per cent of the population, is not content to see, served on the family table, bones already picked over by the lion.

Let us be frank. We are still divided on an extremely serious matter: the interpretation and the execution of the Confederation agreement. The increasing disagreement on the very principle of the federal State bodes ill for the future. A conviction is slowly developing in the uneasy mind of one of the mother provinces and of one nationality that she can no longer rely on the central power to be protective or impartial. More than that, placing itself at the head of the most hostile elements, this central power plots against the most sacred rights of one province and against the national future of almost a third of the Canadian population.

✷ Misunderstanding as to Patriotism

The misunderstanding unfortunately does not stop there. While deceiving us so completely, the men of Ottawa found means of sowing between the races

other seeds of division. When the ethnic groups of a country are too diverse by
blood, history, and cultural inheritance, there is still the possibility that at least
they may meet and come to an understanding through common affection for the
same country. A country, to give to the Canadians a country, this was one of the
dreams and one of the solemn promises of the men of 1867. Did they proclaim
so loudly their design to create a Canadian soul and spirit, a 'new nation', as they
said, and yet to this new nation bequeath nothing but the earth we live on?
Having hesitated over the name by which they would call it, having thought of
Columbia, New Britain, etc., they rallied to that of Canada, for the name evoked
a great history and a superb geographic entity, one built by the immortal
explorers. Then, that this Canada might really be for the Canadians, John A.
Macdonald talked of making it a 'great British monarchy'. He wished to make
the Confederation a vice-royalty with a member of the royal family at its head.
He and his colleagues proposed to call the new country, 'Kingdom of Canada'.
You know what has become of this dream of greatness and liberty. For forty
years an offensive return to the most abject colonialism has made Canada
retrogress toward political infancy, has brought us back, in several particulars,
to the condition of 'Crown colony'. What have they not done to uproot us, to
kill Canadian sentiment? They have exacted of us, for another country, sacrifices they would hardly dare ask for our own land. I understand that some good
souls question and no longer know who directs our external policy. Briefly, at
the present hour, nothing so much divides Canadians as the equivocacy, the
disagreement as to the very reality of the country itself. Honest opinion will tell
you that seven out of ten million Canadians see themselves deprived of the right
of loving their own country most of all, for the benefit of the country that it
pleases a minority of imperialists to impose upon them.

Was it to produce these miseries, this return to colonial servitude, that the
Fathers created Confederation? Ladies and gentlemen, I am not a separatist,
whatever may be said. I believe and I teach my students of the University of
Montreal that Confederation might have been welcomed in 1867 as a great
French victory. The ills we suffer, I maintain, come less from institutions than
from men. I mean the sort of men who for seventy-six years have held, or rather
have degraded among us, the role of leaders. I believe that an intelligent and
energetic race that would not allow its politicians to betray it, might, in spite of
this political statute, develop freely its whole life, including its economic life.
On the other hand, I believe that I state the fundamental thought of my compatriots, at least of those who still hold themselves erect, when I speak thus:
we want a central power at Ottawa, we do not want a centralizing power. We do not
want a super-state whose principal care is to demolish the provincial States.
Nothing in the world, and certainly not the interests and combinations of the old
parties, will make us stay in the Confederation to play there the part of Cinderella
or to allow the men of Ottawa to place the burden of national peace on the back
of the Province of Quebec. They are not going to make of us a perpetual Jonah to
be thrown upon the waters whenever the boat gets into trouble. Furthermore, in
the family residence we want our place in the living-room with the others. We will
not be relegated to the servants' quarters. Finally and especially, enrooted in this

land for three centuries, having contributed gloriously to the conquest of its independence, at least theoretical, convinced by historical experience and natural law that a free and reasoning man has but one country, and one country only, we shall accept none other than the land of our fathers, Canada. We shall sing no other national song than a Canadian anthem, nor bear any other flag than that of Canada.

✗ Possible Remedy

I have tried to tell you the real causes of our divisions. Not being a politician, at least I hope not, I have not tried to hide the seriousness of the situation from you. I ask you if the citizens of a country can argue on more serious points than these: disregard or limited acceptance of the French fact and of the Confederation pact, that is, disagreement concerning the national and political structure of the country; and disagreement on the reality or very idea of a native country. That is our subject of disagreement in its stark reality. Is this to say that there is no remedy for such an evil? I do not believe so. But in order to be clear about the remedy, I repeat that we must realistically decide to what degree, among us, the evil of division can be cured, or, more exactly, how far we can go with this so-called union of races or *national union*. I do not say *national unity*, I say *national union*, according to the advice given us a few years ago by a man of law who knows the value of words, M. Antonio Perrault. Union, unity; it is the difference between the possible and the impossible. Since our country has been built as it has, with geographic differences, a mixture of races and beliefs, the federal character of its political constitution, let us ask objectively what can be humanly achieved, what legitimate hope does history allow. Let us ask, also, if there is not a perfection, a summit of *bonne entente*, for which it would be folly ever to hope. For some of our people, as you know, a supreme, transcendent reconciliation of races must come, cost what it may, even though we should have to pay all the cost and become, as a result, less French.

⤳ Bilingualism or Contacts

From this came the demands for bilingualism, an unlimited assimilation of teaching methods and ways of living, and undiscerning contact. I do not fear to call this false orientation, vain strategy. What good comes of dreaming of the impossible? All history follows strong lives which mark out their own direction. Peoples different by faith, language, law, traditions, and philosophy of life will never be able to think, feel, or act alike. Our land is too vast and too diverse to prevent the formation of irresistible regionalism, even in the English-Canadian provinces. We, the French Canadians, are too different. To attempt, under pretext of national union, to reshape our characteristics, the very foundation of our being, is to risk damaging or losing them without profit to our neighbours. Let us remember that it is not healthy or advantageous to a land to seek absolute uniformity. This truth, old as the world, an English-Canadian newspaper, the Halifax *Chronicle*, recalled to us a short time ago: 'But national understanding is a god which Canadians could not adore without danger. For, to give the term its full meaning, embracing the social, cultural and economic realms, would be a stupidity of the worst kind.'

Let us beware, consequently, of the illusion of bilingualism as a miracle worker of national union. English Canadians and French Canadians would need to talk more together only if their variances rested on misunderstanding. But we have seen that there is something very different from misunderstandings. The Irish of Ireland eventually learned the language of their oppressors. Did they become reconciled thereby? In general, Irishmen and Englishmen speak the same language today. Do they get along any better? We ourselves have pushed bilingualism to the point of imprudence. We have scorned universal experience, forgetting that bilingualism generalized is usually the first phase of a nationality's pangs. We have been led into this imprudence in the name of economic liberation and national unity. However, bilingualism has not prevented us from becoming more than ever the servants of the minority in our province. I do not see our Anglo-Canadian compatriots taking us more closely to their hearts for having learned their language more than they have learned ours.

Let us beware, for the same reasons, of enrolling *en masse* in Anglo-Saxon societies and clubs, infallible recipe, it appears, for ending all racial prejudices. I see clearly what French Canadians too often lose in these contacts; I have yet to discover what they gain. Whatever may come, we cannot enter like a herd into the societies of others, take part, by affiliation, in all the neutral associations, English or American, show ourselves consequently incapable of forming societies of our own, suited to our own spirit, and keep up any pretension to being a proud race, Catholics of initiative and creative imagination, and, in addition, *leaders* of social life in our province. We cannot play, dress, build, eat, think, feel like Englishmen or Americans and flatter ourselves that we shall remain indefinitely French. Enough of chimerical visions and vain dreams. To come to an understanding with the English, said Jacques Bainville, it is hardly necessary to cough or spit like them. We can unite; we cannot and we never should become unified. In the name of common sense, let us stop dreaming of a marriage of love where only a marriage of reason is possible.

×False Strategy

You ask me how to achieve this marriage of reason, this reasonable and realizable *bonne entente*? Have we so far manoeuvred wisely? If we were to credit the advice of a school of politicians and invertebrates, the good, the only method to appease, to subdue fanaticism is always to give in to it, to attack it with kindness, moderation, and resignation. This would mean never to forget that we are a minority, and that cleverness and prudence would order us to never talk too loudly, to walk softly, to abdicate our liberty of thought and our right to criticize, to listen to and perform on bended knee every wish of the majority, to say 'amen', indeed, to every imperialistic extravagance, to regulate our reflexes according to the reflexes of Anglo-Saxons. 'When an Englishman loves France,' said Sir Austen Chamberlain, 'it is as one loves a woman.' There are those amongst our *bonne ententistes* who, to become liked by the English, would be capable of changing their sex, if they have actually not already done so. Once more: wrong method; wrong strategy. I call to witness every realist who knows a little of the psychology of the Anglo-Saxon: to appear timid, fearful, to play the fool before him, are these the tactics that can win his respect? Is it within the means of the lamb to tame the wolf? The historian of the future, I am sure, will reproach us more than anything else for having acted like poor psychologists in our relations with the English Canadians. We have learned nothing of the psychology of the strong. I do not wish to ignore the existence of an English-Canadian élite, animated by the spirit of justice toward French Canadians, ready to admit the duality of culture in Canada, and who even have no other country than ours. The merit of these English Canadians is great enough, in being, and in appearing to be, what they are, for us not to economize in our esteem and our admiration for them. Is this any reason for hiding from ourselves the fact that for perhaps one-fortieth of the English Canadians who have their eyes open, thirty-nine-fortieths have their eyes still closed. If there exists an intelligent and generous élite which seeks to open these eyes, there is also an élite of the wrong sort which devotes itself to closing eyes that wish to open. You wish to deal with this Anglo-Saxon? Begin by remembering that he belongs to an imperialist race which, for two hundred years, has held an incontestable hegemony in the world. One does not wield such power, one does not play such a role for two centuries, without the idea of domination becoming instinctive and awakening a terrible racial pride. To this dominating passion, the Anglo-Saxon of Canada adds a somewhat troubled element. Paradoxical as may appear my assertion, I dare to say that he suffers from an inferiority complex. Recollect that, in Lower Canada before 1867, he lived for about a hundred years as a minority; in the United Canadas until about 1850, he remained a minority. Today, in this diverse country of nationalities so ill-mixed, in the dilemma of becoming again a minority, it seems as though he always fears losing the reins. To safeguard his supremacy, you will see him periodically seize upon projects for massive British immigration, but above all upon the ever-present imperialist idea. Imperialism is for him a motive force, his insurance premium against anxiety. In the final analysis, the Anglo-Canadian is an uncompromising imperialist, fiery, more imperialist than the imperialist of England, because he is an uneasy imperialist with an always exacerbated racial passion. Very attached, moreover, to the little European island that has made him one of the great world's great, he needs time to take root in another earth. It is not unusual, you will have observed, that in setting foot on Canadian soil, a new arrival from England takes on the airs of a young squire because he still thinks he is treading the soil of a colonial possession of the motherland, strengthened in his conviction by the childish attitude of a land that unceasingly clings to the skirts of the motherland. 'Metropolitan mentality, a newly arrived immigrant,' we say, with a smile. Nevertheless, let us not forget that to lose this newcomer attitude the Anglo-Canadian needs at least a four- or five-generation stay in Canada. How unwise then to act the colonial before him more than we need. You wish to know why we are divided? To those who are always looking beside the question, I can answer simply: because there is too much arrogance and pride on one side and not enough on the other; because, on one side, there is abuse of the desire for power and domination, and on the other there is abuse of resignation and of naïveté.

✕ Failure of Appeasement (*Diplomatie roucoulante*)

If time and experience can teach anything, it is the startling and complete failure of our policy of excessive candour, of unconditional co-operation, and, more than that, of what I would call our languorous or sighing diplomacy; others would call it bleating or servile. For, after all, if French Canadians are still ill-treated at home, could it be because they have refused to co-operate in the edification and the peace of this country? They have always co-operated to the point of feebleness, to the sacrifice of their most sacred interests, consequently to the point of silliness. We have co-operated, collaborated since 1760. 'While the said inhabitants obey and conform to the said orders, they shall enjoy the same privileges as the ancient subjects of the king,' promised Amherst. Lord Egremont wrote him from England: 'As you observed very truly, they have become the equals of the other subjects of his majesty.' Subjects equal to the others. Have you ever heard that any governor of the period reproached us for lack of docility? Yet, as early as 1764, the metropolis hastened to declare that our fathers, being Catholics, were shorn of all civil and political rights and were second-class subjects. Even so, we co-operated in 1776, when our nobles and clergy by their loyalty, and our people by their neutrality, saved the country for England. We co-operated in the time of the French Revolution; we even, at that time, called the English Conquest a 'providential blessing'. We co-operated in 1812 on the morrow of Craig's bullying. We co-operated in 1842, when the Union set-up pointed against Lower Canada would have justified a revival of insurrection. We co-operated in 1848 to endow the country at last with 'responsible government' and to prevent, in spite of the Tory loyalists, annexation to the United States. We co-operated in 1867, despite the dangers that Confederation meant for us. And, since 1867, although the federative pact, as we have seen, has been made into a dupe's bargain, and often into a trap, we have continued to collaborate; we have done so in spite of the unworthy treatment inflicted upon our minorities, upon our language, too often looked upon as though it were a Hottentot dialect. Each time that one of our rights was disputed, we have had political chiefs to ask us, in the name of peace and national unity, to give up a share of our rights. For peace and national unity we gave way every time. Decoy-ducks for M.P.s, Senators, decoy-ducks for ministers, trained to entice their compatriots toward the hiding-place of those great hunters who are the masters of Ottawa, or toward the princes of financial dictatorship. We have had enough of these to tear from us, shred by shred, our patrimony and our ancient pride. Political history since Confederation teaches that the majority of our supposedly great leaders have been more than anything else 'yes-men'. We collaborated during the war of 1914 and during this war, regardless of what so many decoy-duck majors may say. Certainly we have not gone, like others, to the point of hysteria and delirium. We have refused to confuse collaboration with a policy of colonial servitude or a policy of national suicide. As much as anyone, we have, none the less, given our money and our children. In our criticism of the war policy, we have never gone beyond the limits of a just freedom, of that liberty that we are supposed to defend on every shore of the world. We collaborated in 1914 when they took advantage of the war to cut the throats of our minorities. Since 1939 we have been collaborating while they take advantage again of the war to oust us more than ever from the services of the State, to begrudge us the positions of command in the navy, the air force, and the army. We collaborated even when they tore up the constitution, to make us understand, no doubt, that the cult of democracy, the franchise and the rights of small peoples, are all articles for export. In a word, of all possible concessions, which have we not made, even of those we ought not to have made? What have we gained? Crumbs, nothing but crumbs, and, for added measure, that haughty and subtle disdain of our English-Canadian compatriots who, in giving crumbs, act as though they are always according too much. The most flamboyant proof of the failure of collaboration without return and of languorous diplomacy has been provided us recently when to amend the federal constitution, they overlooked the formal wishes of Quebec. In this serious situation what attention did the Ottawa government pay to the warnings of the highest authorities of the province? As much attention as a locomotive does to the dust on the rail. It hastily confronted Quebec with the most dangerous act the central government has ever committed. So dangerous that Mr. Godbout, who in such circumstances is not accustomed to sin by extreme pessimism, was unable to keep back this word of disillusionment: 'If they can amend the constitution without consulting the provinces, the constitution is no longer worth anything to us.'

ˣ Realistic Diplomacy

What is to be done? A child would reply: 'Do not persist in your failure, and in the absurd; change your strategy.' Particularly at Ottawa. For our languorous diplomacy we should substitute the diplomacy of dignity. For collaboration without return or without profit we should substitute a collaboration based on interest, on give and take. Note well: I do not suggest a policy of unnecessary stiffness, even less of violence. I do not ask for war and I do not urge war. I propose the only course left to us, the course of legitimate defence. I do not preach an attitude of retreat; I want a policy of being present whenever there is need of being present, but only on a footing of equality and dignity. We do not need to show that we want national peace in Canada more than anyone else, since we have made more sacrifices for it than anyone else. We always keep our hand open and outstretched, but we no longer hold out a soft hand to be crushed. We cease to beg for union as if guilty of disunion, or as if the problem of understanding were not at least ninety-five per cent an English-Canadian problem rather than a French-Canadian problem. To sum up, we do not refuse to collaborate; but it must be two-sided collaboration. Our collaboration is no longer inspired, guided, by party servility, but by the interest of the province and of nationality when this interest is not contrary to the general interest. And we always retain the freedom to withdraw our collaboration. A policy of the earth, earthy, they will say to me. A realistic policy; a compulsory policy. The time has passed when there were for us optional policies or strategies. Since the spirit of justice and of charity proved incapable of producing national peace in Canada, what else can we try except to create it along the lines of interest? Agreements between nations are reached every day and have been for a long time on this prosaic basis. Let us call it, if it pleases sensitive souls, an *entente cordiale*. We all know those *ententes cordiales* where all that is lacking is cordiality. The *entente cordiale* between France and England was born, writes Jacques Bainville, 'the day England began to fear the German fleet'. It remains cordial, we know, as long as the German peril lasts and as long as the French army is worth something. Certainly, a Christian people can and should put some feeling in its political relations. Let us not put sentimentality into them, especially when the others do not do so.

⋊ In Quebec

In Quebec let us be strong with all our strength. Let us take heed of the incomparable value of our geographic position. In 1867 Confederation could not have been made without us; we have remained indispensable to Confederation. We are the arch that links the East and the West. By the river we guard the great door to the sea; through our territory we give passage to the transcontinental railways on their way to the ports of the Atlantic and the Pacific. Quebec, the nearest Canadian territory to Europe, furnishes aerial transport with its most convenient bases and landing-fields. There may be richer lands than ours; nevertheless, we possess some of the most opulent riches of Canada and of America. We possess them in sufficient variety to build one of the best-balanced economies of the world. These riches should no longer be offered to the stranger for some handfuls of cents or dollars. Let us regain those we have lost by every means that we can learn from our economists, particularly by the co-operative system. We have considerable purchasing power. Following the example of the whole world, let us use it for our own benefit first. Would certain mercantile races insult or frown upon us if we ceased to make their fortune for them? We have labour; let us not lower the market for it. Let us exact a just return from those who live and grow rich at our expense. Let us not abandon our workers to leaders from beyond our borders or elsewhere who ask nothing better than to sell us a Trojan horse.

We have political power. We should keep it entirely for ourselves. We should tear it from the domination of financial powers, from the claws of Ottawa. Let us above all have a definite policy. We must play an important part in the federal capital. We should remember that for a State the first condition for a strong foreign policy is a strong internal policy. See where a policy empty of all French-Canadian national interest has led us. In Quebec, it has led us to become the tools of the minority; in Ottawa, of the majority.

In Quebec, the minority has profited by it to undermine our economic and social structure; in Ottawa the majority has profited by it to undermine our political and national structure. As to the constitutional position of the provinces in regard to the central power, let us clear our minds of any obsolete idea; let us revolutionize our political concepts. The political authority of Quebec does not rest on any delegated powers. It is in no way 'an emanation of the Canadian government or of the English government'. In other words, and contrary to what they have too long taught us, the provinces do not hold their authority from the government at Ottawa; nor are they subordinate to it. As for the power that Article 92 of the federal constitution concedes to them, their powers are exclusive and supreme; thus, in internal sovereignty, the Canadian provinces are properly sovereign States. And I did not do this, need I add. I quote the teachings of our best jurists, themselves commentators on many decisions of the Privy Council of England. Let us then leave to others the denunciation, in season and out, of provincialism. Let us recollect rather that the provinces have every reason in the world to refuse to become colonies of Ottawa. To sum up, when we have our economic life well in hand, we shall begin to be respected. When we find the courage and the means to govern ourselves for ourselves, others will court us. Then we shall be able to dispense with *bonne ententistes* preachers.

⊁ Policy of Provocation?

Some will mistake this realistic policy for a policy of provocation. What could be better calculated, they will say, to raise against us the majority of this country. You can see them already, brandishing the English bugbear at us as though we were children, after the manner of our politicians. My response will be brief. The English bogeyman does not exist. The British no longer form the majority in this country; and, as we have said, it *implies* that all Britons are fanatics. Just and sincere men are able to understand that to defend one's right is not to attack the rights of others. And if they could not understand, what good would it do to talk any longer of an *entente* or of national peace? The proof that the bogeyman of our neighbours is not formidable is that they dread us as much as we dread them. As a matter of fact, while our opportunists raise before us the Anglo-Canadian bogeyman, the Anglo-Canadian fanatics raise before their people the French-Canadian bogeyman. Moreover, we are not alone in this land. If the English Canadians do not want our alliance and our collaboration, or even if they do want it, we should turn more than ever to the New Canadians. With them we have at least this in common, that they have no other native land than Canada and desire no other. They came here to live, like us, an ideal life of generous liberty. We are not alone in America. An interrelationship and a balance of forces have been established that can never be broken. If it happens that political leaders menace us, and that has been known to happen, and we are assailed by anxiety, we should remember that our situation is no worse than that of the Ireland of de Valera, now free, but still at the very doors of its former jailor, a jailor ill-reconciled to his expulsion from the Emerald Isle. We should remember especially that we are three million souls in Canada and that it is not in the power of any country, of any State, to govern against the interest of thirty per cent of its population when this thirty per cent refuses to allow it.

Anti-Christian Policy?

Some good souls will ask me: What do you make of the Christian spirit which teaches never to abandon the dreams of a brotherhood of races and nations in the charity of Christ? To them I reply: let us keep intact our Christian idealism, let us keep the dream, the hope of a national peace ever more firm and ever more generous. We must not forget, however, that we live in a world of earth and flesh. The Christian, so great in every way, is not necessarily a great sucker. The 'Christian genius', clearly explained Gonzague de Reynold, is 'a spiritual being who submits to reality'. May the real, the practical remain then, at least occasionally, our landing-field.

I insist that we do not ask better than to set up with our associates what the realist Franklin Roosevelt calls the relationship of 'good neighbourhood'. For peace, for understanding, we remain the same chivalrous race, loyal to its word and to its undertakings, disposed to forget all and to pardon all, always ready to go half-way. However, I do not see that the Christian spirit, which is one of wisdom, even of political wisdom, obliges us to go all the way alone, much less to adopt the attitude of the vanquished bearing the white flag. That this solution, this attitude, may be a solution and attitude exemplarily Christian I recall from the illustrious examples of O'Connell, and of Windthorst, who, to save their country or their Christianity, did not fear to resort to these practical means. This solution is essentially Christian because it applies to the strong, to the immoderate use of force, the only brake that is effective; because it preserves for the feeble and the small a consciousness of their rights and their dignity. Finally, it produces an atmosphere whence cannot fail to emerge respect instead of racial suspicion, esteem instead of charity. These are, and will be for a long time, the only bases for national or realizable union in Canada.

Appeal to Teachers

I see before me, in this audience, many teachers and many young people. Teachers, young and old, I trust that I have convinced you that the only future for our people lies in a sort of sublimation of its life. Raise as high as you can the spiritual ideal of education; raise the moral level of youth. Rehabilitate our race. Cost what it may, the frightening number of renegades or of decoy-ducks amongst us must diminish. From our political life must disappear that abominable ideal by which so many Catholics reach the belief that anything is permissible that hurts their province and nationality, not excepting treason, if it saves or even profits the party. The great sorrow for any man of faith and upright life is not to be discussed, misunderstood, and even insulted, but to see the depressing spectacle of cowardice and desertion among his former fellow-travellers. It is the cynicism of men in the maturity of age, his friends of yesterday, who, to rid their conscience of the corpses of an ideal, try their skill at sarcasm, sneering at the enthusiasms and exuberances of their youth. It is a funeral procession of spineless dogs, floating with the stream, poignant symbol of a race betrayed by its leaders.

Teachers, to put an end to these sorrows, to these moral miseries of a Catholic people, you know as well as I to what good use you may put our Catholicism. I will not dwell on it. May I beg you to pity a poor people, so great yesterday, which today knows not whither it goes, nor what it wishes, nor what is desired of it. Teach the young a greater sense of the continuity and beauty of our destiny. Teach them especially that we have a destiny and a magnificent one. Tell them more often that if we remain French in essence and a people of faith, we can be for the good of Canada, esteemed by those who do not stop at material greatness. We can be a ferment of marvellous life also for the whole continent, the dispenser of one of the greatest cultures of the world. Recall also to this youth our historic greatness, our titles, our right to be proud in the presence of English Canadians. Remind them that we are neither a nuisance nor a shame to Canada and that, in the building of our common homeland, our share, though different, is as great as that of anyone. To recall our services to Canada, or to old England, we are accustomed to name two dates: 1776, 1812. It is to belittle our history. For one hundred and fifty years we built this land alone; we discovered, explored, cultivated, evangelized it. Without intending it, but at no less profit to her, we prepared a jewel for the British crown. Today, we may assert it strongly: if there was once a Canada that was a British possession, and if there is today a Canada pure and simple, it is because there was first of all a French Canada, kept French by us in spite of her conquerors. If, at the treaty of St. Germain-en-Laye, New France had remained with Kirke and all North America had become an English possession, who can doubt that this Canada would not have been torn from England's possession in the struggle for American independence? If, on the morrow of the treaty of Paris, the Canadians had emigrated as they had the right to do, and if they had left the field clear for Americans from the south and British immigrants; if, in 1763, we had submitted to the harshness of the Royal Proclamation, and, having surrendered to London's policy of assimilation had lost or allowed reasons for remaining Catholic and French to grow weak, who can say that Canada would have resisted the seductive call that came from Philadelphia in 1776? If in 1849 we had made common cause with the annexationist Tories, that is to say with the fine flower of British Loyalism in full revolt against the English mother-country, who could have prevented Canada from passing under the American flag? Let us say it; let us repeat it to these gentlemen of the *Gazette*, of the *Star*, of the *Globe and Mail* of Toronto, of the *Free Press* of Winnipeg: If a Canada exists of which they can make today a bulwark of empire, it is because a share of it was built in the French way and because, in 1776 as in 1849, we refused to join their ancestors who wished to cede her to the United States.

Appeal to Youth

Young French Canadians, men and women, never has a more difficult task, nor a more inspiring one, been offered to a more ardent youth. Do not talk too much: a generation led astray robbed us of everything: our present, our future, and even the pride that gave us love of life. One thing remains to you that they could not take because it is untakable: your souls as young Frenchmen and as young Catholics. Become for us a strong, proud people. A proud people – one that has done with submission to the mighty, because they carry almost on their skin their sense of right, pride in their past and in their mission, and their dignity as a human nation. A strong people would be first of all a united people. Through ignorance, passion, or the folly of party spirit, politicians of the old school have destroyed our great ideas, the great feelings that are basic to the idea of patriotism or of national brotherhood. These ideological vacancies in our spirits have deplorably increased our individuality as Frenchmen. Today, not only are we disunited, but so much has this anarchy become a part of our blood that the best among us seem unable to exorcise the devil of discord. Youth who have thrown to the nettles the old empty partisan shells, you of a generation more homogeneous because of a firmer national doctrine, you will have understood that, in these evil days, the first duty of French Canadians is to establish a united front at home before trying to do it elsewhere. In this way, young people, you will serve, far better than anyone else, better than the professional *bonne ententistes*, the cause of Canadian union. If disunion exists between the races, particularly because the French Canadians are too divided to make themselves and justice respected, we conclude that there never will be union in Canada until there is national union among the French Canadians.

A strong people would still be a people attached to its moral strength, to its faith, to its Catholicism, by all the fibres of its soul, planted in its past, in its traditions, in its Quebec earth, as solidly as the maple. It would be a people possessing a well regulated organic life: economic life, social life, political life, cultural life. This masterpiece of strength and faith you will create, you will give to us. You will not build it by borrowing right and left, from foreign philosophies, from programs for social restoration that are not of our land and not of our atmosphere. A Catholic is too rich to borrow from communists or socialists. The French Canada of tomorrow, an original creation, will be flesh of your flesh, the flower of your spirit. It will gush forth, resplendent with youth and beauty, from the breath of you young French Canadians, from your sociology as sons of Christ. Whatever may be said, we are a little people who have never had much happiness to spare. You will do these things for us in order that at last there may come an hour in our life, a day of wholesome retaliation, when it will be possible for us to say to ourselves as others do: 'I have a land of my own; I have a soul of my own; I have a future of my own.'

20 André Laurendeau (1912-1968)
Is There a Crisis
of Nationalism?

In this article, by 'nationalism' I shall mean a very precise, conscious grasp of French-Canadian values and of the dangers that threaten them, as well as a fervent desire to work for their defence and development.[1]

The danger of such a broad definition is that it appears to include everyone. But without an arbiter how do we pass judgments on the supporters of nationalism? They are so diverse.

I have always found highly amusing the way foreigners who are unfamiliar with our *milieu* are so off-handed in claiming to establish classifications that really do not take our actual situation into account. They think they have defined us by merely recalling the names of Maurras, Barrès, or who knows, even Gobineau.

Having lived almost all my adult life among nationalists, I am still struck by their extraordinary diversity. There are nationalists in language, and their close neighbours, the nationalists of 'right': I mean that, for them, nationalism must be seen first of all as a claim for minority rights, or as linguistic devotion (and even this is quite varied: it can call for the recognition of French in places where it is forbidden, or for its purification, etc.). There are economic nationalists who give real priority to problems of this nature, and there are social nationalists. Besides, there is cultural nationalism, political nationalism, not to mention pure and simple traditionalism when it takes itself for a doctrine.

Other groups crop up from among these groups. Among the nationalists who are chiefly interested in politics, one finds an authoritative tendency and a democratic one (the tradition of which goes back for more than a century). Among 'social' nationalists similar distinctions arise, since there is a 'left' and a 'right'.

In some cases it is pure and simple predominance, but in others the preference for a certain aspect of nationalism tends toward exclusiveness. There are very few who succeed in setting up a hierarchy of the frequently contradictory demands of the nation.

Translated from 'Y a-t-il une crise du nationalisme?', *L'Action nationale*, XL, December 1952, pp. 207–25, and XLI, January 1953, pp. 6–28.

Add to this diversity real ambiguities that come from the fact that French Canadians live under double or triple allegiance: are we chiefly Canadians, French, or French Canadians? Four men whose thought and influence in such matters have been considerable are Henri Bourassa, Olivar Asselin, M. Edouard Montpetit, and Canon Lionel Groulx. All four are undeniably French-Canadian nationalists. Bourassa placed more and more emphasis on Canadianism. With Asselin nationalism was first of all French and cultural; with M. Montpetit there are economic considerations and a generally more subtle thought; starting from an interpretation of history, Canon Groulx develops a nationalism that is first of all French Canadian and *québécois*. Such divergencies as these are enriching, provided one does not stimulate them just for the sake of it.

Indeed, we are concerned here with remarkable intellects that have brought about syntheses. However, these syntheses alone are incapable of resolving all the problems. Temperaments are expressed through doctrines, and even an ardent love for the nation does not necessarily lead to identical answers to political, economic, or, least of all, intellectual questions. Unless nationalism is seen as a whole, the arising of these divergences is fatal.

You may say that this is all very categorical, but nationalists have traditionally given a great deal of importance to categorical discussions. Nationalist 'personalities' have always expressed themselves forcefully; I suspect them and their disciples (and therefore myself as well) of having preserved a strongly individualistic streak. There are times when the trees are so thick that we cannot see the forest. Contemporaries are, by definition, always a little too close to the trees to make out the forest clearly.

Consequently French-Canadian nationalism has been through many crises. Great names symbolize past successes and failures: Papineau, Etienne Parent, LaFontaine, Cartier, Mercier, etc. I myself have been present at three crises: the first around 1925–9 when the movement seemed to be caught in indifference; the second from 1936 to the war, and coinciding with the first Duplessis régime. The third will make up the subject matter of these articles.

Let us say right away that it is the most serious.

How are we to recognize it?

First of all, nationalism is not sure of itself. The divergences mentioned above are increasing. The fact that the present provincial government is considered to be nationalist, and really is in a few of its attitudes, tends to separate nationalists even more. We have seen them seated in opposing camps and seen them wound each other as only brothers who hate each other can do.

Another, more significant, symptom is that in most of the movements the recruiting of new blood is difficult. A good part of the young generation seems indifferent or hostile to nationalism (it is a different question whether misunderstandings and mutual ignorance enter into this attitude). Some of the nationalist movements look like families without children. This is not a promise for the future.

If the phenomenon is easily recognized, it is less easily explained.

General Causes

I see in this some general causes. First of all, the idea of a homeland is losing its force in the Western world (except in the United States where, moreover, it does not correspond to the traditional idea). This current of thought is running across the hemisphere. In Europe the homeland has demanded too many great sacrifices that led to the impoverishment of nations. The most serious questions (peace, trade, etc.) lie outside the scope of the homeland; other 'awarenesses' develop: class consciousness, awareness of belonging to a common civilization, European or American awareness, etc., such that the homeland appears as one value among others, and even as a value that harms the growth of other, more worth-while, values. The homeland loses its sacred character. Ideologies such as Marxism help speed up this movement, even in strongly anti-Marxist *milieux*. Finally, there is the pressure of facts that physically link peoples by increasing their means of rapid communication: from the press, the cinema, and the radio to the jet airplane; because of these phenomena the idea of a homeland seems outdated to many people.

However, there are other, more specific, causes at work here. They are very numerous and overlapping. Let us group the main ones under four chapter headings:

1. First of all there are concomitantly: (a) the decline of English imperialism and its influence in Canada; (b) the rapid rise of American influence and its effect on us; (c) the (apparent) decline of French vitality. Now, our entire life for three centuries has moved among these three countries; our external equilibrium is now entirely changed.

2. And at the same time the internal political equilibrium of Canada has been destroyed. The central government has acquired a power, dynamism, and stability that no provincial government possesses. This tendency, started during the First World War, has grown with the economic crisis, and it has developed a catastrophic attraction since the Second World War.

3. The industrial revolution that began in Canada at the beginning of the century displays before our eyes its social and demographic consequences. Now we are becoming aware of them.

4. One final problem has arisen: it is, on one hand, the attitude of the laymen toward the clerics and, on the other, the attitude of the Church toward the national problem. In the last twenty years or so they have both changed, and now attempts at readjustment are being made.

But let us examine more closely the four questions we have just listed and ascertain their repercussions in daily life and thought.

1: External Equilibrium

For as long as it has existed, Canada has been affected by various external factors. For a long time the predominant influence was British. Then the United States began to arouse in us the fascination that every large, free neighbour must necessarily arouse in a colony that is labouring impatiently under a yoke.

Due to the feeling it inspired in us, and due to its cultural brilliance, France had a more subtle, but nevertheless very strong, influence on us.

Let us split history into three periods to correspond with the three generations that are still alive. When my father was young, that is before 1914, Great Britain seemed to be the largest world power, its imperialism had just been affirmed in the Boer War, and many Canadians agreed with Henri Bourassa that our first duty was to fight for autonomy (if not independence) within the Empire. After Germany, France was the great European power; it showed extraordinary intellectual vitality. As for the United States, they thought it had a bright future and thousands of Canadians were drawn there; but despite the comings and goings of many of our fellow-countrymen, its already massive presence was not felt here (as a danger or a real temptation) except by a few alert minds.

My generation – those who were in their twenties in 1930 – began by seeing things as our elders had. France appeared to us as a still-great power and was recognized as a master, if not the master, in intellectual matters. We saw Great Britain rise again, keep its Empire intact, and assert itself in Canadian affairs despite the Statute of Westminster; and it was through Great Britain that we entered war again in 1939. The United States had shown what it was capable of at the end of the First World War; its products (even in the cinema and popular art), its business methods, its technical methods, and its capital were established in Canada. Denunciations of 'Americanism' had already become common but ineffectual complaints; they were far from arousing the same outcry as the struggle against British imperialism.

Today the situation is reversed. One need only consult our daily papers: our newspapers are filled with despatches coming from the States; everything coming from Washington or New York has priority; and since it is the same all over the world, how can we escape from the United States when it is our only neighbour except the North Pole? Washington possesses power and prestige: it is the central point of a coalition in which we take part with Great Britain and France (which are now secondary powers). The war brought about an extraordinary change. Words that would have stirred up the masses around 1938 or 1941 now seem somewhat anachronistic. Yet there still remains in many hearts an emotional charge of anti-Britainism that now has no object. But the 'American way of life' is a subtle and omnipresent phenomenon of quite a different kind, as omnipresent as the air we breathe in Canada, a permeation more persistent than the slyest British diplomatic moves, even those of St. George's cavalry!

The Massey Report describes the constant wave of American publications and despatches that inundates Canada. It shows to what extent this penetration goes, even in halls of learning and universities; and this is true for French Canada to a certain degree, despite the less and less hindering obstacle of the language. Thus the war signalled a split: our sociologists, scientists, doctors, and technicians are going more and more to the United States rather than to France for their university education. For one traveller who goes to Europe, ten, fifteen, or twenty tourists cross the forty-fifth parallel to look for rest and relaxation, and (less and less) to emigrate; in winter *la Presse* has hundreds, if not thousands, of subscribers in Miami.

Although one hears weak sounds of resistance, and Canada still remembers it belongs to the Commonwealth, our political direction is now toward Washington. In the broad sense we have become a political satellite of the United States.

And in economic matters we are their branch office – with a margin of local autonomy. Figures prove this beyond a doubt. They show that as the British Empire declined, an immense American influence arose. For example, in 1939 sixty-six per cent of our imports came from the United States, while we sent forty-one per cent of our exports there, which already shows a strong dependence. In 1950 the proportion of imports had hardly changed (sixty-seven per cent instead of sixty-six), while Canadian exports to the United States jumped from forty-one per cent to sixty-five per cent. Now, we know that exports are much more important than imports, at least in a case like ours; a merchant is more closely linked with his biggest customer than with his supplier.

Let us examine the movement of foreign capital invested in Canada:

Foreign capital invested in Canada

	1926	1949
American capital	$3,200 million	$5,900 million
British capital	$2,636 million	$1,742 million

In 1926 American investments were already larger than the British, and in twenty-three years they increased ninety per cent, while British investments fell by thirty-seven per cent. The case of Canadian railways is quite typical. We know they were largely run by British capital, and therefore not autonomous. During the war Canada bought back a slice of the shares in Canadian National Railways from Great Britain; at the same time Britain sold a part of its shares in C.P.R. to the United States. The over-all result was this:

Canadian Railways

	1939	1948
American capital	$588 million	$718 million
British capital	$1,215 million	$724 million

Here Canadians register a gain; but the United States rises while Great Britain falls seriously.

A last example. We estimate that thirty per cent of *all* capital invested in Canada is controlled by Americans, and because of this they exercise a determining influence on *all* of the Canadian economy.

Now an interesting reaction results. One part of English Canada rises up against the threat of absorption. Do they do this from British or from Canadian sentiment? It is not easy to untangle these still-confused feelings, but whatever the motive may be, the attitude is a good one.

It was expressed forcefully in the Report of the Massey Commission which still remains the strongest plea against the excesses of American influence in Canada. The members of the Commission limited themselves to cultural matters, but the principles put forward are valid for all the questions not treated there: if, for example, New York magazines invade the Canadian market to the point they do, the economic situation is chiefly to blame. The strong reaction of the Massey Report is an event of prime importance. It indicates that a part of the Anglo-Canadian intellectual élite is aware of the obstacles that hinder Canada's very existence as an independent and unique country.

This 'discovery' implies the revelation of an interior weakness, for if French Canadians feel weak in the face of American pressure, how much more at the mercy of events must the English Canadian who means to remain Canadian feel?

Would it not be risky to keep separate, on one continent, without natural borders, two groups of men who speak the same language, who have almost the same background, one of which is made up of one hundred and fifty million people and figures as the largest world-power, and one of which is made up of eight million people within a State of third-rate importance? It is a paradox that Great Britain successfully carried off when it played the world role that the United States has since assumed; but Britain has more pressing problems to resolve now. English Canada's 'guardian' has almost disappeared, and one seriously wonders if the plant is not too weak to stay alive.

To what does Canada owe its survival as a distinct country against the disquieting presence of its American neighbour? To English politics on one hand and to French Canada on the other. We have been one of the prime factors. Let us not draw excessive glory from this, unless it is for having preserved the French way of life by not speaking another language and thereby weakening and diversifying our *milieu*.

Now the British factor has decreased until it is little more than the shadow of itself.[2] The English Canadians who stand by their country and try to look ahead are growing closer to us. Will we receive them badly?

Here many opinions are possible, and traditional replies are not good enough. Also, we can see the French Canadians are divided on the matter.

Some say we must bring about a reconciliation with English Canada at all costs. Since we are already small compared to the immensity of the United States, we should at least stop arguing with each other; we must not fight among ourselves. Moreover, it would be ideal if we were to gather round a strong government, the government in Ottawa of course. For all provincialisms tend to scatter Canadians and dangerously multiply allegiances. These French Canadians believe in centralization with disarming naïvety and I would not dream of questioning their good faith.

Other people think this is a great illusion. They want to abandon an English Canada that is more British than Canadian, and that, on the eve of being devoured itself, has not given up the hope of devouring us. But reality is not that simple. Among the intellectuals who see the American danger, several still keep their old prejudices against the French; their 'centralism' is not always as innocent as some would have us believe; even when there is a break history continues somehow, and old feelings live on within a new viewpoint.

And so, as a consequence, one can see among us elements of a new separatism that would be based on new causes, all of them serious but lacking in one essential point: and that is that separatism, the splitting of Quebec from the rest of Canada, is a dream, a fantasy that we should abandon on leaving adolescence. The economic, technical, political, and military causes that made this ideal difficult in 1920 now place it among other anachronisms.

Between these two extreme attitudes there is a whole range of intermediary positions. To my mind they must obey a double will: one is the desire for the friendship of the two cultures, for the upholders of reconciliation are right, their view is based on a deep intuition of Canadian life. Canadians are not so numerous or so rich that they can afford to tear themselves to pieces or cordially hate each other so that they risk one day wanting to throw themselves into the arms of their great giant neighbour that is so sure of his strength that he does not even dream of taking them.

The other will is the desire for isolation. But this brings us to our second question.

11: Internal Equilibrium

Around 1920 the provincial States were almost all solid entities in Canada. However, the bases of their future weakness existed already. But Quebec and Ontario gave the impression of being stronger centres than the government in Ottawa, which, while much larger, was more faint-hearted. It was admitted that social life and education were solely and exclusively provincial powers, and the provinces were jealous of their autonomy. Despite the bitter experience of the First World War they remained stable and, along with their municipalities, received more than half of all the taxes collected in Canada.

In 1952 this solidity no longer exists. The central government pays pensions, looks after unemployment insurance, and threatens to impose centralized health-insurance. It pays family allowances and 'helps' universities and secondary schools. Nine provinces are included in the system of fiscal agreements; they will receive from Ottawa (like pensioners) and no longer from the taxpayer (like sovereign States) the largest part of their revenue. Powerful Ontario lines up grumblingly with the poor provinces that wait for their pittance from the federal wicket. Quebec alone resists, and it is not easy. The prime minister of a province that is in its third agreement in ten years, gravely asks a question that would have seemed improbable to his predecessors: '*Do we want to continue as a federal State?*'

What has happened then? Two wars and the threat of a third, a world trend toward the concentration of powers, Ottawa's desire to profit from circumstances, and unusual provincial weaknesses. It is a process we have examined too often to do it again here.

Let us be satisfied with quoting the (Liberal) prime minister of Nova Scotia again: 'I believe that certain acts during the last thirty years or so betray a trend toward the unitary State.' Among these acts the one of most consequence is, perhaps, the act that allows the central government to take seventy-seven per cent of all the taxes gathered in Canada for itself, leaving a meagre twenty-three per cent to be gobbled up by the ten provinces and all the municipalities.

Here is a new situation, equilibrium, or more exactly new disequilibrium that endangers Canadian federalism. For if the central government keeps growing while the provinces continue to diminish, the unitary state is inevitably at the end of this evolution.

This political crisis is bringing on a national crisis. Although a minority within Canada, the French Canadians are the majority in the State of Quebec; they found in this fact a weapon, a possibility of expressing themselves through their own institutions, and a meeting-place of great psychological importance. Once Confederation is questioned, they risk being only a minority everywhere. Are they going to react unanimously?

No, this new situation will generate new attitudes, or, more precisely, it will soften the irreconcilable positions already taken. And here we come back to the problem outlined at the end of the preceding section.

The problem is basically this: what is a Canadian? People have never agreed on a definition, but the double crisis Canada is experiencing forces us to re-examine the problem.

We used to think of ourselves as *the* Canadians because we alone merited this name. Since men of another culture share the name with us, it has been necessary to stipulate that we are French Canadians, the two words being inseparable since they do not express two superimposed entities but a unique being. Now people would like to call us *French-speaking Canadians*, as if language alone separated us.

Father Richard Arès examined the meaning of these various expressions a year ago in this magazine.[3] I do not intend to review his analysis, but I recall that 'French-speaking Canadian' is a poor and inadequate expression. Except from the political point of view, we are not Canadians who speak French along-side other Canadians who speak English: the difference between us is profound in a different way, it is a difference in culture, and this culture is rooted in a thousand years of history. Language is the most obvious sign and one of the chief riches of this culture, and its protector as well. But to reduce all to a question of language would be to impoverish ourselves senselessly.

Our culture expresses itself through human attitudes, customs, institutions, and laws. And it must be able to do so. If we let it grow weak, if we reduce it to a narrow, linguistic phenomenon, we cut it off from its sources and hinder its free development. To attach importance to the national State of Quebec is to recognize this and to assure Canada of one of its best defences against the temptations of suicide. To unify ourselves in the strict sense of the word would be to work for the King of Prussia – I mean for the President of the United States. We will live decentralized or risk dying paralysed around Ottawa.

When the Massey Report recorded the danger of the 'American way of life', it saw clearly. When it lent its support to centralization, it opted for the worst remedy. For one does not help the defence of Canada by contributing to the dismantling of one of its bastions.

Even if one alleges, as a pretext, that it is in hopes of saving the outposts.

For the centralizers, avowed or not, have found this splendid alibi. By coming to Ottawa, they say, French Canadians will bring about a joining of their forces: thus the minorities will be better defended. Instead of being given over defenceless to a hostile provincial State, they will add their influence to the Quebeckers' to obtain justice from the federal State.

The amount of illusion, naïvety, and often stupidity that such a viewpoint is based on strikes anyone who knows a little of his history.

When, in federal matters, have French Canadians ever had a determining influence in Ottawa? Their opposition to the policies of two wars prevented almost nothing, either under the Conservatives in 1917 or under the Liberals in 1942. The central government does not even respect bilingualism in its services outside of Quebec.[4] Why would the situation change by a miracle *in extremis*?

No, the 'defence of minorities' is nothing but a pretext. It will turn us *all into a minority* in a country where the French-Catholic minority has never succeeded in getting its rights. It will weaken everyone without seriously reinforcing any group whatever. The best defender of minorities is still Quebec, and it will defend them as long as it exists and progresses.

But it still remains that at the present time this question divides French Canadians and even the nationalists. We saw this when the question of federal aid to the universities was discussed. Perhaps we will still see it when the problem of federal health-insurance finally comes up. In short, new facts give rise to divergent interpretations.

III: Discovering the Industrial Revolution

The industrial revolution overwhelmed us more than 1789 changed France. Since no violent military or political events accompanied it, it had long been a fact before individuals became fully aware of it. Eighteen thirty-seven is an historic date, but the construction of factories or the opening up of a few mines does not strike one's imagination.

Of course it is only a small chapter in world history, in the chaotic passage from one age to another. But we have lived this drama in our own time.

Urbanization

Already there was an unresolved population problem in the rural areas. From the beginning of the nineteenth century the country was so badly managed that, in spite of the immense territory, its farmers were smothering in the former seigniorial lands, and so went elsewhere to look for means of survival: part of the surplus rural population poured into the United States, all during this century. Much later, industries were set up here, and they created a demand for labour. A part of the population moved to our cities and began to increase rapidly without much help from immigration. Montreal had less than 60,000 inhabitants (mostly English) in the first years of the Union, then 100,000 at Confederation, and 500,000 during the 1914 war.[5] However, the countryside was not depopulated, since at the same time we were consolidating our conquests in the Eastern provinces, moving into Temiscamingue, and sending several thousand farmers to Ontario, New Brunswick, and the Prairie provinces.

But what changed was the population balance. Twelve per cent of the population of Quebec lived in cities in 1825, by 1871 the proportion had grown to twenty-three per cent, and then to forty-eight per cent in 1911: the First Great War was the turning point. By the census of 1921 the urban population had reached nearly sixty per cent of the total, while rural residents occupied in farming made up less than ten per cent of the whole.[6]

Proletarianization

What happened has been described a hundred times. The *habitant*, a semi-autonomous producer, became an unskilled worker in the cities, a proletarian. The son of an owner of a small farm and a house now lived in lodgings he did not own. In the country experience was passed on from father to son for want of vocational education; in the cities the newcomer received no technical instruction at all. He received more money, but in other things was content with less, and was not organized into unions: he suffered from constant competition that tended to lower his worth, and from the relentless habits of powerful liberal capitalism. The pattern of his life changed completely: formerly an integral part of a community, he became an atom in a large city. The urban section where he lived also tended to lose its homogeneity, while the urban parish's influence became weaker and weaker. The family itself had less and less unity, it ceased to fulfil the economic functions that it had in the rural environment, and parental authority decreased; a hundred factors from inadequate housing to the easy morals of the cities helped break down the family unit. From an early age the urban man of all classes, but especially of the proletarian masses, was submitted to different influences, and so acquired a new psychological make-up.

A Long Delay

For a long time no one seemed aware of this. One can read most of the books written at the end of the nineteenth century and the beginning of the twentieth and look through the reviews and even the newspapers without finding any mention of the crisis in the French-Canadian *milieu*. Men continued to look for old solutions to old problems. They lived through an overwhelming collective transformation without realizing it. When they began to notice it, they explained it badly: they interpreted it as a passing accident due to the ill will of men. They did not see the action of economic forces clearly. When they took the trouble to think about it, the city was for them a kind of bad place that developed because French Canadians had degenerated, or because there was insufficient political aid for agriculture and colonization (and for a long time this was quite true). They thought it was more important for the townspeople to settle on the land again 'like their fathers' than to organize the cities.

For the intellectuals of the time the real French Canadians were the rural people and perhaps the middle class in the towns. In all our literature, or in what passed as literature, there is a persistent and virulent nostalgia for a highly idealized farm-life. And even just before the First World War, when scarcely ten per cent of those living in Quebec worked on farms, many French Canadians continued to think of themselves as attached to the land. This historical cliché persisted in most halls of learning: our future, like our past, is with the land, the cities are (morally and nationally) places of perdition.

Moreover, the irony here may be unfounded. Some touch of genius or knowledge of previous and similar experiences would have been necessary to understand fully the realities of the situation. The English have this superiority over us in that they experienced a similar upheaval at home. Since the industrial revolution began in Great Britain a century before it did in Canada, they had points of comparison and became aware more easily of the evolution Canada was undergoing: an awareness that prepared them admirably to profit from it. But we were enclosed in our historical *milieu*, did not even possess an upper *bourgeoisie*, and were struck solely by the all too real damages that proletarianization caused among our masses.

The Veil Is Torn

Slowly we made two discoveries. First, we realized that the agricultural land in Quebec was very limited and that it would soon be all taken up. Then the scope of the urban phenomenon finally struck us.

The physical geography of Quebec implies the opposite of an agricultural vocation. This is determined by the very nature of the land: however, for a long time we ignored this fact. I remember that when Esdras Minville underlined this, several writers called him a traitor to the race. To recognize a brutal fact sometimes requires as much courage as clear-sightedness.

Statistics were just as convincing. However, they provoked mainly surprise, and while they remained on the surface of our thoughts, we needed some time to digest them. One day we perceived the truth: we had to struggle whole-heartedly against ill fortune; we could not send out all the unemployed to colonize Abitibi. Every ten-year census from 1921 rang the knell of an anachronistic concept.

Some foreigners helped us to see ourselves more clearly. Note the importance of E. C. Hughes's book *French Canada in Transition* in this arousing of awareness. Almost at the same time the novel pointed out that awarenesses were finally awakening. *Trente Arpents* and *Menaud* in their own way marked the end of a cycle,[7] while *Bonheur d'Occasion* and *Au pied de la pente douce* started another. Almost all of the urban novels and the novels of mental anxiety date from this period, the earliest not fifteen years ago.

It had taken half a century of existence to arrive at this result. For if the intellectuals and the artists, with a few exceptions, took refuge in a retrospective dream, hundreds of thousands of families were leading an urban life, looking for their daily livelihood and undergoing their own internal evolution. Others were preoccupied with it and in a down-to-earth way reflected on the immediate difficulties that were arising. Trade-unionism, at first imported, became deeply rooted here due to agitators who did not have broad horizons but who grasped the real situation; as everywhere it was judged subversive, then tolerated, sometimes bitterly opposed and at others accepted with distrust. It received Bourassa's stamp of approval. Its aggressiveness and mysticism are recent developments. Historians, economists, and sociologists have gathered some of the facts, determining them little by little, and legislations confirmed their first discoveries. Little is known of this part of history and it might be exciting enough to tempt young researchers: it would allow us to see more clearly and no doubt would explain why the conscious grasp of such a general phenomenon was so difficult.

A change in vocation is a great upheaval for a people. They experience it profoundly, without admitting what is happening. Helplessly they stand by and watch the crumbling of old social frameworks, which are not immediately replaced. In vain the people tries to reaffirm tradition, but slowly realizes it is speaking empty words. Then it begins to doubt itself, and has periods of despair followed by bursts of irrational faith. Instead of seeking within itself the answer to new problems, it opts out temporarily either by repeating ineffective clichés like a deaf man or by ponderously importing ready-made solutions. When tragedy strikes a people whose existence has already been precarious, it produces the sensation of falling into an abyss. Only little by little will the crisis be overcome and the people gain a new equilibrium.

The Role of the Nationalists

What has been the nationalists' role in this grasping of awareness? It has been disregarded, especially by the young who, because of the pressure of circumstances, are ignorant of recent history and feel forced to assert themselves, and who seem to be so astonished at the newness of the problems that they quickly deny all that is worth while in past history. We have all been this age.

In fact several nationalists have played important roles. They were basically concerned with the economic and social problem. Precursors like Etienne Parent and Errol Bouchette showed the importance of the economic factor and explained how French Canadians must not simply endure the industrial revolution but must take part and find their place in it. Israel Tarte provided an active stimulus to the port of Montreal. When the provincial governments distributed natural resources rather haphazardly, it was Henri Bourassa who rose up against the weakness and waste of such policy. Olivar Asselin, Edouard Montpetit, then the group from Action Française were among the first to see the need for economic and social policy. I have already mentioned the role of Bourassa and of *Le Devoir* with regard to local and national trade-unionism. Canon Groulx added to history his economic, and especially his social, preoccupations. The social-reform movement begun during the economic crisis was conceived and spread by the nationalists: first by sociologists like Esdras Minville, then by men of action like Paul Gouin and Dr. Philippe Hamel. All these men were ahead of the politics of their time. Moreover, the co-operative movement had nationalists as its founders and as its fighting men. Nowhere else can one find such (relative) brilliance of thought and success in realizing it, at least among the original founders.

Since the Crisis

But the problem has grown in size, and we have traversed the last stages at great speed. And at the same time intellectual horizons have broadened. All modern interpretations of socio-economic facts have engulfed us: socialism, social security, co-operatism, labour promotion, trade-unionism, etc.

And so the already latent divisions between the nationalists have become more precise and accentuated. They did exist at other times (do not believe that everyone accepted M. Bourassa's trade-unionism in 1919, or that all classes rallied around the anti-trust movement in 1935-6!), but now they are more bitter. We used to be in agreement on the essential matters when we were unaware of the world we were entering. The coming of awareness broke up all that was unreal in this unity, and we now see only the divisions. Nationalism does not say what one must think of family allowances, of the Louiseville strike, of health insurance, or of social and political institutions. A 'right' and a 'left' will continue to separate yet further, each one accusing the other of betraying the nation. Love for French culture – and even adherence to the social doctrine of the Church – does not bring agreement between employers and employees or accord between wage-givers and wage-earners.

Politics Emphasizes the Divisions

When politics joins in, a strong cacophony results. And how could it stay out of it? The majority of French-Canadian nationalists agree on the need for a strong provincial State to oppose the government in Ottawa, and they nearly all rally around the idea of political decentralization.

But if the central government offers the social reforms deemed necessary, while for all intents and purposes the provincial State refuses to bring them about, would it be necessary in the name of national feeling to push aside the reforms undertaken by Ottawa? In the long run would the nation herself not suffer because of it? And, indeed, do not some forms of modern life imply centralization? For example, can unemployment insurance be administered at the provincial level? In order to be effective does labour legislation not have to have some uniformity, and how do we get this if not by a federal labour law? And so on. These questions and many others disturb several 'social' nationalists.

Now an autonomist and conservative (in the social sense of the word) administration comes to power in Quebec, while the opposition is bluntly 'collaborationist' or vaguely resistant. There are few or no problems for the conservative nationalists: they would support it even if they were not followers. But for the others? Just because they are nationalists should they proceed on their social convictions and support a conservative government because it is the only one that would offer resistance to Ottawa? Or, on the contrary, should they run the risk of weakening the provincial State by severely criticizing the government currently in power, which, in their eyes, is reactionary? The recent failure of the social-nationalist parties keeps them from calling upon a third solution. Therefore it is necessary at the present time to choose between two lesser evils: which is really the lesser evil?

Now the problem of the State is more central than it was in 1867. Just think of the governments of the Liberal period, which in self-defence intervened in the construction of the railways (because capitalism, although aggressive, decidedly needed help), but which refused to regulate social and economic life. And think of today's governments, which are all more or less interventionists, all engaged in vast projects in social security, education, public health, etc. The question of autonomy is acute in a different way since it implies human consequences that are very much different in 1952 than they were in 1867!

The choices are not all one-sided. The conservatives fall in line with the government, and some of the 'social' nationalists rally around it on election day while still leaving many unresolved problems deep down. Another group throws itself into the arms of the opposition. Between these extreme positions we find as many intermediary attitudes as we could want. Since men always know how to adjust their ideas to suit their interests, they sharpen the former against the latter with admirable arguments for the occasion. It is no longer a matter of unity.

At the same time young people are turning away from nationalism, which they regard as poorly adapted to the times. They confuse it with social ignorance, vain and outdated words, and a long-standing indifference to reality. The industrial revolution lasted too long without our noticing it: since they see it (and with what intensity!) they reject all the rest, confuse lasting things with transitory ones, and are blinded by their discovery to all that does not pertain to it. Since nationalism does not imply a definite social position, they think it is useless. Indeed, some of them go much further. They make the same reproach to religious thought. They deify social matters and ignore the need for authentic divinity. From the Bible they retain only the second commandment, love thy neighbour.

In short, toward the industrial revolution and the problems it gave rise to, there is no nationalist position *as such*, there never has been, and there never can be: unless we call a position the will to persist despite changes and to draw forth all that is lasting in French-Canadian culture. The best we can hope to have are propitious circumstances like those in 1935–6, or a personality so powerful that it imposes itself on others, like M. Bourassa.

However, nationalists know that they possess some common convictions. How to make use of them? How to find a rallying-point?

iv: The Clergy and French Canada

For a long time they have found this rallying-point, even for national matters, in the Church of Quebec. I do not mean by this that the nationalists have generally been satisfied with the attitude of the higher clergy, especially since our relations with the Empire have been in question: from Mgr Plessis (and even from Mgr Briand) to Cardinal Villeneuve there has been a tradition of loyalism that has annoyed many generations.[8] Moreover, in this area history has not been thoroughly enough examined for us to know all the nuances of the high clergy's attitudes toward the French-Canadian national problem. However, since the interests of the Church have been confused for a long time with those of the French-Canadian group to a large extent (of course I am talking of ecclesiastical policy and not examining deeply the spiritual problem), it certainly seems that the Church has been the protector of French life and institutions in Canada. This is quite obvious in the case of the low clergy who have lived with the people.

Now other ideas come forth. We see them in the incident of Notre Dame: I mean in Cardinal Bourne's speech to the International Eucharistic Congress of 1910 in Montreal, and especially in Henri Bourassa's famous clarification. In certain respects there is no text that is more up-to-date than these two improvised speeches (in which two positions are crystallized) delivered forty-two years ago at a dramatic moment. Mgr Bourne adopted the attitude of the Irish-American and Anglo-Canadian clergy, but in such careful terms that one must read it very carefully to see what provoked Bourassa's retort. In brief the Archbishop of Westminster saw the future of the Church in Canada and in the United States as in the hands of the English language, seen as an instrument of apostolic conquest. Bourassa knew how this worthy ideal was growing day by day, and that it tended to favour the religious imperialism of the Irish to the detriment of our minorities and perhaps, one day, of our central group. He framed a splendid and lofty reply, pointing out the real French-Canadian situation, humble no doubt, but real and consistent. A few days later he explained:

> While waiting for the time, so ardently desired by all Catholics, when the English language, literature, and mentality will be devoted to Catholicism, these moral forces are no less devoted, to a large extent, to the service of Protestantism, agnosticism, and in the United States especially, to the cult of gold and all material appetites. As long as this is the case, would it not be unwise to misjudge the power of religious and moral preservation offered by the upholding of the French language, not only among French Canadians and Acadians, but even among Catholic European immigrants, who already speak French or who would learn it in preference to English?[9]

Is that not conservatism? Would it be necessary to choose between a meagre *status quo* and hopes of conquest on a continental scale? Farther on Bourassa refused the alternative:

> Neither as a Catholic nor as a Canadian and a British subject can I accept that the Church be reduced to the alternative of choosing between giving up the French language and the stopping of its apostleship – between 'a calamity' and a 'great misfortune'.

Against the thesis that the future of Catholicism depends principally on the spreading of the French language, I put forward the thesis that, in the future as in the past, Catholicism cannot and must not be English or French, but essentially Catholic.

To the opinion that the Church must find support now in one race, now in another, and spread one language today and another tomorrow, I reply humbly that it must find support in all races and preach the Gospel in all their respective tongues.[10]

Moreover, a certain meaning of 'preservation' is nothing else but realism. It is a fact that *milieu* moulds the individual. What remains of Catholicism among us, in habits and institutions, carries individuals along and allows them to adhere to a faith that they would preserve otherwise only with heroism. I am not talking theology, and for good reason: I am recording the lessons of statistics. And the *milieu* certainly does not promise eternal life; it evolves at a terrifying speed; it can dechristianize slowly and no longer give the natural support to the faith that it did for more than three centuries; therefore we must till the land, sow seeds continually, and care for it with the farmer's productive concern that helps the fields to bloom. But it still represents an authentic value.

I believe that all the higher clergy, that all the clergy, shared this conviction with Bourassa. Do they still? A few occurrences in the last fifteen years or so permit us at least to raise the question. One could not speak of a radical change in attitude, but must we not admit that in the main this conviction has cooled off?

A Few Examples

Here are a few examples.

In 1937 the A.C.J.C. was to all intents and purposes suppressed and became little more than a branch of the Action Catholique Spécialisée. At this time within the latter group there was no national training, and in some sectors even a strong desire to give none whatever, reinforced by a gloomy attitude toward everything that was called French Canadian; among several chaplains and some directors there was an apparent confusion between the sense of the universal and the wish to uproot themselves, as if it were necessary to stop being actively involved in a *milieu* in order to be Catholic, and as if one had to begin by denying all warm solidarity with one's national *milieu*. I realize that at the time it was necessary to destroy the quasi-real identification some people had succeeded in establishing between faith and language; and from this point of view the excesses of the anti-national or a-national reaction do fill a historical role. I realize that the young people did not feel attracted to militant national action (which was and still is too burdened with clichés and almost uniquely founded on vague feelings) and that they refused all that was distorted and strained in the nationalist attitude. Finally, it was a matter of a universal call that our youth could not refuse, and this motive suffices for them. But those I am speaking about went further. Often, by their conduct, they denied the very *milieu* they wished to conquer, at least in its national aspect (but the strange thing is that they did not refuse its social aspect). They had a way of smelling sin wherever they detected a national value, a way of turning up their noses as if they had come upon rotting garbage. These attitudes have changed, and if there still is distrust of 'nationalism', we can see again respect and almost solid esteem for the national situation. But in the meantime the A.C.J.C. had disappeared. It was set up again, but without enthusiasm. It vegetated for a long time, and today the A.C.J.C. is resuming existence with difficulty. Now this is a considerable phenomenon. For more than a quarter of a century the national movements had drawn their militants from the A.C.J.C. and it gave them a large part of their membership. This spring has dried up. The new groups have a decidedly inadequate training.

Recently the University of Ottawa has turned toward unilingualism. And so the French school system in Ontario, constructed with the help of many sacrifices, has been deprived of natural completion. When it was known, the event caused a stir, but the reaction was not widespread and it still has gained almost nothing positive. It is a curious thing that those who were denounced the most were not the men responsible for this change, but the journalists who attacked them. It seems to us that thirty or forty years ago the reaction of the clerics in Quebec would have been more unanimous and effective. For more than half a century the clergy has closely watched the attempts, no matter how indirect they were, to centralize the control of education in Ottawa.[11] Now the Massey Report has succeeded in making a breach in the defence system, which had been untouched up until then. Federal aid to universities and secondary schools has raised no protests in high circles. Behind the scenes, provincial politicians of both parties have even claimed that if they fought too strongly against federal aid, they would have the clergy against them; when one has frequented political circles, one knows to take such insinuations with a grain of salt. Nevertheless, in 1952 the federal grants were passed as easily as one puts a letter in the mailbox; the only discussions the public heard echoes of arose between the classical colleges and the University of Montreal over the dividing of the grant.

Of course, the honest, simple man does not take part in the guiding of the Church and he has no lessons to give. However, he is permitted to record facts and carefully to draw his conclusions. Matters passed as if the Church no longer intended to act as tutor to the French-Canadian groups (for reasons I do not have to examine) or at least not to the same degree. The Church seems to imply that French Canadians henceforth cannot count as much on her; that they must consequently take their secular fate in their own hands, even in such fields of common interest as education.

The case of the University of Ottawa is surprising nevertheless. Here is an institution that French Canadians, and not only those in Ontario, have sustained with their sympathy and their dollars; of course at first these were demanded of them in the name of faith, but also in the name of the language and the culture the University was serving. The University turned to the Quebec legislature and was not badly received. And then overnight it changed its direction. It did not consult the heads of families and even led a real campaign of disparagement against the rebels who dared to display publicly their surprise at the revolution: they were called anti-clericals, but they did not reproach the clerics in their clerical activities, but became indignant that anyone could so radically modify the character of an institution without even warning those most intimately concerned – the parents of the Franco-Ontario community. This fact overwhelmed thousands of French Canadians among whom there are certainly many clerics; but it continues. It opens up strange prospects and inspires among the nationalists – at least those whom it does not push to defeatism – frightening question-marks.

From all we have just talked about, new doubts arise in the French-Canadian consciousness, or very divergent attitudes: some think it is unwise to dare pose the problem, while others go to the opposite extreme and dream of a purely lay, not to say anti-clerical, nationalism, to openly oppose the Church if immediate national interests seem compromised; here we are not far from Maurassism. These questions are little discussed in public, but they are privately, and they occupy several minds, especially among the young.

The Other Dispute

At the same time another dispute was going on about the role of the clergy.

Historical circumstances have given to the French-Canadian clergy additional functions that go beyond the specific role of the clergy. It has fulfilled these functions admirably. Laymen now think that they can take over these functions (and maybe even a little more). For example, in union matters they assert that direction is coming back to them, and they remind the chaplain that he is first of all a moral adviser. In education they believe they can legitimately aspire to all offices, from a professorship to the running of an institution, and they revolt against the 'monopoly' of the clerics in secondary-school education. In the intellectual realm they complain that dogmatism has invaded the domains where hypothetically there are no dogmas. In a general way they demand to be treated as adults (although their complaints sometimes sound like those of adolescents). Others are more far-sighted and wonder if they are not going through a religious crisis in which the very role of the Church, as a Church, is being put in question.

But I do not mean to raise here the problem of anti-clericalism: an old question, renewed, however, by the fact that most of the critics are at present 'within the Church'. It has no real connection with the subjects brought up in these pages. Nevertheless, it adds its share of anxieties to the present doubts.

In short, the French Canadian used to have solid points of support. He found them in rural values and even more so in the Church, which was universal in itself but in his eyes confused with the national group, and with which he had special relations. Now, on one hand, it seems that the Church is retiring a little; and on the other, that he, or some of his friends, although strongly religious and acquainted with certain fundamental distinctions, call for a new kind of contribution from the priest from now on.

His lack of interior balance has increased because of this, even if he does not admit it, even if he sees it subconsciously, and even if he violently takes one side or the other. And so the divisions are taking an inexorable turn. If he opts for tradition he is hardened in a stubbornness that makes him curse his divided brothers; if he chooses newer views he feels cut off from his natural group. Often he remains undecided, calling it the 'happy medium', and he remains a divided person, that is, an ineffectual person.

We have isolated various factors, but in daily life they all interact. The most important is undoubtedly the industrial revolution: for it causes political, social, and cultural disturbances that bewilder us.

Our little world has undergone great changes within a universe in revolution. We are aware of it now, and we are beginning to bring new answers to new problems. *These answers divide us* – they divide the nationalists internally because love for the nation and the awareness of its dangers do not necessarily imply identical answers to the questions that come up.

In these pages I have tried to analyse psychological behaviour; I ought not to end with a slogan. However, in conclusion I would like to formulate two thoughts.

The first is that we are still very ignorant of the phenomena that take place around us and within us. We are beginning to realize this, but it is a widespread awareness, still very vague and often inconsistent. Research is necessary in all areas. This often unproductive analysis is perhaps the first to be demanded from the present generations. The nationalists must participate as best they can unless they wish to see their attitude quickly debased, as particularly sentimental faiths always are.

And this is our second observation. I take sides in some of the divisions between nationalists – they are fatal as we have seen – but not in *all* of them. Since they are often separated in daily life, the nationalists must learn to secure unity through a few essential values – values that can be reaffirmed whenever it is a question of the truths that make them nationalists.

2I Paul-Emile Borduas
(1905-1960)
Refus Global

We are the offspring of modest French-Canadian families, working-class or lower-middle-class, who, ever since their arrival from the Old Country, have always remained French and Catholic through resistance to the Conquest, through arbitrary attachment to the past, by choice and sentimental pride, and out of sheer necessity.

We are the settlers who, ever since 1760, have been trapped in the fortress of fear – that old refuge of the vanquished – and there abandoned. Our leaders set sail to sell themselves to a higher bidder, a practice they have continued to follow at every opportunity.

We are a small people sheltering under the wing of the clergy – the only remaining repository of faith, knowledge, truth, and national wealth; isolated from the universal progress of thought with all its pitfalls and perils, and raised (since complete ignorance was impossible) on well-meaning but grossly distorted accounts of the great historical facts.

We are a small people, the product of a Jansenist colony, isolated, defeated, left a powerless prey to all those invading congregations from France and Navarre that were eager to perpetuate in this holy realm of fear (fear-is-the-mother-of-wisdom!) the blessings and prestige of a Catholic religion that was being scorned in Europe. Heirs of papal authority, mechanical, brooking no opposition, past masters of obscurantist methods, our educational institutions had, from that time on, absolute control over a world of warped memories, stagnant minds, and crooked intentions.

We are a small people, who yet grew and multiplied in number, if not in spirit, here in the north of this huge American continent; and our bodies were young and our hearts of gold, but our minds remained primitive, with their sterile obsession about Europe's past glories, while the concrete achievements of our own oppressed people were ignored.

It seemed as if there were no future for us.

Translated from *Refus Global*, Mithra-Mythe Editeur, Montreal, 1948.

But wars and revolutions in the outside world broke the spell, shattered the mental block.

Irreparable cracks began to appear in the fortress walls.

Political rivalries became bitterly entrenched, and the clergy unexpectedly made mistakes.

Then came rebellions, followed by a few executions, and the first bitter cases of rift between the clergy and a few of the faithful.

Slowly the breach widened, then narrowed, then once again grew wider.

Foreign travel became more common, with Paris as the centre of attraction. But the distance being almost prohibitive, and the city too active for our timid souls, the trip was often no more than an opportunity for a holiday spent in improving a retarded sexual education or in acquiring, through the prestige of a prolonged stay in France, the necessary authority whereby better to exploit the masses on one's return home. With a very few exceptions, the behaviour of members (travelled or not) of our medical profession, for instance, tends to be scandalous (how-else-is-one-to-finance-these-long-years-of-study?).

Revolutionary publications, if they ever attracted any attention at all, were considered as the virulent outpourings of a group of eccentrics. With our usual lack of discernment we condemned such publications as devoid of any academic merit.

Travel was also, at times, an unhoped-for opportunity for a new awakening. Minds were growing restless, and everywhere the reading of forbidden books brought a little hope and soothing comfort.

Our minds were enlightened by the *poètes maudits* who, far from being monsters of evil, dared to give loud and clear expression to those feelings that had always been shamefully smothered and repressed by the most wretched among us, in their terror of being swallowed up alive. New vistas were opened to us by those literary innovators who were the first to challenge the torments of the soul, the moral turpitude of modern life. How stirring was the accuracy, the freshness of their answers, and how different from the hackneyed old lectures delivered in Quebec and in seminaries the world over.

We began to aspire to greater expectations.

We giddily watched the worn and tattered boundaries of our old horizons vanishing into space. Instead of the humiliation of perpetual slavery there came new pride in the knowledge that freedom could be won.

To hell with Church blessings and parochial life! They had been repaid a hundredfold for what they originally granted.

We had our first burning contact with the brotherhood of man to which Christianity had barred the door.

And fear in all its facets no longer ruled the land.

Its facets were legion, and in an attempt to expel them from memory, I shall enumerate them:

fear of prejudice – fear of public opinion, of persecution, of general disapproval

fear of being abandoned by God and by a society that invariably leaves us to our lonely fate

fear of oneself, of one's brothers, of poverty
fear of the established order – fear of absurd laws
fear of new acquaintances
fear of the irrational
fear of needs to be met
fear of opening the flood-gates of our faith in man – fear of the society of
    the future
fear of the unsettling experience of love
deadly fear – holy fear – paralysing fear: so many links to our chains

Gone were the days of debilitating fear as we entered the era of anguish.

It would take an iron constitution to remain indifferent to the sadness of those who grimly assume an artificial gaiety, of the psychological reactions to the refinements of cruelty that are but the transparent cellophane wrappings to our current anguished despair. (How can one stop screaming upon reading the account of that horrible collection of lampshades pieced together out of tattooed skin stripped from the flesh of wretched prisoners on the request of some elegant lady; how can one stifle one's groans at the long list of concentration-camp tortures; how can one stop one's blood from curdling at the description of those Spanish prison cells, those meaningless reprisals, those cold-blooded acts of vengeance?) How can one fail to shudder at the cruel lucidity of science?

And now, after the reign of overpowering mental anguish, comes the reign of nausea.

We have been sickened by man's apparent inaptitude to remedy such evils, by the futility of our efforts, by the shattered vanity of our past hopes.

For centuries the many sources of poetic inspiration have been doomed to total failure in a society that tossed them overboard, and then tried to retrieve them and force them into the mould of integration, of false assimilation.

For centuries lusty, seething revolutions have been crushed after one brief moment of delirious hope during their fatal fall:

the French revolutions
the Russian Revolution
the Spanish Revolution

all ended in international confusion, despite the vain hopes of countless simple souls throughout the world.

There again, fatality was stronger than generosity.

It is nauseating that fat rewards should be handed out to practitioners of gross cruelty, to liars, to forgers, to those who manufacture abortive projects, to the plotters of intrigue, to the openly self-seeking, to the false counsellors of humanity, to those who pollute the fountain of life.

It is nauseating to realize our own cowardice, our helplessness, our weakness, our bewilderment.

Our ill-starred loves . . .

And the constant cherishing of vain delusions rather than enigmatic realities.

Where is the cause for man's self-imposed efficacy for evil to be found, if not in our stubborn purpose to defend a civilization that ordains the destinies of our leading nations?

The United States, Russia, England, France, Germany, Italy, and Spain: all of them heirs to the same Ten Commandments, to the same gospel.

The religion of Christ has dominated the world. See what has been made of it: a communal faith exploited for the satisfaction of personal ambitions.

Abolish the individual thirst for competition, natural riches, prestige, authority, and these countries will be in perfect agreement. But whichever of them were to gain total supremacy over the world, the general result would be the same.

Christian civilization has reached the end of its tether.

The next world war will cause its total collapse, when international competition is no longer possible.

Its moribund condition will strike those who are still blind to it.

The least sensitive natures will be nauseated at the sight of the gangrene that has been setting in since the fourteenth century.

The despicable way they have been exploited so effectively, for so many centuries and at the cost of life's most precious values, will at last become obvious to its countless victims, to all of its submissive slaves who, the more wretched they were, the more they strove to defend it.

But there will be an end to torture.

The downfall of Christianity will drag down with it all the people and all the classes that it has influenced, from the first to the last, from the highest to the lowest.

The depth of its disgrace will be equal to the height of its success in the thirteenth century.

In the thirteenth century, once man's spiritual awareness of his relations with the universe had been allowed to develop within permissible limits, intuition gave way to speculation. Gradually the act of faith was replaced by the calculated act. Exploitation fed on the very heart of religion by turning to its own advantage the limitations of man's reasoning powers; by a rational use of the holy texts for the maintenance of its easily-won supremacy.

This systematic exploitation spread slowly to all levels of social activity, expecting maximum returns for its investment.

Faith sought refuge in the heart of the populace and became their last hope, their only consolation. But there, too, hope began to fade.

Among the learned the science of mathematics took over from the outmoded tradition of metaphysical speculation.

The process of observation followed that of transfiguration.

Method paved the way toward the elimination of restrictions. Decadence became convivial and necessary, prompting the advent of agile machines moving at frightening speeds, enabling us to harness our riotous rivers pending the day when the planet will blow itself up. Our scientific instruments are wonderful devices for the study and control of size, speed, noise, weight, or length. We have unlocked all the gates of the world with our rational thinking; but it is a world where we are no longer united.

The growing chasm between spiritual and rational powers is stretched almost to breaking-point.

Through systematically controlled material progress – the privilege of the affluent – we were able, with the help of the Church (and later without it), to secure political progress; but we have not been able to renew our basic sensibility, our subconscious impulses; nor have we been capable of seizing our only chance of emancipation from the grip of Christianity by allowing for a free development of man's true feelings.

Society was born through faith, but will perish through reason: A DELIBERATE PROCESS.

The fatal disintegration of collective moral strength into strictly individual self-indulgence has lined the formidable frame of abstract knowledge with a patchwork quilt under which society is snuggling in concealment for a leisurely feasting on its ill-gained prize.

It required the last two wars to achieve this absurd result. The horror of the third war will be decisive. We are on the brink of a D-day of total sacrifice.

The European rat-race has already started across the Atlantic. But events will catch up with the greedy, the gluttonous, the sybarites, the unperturbed, the blind, the deaf.

They will be swallowed up mercilessly.

And a new collective hope will dawn.

We must make ready to meet it with exceptional clear-sightedness, anonymously bound together by a renewed faith in the future, faith in a common future.

The magical harvest magically reaped from the field of the Unknown lies ready for use. All the true poets have worked at gathering it in. Its powers of transformation are as great as the violent reactions it originally provoked, and as remarkable as its later unavailability (after more than two centuries, there is not a single copy of Sade to be found in our bookshops; Isidore Ducasse, dead for over a century, a century of revolution and slaughter, is still, despite our having become inured to filth and corruption, too powerful for the queasy contemporary conscience).

All the elements of this treasure as yet remain inaccessible to our present-day society. Every precious part of it will be preserved intact for future use. It was built up with spontaneous enthusiasm, in spite of, and outside, the framework of civilization. And its social effects will only be felt once society's present needs are recognized.

Meanwhile our duty is plain.

The ways of society must be abandoned once and for all; we must free ourselves from its utilitarian spirit. We must not tolerate our mental or physical faculties' being wittingly left undeveloped. We must refuse to close our eyes to vice, to deceit perpetrated under the cloak of imparted knowledge, of services rendered, of payment due. We must refuse to be trapped within the walls of the common mould – a strong citadel, but easy enough to escape. We must avoid silence (do with us what you will, but hear us you must), avoid fame, avoid privileges (except that of being heeded) – avoid them all as the stigma of evil, indifference, servility. We must refuse to serve, or to be used for, such despicable ends. We must avoid DELIBERATE DESIGN as the harmful weapon of REASON. Down with them both! Back they go!

MAKE WAY FOR MAGIC! MAKE WAY FOR OBJECTIVE MYSTERY!
MAKE WAY FOR LOVE!
MAKE WAY FOR WHAT IS NEEDED!

We accept full responsibility for the consequences of our total refusal.

Self-interested plans are nothing but the still-born product of their author. While passionate action is animated with a life of its own.

We shall gladly take full responsibility for the future. Deliberate, rational effort can only fashion the present from the ashes of the past.

Our passions must necessarily, spontaneously, unpredictably forge the future.

The past must be acknowledged at birth – but it is far from sacred. We have paid our debt to the past.

It is naïve and unsound to consider famous men and events in history as being endowed with a special quality unknown to us today. Indeed, such quality is automatically achieved when man follows his innermost inclinations; it is achieved when man recognizes his new role in a new world. This is true for any man, at any time.

The past must no longer be used as an anvil for beating out the present and the future.

All we need of the past is what can be put to use for the present. A better tomorrow will emerge imperceptibly from the present.

We need not worry about the future until we come to it.

The Final Squaring of Accounts

The social establishment resents our dedication to our cause, our uninhibited expression of concern, our going to extremes, as an insult to their indolence, their smugness, their love of gracious living (the meaning of a rich, generous life, full of hope and love, has been lost).

Friends of the prevailing political system suspect us of being promoters of the 'Revolution'. Friends of the 'Revolution' suspect us of being downright rebels: '. . . we protest against the established order of things, but reform is our sole objective, not complete change'.

However tactfully it may be worded, we believe we understand what they are getting at.

It is all a matter of class.

It is being conjectured that we are naïvely trying to 'change' society by substituting other, similar men for those currently in power. If that were the case, then why not keep the present ones?

Because they are not of the same class! As if a difference in class implied a difference in civilization, a difference in aspirations, a difference in expectations!

They dedicate themselves, at a fixed salary plus a cost-of-living allowance, to organizing the proletariat; they are absolutely right. The only trouble is that once they have strengthened their positions, they will want to add to their slender incomes, and, at the expense of that self-same proletariat, they will always be demanding more and more, ever and always in the same manner, brooking no rebuttal.

Nevertheless, we recognize that they follow a time-honoured tradition. Salvation can only come after an unbearable exploitation.

These men will be the excess.

They will inevitably become so without anyone's assistance. Their plunder will be plentiful. We shall want none of it.

That is what our 'guilty abstention' will consist in.

We leave the premeditated carnage to you (premeditated like everything else that belongs to complacent decadence). As for us, give us spirited action, and the full responsibility of our total refusal.

(We cannot help the fact that various social classes have superseded each other at government level without any of them being able to resist the compelling pull of decadence. We cannot help the fact that history teaches that only through the full development of our faculties, and then through the complete renewal of our sources of emotional inspiration, can we ever hope to break the deadlock and make way for the eager passage of a new-born civilization.)

All those who hold power or are struggling for it would be quite happy to grant our every wish, if only we were willing to confine our activities to the cramping limitations of their cunning directives.

Success will be ours if we close our eyes, stop up our ears, roll up our sleeves, and fling ourselves pell-mell into the fray. We prefer our cynicism to be spontaneous and without malice.

Kindly souls are apt to laugh at the lack of financial success of joint exhibitions of our work. It gives them a feeling of satisfaction to think they were the first to be aware of its small market-value.

If we do hold countless exhibitions, it is not with the naïve hope of becoming rich. We know that there is a world of difference between us and the wealthy, who are bound to suffer something of a shock from their contact with us.

It is only through misunderstanding that such sales have, in the past, brought in big profits.

We hope this text will avoid any such misunderstandings in the future.

If we work with such feverish enthusiasm, it is because we feel a pressing need for unity.

Unity is the road to success.

Yesterday we stood alone and irresolute.

Today we form a group with strong, steady, and already far-reaching ramifications.

We must also share the glorious responsibility of preserving the valuable treasure that history has bequeathed to us.

Its tangible values must constantly be reinterpreted, be compared and considered anew. Such interpretation is an exacting, abstract process that requires the creative medium of action.

This treasure is the poetic source of supply, the fountain of youth for our creative impulses that will inspire the generations of the future. It must be ADAPTED to suit circumstances if it is to serve its rightful purpose.

We urge all of those who are moved by the spirit of adventure to join us.

Within a foreseeable future, man will be able to develop, untrammelled, his own individual skills, through impassioned, impulsive action and glorious independence.

Meanwhile we must work without respite, hand in hand with those who long for a better life; together we must persevere, regardless of praise or persecution, toward the joyful fulfilment of our fierce desire for freedom.

Paul-Emile BORDUAS

Magdeleine ARBOUR, Marcel BARBEAU,
Bruno CORMIER, Claude GAUVREAU,
Pierre GAUVREAU, Muriel GUILBAULT,
Marcelle FERRON-HAMELIN, Fernand LEDUC,
Thérèse LEDUC, Jean-Paul MOUSSEAU,
Maurice PERRON, Louise RENAUD,
Françoise RIOPELLE, Jean-Paul RIOPELLE,
Françoise SULLIVAN.

22 Michel Brunet
Canadians and Canadiens

The words 'Canadian' and '*Canadien*' have a long history. Without reference to the past it is impossible to grasp the complex realities that the words represent, and to put an end to the misunderstanding they constantly generate.

The part of the New World that lay to the north of the Spanish colonies was settled by two great European nations. In the middle of the eighteenth century the English colonies stretched from Georgia to Nova Scotia. The French had established themselves in the valleys of the St. Lawrence and the Mississippi. The French colony in the St. Lawrence valley was called Canada. Its inhabitants called themselves *Canadiens*, giving their neighbours and enemies the name of Bostonians (*Bostonais* or *Bostoniens*). It would have been normal for these two colonies of European origin, the English and the French, to grow into two large nation-states: an English nation and a French nation of America. History decided otherwise.

The Seven Years' War drove France quite definitely out of the New World. The country had shown itself incapable of founding the 'great realm', strong enough to resist English colonial expansion, that Intendant Talon had proposed. The former French Empire was divided between Spain and England. It was an unconditional surrender. At one stroke the Proclamation of George III, published three months after the Treaty of Paris, abolished the old Canada. A narrow strip of land was carved out from its territory and called 'the Province of Quebec'. It thus became the fifteenth colony of the British Empire on the shores of the Atlantic. East of the Mississippi the whole of North America had become English. It was the end of a struggle that had lasted seventy-five years. The future seemed bright for the English in the New World.

If Canada no longer existed, however, the *Canadiens* still did. When it withdrew from the St. Lawrence valley, France left behind a population of about sixty-five thousand people. This nation, though small, had fought valiantly to maintain the Empire that had given it birth and upon which its future and prosperity depended. Despite its courage and energy it had been forced to yield to superior numbers. It had witnessed the departure of its leaders. Unable to

---

Translated from the title article of *Canadians et Canadiens*, Etudes sur l'histoire et la pensée des deux Canadas, Editions Fides, Montreal and Paris, 1954, pp. 17–32.

follow them, its people had stayed behind on their land, in their villages or towns. These sixty-five thousand settlers – peasants, craftsmen, merchants, and priests – had been brutally and much too prematurely severed from their metropolis. They nevertheless retained, to a certain extent, the illusion that they were continuing the work of France in America. For them Canada had not disappeared. It was the country they had always known, the realm founded by their ancestors, the native soil they had defended from invaders. Canada was, in a word, their homeland. The Conqueror himself encouraged them in this belief by reserving them the name of *Canadiens*. That was the word used to designate the 'new subjects of His Britannic Majesty' in official documents of the period. The men who had been vanquished in 1760 still had the feeling that they formed a distinct nation: the *Canadien* nation.

This *Canadien* nation, unfortunately, inhabited a land that no longer belonged to it. The Conquest had fostered new colonization in the fifteenth English colony of America. At the beginning the influx of English immigrants was not very great. A few hundred came from 1760 to 1775. Such a tiny minority, however, possessed an influence that was much greater than that of the *Canadiens*, whose only strength was their number. England naturally entrusted the administration of its new colonies to its own subjects. When *Canadiens* gained the right to hold public office, they had to be content with subordinate posts. In less than fifteen years the whole of foreign trade and a considerable proportion of domestic trade had passed into the hands of English merchants. Because of their connection with the London market they had quickly supplanted the *Canadien* merchants, who were cut off from the support of a metropolis. Control of the political and economic life of the vanquished colony belonged to a group that the *Canadiens* now called 'Londoners' or 'the English'.

The conquered were not unduly alarmed by the situation. Since they could not foresee the ultimate consequences of the Conquest, they remained optimistic. Their illusions were nourished by the marks of sympathy they received from the first two English governors, and by generous concessions from the Imperial government. The colony was relatively prosperous. After a few years there remained no trace of the ruin caused by the war. The *Canadiens* knew that they constituted an immense majority of the population, and everything seemed to indicate that this would always be the case. Carleton himself was convinced of it. The *Canadiens* did not doubt that sooner or later they would regain political and economic control of the country that they still considered as their own, a country belonging to them by right. They secretly thought that the 'Londoners' would not always be on top. A day would come when they would once again be masters of their own destiny. They cherished this fond hope and believed it to be both legitimate and realistic because they refused to see, or had not yet seen, that a new Canada – an English Canada this time – was in the process of rising on the ruins of the old French Canada.

This historical evolution, which had begun immediately after the Conquest, was accelerated by the American Revolution. A profound cleavage divided the Anglo-Saxon family in America. The English in favour of a republic founded the United States. They are now Americans. The English who remained faithful to a monarchic ideal settled in the colonies still under British rule. For a long time they called themselves British Americans. They are now 'Canadians'.

The arrival of the Loyalists caused great anxiety among the *Canadiens*. When they saw that the Loyalists had established themselves outside their own territory, however, they regained hope. The constitution of 1791 almost completely calmed their fears. They became convinced that the Imperial government had given them Lower Canada for their own. Although not unaware of the fact that a few thousand English subjects were living in their midst, they persisted in believing them to be travellers established temporarily in their country. They denied these English subjects the right to be called *Canadiens*. They considered themselves the only true 'native sons' and gave the others the rather clumsy title of 'co-subjects from overseas'. Having obtained control of legislative powers, Papineau and his lieutenants demanded, in the name of the *Canadien* electors who were in the majority, control of executive powers as well. It was an attitude that was totally unrealistic.

The English population of Lower Canada had never approved of the 1791 constitution. It would not tolerate placing itself at the mercy of the *Canadien* majority. Conquerors do not usually submit to the people they have conquered. The English of Lower Canada, who were, on an economic level, uncontested masters of the St. Lawrence valley, did not lack means of defence, and they used them. In 1837 rivalry between the two national groups led to gunfire. The Durham Report at last enlightened the Imperial government on the mistake it had made in creating Lower Canada. The Constitutional Act of 1791 had fostered in *Canadiens* the dangerous illusion that the Conqueror had accorded them an autonomous territory upon which they could rebuild the French Canada that had been destroyed in 1763. Situated in the St. Lawrence valley, this French-Canadian State was a grave threat to the unity of the English colonies in North America. Half a century after it had been made, and before it was too late, the mistake was hastily rectified.

For the descendants of English merchants and the heirs of the Loyalists of the American Revolution, the Act of Union at last provided an opportunity of building the British kingdom that had been their dream when they established themselves in the new colony. English political leaders, especially Hincks, tried to convince the two main representatives of the *Canadiens*, LaFontaine and Morin, that it was in their interests to associate themselves with this enterprise. Papineau's program had never been very precise. The entire structure of French-Canadian political thought, erected painfully between 1760 and 1837, was still riddled with confusion. That is why it was so easy to gain the support of Papineau's former lieutenants. In any case everyone was tired of the sterile parliamentary conflicts that had been raging in the Legislative Assembly of Lower Canada for the past thirty years. The revolt had brought the old French-Canadian political leaders into disrepute. They were delighted to be able to tell the electorate that it would at last obtain 'responsible government'. But they were careful not to explain that this 'responsible government' would be run by a non-*Canadien* majority. A new illusion replaced the old ones: French Canadians now believed that it was they who had achieved ministerial responsibility. They all too readily forgot that the leaders of English Canada had fought for self-government in Montreal, the Maritimes, and Upper Canada.

After 1840 the *Canadiens* were forced to realize that their old dream of dislodging the 'Londoners' and their 'co-subjects from overseas' would never come true. LaFontaine, their leader, invited them to share with others the country they had always considered their own. He asked them to give up the idea that only they could be called Canadians. Let us look at his electoral manifesto, dated August 1840:

> The events that the future reserves for this country are of the highest importance. Canada is the country of our ancestors; it is our homeland, as it must be the adopted homeland of the different peoples who come from various parts of the globe in order to exploit its vast forests and find a permanent site for their homes and their interests. Like us, they must desire above all the happiness and prosperity of Canada. Such is the inheritance that they must strive to hand on to their descendants in this young and hospitable land. Like us, their children will have to be, above all, CANADIANS.

Thus was born Canadianism, short and simple. From the *Canadiens*, who had already lost control over their destiny, even their name was taken. This historical evolution was a natural consequence of the Conquest. English Canada, a realm of the British Empire, had replaced French Canada, a realm of the Bourbon Empire. A few French-Canadian political leaders, still faithful to the chimerical ideal of former generations, tried half-heartedly to oppose this evolution. They remained isolated and misunderstood men. The last opposition was bought out by the material prosperity of the country – it was the era of the construction of canals and of the first railways. Soon the immense majority was congratulating itself on the new order of things. Alliance had been concluded between the two uneven opponents.

In writing his manifesto LaFontaine had been entirely realistic. The die had been cast. The Londoners had won, and the descendants of the vanquished of 1760 found themselves forced to acknowledge that, whether they liked it or not, this new Canada was no longer the country founded by their ancestors. It was a British Canada, which did not, and would never, belong to them. A few years later the population of Upper Canada was greater than that of Lower Canada. The fate of the *Canadiens* was definitely sealed: they were to be a minority. A conquered nation can retain the hope of a return to the past as long as it retains its numerical ascendancy. Such was the situation of the *Canadiens* from 1760 to 1837. When the conquerors have themselves become the majority, the conquered can only rely upon their own skill or their masters' generosity. Such has been the situation of the *Canadiens* since 1850.

Historical evolution did not cease with the Union. The country developed rapidly. A new constitution became necessary. In 1867 three British colonies of North America, United Canada, New Brunswick, and Nova Scotia, deemed it expedient to form a federation. This, it was thought, would contribute to everyone's prosperity, as well as protect the British population from the American threat. The first of these colonies was divided into two provinces: Ontario and Quebec. The latter province provided, for the French and Catholic minority, a source of support and a framework within which its national life could be organized. That is, providing it were used. The new federal State took the name of Canada. Someone had suggested calling it Borealia. Had Australia not just been created? If this suggestion had been accepted, it would have removed the cause of a great number of misunderstandings obstructing French-Canadian political thought. It would have been simple enough to distinguish between a Borealian and a *Canadien*, between Borealian policies and *Canadien* policies. The name 'Canada' won the vote of the majority, even the votes of the *Canadiens*, who imagined that they were helping to make La Vérendrye's dream come true as they witnessed the birth of a Canada *a mari usque ad mare*. Another illusion was added to French-Canadian folklore. Nations that survive after having lost control of their destiny seem doomed to sustain themselves with beautiful myths. These temper the bitterness of reality. Unfortunately, they also stifle action. The new Canada was not the work of *Canadiens*, it was an English realm created by 'British Americans'. The new State constituted a victory for British nationalism over the provincial particularism of the old English colonies of North America.

This victory of British-American nationalism was not complete. The principal architects of Confederation had not concealed their intention of organizing a very powerful central government. The new constitution provided that all provincial laws be subject to federal veto. Macdonald and his colleagues had dreamed of creating a nation that would be 'British American' or 'Canadian'. They had wished to establish a nation-state. As soon as the new constitution came into effect, however, their ambition began to conflict with the provincialism of the majority of the population. In 1867 Canada was merely an English colony whose inhabitants still lacked a sense of nationality. Their first allegiance was to their little provincial homeland. Their second allegiance – at least that of the Anglo-Saxon majority – was to the Queen and to the government of the mother country. As for the government in Ottawa, it had to resign itself to playing a very modest role. The citizens of the various provinces considered it, at best, as an agent in charge of building transcontinental railways, promoting trade, protecting budding industry, securing the military defence of the country against the United States, and maintaining colonial links with the United Kingdom. For a long time the provinces kept a jealous watch over their rights, vigorously opposing any initiative on the part of the central government that seemed to threaten their autonomy. Several decisions of the Privy Council, especially between 1883 and 1896, limited the jurisdiction of the federal government in favour of provincial governments. The latter came to think of themselves as the free agents of sovereign States. The provinces maintained the illusion that they had, themselves, created the central State. Provincialism had been stronger than nationalism, whether British American or Canadian.

After 1930 the situation changed. The economic crisis of 1929 had placed several provinces in financial positions that were extremely precarious. The provincial governments appealed to the central power for help. The government of Ottawa replied to the appeal, taking advantage of it to extend its jurisdiction. The Rowell-Dafoe-Sirois Report on federal-provincial relations (1937–40) outlined an immense program for the central government, with the aim of making it a truly national government. The setting up of old-age pensions (1927), the foundation of the Canadian Radio Broadcasting Commission (1932), and the creation of the Bank of Canada (1934) had already indicated that federal leaders intended to move deliberately in this direction. The inquiry into Dominion-provincial relations had the precise aim of re-examining the position of the central government in the Canadian federation and of promoting the public support of genuinely national policies.

This constitutional evolution was favoured in a direct way by the Second World War. The central government took the initiative in all spheres. It has kept it ever since. We need only recall certain developments: the national scheme of unemployment insurance (1941); the war-time fiscal agreements with the provinces (1942); the Marsh report on social security (1943); the Family Allowance Act (1945); the federal-provincial conference on post-war reconstruction (1945–6); the Canadian Citizenship Act (1946); new fiscal agreements with the provinces (1947); the admission of Newfoundland into the Canadian union (1949); the setting up of a Royal Commission on National Development in the Arts, Letters and Sciences (1949); the abolition of appeals to the Privy Council, and the reorganization of the Supreme Court of Canada (1949); the constitutional amendment allowing the federal Parliament to act alone in modifying the Canadian constitution with regard to the powers of the central government (1949) – in all other federal States of the world, the central Parliament cannot modify any part of the constitution without the co-operation of the other legislative assemblies of the country; the federal-provincial conferences on constitutional reforms (1950); the *Report* of the Royal Commission on National Development in the Arts, Letters and Sciences (1951); federal grants to universities (1951); the visit of the future sovereign of the Empire (1951); the appointment of a Canadian-born governor general (1952); the new fiscal agreements with all provinces except Quebec (1952).

Instead of the old provincialism there is now a new kind of thinking, which is Anglo-Canadian, or simply 'Canadian'. The English Canada of 1953 is a true nation-state. Its national government is that of Ottawa. This powerful government provides English Canada with the framework that every nation needs to develop and expand. The national, centralizing tradition that inspired the main architects of the 1867 constitution has been renewed in the past thirty years by an élite group of political thinkers, well-known university professors, writers, historians, economists, and eminent jurists. These men have often formed the core of federal cabinets. Their followers occupy the main administrative posts in Ottawa as well as in provincial governments. From Halifax to Vancouver they are to be found in the higher education of English Canada. They are responsible for the Rowell-Dafoe-Sirois inquiry and the whole program of internal policies pursued during the past twenty years. Their work has received the enthusiastic support of the immense majority of Anglo-Canadians. All federal political parties have been based on this majority. Throughout English Canada no one seriously questions the legitimacy of the aims pursued by the central government.

Canada's international responsibilities have brought Ottawa increased prestige and authority. The central government can, for the collective security of the Atlantic world, use all its emergency war-time powers. It has sole control over the development of nuclear energy. Its financial resources are unlimited. It is even considering a system to ensure rational exploitation of the natural resources of all provinces, should this be warranted by international conditions. In the last ten years this government has shown that it is as powerful as that of any unitary State. It has not the slightest intention of sharing its power with the provinces. Nevertheless, it is quite willing to grant them generous subsidies. It can act in this way because it has been able to win the consent and collaboration of the majority of citizens. Modern means of communication and propaganda (radio, films, television, pamphlets, newspapers, official inquiries and reports, articles from semi-official publicity-agents, publicity organized by various ministries, popular manifestations, etc.); social legislation (old-age pensions, unemployment insurance, family allowances, grants from the federal Department of Health, housing laws, preparation of a national plan of health insurance); the training of military personnel (cadet corps, training-camps, naval colleges, military colleges); the new political economy (the Bank of Canada, the Industrial Development Bank, Crown corporations, production subsidies, price-support schemes, anti-cyclical fiscal policies, control of money and credit); transportation (railways, commercial airlines, the trans-Canada highway, the St. Lawrence Seaway): such are the levers that have been used to arouse national feeling throughout the country and thus unite the inhabitants of ten provinces. This gigantic work of unification has been accomplished in less than twenty years. It is a masterpiece of human planning which deserves the admiration of any impartial observer.

This national unification has been accomplished in the name of Canadianism. That is to say, in the name of the political ideal that has inspired founders of English Canada since 1760: the ideal of building here in North America a loyalist, monarchic, British country in opposition to the rebellious, republican, and cosmopolitan United States. Now, as in 1840, an English-Canadian majority, which is more sympathetic than ever toward the French-Canadian minority, counts on its collaboration to build this Canadian, or British-American, nation-state. Many French Canadians whose devotion to their compatriots is beyond doubt rejoice in this historical evolution. A few, still misled by past illusions, are so naïve as to claim that a Canadian republic is in the process of being formed. These French Canadians think that their destiny is to carry out Intendant Talon's program. They are quite simply three centuries behind the times. The Canadian realm of the twentieth century can never be the *Canadien* realm described by Talon in 1665. When this objection is raised, they maintain that we are at last headed for the creation of a Canadian nation in which two distinct cultures will develop on parallel, and mutually enriching, lines. Such an ideal is not devoid of generosity, or splendour. It is apt to appeal to those French Canadians who have kept, deep down within themselves, some vestige of the imperial dream their ancestors cherished when they dominated the whole of North America from the Gulf of St. Lawrence to the mouth of the Mississippi.

The descendants of eighteenth-century *Canadiens* must be a bit more humble, and more realistic. It is imperative that they abandon all their illusions about their real strength in the Canadian union. True, French Canadians represent thirty per cent of the country's population. It is, at first sight, a most impressive figure. There are, however, other factors to consider. The French-Canadian population does not possess ten per cent of the national wealth. In the Province of Quebec, where they constitute eighty per cent of the population, French Canadians do not control twenty-five per cent of the economic life. If the French-Canadian minority's economic strength equalled its numerical strength, the situation would be entirely different. Under actual conditions, however, a Canadian nation, held together by a national government with its headquarters in Ottawa, could only represent and defend a single culture: that of the majority forming the nation-state. The only issue – a more or less long-term issue – is the assimilation of the weaker culture by the stronger. The most enthusiastic supporter of federal centralization and recent constitutional evolution cannot deny this elementary law of anthropology, unless he is so rash and unrealistic as to maintain that French-Canadian culture is the strongest, which would be nonsense.

It is in the interests of French Canadians to take a realistic view of the matter. They must first of all realize that the Ottawa government has become, and will remain, the national government of English Canada. A Canadian, or British-American, nation-state has been created since 1760. Especially since 1867. The French-Canadian minority was powerless to prevent it. This nation-state is monarchical, British, and Protestant. It could not be otherwise. The national government of this nation-state has the responsibility of guarding Canadian culture and civilization and of fostering their expansion. It carries out this duty admirably. However, when this government suddenly takes upon itself the mission of helping and protecting French-Canadian culture, it steps into a field not granted to it by the 1867 constitution. French Canadians themselves have encouraged it to do so by using a form of power politics to obtain the enforcing of a bilingualism that was never in the plans of the Fathers of Confederation. While they may rejoice at the results obtained or praise the conciliatory spirit of the Anglo-Canadian majority, French Canadians must not blind themselves to the fact that the project of creating a bilingual and bicultural nation is, politically speaking, an entirely chimerical one. A minority accepting such a program without the political and economic means of assuring its normal development would be committing suicide.

French Canadians have only one government to which they may confidently entrust the safekeeping, defence, and enrichment of their culture and civilization. This is the government of the Province of Quebec. Two hundred years after the Conquest the province remains the sole geographic, economic, and political framework within which the descendants of the *Canadiens* of 1760 can hope to organize their national life. Providing, however, that they are energetic in desiring it, and that they abandon once and for all the fancies and illusions that have distorted, and still distort, political thinking in French Canada. As far as a French Canadian is concerned, the Ottawa government can never be anything but the central government of a federation uniting Quebec and English Canada. A close and harmonious relationship can and must exist between provincial and federal authorities. Nevertheless, for the French-Canadian nation the government in charge of the defence and promotion of the common good is the government of the province that is the home of the immense majority of French Canadians. That is why Quebec must not be considered – nor must it consider itself – as merely one of ten provinces. It has the right to demand a special status in the Canadian federation, since it represents and defends the minority. If the majority of French Canadians do not accept this political truth, it is because they will not give themselves that minimum framework essential to any nationality that does not wish to die. If there are French Canadians who favour the total assimilation of their compatriots through fusion of the minority within the majority, let them at least have the courage to say so openly and not conceal the fact by pretending to elevate themselves to a kind of Canadianism 'at large'.

Should French Canadians decide to resist complete assimilation to English Canada, the only kind of Canadianism they could approve of or practise would be one that gave them the political and economic means of maintaining the independence of their culture. For this culture would be doomed on the day it came to depend entirely upon the goodwill and charity of the Canadian majority in order to strengthen and perpetuate itself. A ruthless observer might even claim that this day had arrived a long time ago. English Canada makes sure that it has adequate protection against the economic and political influence of the United States. It relies, quite rightly, upon French-Canadian collaboration to reinforce its policies of cultural defence. It must not be forgotten, however, that the French Canadians of Quebec have themselves the right and the duty of reducing, as far as possible, the pressure exerted upon their national life by English Canada. They will succeed only if they are able to keep all their institutions free and autonomous. To achieve this legitimate aim, they have need of maximum provincial autonomy.

A nation cannot live or act indefinitely on the basis of half-truths, misunderstandings, sentiments that are generous but unreasoned, ideals grandiose but empty, hopes persistent but divorced from reality. There comes a time when the decision from which former generations shrank can no longer be postponed by their descendants. Such a time is rapidly approaching. The younger generation must choose: either to become purely Canadian, thereby accepting the fact that the minority nation that is its inheritance will gradually or brutally disappear for the greater good of the majority and for the creation of a British, monarchic nation-state *a mari usque ad mare*; or to remain *Canadiens* by turning inward to Quebec, the province that can support and maintain the French-Canadian nationality. The latter solution will require a realistic reinterpretation of the exact roles, where the French-Canadian minority is concerned, of each of the two governments involved: the national government of the Canadian nation-state, and the national government of French Canada.

The younger generation remains entirely free to choose the first or the second solution. However, let it be honest enough to say in which camp it wishes to be. As opposed to preceding generations of *Canadiens* since the Conquest, it has the advantage of seeing clearly that to which it is committing itself. The time for a definite choice has arrived for *Canadiens*: either to opt for the fusion that was the dream of some of their ancestors as far back as 1790, or to set up the political and economic framework essential for any nation wishing to survive. It is not for historians or professors of political science, but for men of action to make this decision, upon which rests the future of a nation that, like other nations whose history is more than a mere memory, would perhaps be worthy of a free and rich life.

23 Léon Dion
Pessimistic Nationalism: Its Source, Meaning, and Validity

During an address given at the University of Toronto in February of 1957 as one of the 'Grey Lectures' series, Albert Faucher discussed recent French-Canadian nationalist tendencies, in particular those of Guy Frégault and Michel Brunet. He said he was struck by the contrast in atmosphere and attitude between these two men and the older nationalists of the Groulx school. While the nationalists of the Groulx school, and especially Groulx himself, remained, even in the face of economic and cultural crises and in spite of everything, stimulating and optimistic, their successors are depressed and tragic at a time when French-Canadian society has relative economic prosperity and is showing signs of a cultural awakening. If this opinion is true, as I believe it is in the main, the nationalist awareness must have changed radically in the course of the last fifteen years. In an attempt to explain this contrast Faucher even talked of 'neo-nationalism' and 'historical revision'.[1]

This seems to me to be a profitable line of reflection, on condition that it is realized from the start that the 'revision' has bearing only on the interpretation of history, and not on the construction of the historical object. In fact the object has remained the same: it is always a question of national history. The problem that arises is exclusively one of the radical differences in interpretation and general conclusions about the French-Canadian nation. How do we explain this new pessimistic state? What does it mean? Is it valid?

The Source of Pessimistic Nationalism

The divergence between neo-nationalism and the nationalism of the Groulx school cannot be explained by differences in individual temperament. Similarly it would be impossible to elucidate the nature of this contrast by recalling the

Translated from 'Le Nationalisme Pessimiste: Sa source, sa signification, sa validité', *Cité Libre*, November 1957, pp. 3–18.

unquestionable differences between the two schools with regard to the conception and the practice of the vocation of historian.[2] This contrast could not be explained without raising the complex problem of intellectual generations.

Let us briefly state what we mean by 'intellectual generation'. This notion does not refer directly to age nor to historical time; rather it is linked with what we shall call 'mentality'. A mentality can be discerned by the kind of definitions individuals or groups give to situations. But each change in the definitions of situations, if it implies an evolution in mentality, does not necessarily mean that a new generation has appeared. For this to happen it is necessary for both the definitions and the situations to have changed. Moreover, situation is not synonymous with 'objective' conditions, i.e. economic, political, etc. . . . No matter how compelling conditions may appear, they never constitute anything but the opaque and exterior aspect of a situation. They refer to the phenomenon of 'appearance' and as such naturally refer to their correlative, that is, 'sight', the consciousness that is aware of itself as 'conditional' but that moves toward 'self-liberation' and 'transcendence'. What makes up the generation is a specific relationship to the total situation (considered at one and the same time as 'appearance' and 'sight') and not directly any particular kind of definition or any method of conditioning. To describe a situation is essentially to explain a given state of awareness – it is to seek at the level of a universal law the real origin not only of judgments but also of myths and dreams. Now, it is precisely by these judgments, myths, and dreams that a mentality is expressed and that the characteristics that make up a generation are revealed.[3]

A few general observations will suffice to show, first, that a generation separates the nationalists of the Groulx school from the neo-nationalists, since the change from one generation to another is revealed by the substitution of a secular approach for an ecclesiastical one in the interpretation of national concerns; and second, that these two viewpoints have given birth to two different myths.

It is impossible to understand the neo-nationalists unless one first of all sees them as 'lay' historians; just as one cannot understand Groulx unless one sees the 'cleric' behind the writer. Certainly Groulx has also directed his attention, sometimes sorrowfully, toward the objective context of past and present. His view of history is influenced by the First World War and by the economic depression of the thirties. Outside this context, or perhaps across it, he thought he discerned possibilities for salvation and reasons for optimism; the reason for this is that Groulx and those who were directly influenced by him had an ecclesiastical view of national history. They delighted in reflecting on the distinguished position held by the Church, and they tended to define the French-Canadian nation with reference to its religious character. Other peoples, so they said, surpass the French Canadians in industry, trade, and political strength; but the French-Canadian nation surpasses all others in its religious feeling and in its faithfulness to the Church, a flawless institution that may not have entirely determined the society, but that has, nevertheless, permeated it through and through. On the other hand, the neo-nationalists have substituted a secular approach for Groulx's ecclesiastical one. Their viewpoint is derived from the new status of laymen that French-Canadian intellectuals have accepted for the past fifteen years or so.[4] They realized immediately that the reason for the dominant position of the Church in the French-Canadian society was at first, and to a certain extent still is, the weakness or complete absence of the 'secular' institutions, organizations, and groups that one expects in a 'normally' formed society. Besides, they believed that the 'secular' aspect that had developed in the social structure in Quebec was either imposed or implanted from outside – recent industrialization being only an intensification of this constant process – and they believed that national history must consequently be viewed in terms of a progressive 'assimilation' to foreign cultures. According to Groulx the essential element, the Church, has survived admirably throughout all of national history: therefore optimism is permitted. For the neo-nationalists, who are representatives of the new lay generation, national concerns are made up of the entire social structure in terms of its political, social, and economic factors, of which the Church is only one part, and of which the essential parts are the State and the economic system. Now, from their secular, nationalist viewpoint, this social structure seems to them to be irrevocably and radically foreign to the spirit of the French-Canadian people, or at least to the original intention of this spirit as it was expressed before 1760: hence their pessimistic conception of national history.

Two viewpoints and two myths are advanced to explain these viewpoints.

Groulx's and his disciples' most important myth – the myth of the land and a rural civilization – was constructed in such a way as to depict eloquently and simply the happy and triumphant aspect of national history: that aspect embodied in the patriarchal family; the hard-working, clean, and independent life in the fields; that beautiful web of traditions that linked the present generation with their ancestors; and the stable uniformity of customs and beliefs that bound the parish to the region and the region to the whole territory of French Canada. All this was deeply and firmly permeated with religious values and placed under the attentive and benevolent authority of the Catholic Church. This was a positive myth, capable of releasing sufficient energy to satisfy not only the aspirations of certain individuals and social groups, but also the need for action in the realm of actual existence. How many slogans calling for action it inspired: 'return to the land', 'buy French Canadian', 'give us a leader', etc. – catch-phrases that nowadays seem to be just so many illusions, but that were methods of salvation to those who repeated them, even in the realm of economic and political activity.

Apart from the fact that the rapid changes due to the recent intensification of the industrialization process have irremediably dashed the hopes stimulated by these slogans in the beginning, all the alluring symbolism of the myth of the land is repugnant to the lay mentality.[5] So far the secular viewpoint has been unable to arrive at an optimistic conception of Quebec's national concerns, and it has found expression in the most depressing myth for a people: the myth of irrevocable defeat. Hence the contempt it directs at French-Canadian society. From the neo-nationalist's point of view the relative economic prosperity and the cultural growth are definite symptoms of the destruction of the French-Canadian character.[6] Continually this formidable rock looms up: defeat, the Satanic force that weaves its spells under many guises. Neo-nationalist thought is dominated, even overwhelmed, by the very significant historical accident of England's conquest of New France. It is so obsessed with the memory of this event that it has made a myth of it – the central myth through which it sees all of national history[7] and evaluates the future of the French-Canadian nation.

The Meaning of Pessimistic Neo-Nationalism

We must not look for the deeper meaning of neo-nationalism in its concrete expressions nor even in the myth it propounds, as one can do in all other forms of nationalism. Although national myths have the peculiarity of presenting themselves as being most 'real', it is not as an 'historical reality' that nationalism has exercised its great hold on modern peoples. In fact no one has succeeded in defining precisely what the words 'nation' or 'national' mean. When the 'nation-lover' describes the link that binds him to the nation, he borrows the language of religious mystics: he speaks of 'communion', 'mystery', 'devotion', and 'faithfulness'. According to him one can only feel and never express concretely what a 'nation' is, because what is human is national and what is national is human. It is easy to discover the origin of the need that forced modern Western man to develop this mystical conception of the national. Since his life, labour, disappointment, and suffering all are defined in terms of what is national, it is only normal that his aspirations, hopes, and plans should be too. Thus all of modern man's consciousness tends toward the adoption of 'national' frameworks. But, in order for this to come about, it was necessary for the notion of the 'national' to be defined so that it might transcend the sociological conditioning imposed by history. In carrying out this transcendence, the historian of the 'national situation' was a creator of dreams. In his interpretation of the 'national situation' beyond social, political, and economic conditions, he discovered or invented a design of liberation and transcendence. In fact for him the 'national situation' is a fabric whose social, political, and economic weave might follow the pattern of a dream. It is precisely because national histories have succeeded in expressing and integrating man's existential hopes and plans, especially among the *bourgeois* classes, in a collective dream, that they have caused the psychic reverberations we know and that we generally call 'national feeling' and 'nationalism'.

The importance of the dream in Groulx's nationalism has often been evaluated. For the most part this dream conformed to his ecclesiastical viewpoint and was no more than a projection of the myth of the land toward liberation and transcendence. Groulx's dream, a powerful one in its time, found its most lofty expression in the form of the apostolic and missionary vocation of French Canadians. We must point out here that this dream gave at the same time a possibility of internal liberation from the depressing aspects of national conditions and a possibility of transcendence above these same conditions by broadening the national to the universal. The school of Groulx also delighted in bringing its mind to bear on other ranges of the national dream, particularly through the unveiling of a few scenes from the lofty and ideal *tableau* of the Laurentian State. But in the work of the Groulx school, taken as a whole, the political note was most often muted, since the religious viewpoint made it almost impossible to elaborate an openly and frankly political dream.[8]

Neo-nationalism, like all kinds of nationalism, seeks to enclose within a formula a dream that at the same time is appropriate and satisfies its need for liberation and transcendence. In the secular approach to the national there is only one dream that can hold all the aspirations of the nation: the dream of the State. This dream, in the form of complete national autonomy and self-determination, has made a synthesis of existential aspirations – especially economic and cultural ones – toward freedom and independence as they are seen by modern Western man, especially among the *bourgeois* classes. Among modern peoples this dream has been lived with such intensity that the State has been conceived as the final and perfect expression of the nation's development. And so, as an object of mystical contemplation by the whole gamut of aspirations directed toward it, the nation has become a quasi-judicial category through its association with the State. It has been defined both as the normal end to which modern man's thoughts and hopes for existence must refer and also as his normal framework of existence.

In this context one can grasp the meaning of the neo-nationalists' pessimism with regard to the present situation in French Canada: the nation has neither the framework nor the support to sustain the dream of a national State;[8a] there is no 'Canada' for '*Canadiens*' as Frégault said in the introduction of his splendid work *La Guerre de la Conquête*: the neo-nationalists are faced with an impossible dream. They must be content with imagining what this dream might have been, in a different context, a different time, if not a different world, something to be savoured voluptuously. Three images haunt their imagination: the image of a Canada already sociologically integrated and delineated before the Conquest and, as Frégault says at the end of his book *La Civilisation de la Nouvelle-France (1713–1744)*, 'based on a past whose irresistible force propels it into the future';[9] the image – or rather the 'probable' pattern of evolution in New France – of the American society that liberated itself at the right moment from the imperial yoke and then became a great modern nation; and, finally, the image of present-day Canada, on the road to great expansion but not conforming to the usual concepts of the nation.

When these images are transposed over the present situation, they are quickly led to think: what a beautiful dream we could have lived if only there had not been the Conquest. Despite the present existence of Anglo-Saxon and political America, they delight in mentally reviving a second America that might have been: French America.

To imagine oneself in a state of dreaming is to have an inverted dream. One would be tempted to say that with neo-nationalism the national ideology becomes utopian, but this would be to misjudge the nature of utopia as a mental exercise: it would also be to misjudge the real state of neo-nationalist awareness. One often attributes the pessimism of neo-nationalism to its more 'realistic' approach to history. This is not accurate. The neo-nationalists are not sad because they are 'Darwinian' or 'Newtonian' in their approach to history.[10] Von Treitschke was a Darwinist and a Newtonian, but he did not lack optimism. While to him the dream of the State might suggest all kinds of delightful images, to the neo-nationalists it provides nothing more than the rather repugnant sensation of the small being eaten by the large. All our sickly, pessimistic, neo-nationalist historians would need for their attitude to change into irritation and their downhearted demeanour into triumphant and threatening gestures would be one ray of hope that this situation might one day be reversed. Inverted von Treitschkes, their national aggressiveness turned into a suicidal impulse, this is what the neo-nationalists are. The awareness of the secular type of nationalist is pessimistic or exultant according to its appreciation of the 'physical' and political possibilities of the nation, which is depicted, according to the circumstances, as a 'devouring wolf' or a 'devoured lamb', the wolf supposing the existence of the lamb however, and vice versa. This position has nothing directly to do with the personality of the neo-nationalists; it depends exclusively on their secular viewpoint of national concerns. From such a viewpoint, for the nation to free itself would be to acquire powerful teeth and a large greedy stomach; to transcend would be to devour the weaker nations and thoroughly 'assimilate' them. The distinguishing feature of the two forms of secular nationalism, the exultant and the depressed, is whether one sees oneself as the subject or object of the digestive process.

The Validity of Pessimistic Nationalism

For many reasons French-Canadian nationalism has not shown signs of the explosive force common to European nationalisms, especially those of the peoples of Central Europe, whose situation had, at least in outward appearance, certain characteristics similar to those of the French Canadians. From existing research we possess little positive knowledge about the actual behaviour of French-Canadian social groups, especially of the *bourgeois* class, but it does seem that this behaviour has been disappointing from the nationalist, secular viewpoint.

Groulx's nationalism seems to have had only slight foundation in the condition of the French-Canadian capitalist *bourgeoisie*, and indeed it is doubtful if it expressed its basic aspirations. In reality Groulx saw himself less as a reformer or a national liberator than as an educator. Particularly during the thirties his influence was very great among college students. Even those who later detached themselves intellectually from his position on nationalism seem to have retained the profound inspiration of this nationalism, cultivating their fighting qualities and preparing for action.

Even if, as a result of his ecclesiastical view of national concerns, Groulx did not feel forced to find a firm sociological basis for his nationalism and preferred to see himself as the leader of a school that drew moral lessons from national history, it could not be the same with the neo-nationalists, since they are forced by their secular view of national concerns to concentrate on the sociological aspects of national concerns in Quebec, or else to function without meaning. When one considers what kind of documents they are taking from archives and to what use they are putting them, one realizes that they are seeking a *bourgeoisie* that both in sentiment and in fact would be a clearly defined part of the French-Canadian national context. Their research has centred particularly on the French régime, and they believe they have proved the existence of a relatively strong merchant-class before 1760; this research is much less extensive for the years following 1760, but likely they are already sure that no real French-Canadian *bourgeoisie* developed after this time, since, as Frégault says, the structure of society was 'demolished' by the Conquest and 'never properly rebuilt'. It is in this direction that I would see the reason for their ultimate failure. In fact the secular viewpoint of neo-nationalism can only lead to pessimism and defeatism as long as historiography continues using the uncertain and incomplete information on the true nature, orientation, and actual aspirations of the French-Canadian capitalist *bourgeoisie* that is now being used. The neo-nationalists delude themselves and mystify their critics when they pour forth their pessimism about the myth of conquest,[11] and especially when they conclude from the fact that the French-Canadian nation does not have complete direction of the collective instruments for initiative and control (especially of the State and the economy) that a national destiny is impossible. The European nationalists who are most virulent and most open to the future had their origins in similar conditions. It seems to me that their pessimism results from the inability of nationalist historiography to prove with the aid of numerous unambiguous documents that the French-Canadian capitalist *bourgeoisie* ever really wanted economic self-sufficiency and a national State ruled by it. This amounts to saying that a secular nationalism based on the French-Canadian ethnic group is neither viable nor valid, because this kind of nationalism, unlike Groulx's nationalism, cannot be satisfied with support from the clergy, the liberal professions, some categories of intellectuals and students, and other groups that are, from the secular nationalist point of view, not essential elements of national concern. Furthermore, since they despair of finding any deep-seated response among the capitalist *bourgeoisie*, the neo-nationalists must realize that the new direction they are imparting to nationalism will deprive them of the support of some groups that are in favour of Groulx's nationalism, in particular the clergy. In the final analysis the pessimism of the neo-nationalists comes from the fact that, recognizing the absence of national feeling as they imagine it, they become aware of their uselessness.

One can see very clearly in the divergence between the chronic state of pessimism of neo-nationalist historiography and the more or less pragmatic way in which social groups, particularly the *bourgeoisie*, conceive and imagine their future, starting from the experience of their present situation, that present-day historiography in its double mode of secular and nationalist is developing entirely outside of the social structure that concretely defines French-Canadian social groups. This is the real reason for the neo-nationalists' discovering that French Canadians are not responsive to secular nationalism, and, consequently, in their eyes are not worthy of existence. However, a more general and objective conclusion is also possible: a historiography that does not succeed in establishing a positive, real, and immediate link between its people and its past should be abandoned or ignored, since it has no justifiable meaning.

The tragedy of the neo-nationalist position results from its inability to find an alternative to the unsolvable dilemma in which it is locked: either complete nationalism according to the secular viewpoint or the permanent position of inferiority, if not the eventual disappearance, of the French-Canadian ethnic group. And yet they could find the alternative in the debates, the 'examinations of conscience' and the 'searches for solution' that are everywhere inscribed on the agendas of traditional institutions and organizations representative of various social groups. In the language of sociology let us say that the alternative is expressed in institutions and groups as a process of adaptation to new structures, or at least recently 'accepted' ones. It consists of the search for a sound sociological reference with the concrete structures within which real, living men work, make plans, and experience physiological, religious, educational, political, and economic needs to which social institutions must and can be adjusted.[11a] From the point of view of the national historian who would read history instead of making it into teleology based on categorical presuppositions (taken from the classical secular conception of national concerns), the alternative would consist of the search for a good historiographical relationship, which he must establish here and now in national matters, between the 'cultural' in the strict sense of the word on the one hand, and, on the other, the cultural tools at the disposal of our society, such as the Catholic Church, the federative State, the capitalist system in its present form, and trade unions.

It is easy to understand, moreover, that, from the viewpoint of secular nationalism, the way of being national that the great majority of French Canadians accept without either much enthusiasm or many regrets while still trying to extract from it the best possible advantage can characterize only a bastard nation. Nevertheless, on the basis of this present study, it is possible to apply two correctives to the pessimistic conclusions of the neo-nationalists. In the first place, the nation they speak of, and for which they prophesy a dreary future, has never existed; or at the very least has no present sociological existence. In the second place, as far as the French-Canadian ethnic group – as it really is – is concerned, no matter how repugnant it may appear to the national, secular historian, it would be most indiscreet for anyone to proclaim its progressive assimilation, for ever partial according to Brunet, but eventually complete, it seems, according to Frégault, to the Anglo-Saxon group in North America without drawing this conclusion from a rigorous analysis of the meaning and probable direction of the existing relations between French Canadians and other peoples – as much the Americans as the Europeans, and especially the French – within the system of generalized interdependence where all Western peoples and, to an increasing extent, all peoples of the world live. Supposing such an analysis were to confirm the gloomy prediction of the neo-nationalists, the French Canadians as individuals would still be free to claim against all theorists their right to choose their own destiny. But it is not certain that the analysis would corroborate neo-nationalist pessimism, the

logical condition of an inverted nationalism that simply reproduces the theme
of survival in a new form, as the theme of decline.

Conclusion: Balance-Sheet and Prospects

One might be tempted to attribute the failure of the neo-nationalists to their
secular view of history, but this is not so. The acquiring of a secular viewpoint
marks a step toward intellectual maturity among us; it is a definite gain. The
problem lies with the construction of the historical object.

Could the failure of the neo-nationalists be explained by the fact that they
were mistaken about the reality of the French-Canadian national object, since
it has to be defined today with reference to all of Canada and not just to French
Canada? Indications of a new Canadian nationalism, which is sometimes called
Canadianism, can be seen here and there. The positive expressions of this new
nationalism, which I would call an attitude of mind, are in no way systematic.
They usually show up in the form of a contemplation of the riches that the
Canadian people have received as the result of their cultural duality. More
recently people have been talking of biculturalism. Biculturalism seems to
suggest something more integral than 'cultural duality'. It emphasizes cultural
interrelationships and reciprocal influences as well as the apparent similarity
in the political and economic context; beyond the cultural duality that would
persist, a certain specifically Canadian culture should result, so they say, the
final form of which is largely problematic. On the other hand, it is easy to find
the negative motives that support this nationalism: first, the desire to overcome
the awareness of the differences, if not oppositions, between Canadians, that
are rooted more in prejudices and narrow-mindedness than in undeniable
differences in daily patterns of existence, mentalities, or basic purposes in life;
next, recognizing the fact that the Canadian framework is more of a whole,
and more complete, than the Quebec framework, the conviction that men will
be more satisfied and fulfilled from a human point of view if they determine
national concerns with reference to the larger framework rather than to the
more restricted; finally, and above all, the search for protection against the
danger of a pan-Canadian cultural 'assimilation' due to the growing penetration
of Americanism into Canada. It is too early to evaluate the future possibilities
of this orientation. On the contrary, it really seems that such an orientation is
not sufficiently well rooted to be considered as a concrete alternative to pessimistic nationalism for the mass of French Canadians. History that might be
acceptable to all Canadians, French as well as English, as of a nation inspired
by a common will to live, is still to be written and, I believe, on many counts
still to be made.

The neo-nationalists seem to have constructed their object less from the
historical matter provided by documents than from an idealized vision of the
nation. Two comments come to mind: first, without doubting the authenticity
of their dream (the dream of the nation from the secular viewpoint) as their
own nationalist historians' dream, it seems to have no correspondence in fact
with the sociological reality of the French-Canadian ethnic group; second,

there is nothing really depressing about the fact that the national dream (in the quasi-archetypal form in which it has been viewed since the French Revolution and particularly since the middle of the nineteenth century) be recognized in Canada as an impossibility and be abandoned, since throughout the Western world national viewpoints are being questioned, but not necessarily abandoned. One sees the opinion gaining credence that the old ideal of the exclusive possession by each people of cultural tools (especially economic and political institutions) must be forsaken; on the contrary, one sees very well that there are times when they must be distributed as joint property so that each people, being enriched by the common ownership of resources and by the internationalization of certain political functions, may also have the culture that history gave it enhanced. Thus the French-Canadian ethnic group is in no worse a position than other peoples: following the proper methods in the situation, they also can legitimately search for the best means of using the cultural tools they share with English Canadians, or even with foreign peoples, to the best profit of their own culture. Everywhere the emphasis is on the re-evaluation and re-creation of societies. Everywhere there are 'fundamental' problems and 'crucial' areas. So there is nothing abnormal about the position of the French-Canadian ethnic group. The abnormal part might be that this group sees in the Conquest of 1760 an irremediable cause for its present situation, and, believing in the uselessness of all searching for solutions, it waits for death. In other words the burden of constructing its present and its future rests squarely upon it, and, while realizing the conditions that both constrain and stimulate its impulse to act and placing in parentheses the possibility of a catastrophe from within, one can say that its future will be whatever this group decides it will be.

To conclude that the neo-nationalist position is incompatible with the tasks that must be pursued or undertaken in our society does not mean that we must turn away from the conception of a national form of history. On the contrary, the national historian must have the opportunity to exercise his essential and irreplaceable role – here as well as elsewhere: that of a stimulator of awareness.[12] Nevertheless, one must realize that national concerns cannot include all of reality and all of the intentions of individuals, social groups, and institutions. Being 'national' must not be considered as the synthesis, and still less as the common denominator, of the many modes of human existence. It is time that, alongside national history, a social history grew that would re-examine in a new light the political, economic, and cultural experience of French-Canadian workers, peasants, and *bourgeoisie*, that is, of the men who worked and tried to establish themselves with regard to the actual structures within which their existence took on its real meaning, men who undoubtedly aspired to certain forms of liberation and transcendence.

24 Jean-Marc Léger
Where Does Neo-Nationalism Lead?

At the beginning it seemed to be a quiet revolution – to use a fashionable expression. Saint-Just, who asserted '*qu'on ne gouverne pas sans laconisme*', would no doubt find our conception of 'quiet' strange. As for the revolution, at first glance it presents a reassuring and good-natured appearance, something it rarely exhibits under other skies. But this is understandable; in their first stage reform movements almost invariably resort to the magic of words and to a kind of lyricism that feeds their own fervour and sustains, let us not say illusions, but what Camus accurately called the great, rejuvenating myths that man often needs.

In Quebec for the last three or four years we have witnessed a veritable verbal inflation, which extends from the 'policy of greatness' to 'masters of our destiny' by way of 'emancipation' and 'liberation', to the point where we are inclined to believe for a moment that we are at the heart of a sweeping, national revolution and that November 14, 1962, may have had some of the significance of July 14. At one extreme – and it is not a negligible one – people have already begun to bring together some of the basic conditions necessary for the launching of a real national emancipation. Having been for so long in a state of torpor and stagnation explains why today we view with delight, indeed with exaltation, the simple return to normal; but the debasement of language carries with it serious dangers, such as the tendency to give the appearance of a revolution to something that is only sensible reform.

In the festival of fashionable expressions it was inevitable that 'neo-nationalism' should make its appearance. To speak of neo-nationalism presupposes that there already was a nationalism, and that today we are witnessing a new form of it, with a tone and content new to Quebec nationalism.

This is a classic phenomenon among peoples, and particularly among colonized peoples. Should we then conclude that between traditional nationalism and what is called Quebec neo-nationalism there is much the same difference

Translated from 'Le Néo-nationalisme, où conduit-il?', *Les Nouveaux Québécois*, 3e Congrès des Affaires Canadiennes, 1963, Les Presses de l'Université Laval, Quebec, 1964, pp. 41–58.

as, for example, between the old Destour and the Neo-Destour movements in Tunisia before independence? Actually it is the appearance of neo-nationalism that we must try to sketch, and its reality with which we must try to come to grips, by comparison to – and perhaps as distinct from – the corresponding aspects of classical nationalism, before we ask ourselves where this neo-nationalism is leading us, if indeed it does exist.

From the 'National' to Nationalism

If for some time now there has been talk of 'neo-nationalism', and if it has been thought necessary to use this expression, perhaps it is because people have had a distorted view of nationalism. The lasting association made in some circles between French-Canadian nationalism and traditionalism of all kinds is as false as the identification of nationalism itself with conservatism and with the right.

Moreover, internationalism, considered today, in an oversimplification, as a 'leftist value', was an adjunct to the conservative forces and to the holy alliance among dynasties before the French Revolution. And who would dispute that even today there are international bonds among the great leaders of industry and of the large monopolies?

In Canada nationalism was at first liberal and revolutionary: what one would call today a 'leftist' phenomenon; almost throughout our entire history there has always been a leftist, nationalist current among us; varying in strength according to the times, often relegated to obscurity by the national conservatism, but never entirely eliminated. From the time of the American Revolution and its extension in the form of the invasion of Canada, newly conquered by Great Britain, until Confederation in 1867, including the Rebellion of 1837, nationalism has been a popular phenomenon, the expression of a desire for liberation, democracy, and, in certain respects, secularization in the face of the coalition of the *seigneurs*, the higher clergy, and a part of the new *bourgeoisie* that had rallied to the support of the new masters. They had done so for various reasons: a tradition of obedience and resignation, an automatic respect for established power, an unhealthy fear of revolution, short- and long-term interests, and, in some cases, a propensity for servility.

Perceptible from the time of the American Revolution, the liberal and secular currents became stronger among a part of the *'patriotes'* in the decade between 1830 and 1840, notably among the *'fils de liberté'*. At about the same time the first expression of the internal logic and the normal evolution of nationalism was recorded when an attempt was made to create the Republic of Lower Canada. Signs of this tendency were seen later in the bitter opposition to the plan of federation, which was finally accepted by a resigned French-Canadian opinion only under the pressure of a part of the higher clergy and through the influence of Cartier. Note that while the priests joined with the most dynamic elements of the nation in the attempts at liberation in the years 1830–40, the higher clergy were constantly faithful to the established power.

During the period immediately preceding Canadian federation, and especially from that time, the nationalist left began to lose its influence and its vitality,

306 French-Canadian Nationalism

and nationalism gradually took on a conservative appearance. Having lost all power of invention and imagination, it took refuge in the sterile defence of traditions and became identified to a large extent with the survival of a folk culture. From the 'Castors' to the Phalange, conservative nationalism was out to win its laurels, so to speak, and by closely and indissolubly linking language and faith, was to nourish a tradition of francophobia, of which we are still the witnesses and the victims.

The democratic, liberal, and secular dimensions disappeared, or rather, people watched the quasi-elimination of one form of nationalism in favour of another. This nationalism – which really was not nationalism – that had an enormous influence on the evolution of French-Canadian society, displayed five main characteristics: (1) defensive, it emphasized the preservation of the traditions and position of the French-Canadian community; (2) it became directed essentially toward the defence of language and culture, being interested in politics only when the autonomy of Quebec seemed at stake; (3) apostolic and formalistic, it tended to act more by means of propaganda and campaigns to influence public opinion than by the modification of political structures; (4) traditionalist, it stood aloof from the industrial revolution without complaint, it willingly abandoned the world of big business to the Anglo-American element, even in Quebec; (5) conservative and bourgeois, it became an adjunct of the middle classes, and was impervious to economic and social transformations. It was gradually cut off from the masses – except in times of crisis – and became a partisan of economic liberalism.

This nationalism also had another characteristic, and an extremely important one: the close association of cultural and religious values, seen as mutually interdependent and destined to survive or die together. Certainly there were men and groups who, while supporting nationalism, did not fit this description, but they were the exceptions in the large nationalist element.

The result was a constant ambiguity about the nationalism that was eventually to appeal to the majority of French Canadians. Elsewhere the word 'nationalist' is applied to the men and parties who seek the greatest possible expansion of their nation, and who hope, above all, that their nation will attain complete sovereignty if it does not already possess it. Here in Canada the word 'nationalist' was generally applied to anyone who was specially preoccupied with the survival of the nation and who was fighting either by the spoken or written word for the salvation of the language, the maintenance of the semi-autonomy of Quebec, and justice for our minorities. And so, when real nationalists appeared, preaching political independence for Quebec, the need arose to look for new names, such names as séparatistes, indépendantistes, souverainistes.

Alas, like so many things in French Canada, our nationalism was mediocre at first, yet it was not contemptible, but, rather, a cut-rate enterprise in which it was more a question of holding on, preserving, and defending than of inventing, creating, and giving to the nation a State and institutions that really suited it.

The word 'nationalism' in French Canada has gradually acquired an acceptance appreciably different from the one currently recognized in the West and, in a more general way, in the contemporary world. A clear definition of nationalism is difficult to obtain: it takes in widely diverse phenomena, ranging from the most basic will to live or to survive to the most extreme desire for power, imperialism, and State-worship. The word 'nationalism', which makes a part of the left in the West bristle when applied to Europe, for example, gives rise among these same leftists to warm, emotional approval when it is used to express the aspirations of a people in Africa or Asia.

In the Western world, especially since the Second World War, it is necessary to qualify nationalism in some way, since, for a large part of public opinion, it has become synonymous with fascism, Nazi-ism, and even racism. Let us not forget the rather sketchy definition of the word given in even the best dictionaries, according to which 'nationalism' is 'a preference, sometimes excessive, for everything that is related to one's own nation'. Really that says nothing and only demonstrates that the perplexity of lexicographers in these circumstances is scarcely greater than that of political writers.

Basically it does seem that in Canada more than elsewhere there has been lasting confusion between the 'national' and 'nationalism'. 'National' feeling corresponds to the natural, normal, and legitimate tendency of every nation, first of all to survive, then to be as completely as possible the master of its destiny, and finally to enjoy complete autonomy or independence. Nationalism is more than the will to live or to survive, more than the daily defence of the cultural values and the political rights of a group: it promotes a form of national organization, seeks for the system it needs to assure it the greatest degree of growth and expansion, is frequently in the form of a doctrine, and aims at conferring on the nation the largest possible measure of prosperity, power, and prestige. If this distinction is admitted, it must be agreed that French-Canadian nationalism has been principally 'national', without, as a general rule, even going so far as to seek complete autonomy, but attempting, not without merit, to preserve language and culture as well as the accepted powers of the provincial State. Indeed, there has been an economic constant to this national action: it took the form, in turn, of buying French Canadian and of attempting to implant the co-operative system. The results were not negligible, but they never did reach dimensions large enough to bring about a transformation of the nation's over-all position in the economic and social spheres.

All things considered, whether it was a matter of trying to recover even partial control of the economy, of struggling for respect and purification of the language, of defending French-speaking minorities outside Quebec and of helping them, and of fighting continually for both the independence of Canada and the preservation of autonomy in Quebec, these various undertakings had two kinds of effects: first, the generally modest and always precarious results obtained as a by-product of their real objective; then, the permanence of national vigilance, at least in a few important sectors of society, and a kind of psychosis of mobilization.

However, between the two world wars, in the most clear-minded circles, the particular limits of such action, the need for an organic bond among the scattered fighters, the recourse to the intervention of the provincial State, and the need for a change in structures and institutions could already be felt: in brief, it was apparent how vain, formalistic, and harmful it was to struggle against the effects without attacking the main causes. But the time was not ripe: a long crisis and a long sleep were necessary before a new, and in some respects revolutionary, conception of nationalism or of French-Canadian national concerns appeared. The reign of Duplessis marked both the zenith and the twilight of a certain kind of traditionalism and formalistic nationalism and, while seeming to force all the progressive elements into the anti-nationalist camp, would unknowingly prepare for the rise of what is called 'neo-nationalism'.

The Appearance and Outlook of 'Neo-Nationalism'

To say that everything began in 1960 would be too easy, and, what is more, it would be inaccurate and an oversimplification. Rather let us say that something new began in 1960, or more correctly, that something took shape and began to express itself, something that had been gestating for a long time. It was what has been a little too summarily called the reconciliation of the 'social' and the 'national', the link between the political and the cultural, the movement or transference of national feeling from resistance and preservation to conquest and invention. Men who called themselves 'anti-nationalists' and thought they were, when they were really anti-conservatives, who rose up against nationalism in the name of democracy, progress, respect for human values, social justice, and intellectual freedom, discovered that these values were eminently national, that in Quebec's particular situation nationalism could only be of the left, and that they had made the error of comparing nationalism with the caricature of it that had existed from around 1945 until 1960 in some *milieux*. Almost alone during this period the staff of *Le Devoir* (I say this without hesitation, since I did not belong to it at that time) declared that nationalism was not an enemy of progress, that the defence of autonomy in Quebec had nothing to do with the concrete policy of the régime then in power: an eminently uncomfortable position that caused the paper to be attacked by the far right as well as by the group of 'young Turks' of the period, however brilliant many of them were.

Think back ten years or even five: there was no question then of the nation, nor of independence, nor even of special status for Quebec, not to mention a difficult step-by-step defence of provincial autonomy or semi-autonomy. What was the position then of most men who counted – that is, those who thought and who spoke out – in the universities, at union headquarters, in socialist circles, and among intellectuals and journalists?

Look at these same men, these same groups, today. Their objectives and their chief concerns have not changed; but their perspective has changed greatly: they have again found a homeland, a homeland at the same time of the spirit and of the flesh, by rediscovering the true sense of the word 'national'. They have discovered that authentic nationalism is humanism, and that the nationalism of a colonized people can only be progressive, intensely concerned with reform, and, in some respects, revolutionary. Those who yesterday jeered at our mediocre autonomy, who prayed for the taking over of large sections of

social security, of cultural matters and education, of economic planning by an
all-virtuous Ottawa, now often consider the present Quebec government
needlessly timid and hesitant in its dealings with the central government.

What has happened? Simply the return to the normal situation, but, because
of the history, attitudes, and direction of French-Canadian nationalism for half
a century, it has come to look like a radical change. By a return to the normal
situation, I mean basically a universal awakening of awareness to the national
fact, the concrete recognition of the reciprocal interaction of political, economic,
cultural, and social factors, the admission of the need for State intervention,
the search for a growth that would provide at one and the same time for the
internal progress of the French-Canadian society and for the emancipation of
this society. From the time that the mortgage that conservatism and stagnation
held on political nationalism was at least partly lifted, nationalism has quite
naturally returned to its vocation of defining the ways and means necessary
for the advancement of the nation and for the true promotion of the national
community. This promotion must also be carried out in the political, cultural,
economic, and social spheres: it presupposes human and financial resources,
institutions, an over-all plan, means for action, a State. We have realized that,
in our position, nationalism was a requirement for realism and dignity. What has
been called the struggle for survival could make no sense unless it were concerned not with maintaining a vast museum, but with helping spiritual and
cultural values to bloom in terms of invention and creation. And so it gradually
appeared that nationalism was the search for the future shape of the nation,
for the means of erecting a modern, original, appropriate, and progressive
society; it appeared that such an undertaking was impossible if the nation had
to remain economically subordinated, politically dominated, and culturally
backward.

At the same time people discovered not only the limits, but the mortal
dangers, of the kind of national handiwork we had persisted in doing until
then in conjunction with a rather weak resignation to our historical situation.
The salvation of the language by campaigns for good French, mastery of our
economy by buying French Canadian, the illusion of equality in the federation
through periodic gestures, such as bilingual cheques, and other painful play-
things, all this rather disgusting mythology was finally criticized. The refusal
of mediocrity had finally come.

'Neo-nationalism' is perhaps first of all demystification, then lucidity, and
finally maturity. In 1963 in North America it is no longer possible to ask a
national community to stake its existence on images of a crown of thorns, to
teach it the virtues of poverty, submission, resignation, and to persuade it to
fight for the defence of values that convey nothing concrete, dynamic, or
progressive. In this regard I was delighted by the worker who said to me after
a chat about the pitiful state of French in Quebec: 'You are one hundred per
cent right, sir, but I will go along with you and ask my kids to speak real French
only when they can earn a living with it, and when it is the language of labour
and economy in Quebec.' He was right, as, on a different level, was an engineer
with Quebec Hydro who told me: 'You do not know what it is like to find one

can work in a large enterprise in French, to find that one can think, speak, and do one's job in French.' We were smothering in the dust of the museum; we were becoming an anachronism in North America. But from the very depths of stagnation and humiliation the profound desire for movement and emancipation were to rise.

Actually, what is surprising is not that what is called neo-nationalism has appeared, but the fact that traditionalism and conservatism were able to side-track us so long, and that classical nationalism remained so long apart from the fundamental realities of the economic and social spheres. Neo-nationalism refuses the labels that are often deceptive, refuses survival for the sake of survival, rejects the sentimental heritage that goes from Carrillon's cult of the flag to the passing out of allegorical cardboard chariots to receive public donations for our unfortunate minorities. What we pretend to be, to represent, to embody, can have no meaning unless it animates a modern, passionate, creative society that is a place of progress, justice, and prosperity for all its members. Otherwise it is really a deception to urge people, and particularly young people, to efforts, sacrifices, and a kind of everlasting crusade to maintain at all costs the semi-autonomy of a prostrate nation expressing in a painful patois the vestiges of its culture and the signs of its growing assimilation in all areas. Coming after a long winter of grey and monotonous survival, neo-nationalism is French Canada's spring: it is youth, earnestness, the new realism in Quebec.

We start from the fact that as a group we are a proletarian and tenant people in our own homeland, and, given that, the defence of our cultural values and the attempt to improve them, as well as the search for a kind of economic strength, are all doomed to failure as long as the fundamental characteristics of our over-all situation remain unchanged.

For example, consider the amount of energy we have spent in the last fifty years in the struggle over language, and measure the results obtained: ridiculous results compared to the effort made. The same is true of all the campaigns to buy French Canadian. It could not be otherwise. In both cases – and in so many others – we practised a kind of apostleship, without trying to take action against the main causes of the evil, and without trying to change our institutions and structures.

Neo-nationalism has understood all this, and it has contributed an entirely new orientation, a quite different accent, means hitherto unknown to us (but completely normal elsewhere), accents and means that are sure to upset both a part of the ruling minority and the conservative elements of the nation. To return to the example of the language, it is obvious that its salvation, that is, its existence as the deep-rooted expression of the *milieu*, will remain an impossibility until there are powerful economic and social motives for speaking French, until French is the language of labour and activity in all spheres, the language of economic success and social progress. Now, this result depends to a large extent on our economic emancipation, which, in turn, is conditioned by the policy of the State of Quebec as well as the extent of its power and resources. Similarly, if one approaches the problem from the bias of the economic situation in the French-Canadian nation, one readily sees that in the Western world, and especially in America in 1963, a nation economically dominated and colonized does not free itself by buying at home or through co-operatives. It needs a unified economic policy that only the State can set up and direct. It needs to possess some large, basic, natural resources, some large industrial complexes, and it must have the use and direction of a part of its savings: all measures only public powers can apply. It is the same with education and social security.

In all of the Western world, formerly and still officially liberal, the amount of State intervention continues to increase: it is inevitable where nations are complete masters of their destiny. How much more will this be so in the case of a nation like ours, whose future depends on the vigour, the dynamism, and the political and financial means of the State.

All things considered, what is called 'neo-nationalism' appears to me, first of all, as a passionate desire for life and dignity; next, as a universal awakening of awareness to the national situation and to the factors of this situation; finally, as the passage from formalism and sentimentality to clear-sightedness and, consequently, to the desire to act positively on the causes of our plight, on our institutions and structures, while keeping in mind the urgent nature of the State's motivating action and the indivisibility of national emancipation. We can no longer be preoccupied with the salvation of the language without also being preoccupied with economic freedom; we can no longer seek social security for workers without accepting the fact that their fate is closely linked with Quebec's evolution in matters of economy and education; we can no longer struggle for the strengthening of Quebec's autonomy without making the new powers and resources serve the intellectual and material betterment of all the classes in the nation.

There are other less important but equally meaningful elements that should be briefly outlined. On one hand is our presence in the world, by which I mean our active interest in international affairs, in the evolution of international relations, and particularly our interest in the young French-speaking States: in this one can see a comforting sign of the end of our withdrawal, of this isolation to which we had been led until now by a tradition of distrust and resignation, as well as by our joining the Canadian federation. It is no accident that Quebec is beginning to acquire a taste for, and an interest in, international affairs at a time when it is undertaking to regain the mastery of its destiny.

People ask us: where does neo-nationalism lead, where can it lead? It seems to me that it leads logically and naturally, by stages that are more or less related, and following, perhaps, unforeseeable processes, to the full realization of the nation, to the passage from survival to life, from defence to action, and from resistance to expression and creation. At the same time it leads toward the definition and erection of a national State.

In quite varied terms like 'a province different from the others', 'special status', systematic provision for opting out, etc., there is already an implicit recognition of Quebec as the political expression of the French-Canadian nation, that is, as a national State. Now, it is obvious that one cannot invite a nation to the mastery of its destiny, to liberation, to expansion, and then say to it:

this entire undertaking must stop at such a time, cannot go beyond this stage, and you must build up a 'strong Quebec' – to use a current expression – in order to reinforce and consolidate the Canadian federation. One cannot push back the due dates indefinitely, let problems lie rotting, multiply the unsatisfactory compromises that irritate the majority as much as the minority, and then in the long run forbid both minority and majority to work out their own destinies. One cannot suppress differences indefinitely with token gestures, veiling them in the euphemism of unity in diversity, and carry on, between the central government and the provinces, particularly Quebec, tricky dealings that are raised to the level of an institution.

To what is neo-nationalism leading? First of all, toward demystification, to give our people a clear vision of Quebec's situation in itself and by comparison with the rest of Canada. Second, to seek, and then to lay hold of, the means that will allow the French-Canadian nation to be in tune with the Western world, to become master of its destiny, and to possess the tools for progress and growth. Finally, to endow the State of Quebec with the means for assuring national emancipation, political and financial means principally, which leads naturally to a complete revision of its relations with the rest of the country and, more important, to a revision of the constitution.

What neo-nationalism demands concerning constitutional matters is, at the least, a new association to replace the federation of the ten provinces. Explicitly or implicitly, several members of the Quebec government have already asserted that judicial recognition of the two nations and the acceptance of a formula by virtue of which these two nations might seek to erect a new association based on equality and mutual respect is just a bare minimum. Each national State will have to enjoy complete and total internal autonomy; the federal régime will serve as a hyphen between the two States and deal with external relations and common defence, on the condition, of course, that the two partners participate equally.

This is one of the situations to which neo-nationalism can lead. The other would naturally consist of Quebec's complete sovereignty, matched with strict and friendly co-operation with English Canada. But it is not a matter here of becoming involved in the rather useless game of predicting. What does seem certain to me is that neo-nationalism, as it persists and spreads, will necessarily lead both to a profound internal transformation in Quebec and to a no less radical transformation in Quebec's relations with Canada. Basically, this quiet revolution, this boiling over, this effervescence, in brief, everything in present-day Quebec that attracts attention, uneasiness, interest, or irritation, according to the situation, is the awakening of a nation that wants to be a real nation, and whose highest aspirations are expressed in this current called 'neo-nationalism'.

After merely existing for two centuries, the French-Canadian nation wants to live, to create, to express itself, and to acquire for itself institutions that its growth demands in all fields. Naturally it is led to question a part of its own habits, conceptions, and traditions, the economic and political régime that up until now was its own, and the constitutional régime under which it lives with the English-speaking community.

It would be premature to call neo-nationalism a 'doctrine'; it is the expression of this aspiration for a real and complete emancipation. It is the image and promise of a new Quebec. It expresses the desire of French Canadians to have their own homeland, one that reflects their hopes and dreams, one that suits them.

Many events can happen that would block this impulse; however that may be, neither Canada nor Quebec will again be what they were before 1960. But all these signs that we can collect lead us rather to think that the present movement is a strong one, that it is naturally going to be strengthened with the coming of younger generations, and that a certain kind of false patience and satisfied resignation is over. More bilingual signs and the end of the injustices done to the French minorities in the West are not going to solve the problem or make the crisis magically disappear. For neo-nationalism has no intention of swapping its desire for a Quebec that is master of its destiny for a mixture of languages and cultures spread from sea to sea. Quebec will not be deceived by an extolling of the opportunities open to the French element from sea to sea; just because of its realism, it will not give in to this unwise sentimentality.

Neo-nationalism is what is called elsewhere decolonization. It is the alliance of clear-sightedness and passion called 'fervour'. Without hate, but rather from a perspective of broad and friendly co-operation with others, it is the awakening of a nation that intends to secure a homeland for itself. How much sovereignty will the national State of Quebec have? Events, concrete conditions, and the people will decide.

25 Jean-Marc Piotte
From Humiliation
to Revolution

This article is a reflection on the present situation of French Canadians. In other words, I shall attempt to understand the significance and trends of our collective being. Therefore, do not be surprised if you find no learned ontological speculation in this article. It is an attempt at practical philosophy, an attempt to understand what Quebec really is.

It is difficult to grasp the underlying structure of a society; one must try different approaches and place oneself in different points of view. In attempting to add up the manifestations of the being called Quebec, I shall employ historical and sociological data, some of our writings, but, especially, Marxist thought.

In the first approach I shall try to show that our social attitudes have been constantly determined by our struggles against English-Canadian imperialism. Then a quick look at the political policy of Quebec from the time of Duplessis to Lesage will allow us to understand the political climate in which we live. This historical sketch will entail a review of the dominant ideology – the *bourgeois* one. In the fourth part I shall describe the underlying structures that condition our society. I think double alienation, both proletarian and national, explains quite well all the manifestations of our collective being. Of course, this look at contemporary society will lead to a study of the means for transforming it so that new conditions of existence may be established.

A Colonized People

The political history of French Canada is essentially the history of the confrontation of French-speaking Canadians with the 'foreigners', who by the Conquest of 1760 became their rulers.[1]

The Conquest of 1760 separated French Canada from its mother country and subjected it to the rule of Anglo-Saxon imperialists. These imperialists did not

Translated from 'De l'humiliation à la révolution', *Essais philosophiques*, No. 9, L'Association Générale des Etudiants de l'Université de Montréal, Montreal, n.d., pp. 30–40.

come to further the venture of French colonization, but to found another colony: an English colony. Immediately after the surrender of Montreal a large part of the upper-class *bourgeoisie* set sail for France. The few French-Canadian leaders who remained in the country were reduced to acting as servants to the members of the Anglo-Saxon administration. The English merchants 'seized economic control of the English colony, thanks to their commercial relations with the British market . . . The Canadians who stayed in business became mere sub-contractors, small-time producers, and shopkeepers.'[2] The French Canadians were placed in the situation all colonized people face, and this was only to be expected.

In 1837 the people took up arms against Anglo-Saxon imperialism. But the shortcomings of the revolutionary organization, the lack of agreement within the *parti patriote*, and the betrayal by the clergy brought about the defeat of the insurrection. This defeat reinforced the pessimistic attitude that had slowly become a part of French Canadians since the Conquest.

Confederation established, once and for all, political and economic inequality between French and English Canadians; it made us permanent subjects.[3] The constitution of 1867 gave very great powers to the English-Canadian majority: control of trade, taxation, transportation, defence, immigration, etc. But 'the new constitution conceded an important advantage to French Canadians. It provided for a provincial government where the French would constitute a majority.'[4] Instead of trying to restore the economic framework of our society with the aid of this provincial government, the French Canadians ignored it. They even made an English Canadian provincial finance minister!

In the second half of the nineteenth century the extensive proletarianization of French Canadians began, to the profit of English-Canadian and American capitalists. As the industrial age took root in Quebec, the power of foreigners increased. The French Canadians were content with the modest functions with which they were entrusted. Capitalism 'found us in a state of steadfast passivity, wanting only peace, and willing to endure adverse conditions much like ducks in the rain . . . The capitalist invasion could have passed very easily for one of those unquestionable facts one simply endures somehow or other.'[5]

French-Canadian nationalism rose again over the question of conscription in 1917 and between 1939 and 1945. At the time of the First World War English Canadians had to send troops from Ontario to Quebec City to bring to heel the citizens who did not want to participate in the war. At the beginning of the Second World War conscription was forcibly put into effect by the English-Canadian capitalists, despite the almost unanimous vote of French Canadians against it. These two events confirm the fact that the destiny of our society has been determined by foreigners.

From Duplessis to Lesage

During 1935–6 the Union Nationale overthrew Taschereau's corrupt régime with the help of the working class and part of the peasant class. At that time the platform of the Union Nationale was reformist. But once in power Mr. Duplessis learned that he could not maintain control without the support of the rural constituencies, since they were much more numerous than the urban ones. Because of its conservatism the farming class forced the Union Nationale to lean toward the maintenance of sterile traditions. The reign of Duplessis was 'the time of the most persistent romance between the financial powers and the ultra-conservative clericals and *bourgeoisie*, on the one hand, and the political gangsters on the other'.[6] And all this reactionary politics came about in the name of a kind of nationalism that was as negative as it was useless. The working class, which had struggled desperately for years to overthrow the Duplessis régime, succeeded on June 22, 1960.

The very long time the Liberal Party spent in opposition forced it to acquire new blood. The platform it presented to the electorate in 1960 was not negative, it even proposed some reforms. Partly due to the death of Duplessis, a certain number of the rural constituencies united with the working class to elect Mr. Lesage's party. After a vigorous campaign of public education Mr. René Lévesque forced his party to adopt the nationalization of electric power. A surprise election, triggered by this question of nationalization, returned the Liberal Party to power.

If they are to continue to direct the destiny of Quebec, the Liberals must revise the distribution of seats in the legislature so that the working class receives a fairer deal. If they do not change the electoral map, they will soon be forced to practise 'end of the road' politics. They will be condemned to the same kind of regression as was the Duplessis régime.

The victory of the Liberal Party was only one sign of the deep dissatisfaction of the Quebec people. But this first sign brought on others. The M.L.F. surprised our *bourgeois* clerics by asserting the plurality of our society. With more and more violent accusations people attacked our entire educational system. Separatist movements began and attracted more and more of the population's attention. Finally, in June of 1962, a part of the rural population showed its dislike for the old parties by electing twenty-three of their own men to represent them in Ottawa. It was a blow to the labour leaders and the leftist intellectuals: it taught them that political action does not come from learned discourses delivered from behind a rostrum, but begins in the street, among the people, and in a language they can understand. On the other hand, this election brought nothing new: the support of these constituencies was given to a doctrine that favoured the individualistic capitalism of the nineteenth century.

The social turmoil in Quebec is still going on: it seems that three new parties will run in the next provincial elections: the P.R.Q., the R.I.N., and the N.D.P. But this is not the first time the people of Quebec have shown their discontent with the situation in which they find themselves. The danger is that they will scatter their forces and slowly come to an acceptance of their lamentable condition: such a submission to 'destiny' would not be new. . . .

The Bourgeois Ideology

The ruling ideas of an era have always been those of the ruling class.[7]

In order to understand *bourgeois* thought fully, one must return to its source: the French Revolution. It was fought amidst cries of Freedom! Equality! Fraternity! A society based on the freedom and equality of all before the law was substituted for a society based on the privileges of the aristocracy and the clergy. But this official freedom hid the actual subordination of the workers. The only true freedom that existed was the freedom of the capitalists. In short, the French Revolution replaced the domination of the nobility over the peasants with the domination of the *bourgeoisie* over the proletariat. In our society, in one form or another, we find this individualistic ideology that masks the real structures of the community.

The *bourgeoisie* alone has enough money to set up great news media; it alone is rich enough to finance the State. Therefore, do not be surprised if it controls the State. 'Modern government is nothing more than a committee that handles the common affairs of the entire *bourgeois* class.'[8] And we know the slogans of our conservative *bourgeoisie*: The government is a bad administrator! Politics based on the Church, private enterprise, the family, and the individual! In the name of individual freedom they advocate the non-intervention of the State. They boldly assert that private enterprise is in the interests of the workers: its final goal is to benefit them! Very impartially our *bourgeoisie* points out our need for foreign capital and hints at how necessary its existence is, as an élite, in the governing of a people.... 'Of course the *bourgeoisie* imagines the world in which it rules to be the best of all possible worlds.'[9]

But there is a more harmful ideology.... The great reformers of Quebec have noticed the existence of certain classes in our society, and, according to them, ideally it would be necessary only to suppress these classes in order to show the unquestionable superiority of the capitalist system. 'In the interests of the working class, *bourgeois* socialism firmly believes that the *bourgeoisie* are the *bourgeoisie*.'[10] They make a few administrative reforms; they establish commissions of inquiry; they create new ministries; they nationalize electric power – and this, it seems, is the key to our economic freedom; they talk of economic planning put into effect by private enterprise, and the State that would be a compromise between the capitalists' insatiable demand for profit and the satisfaction of the proletarians' demands. These small changes the *bourgeoisie* proposes to us will not alter in any way the alienations that condition our existence. Listen to what Marx says: 'By the transformation of the conditions of material life, this socialism does not mean the abolition of the system of *bourgeois* production, since this is possible only by revolution; but it means solely the bringing about of administrative reforms based on these production connections, reforms that consequently alter in no way the relations between the holders of capital and the wage-earning classes and that at best simply lessen the cost incurred by the *bourgeoisie* for its rule, and simplify the State's budget.'[11] The reforming *bourgeoisie* tries to make the proletariat more sensitive to its individual interests. It emphasizes security, comfort.... It would like to transform the proletariat into a small-scale *bourgeoisie*, so that it would forget its alienation. This 'part of the *bourgeoisie* seeks to remedy social anomalies in the hopes of consolidating *bourgeois* society.'[12]

The Double Alienation of the Proletariat

The alienation of the proletarian in Quebec is the alienation common to all workers in a capitalist system. This concrete negation of the freedom of the worker is seen in the object produced and in the very act of production.

The worker must work to provide for his own needs, but as soon as the product of his work is created, it is snatched from him and turned into capital. This means that the worker's labour strengthens the power of the forces that dominate him. The work that should reveal the very personality of the worker is nothing more to him than an absurd task. The alienation from the work resides in the fact that it . . .

> . . . is *exterior* to the worker, that is, that it does not belong to his essence, and that therefore in his work he does not affirm himself but denies himself. He does not feel at ease, but against his will he cannot engage in free physical and intellectual activity. He causes his body to mortify and his brain to ruin. The result is that the worker has a feeling of being involved only when he is not working, and when he is working he feels no involvement. He is comfortable only when he is not working, and when he is working he feels no comfort. His work is not voluntary but enforced, it is *forced labour*. Therefore it is not the satisfying of a need, but only a *means* of satisfying needs beyond the work. This foreign nature of work shows up plainly in the fact that as soon as it is no longer enforced either physically or in other ways, it is avoided like the plague. Exterior work, work that alienates man, is self-sacrifice and humiliation. Finally, this exterior nature of work shows up in the fact that he is not his own property but another's, that he does not belong to himself, and that, while working, he does not belong to himself but to another.[13]

And so man loses his freedom for the benefit of the capitalist. He turns to inferior functions, drinking, eating, etc. But these functions, practised as ends in themselves, become truly bestial: man thinks he can recover his liberty this way, but he loses it irrevocably.

The alienation of man from his product is a correlative of his alienation from nature. While the animal's activity is limited to his surrounding world, man's activity is coexistent with all of nature. Through the activity of labour, man places himself face to face with nature. If the finished work man creates through his activity upon nature takes on a hostile character, all of nature will look strange, hostile, and absurd to the worker.

The opposition between the proletarian class and the capitalist class shows up as an opposition in the very heart of the individual. On the one hand the worker is drawn toward the class that expresses his social being, but, on the other, he has worth only because of his personal work (he must satisfy his needs). This split in the very heart of man is the reflection of social antagonisms: man is a stranger to himself. 'When man is face to face with himself, it is the *other* self that faces him. The relationship between man and his work, the product of his work, and himself is the same as the relationship between man and his other self, his work, and the object of the other self's work.'[14]

The proletarian is not only treated as a piece of merchandise in the service of capitalism, he must also endure the consequences of economic crises. Economic activity is directed exclusively toward profit: one produces as much as possible without trying to co-ordinate supply and demand. The time comes when merchandise begins to pile up in the warehouses. In this case there are two routes open to the capitalists: to fire the workers and face a shut-down, or to start a war and face destruction. In both cases the workers are the ones who bear the cost of the upheavals of capitalism.

Capitalist alienation is common to all workers who had the bad luck to be born in a country of the 'free world'. But in Quebec the capitalists are foreigners. It is a twofold alienation made up of proletarian and national alienations. The workers live with national alienation every day of their lives. In order to work the Quebecker must speak, or learn to speak, English, and this causes disturbances in the linguistic field and, consequently, in the cultural as well. Albert Memmi sums up the situation of the colonial very well: 'Armed with only his mother tongue the colonial is a stranger in his own country. Within the context of the colony, bilingualism is necessary, since it is essential to all communication. The mother tongue of the colonial is the least valued: it has no dignified status in the country. If he wishes to live in the city and in society, first of all he must adapt himself to the language of the others, the colonizers, his masters. His native tongue is humiliated and downtrodden. Eventually the colonial comes to share this contempt for it.'[15] As far as promotions go, the English Canadian has priority: the colonial must be satisfied with inferior jobs.

This national alienation shows up more strongly on the governmental level in Ottawa. The English Canadians, who are in the majority federally, rule Canada according to the wishes of their nation, or, rather, according to the demands of English-Canadian and American capitalists. And so French Canadians have no powers in banking, customs duties, transportation, foreign affairs, defence, etc. Moreover, eighty per cent of the taxes the citizens of Quebec pay goes to Ottawa, where it is used according to the wishes of the majority. It is only normal in these circumstances that Quebec is demanding greater autonomy, greater powers, and a larger portion of the fiscal resources. But it is also to be expected that Ottawa leans toward centralization: it must expand its powers more and more in order to co-ordinate the economy and face the growing demands of the world market.

Towards Complete Freedom

The past will have to be denounced in the name of the future. We must project an image of the future that is vast and wonderfully mythical, one that will place in our now empty sky a compelling vision. The future has never inspired us; it will be beautiful to see what happens to a people who suddenly rise up and learn of the monumental plan of their future.[16]

We have survived since the Conquest, but an uninterrupted succession of defeats and humiliations has accustomed us to the companionship of fear and shame. Now is not the time for compromise and hesitation. We must free ourselves completely from all our alienations, or else agree to continue hugging the walls in a hostile country. This is not the time for sentiment: let us become violent and overthrow the foreign capitalists and their servant, our *bourgeoisie*.

The proletariat is the 'opposite' of the *bourgeoisie*: it is the dominated class that faces the class of oppressors.[17] It is stripped of all real power: it is negative while the *bourgeoisie* is positive. By means of the revolution the proletariat will suppress all separate modes of usurpation. 'The proletarians can take possession of productive social forces only by abolishing their own special kind of usurpation, and consequently every kind of usurpation in force until now.'[18] The proletarian revolution will not be fought for the benefit of a clique of profiteers; it is the revolution of the majority against the minority. Its uprising against the oppressors will bring about a classless society, that is, a society not led by a selfish caste but by the entire community. The men who hold the positions of highest responsibility in this new society will not work to fill their pockets, but will rule in the interests of the entire community. 'The proletarian movement is the spontaneous movement of the vast majority, for the benefit of the vast majority. The proletariat, the lowest stratum of the present society, cannot revolt and reinstate itself without breaking wide open the entire superstructure of the strata that make up present-day society.'[19] The proletariat's realization of the necessity for a world-wide revolution will be conditioned partly by the situation it is in, and partly by the words of sensible men who will reveal to the proletariat the structures determining their condition. 'In the development of productive forces a time comes when emerging productive forces and means of circulation can only be harmful to the existing set-up, and are no longer *productive* forces but *destructive* ones (mechanization and money). A fact related to the above is that a class emerges that carries all the burdens of society without enjoying any of the advantages, and this class is expelled from society, finding itself forcibly in the most open opposition to all the other classes. The majority of the members of the society make up this class and from it springs the awareness of the necessity for a radical revolution, a communistic awareness that can arise just as well in the other classes, thanks to the perspective of this class.'[20]

But must this revolution be fought on the federal or national level? Some people call for the unified revolt of all Canadian proletarians, basing this view on the fact that working conditions are the same here as in Ontario. But this is not accurate: we saw above that our situation as colonials imposes new restrictions on the activity of the French-Canadian worker. And even if this were true, the requirements for action would point up the necessity of centring our efforts on Quebec. It is just as utopian to hope for a revolution of American proletarians as for a revolution of English-Canadian workers in the near future. In Quebec we can rely on the people's resentment of foreign oppressors, a resentment strengthened by two centuries of history.

At the present moment in the development of humanity, the cultural characteristics that differentiate each nation from the other have not disappeared. Perhaps some day humanity will be structured only by culture, but revolutionary action must depend on the demands of the present moment. Our culture (meaning everything organic that structures human relationships in a given society) must be stabilized by a double 'disalienation': proletarian and national. Once our collective being is freed, we can unite with the English-Canadian proletariat. If this union came about today, it would be to the detriment of our cultural being: the English Canadians, the majority in Canada, would rule according to their collective being. We would be forced to submit to the wishes of this majority, and, in the end, to deny our cultural being and become English Canadians.

The society that will be set up will resolve the discrepancies we have seen in the capitalist system, and man will no longer be split between his social being and his individual being. Society will work for the worker, and the worker for society. Each man will take on responsibility for the entire community on the level of his own special job. Man's collective being will no longer be subjected to the impersonal forces of the market, but will direct production according to the needs to be fulfilled. Workers will unite freely and knowingly in the great struggle for universal social progress.

Notes
Part Two

Garneau
Preliminary Discourse to *History of Canada*

[1] The historians of this continent have not had to overcome the difficulties which long embarrassed those of Europe, with respect to the origin of races. They can, without difficulty, indicate the point of departure of the waves of emigration from the Old World, and follow their traces onward, even into the obscurest valley of America.

[2] A quaint but expressive compound epithet, borrowed by the author from Alexie de Monteil, author of *l'Histoire des Français des divers États*; a work of prodigious but thankless research. – B.

[3] *Histoire Romaine.* We adopt here the data of the above-named learned and ingenious historian; also Niebuhr's.

[4] His book, dedicated to Pope Clement XII, bears the title of 'The New Science' (Scienza Nuova). The *Biographie Universelle* contains a long article on this author and his works.

[5] 'The order of St. Benedict gave to the olden world, emasculated by slavery, the first exemplar of labors accomplished by free hands. That great innovation was one of the bases of modern well-being.' MICHELET. The cloisters of the Benedictine monks, whose order was founded in Italy late in the fifth century, became asylums for those who fled before the tyranny of Goths and Vandals. It was the Benedictines who preserved in their cloisters, for the world's after-use, the small remnants of anterior learning and science surviving among men.

[6] M. Maillefer, *De la Puissance et des Institutions de l'Union Américaine.*

[7] The ready amalgamation of these races with the Anglo-Saxons of America was chiefly due to the common Protestantism of all four. – B.

Mgr L.-A. Pâquet
A Sermon on the Vocation of the French Race in America

[1] Encyclical *Nobilissima Gallorum gens* (1884).

[2] Ferland, *Cours d'histoire du Canada*, Part I, p. 31.

[3] Casgrain, *Histoire de l'Hôtel Dieu de Québec*, p. 73.

[4] At the same time as the diamond anniversary of the Saint-Jean-Baptiste Society the fiftieth anniversary of Laval University was being celebrated.

[5] Rameau, *La France aux colonies*, p. 259.

[6] Jeremiah xxx. 22.

Bouchette
Economic Development in the Province of Quebec

[1] Lamartine, Histoire de Jacquard.
[2] Histoire des Doctrines économiques, translated by A. Deschamps, p. 224.
[3] Dictionnaire d'Économie politique, p. 882.
[4] P. Leroy-Beaulieu, Traité des Finances, Vol. I, p. 63.
[5] The phrase commercial wood is in common usage. It shows quite well that up until now we have not paid enough attention to forest industries. If our wood figured in commerce only as a manufactured product, we would no longer say commercial wood but industrial wood.
[6] Traité des Finances, Vol. I, p. 66.

Groulx
If Dollard Were Alive Today

[1] Marie de l'Incarnation, in a letter, June 25, 1660.
[2] This is indeed the hero's real name, and the way he always signed it, as E.-Z. Massicotte has demonstrated in The Canadian Antiquarian, Vol. IX, No. 2 (1912). It is to be hoped that we shall at last be rid of all those 'Daulac' and 'Daulat' which were nothing but the distortions of poor copyists.
[3] É.-M. Faillon, Histoire de la colonie française en Canada (Montreal, 1865–66), Vol. II, p. 414.
[4] Albert Mahaut, Le Chrétien, homme d'action, p. ix.
[5] Quoted by Agathon, Jeunes Gens d'aujourd'hui, p. 209.

Villeneuve
And Our Dispersed Brethren . . . ?

[1] Action française, January 1922, p. 117.
[2] Action française, January 1922.
[3] These remarks were developed in the article in Action française previously cited, as well as in that of M. Durand, ibid., February 1922.
[4] See the brief but substantial summary of this point given by L.-P. Desrosiers in Le Devoir, March 6, 1922.
[5] Cf. the unease in the British Empire in Le Correspondant, April 10 and 25, 1922.
[6] Revue des Deux-Mondes, September 15, 1921; this article was summarized in L'Ami du Clergé, January 19, 1922.
[7] Revue trimestrielle canadienne, December 1921, p. 373.
[8] 'Si la Confédération disparaissait' by Émile Bruchési, in Action française, September 1, 1920.
[9] Cf. 'Le Canada français', by M. le chanoine Chartier, in Revue trimestrielle, December 1921.
[10] Léo-Paul Desrosiers, in Le Devoir, February 4 and March 6, 1922.
[11] Géographie humaine, by Jean Brunhes; Géographie de l'histoire, by Brunhes and Vallaux; cf. Le Correspondant, December 25, 1921.
[12] As is well known, this was the word used by the former Minister, Sir Clifford Sifton: 'A crime against Canada', Le Devoir, April 26, 1922.
[13] January 16, 1922; cf. Semeur, February 1922, p. 166.
[14] Taparelli, Droit naturel. Cf. articles by l'Abbé Robert and l'Abbé Perrier.
[15] See Le Canada apostolique by Henri Bourassa.
[16] See the following pamphlets: La Langue, gardienne de la foi, by Henri Bourassa;

La Langue et la foi, by Albert Foisy.
[17] It is appropriate to recall the letters and articles of the barrister Antonio Perrault, in his controversial but very serious argument.
[18] *Le Devoir,* May 4, 1922.
[19] *Le Devoir,* July 1, 1913; Abbé Groulx, in *Action française,* July 1917, and in his book *Confédération, passim.*

Perrault
Inquiry into Nationalism
[1] See *Lettres,* September 1923, p. 409.

Angers
Why We Shall Never Accept Conscription for Overseas Service
[1] Did not Mr. Gardiner himself, as minister in Mr. King's cabinet, demonstrate that Canada would have been capable of a total war-effort without actually waging war?
[2] Cf. Abbé Lionel Groulx, *Paroles à des étudiants.*
[3] Cf. André Laurendeau, 'Alerte aux Canadiens français' and François-Albert Angers, 'A quelle sauce veut-on nous manger?', in *Action Nationale,* November and December 1940.

Laurendeau
Is There a Crisis of Nationalism?
[1] After the excesses of European nationalism and those that are brewing among Asian peoples, is this a desirable word? I doubt it. It is accurate if one considers it in itself, but when we are not speaking of Quebec, it gives rise to dangerous ambiguities. Nevertheless we are using it for lack of another word and because it is in current use among us.
[2] Meanwhile the immigration of people without roots increases in Canada and we receive people who would be just as willing (perhaps more) to be Americans as Canadians. This aspect of the question is not often enough considered.
[3] Richard Arès, S.J., *Are We French Canadians?,* January 1952.
[4] One single exception: the recent extension of the French network of C.B.C. Radio. But to obtain it the French Canadians in the west had to build their own stations, while the Anglo-Canadians in Montreal obtained without any trouble CBM, as well as CFCF and CJAD.
[5] *Montréal Économique:* Études sur notre milieu, Fides (1943).
[6] *L'Agriculture:* Études sur notre milieu, Fides (1944).
[7] I am not speaking from a literary viewpoint, and a more detailed analysis would show that the phenomenon is indeed more complex.
[8] With regard to this read André Siegfried's chapter 'French Canadians in international politics', in *Le Canada, Puissance internationale.* With several (Protestant) digs, Siegfried summarizes the accepted ideas on the subject, especially in the third paragraph that begins: 'French Canadians accept the British regime because it guarantees them the essentials, their religion and language, that is, the possibility of remaining distinct.'
[9] Reproduced in 'Hommage à Henri Bourassa', *Le Devoir,* 1952, p. 119.
[10] *Ibid.,* p. 119.
[11] Let us not forget the distrust that greeted Confederation itself from a part of the higher clergy, not because it was a confederation, but because it was not confederation enough.

Dion
Pessimistic Nationalism: Its Source, Meaning, and Validity

[1] I shall use these expressions in this discussion. When I am thinking of Guy Frégault, Michel Brunet, and their guiding spirits, I shall speak of 'neo-nationalists', when I mean Groulx and the group who were influenced by his thought I shall speak of the 'nationalists of the Groulx school'. This classification is somewhat oversimplified, and for those who are studying the history of French-Canadian nationalism it will be inadequate. But it is sufficient for the purposes of my study.

[2] In other respects it is partly with regard to the manner in which Brunet, in particular, conceived and practised his vocation that one can understand how he was led to find in the theory of 'power politics' a formula of interpretation that is as valid for national history as it is for universal history, and as valid for relations between independent States as between a central State and the member States of a federation, etc. The historian who interprets history is usually satisfied with a simple formula that allows him easily to isolate his historical perspectives. Brunet believes his formula is borrowed from political theory, but in reality the concept of 'power politics' comes not from political theory but from a political philosophy, or rather, if one studies the origins of this notion in Germany, from nationalist ideology.

[3] It would be wrong to explain the pessimistic side of neo-nationalism by starting with the profound changes in the social structure and ways of life in Quebec as a result of the industrial boom that has come about since the beginning of the Second World War. These are really only conditions and do not constitute a principle for explanation. We must be careful not to slip into facile interpretations starting with the 'effects of industrialization'. Industrialization has effects on men and institutions only because it forms an element, undoubtedly important, of a situation that is intimately connected with a culture and in itself a product of history.

[4] By 'status of laymen' I mean something quite different from what is meant by 'laymen' in legal terminology. Among Groulx's disciples there are several laymen whose viewpoints are as ecclesiastical as his. By the acquisition of lay status I mean the intellectual emancipation from a theological approach to strictly secular matters and, more particularly, to historical questions. The acquiring of this new status is due most of all to the surprising rise of scientific disciplines in our *milieu* during the past fifteen years, especially in the social sciences; and it is due also to the effort the intellectuals, both religious and secular, have made toward assimilating the spirit and methods of these disciplines. Moreover, it is fundamentally this characteristic that reveals the change from Groulx's generation to that of the neo-nationalists. It must be remembered, however, that I do not claim Groulx's descriptions and analyses had no internal validity, since this would be inaccurate, despite the fact that his conception and interpretation of the French-Canadian nation were greatly influenced by the ecclesiastical viewpoint. It may be advisable to add here that there was nothing 'revolutionary' about this lay emancipation. The lay status has nothing to do with anti-clericalism in the vulgar sense of the word, let alone with irreligiousness. On the contrary, certain indications lead us to believe that the new 'lay' generation may have, in several respects, a more penetrating understanding of religious questions than the previous generation.

[5] In many ways the nationalism among the new lay generation, expressed in a pastoral and archaic form by the preceding generation, is tending naturally toward a restatement of the European conception of it, which was urban, *bourgeois*, and political. Thus, the neo-nationalists estimate the value of the French-Canadian ethnic group by calculating how much conformity (or nonconformity) this group has with the national secular pattern. In other words, while continuing to debunk old myths, they turn to the classical myths of lay nationalism in order to arrive at their definition of the

national concerns of Quebec. Moreover, this is the fundamental source of their pessimism, as we shall see, since Quebec national concerns are far from conforming to the national, secular pattern.

6 It would be interesting to find out by what means one moves from the acknowledged fact that in Quebec there were few capitalists, skilled workers, artists, scientists, great philosophers, or theologians, to the belief that all progress in these fields means only one thing: a corresponding decrease in the French-Canadian 'character'. One might see, among other things, how the myth of the land can slyly influence the mental awareness of those who elsewhere reject it, even though they are dominated by experiment and the illusion of an industrial civilization.

7 To come back here to the remark I made at the beginning: my study relates exclusively to the neo-nationalist interpretation of history and not to the analytic or descriptive aspect of the works of the neo-nationalists that would result from internal criticism.

8 Moreover, the dream of a Laurentian State seems more like a borrowing from foreign sources, notably fascist ones, than the logical conclusion of the nationalist viewpoint of the Groulx school.

8a On the subject of a national State there are varying views among the neo-nationalists: while Frégault does not seem to accept any alternative to a completely sovereign national State, Brunet, who is more modest in his hopes, would be satisfied with a provincial State, provided that it legally defined its relations with the central State in terms of political power, and, what is more, that it was based on his own personal ideas. Frégault's position is frankly hopeless whereas Brunet's, despite its greater sobriety, sins through arrogance and deficiency. Through arrogance since he automatically dooms the French Canadians outside of the protecting boundaries of Quebec to 'total assimilation'; through deficiency since he forgets the elementary principles of political federalism. However undeniable and irreplaceable the cultural responsibility of the provincial State of Quebec may be, the political recognition and exercise of the cultural function must be brought about with respect for the attitudes and conduct that conform to the principles of federalism.

9 Frégault claims to have shown that already between 1713 and 1744 New France had become a 'moral entity, a complete being, a new nation'. The criticism of this opinion, which one can call the thesis of the neo-nationalist dialectic (the antithesis being the Conquest, and the synthesis the multinational – or even anti-national – character of present-day Canada), is not important to this study. Moreover, the issue in the debate among historians about this question is inconclusive, since it is not as a historical fact but as a myth bred by the neo-nationalist dream of the State that the image of Canadian society before 1760 is significant. Now, one does not destroy a myth by an act that would be decisive from the logical or factual point of view. The man whose mind is ruled by a myth is impervious to rational evidence, since, if need be, he can lay claim to trans- or infra-rational evidence, to which rational evidence 'must' conform. In other respects the explosive character of the myth, as far as it is a support for the ideology, will diminish as the groups likely to support this ideology recognize that the rational correction of error is *applicable to their situation*. And the importance of a social myth is in direct proportion to the probability of its eventually becoming the core of an ideology.

10 Sometimes the orientation of the neo-nationalists, notably Brunet's, is attributed to their conception of power politics. In fact it is rather because it suited his orientation and his historical perspective that Brunet in particular made the conception of power politics his own. The 'theory' of lay nationalism is necessarily 'Darwinian' and 'Newtonian'.

11 With the Conquest the chance for *Canadiens* to erect a secular, national structure disappeared. And French Canadians today no longer remember having had that chance.

However, they must keep returning to the Conquest if they wish to understand the origin and fatal nature of 'the obvious crisis of French-Canadian society . . .' (Frégault, *La Guerre de la Conquête*).

[11a] You must not take these words 'must' and 'can' as implying on my part a normative methodological position. They refer exclusively to the desire for betterment that cannot help but inspire the sociologist as far as he is a man, a Christian, a citizen, etc. It goes without saying that this desire for betterment remains, as such, extrinsic to the scientific approach, which must be determined by the search for objectivity and positivity that it employs in the practice of its vocation.

[12] Unfortunately for them the French Canadians have only one means of access to their national history, a means of access that often hampers them from arriving at certain deep roots that they seek in the past. Listening to them so often call their present-day problems 'new phenomena', 'revolutionary signs', 'sudden effects of industrialization', etc., one sometimes has the impression that they are thinking of themselves without regard to their past. There is a gap between the historical awareness instilled in the French Canadians and the awareness derived from their present. Moreover, it is this that assures the failure of the neo-nationalists who reformulate the traditional version of history in an inverted form. Is assuming a national feeling more complex and diversified than the one written history has built up until now not formulating an invalid hypothesis?

Piotte
From Humiliation to Revolution

[1] Jean-C. Falardeau, 'Le Canada français politique vu de l'intérieur, *Recherches sociologiques*, II, Nos. 3 and 4 (July–December 1961), 305–6.

[2] In collaboration, *Canada français et union canadienne*, L'Action Nationale (Montreal, 1954), p. 36.

[3] Hubert Aquin, 'L'existence politique', *Liberté*, No. 21 (March 1962), p. 68.

[4] In collaboration, *Canada français et union canadienne*, L'Action Nationale (Montreal, 1954), p. 45.

[5] Pierre Vadeboncoeur, 'La ligne du risque', *Situations*, No. 1 (1962), pp. 29–30.

[6] Pierre Lefebvre, 'Libérer la cité', *Liberté*, No. 21 (March 1962), p. 78.

[7] Karl Marx. *Manifeste du Parti Communiste*, Collection 10/18 (Paris), p. 44.

[8] *Ibid.*, p. 22.

[9] *Ibid.*, p. 56.

[10] *Ibid.*, p. 57.

[11] *Ibid.*, p. 56.

[12] *Ibid.*, p. 55.

[13] Karl Marx, *Manuscrits de 1844*, Éd. Sociales (Paris, 1962), p. 60.

[14] *Ibid.*, pp. 64–5.

[15] Albert Memmi, *Portrait du colonisé*, quoted by *La Revue Socialiste*, No. 5 (Spring, 1961), p. 30.

[16] Pierre Vadeboncoeur, 'La ligne du risque', *Situations*, No. 1 (1962), p. 56.

[17] Jean-Yves Calvez, *La Pensée de Karl Marx*, Seuil (Paris, 1956), p. 216.

[18] Karl Marx, *Manifeste du Parti Communiste*, Collection 10/18 (Paris), p. 34.

[19] *Ibid.*, p. 34.

[20] Karl Marx, *Deutsche Idelologie*, MEGA, I, No. 5, p. 59, quoted by Jean-Yves Calvez, *La Pensée de Karl Marx*, p. 493.

[21] See the noteworthy article by Hubert Aquin, 'La fatigue culturelle du Canada français', *Liberté*, No. 23 (May 1962), pp. 299–325.

Index